BUREAUCRACY AND DEMOCRACY
ACCOUNTABILITY AND PERFORMANCE

FOURTH EDITION

Steven J. Balla

George Washington University

William T. Gormley, Jr.

Georgetown University

FOR INFORMATION:

CQ Press

An Imprint of SAGE Publications, Inc.

2455 Teller Road

Thousand Oaks, California 91320

E-mail: order@sagepub.com

SAGE Publications Ltd.

1 Oliver's Yard

55 City Road

London, EC1Y 1SP

United Kingdom

SAGE Publications India Pvt. Ltd.

B 1/I 1 Mohan Cooperative Industrial Area

Mathura Road, New Delhi 110 044

India

SAGE Publications Asia-Pacific Pte. Ltd.

3 Church Street

#10-04 Samsung Hub

Singapore 049483

Acquisitions Editor: Matthew Byrnie

Content Development Editor: John Scappini

Editorial Assistant: Zachary Hoskins

Production Editor: David C. Felts

Copy Editor: Talia Greenberg

Typesetter: Hurix Systems Pvt. Ltd.

Proofreader: Lawrence W. Baker

Indexer: Judy Hunt

Cover Designer: Anupama Krishnan

Marketing Manager: Jennifer Jones

Printed in the United States of America

Library of Congress Cataloging-in-Publication Data

Names: Balla, Steven J., author.

Title: Bureaucracy and democracy : [accountability and performance] / Steven J. Balla, George Washington University, USA.

Description: Fourth Edition. | Thousand Oaks, California : SAGE, [2018] |

Previous edition lists William T. Gormley as the first author on the title page. | Includes bibliographical references and index.

Identifiers: LCCN 2017019027 | ISBN 9781506348889 (Paperback : acid-free paper)

Subjects: LCSH: Bureaucracy—United States. | Administrative agencies—United States.

Classification: LCC JK421 .G6447 2017 | DDC 352.6/30973—dc23 LC record available at https://lccn.loc.gov/2017019027

This book is printed on acid-free paper.

17 18 19 20 21 10 9 8 7 6 5 4 3 2 1

Contents

Tables and Figures

Preface

Democrats and Republicans agree on very little these days, but most would endorse the proposition that the presidential election of 2016 and its aftermath have brought us all the excitement of a wild roller-coaster ride. Hold on to your hats! After a divisive, bitterly fought campaign, Donald Trump was inaugurated as the forty-fifth president of the United States on January 20, 2017. Just hours after being sworn in by Chief Justice John Roberts, President Trump signed an executive order giving agencies such as the Department of Health and Human Services permission to "waive, defer, grant exemptions from, or delay" provisions in the Affordable Care Act, his first step toward fulfilling a campaign promise to undo one of his predecessor's signature achievements. One week later, he signed an executive order barring residents of seven predominantly Muslim countries from entering the United States and barring refugees from entering the United States for 120 days. The following week, Trump signed an executive order requiring federal agencies to repeal two regulations for every new regulation they adopt. He also launched a review of financial regulations, with the stated goal of weakening regulations triggered by the Dodd-Frank Act. These dramatic actions signaled the new president's intent to reshape public policy and public management quickly, decisively, and unilaterally.

In a democracy, the president of the United States, though enormously powerful, cannot act alone. The ultimate fate of the Affordable Care Act and the Dodd-Frank Act will need to be determined by Congress, which faces sharp divisions (as vividly demonstrated by its failure, in March 2017, to pass health care reform legislation) between and within the two political parties. In response to a lawsuit from the state of Washington, a federal district court judge stayed implementation of the travel ban. Asked by the Trump administration to overturn the stay, the Ninth Circuit Court of Appeals declined to do so, finding that the executive order posed a potential threat to both the First Amendment and the Fifth Amendment. Shortly thereafter, a revised travel ban too was blocked by a judicial ruling.

Political appointees and civil servants also voiced dissent from the new administration's policies and practices. The intelligence community leaked information that led to the resignation of the new national security adviser, Michael Flynn. The information revealed that Flynn had lied repeatedly about conversations with the Russian ambassador to the United States, Sergey Kislyak. Contrary to public assurances and private assurances to Vice President Mike Pence, Flynn had spoken with the ambassador about U.S. sanctions punishing Russia for interfering with the 2016 presidential election. The Office of Government Ethics found presidential spokesperson Kellyanne Conway guilty of an ethics violation after she publicly urged Americans to buy clothing and other products sold by the president's daughter Ivanka.

Many citizens believe that the bureaucracy simply carries out public policies enacted by elected officials. In reality, a large number of the nation's most important policies are formulated inside the bureaucracy. To make the Affordable Care Act operational, agencies have issued thousands of pages of regulations. These regulations, which have the full force of law, are not easily undone by the stroke of a presidential pen. Also, while the bureaucracy normally carries out presidential directives, the executive branch is also subject to judicial review. When President Trump imposed the travel ban, Department of Homeland Security (DHS) officials promptly implemented the ban. However, when a federal district court judge stayed the ban and three circuit court judges upheld the stay, the same DHS officials obeyed the court and allowed travelers to enter the United States. In short, the bureaucracy has many masters.

When presidential appointees and the president himself overstep their legal authority, the bureaucracy can fight back. On the other hand, presidents and presidential appointees can redefine bureaucratic responsibilities, stifle bureaucratic initiatives, redeploy bureaucrats, and suppress bureaucratic reports if they choose to do so. They can also encourage resignations by lowering bureaucratic morale. In the years to come, the balance between presidential control and bureaucratic discretion is likely to be riveting. The success of the Trump administration will depend in large measure on how that balance is struck.

We hope readers of this book will come to view public bureaucracy as important and problematic but also redeemable. Bureaucracy is important because agency officials play a major role in determining the content of the public policies we encounter in our everyday lives. It is problematic because bureaucrats are unelected public officials and because many factors conspire against strong performance in executive branch organizations. It is redeemable because bureaucrats and agencies have shown a significant capacity for reform.

In this book, we focus on bureaucratic accountability and performance. We aim to lay out just how bureaucracy is accountable, as well as to whom, under what circumstances, and with what results. In presenting these issues, we draw on insights from four prominent social scientific theories—bounded rationality, principal-agent theory, interest group mobilization, and network theory. These perspectives provide alternatives to the usual practice of viewing bureaucracy through the lenses of partisanship and political ideology, which, while valid, often obscure our vision instead of sharpening it. Bounded rationality captures the pragmatic side of bureaucratic problem solving and bureaucracy's remarkable capacity to make reasonably good decisions with limited time and information. Principal-agent theory highlights the challenges of delegation from politicians to bureaucrats and the difficulties of overseeing bureaucratic organizations. Interest group mobilization draws our attention to the important role societal organizations play, for better or for worse, in influencing bureaucratic policymaking, as well as the circumstances under which such organizations are most active and powerful. Network theory stresses relationships inside and outside government that cannot be reduced to hierarchical form. In a chapter on the politics of disaster management, we demonstrate the usefulness of these four theories in understanding the bureaucracy's response to some of the most important challenges it faces, including terrorist attacks, natural disasters, and public health crises.

In selecting public policy examples to illustrate our points, we have been deliberately eclectic. Readers will find many examples, such as health care, environmental protection, education, homeland security, regulatory reform, and other areas that receive prominent attention in the mass media. We discuss the dramatic and ultimately successful search to find and kill Osama bin Laden and equally dramatic attempts to cope with hurricanes, tornadoes, and other natural disasters. Readers will also find examples from child care, public utility regulation, transportation, and other activities that receive relatively little public exposure. Although many examples come from the federal government in Washington, D.C., throughout we cite instances from state and local politics. Any treatment of bureaucracy must take federalism seriously, as state and local agencies are important not only because they implement federal laws but also because they make policy in their own right.

In this new edition, we have updated our public policy examples so that they reflect the changes that occurred in the context within which bureaucrats found themselves operating in the latter years of the Obama administration and the outset of the Trump presidency. Throughout the book, readers will discover accounts of the implementation of the Affordable Care Act, education reform, the making of evidence-based law and regulation, and the race to complete midnight regulations in the closing months, weeks, and days of the Obama administration, as well as the efforts of the Trump administration to undo these regulations.

A number of pedagogical tools help bring all of this into focus. We include at the beginning of each chapter a series of core questions to foster critical thinking about a particular aspect of bureaucracy. At the end of each chapter we include a list of key terms for readers to review. An appendix of annotated Internet resources follows the last chapter so readers can more easily pursue further exploration of the topics we raise. Finally, we feature throughout the book excerpts from interviews we conducted with four former cabinet secretaries. Insights from these interviews, featured as "Inside Bureaucracy" boxes within the text, bring bureaucratic decisions and disputes to life and illustrate how prominent practitioners view theoretical appraisals of themselves and their agencies. We would like to thank each of these distinguished public servants—Dan Glickman, Tom Ridge, Donna Shalala, and Christine Todd Whitman—for taking the time to share their insights with us.

We would also like to thank many others for their help at various stages during the preparation of the fourth edition of the book. Brian Harward, Allegheny College; Casey LaFrance, Western Illinois University; Stephen Ma, California State University, Los Angeles; and Jeff Worsham, West Virginia University, offered helpful comments on the third edition that guided us in our revisions. We also received equally useful commentaries as we prepared for a fourth edition from Jerrell Coggburn, North Carolina State University; Chris Foreman, University of Maryland; Lonce Sandy-Bailey, Shippensburg University; Gisela Sin, University of Illinois at Urbana Champaign; and two other anonymous reviewers. Dustin Brown and Marcus Peacock provided valuable advice on key questions. Trellace Lawrimore, a research associate at Georgetown University, provided skillful research assistance. At CQ Press, Elise Frasier persuaded us to do a fourth edition and to adapt our schedules to the rhythms of the electoral cycle. Talia Greenberg did an excellent job as copy editor. And David Felts, our production editor, helped to convert the manuscript into a finished product.

We could not have undertaken any of the book's four editions without the considerable love and patience of our families. We are also especially grateful to our teachers and mentors. Steve dedicates the fourth edition to John O'Connor, his high school Western Civilization teacher, who helped spur a lifelong interest in politics and research. Bill would like to thank Professor Bert Rockman, whose magnificent work on bureaucratic politics convinced him that bureaucrats, like visitors to Oz, have hearts, brains, and, often, courage.

1 | Bureaucracies as Policymaking Organizations

F̲OR DECADES, POLICYMAKERS HAVE CONFRONTED THREE interrelated challenges in elementary and secondary education: (1) finding a way to render public schools more accountable to parents, taxpayers, and other vital constituencies; (2) determining how to improve the performance of public schools so that the confidence of a long-disillusioned citizenry is at last restored; and (3) determining how public schools can best help narrow the achievement gap between whites and minorities, the latter of whom depend especially heavily on the school system for advancement and success.

Two recent presidents, George W. Bush and Barack Obama, placed considerable emphasis on performance measurement and accountability, especially in education policymaking. President Bush signed into law the historic **No Child Left Behind Act** (NCLB), which required standardized tests for students in grades 3 through 8 and which imposed penalties on schools that failed to reach performance thresholds as measured by these tests. NCLB also required states and school districts to publish annual statistics on the performance of certain subgroups, including low-income students, disabled students, and racial minorities. The hope was that the public spotlight would lead to tangible improvements in educational outcomes for these students in particular.

President Obama also promoted performance measurement and accountability in education. As part of the **Race to the Top** initiative, he offered substantial grants to states that adopted certain education reforms, one of which was to establish a system for evaluating teachers based on the performance of their students on standardized tests, after controlling for student characteristics and, in some instances, baseline test data. This approach, known as **value-added modeling,** was aimed at inaugurating a new strategy for evaluating teachers, which would judge them not on their educational credentials or their seniority but rather on the success of their students. The Obama administration also encouraged states to adopt the **Common Core,** a set of standards originally proposed by state officials, which sought to specify learning goals for different subjects in different grades and, more broadly, to encourage "critical thinking" skills in U.S. classrooms.[1]

According to independent assessments, these interventions changed the landscape of K–12 education in the United States. One study found that NCLB boosted math scores for elementary school students.[2] Another study found that the achievement gap between blacks and whites narrowed in some states but widened in others during the years immediately following passage of NCLB. As the authors put it, "In states facing more subgroup-specific accountability pressure, more between-school segregation, and larger gaps prior to the implementation of the policy, NCLB appears to have narrowed white-black and white-Hispanic achievement gaps; in states facing less pressure, less segregation, and smaller pre-existing gaps, NCLB appears to have led to a widening of white-black and white-Hispanic achievement gaps."[3] A third study found that the Race to the Top influenced state education policies, especially the policies of states that won a Race to the Top grant but also the policies of states that applied for such a grant but didn't get one.[4] The study did not fully probe which favored policies were more likely to be adopted by the states. By the end of the Obama presidency, the number of states with some version of teacher performance pay had increased, and forty-two states had adopted the Common Core standards. Some of this was undoubtedly due to strong encouragement from U.S. Secretary of Education Arne Duncan.

The education accountability movement, however, has had its critics. After a brief honeymoon period, NCLB triggered substantial negative reactions from state and local officials, who complained about unrealistic expectations and inadequate funding. Teacher morale declined, and elementary school teachers argued that NCLB left them little time to teach content not emphasized by standardized tests.[5] Parents also joined the chorus of critics. In New York and other states, parents complained that their children were focusing so much on standardized tests that actual learning was taking a back seat. In 2015, some 20 percent of New York state students opted out of standardized tests.[6] In Delaware, Florida, Ohio, Oregon, and other states, parents and public officials fought for the right to exclude their children from standardized tests.[7] In response to growing criticism of the Common Core, a handful of states backed away from these standards. Other states, like New York, delayed the implementation of **"high-stakes" teacher assessments** in which teachers would be evaluated based in part on their students' performance on standardized tests linked to the Common Core.[8] The growth of high-stakes tests led one prominent critic, Diane Ravitch, to recommend that all parents opt out of all high-stakes standardized tests.[9]

As opposition from teachers and parents mounted, Congress responded. In 2015, Congress passed the **Every Student Succeeds Act** (ESSA), which effectively repealed President Bush's NCLB and which voided certain practices used by the Obama administration to influence state and local education policymaking. Under the new law, states will still be required to conduct annual reading and mathematics tests in grades 3–8 and once in high school. However, states will be free to scale back the role those tests play in measuring school progress.[10] States and school districts will still be required to transform their poorest-performing schools, but they will be able to design and implement their own intervention strategies, so long as there is some evidence to back them up. States will also be free to eliminate teacher evaluations based on students' standardized test scores. Under the Obama administration, such practices were expected as a quid pro quo for states requesting a waiver of federal education requirements. More broadly, the new law bars the U.S. secretary of education from requiring or encouraging any particular set of standards, such as the Common Core.[11]

President Donald Trump has promised to open up a new chapter in performance and accountability in education. Under the direction of Education Secretary Betsy DeVos, the Trump administration has pledged to invest billions of dollars in charter schools and private school tuition vouchers. Supporters see such school choice as offering opportunities to low-income students and families.[12] Opponents, by contrast, argue that school choice takes resources away from teacher training, after-school programs, and public schools in general—all without proven results.[13] These ongoing twists and turns in federal education policy illustrate the extent to which bureaucratic accountability and performance have become important issues in public debates.

In this book, we evaluate the operation of public bureaucracies—such as schools, school districts, and education departments—as policymaking organizations in the American democratic system. In this opening chapter, we provide an introduction to the book's basic approach, which is to use several social scientific theories to guide an inquiry into accountability and performance, two key standards by which agencies are judged. This introduction is organized around three *core questions:*

- **WHY ARE ACCOUNTABILITY AND PERFORMANCE IMPORTANT IN UNIQUE WAYS IN PUBLIC BUREAUCRACIES?** Although accountability is vital in all sectors of society, it takes on distinct meanings when authority is exercised by teachers and other public servants. Such decision makers are empowered to serve not shareholders or boards of directors but families and the public.

- **WHAT ARE THE DIFFERENT FORMS OF ACCOUNTABILITY, AND HOW HAVE THEIR USE AND EFFICACY CHANGED OVER TIME?** In recent years, elected officials at all levels of government have sought to make school systems more accountable to political, as opposed to professional, concerns. The imposition of such external standards has important implications for teacher quality, satisfaction, and retention, all of which are in turn linked closely with student achievement.

- **WHY HAS PERFORMANCE BECOME SUCH AN IMPORTANT STANDARD BY WHICH TO EVALUATE PUBLIC BUREAUCRACIES?** Outputs, such as the amount of instructional time devoted to reading, and outcomes, such as student performance on standardized tests and high school graduation rates, have long been vital to education policy. But measuring these facets of performance is difficult, and it is even harder to demonstrate an unambiguous link between specific school activities and the growth and development of different types of children.

In addressing these questions, the chapter lays the foundation for a systematic inquiry into public bureaucracies, organizations where some of society's most fundamental decisions are made.

The Contours of Public Bureaucracy

As the uncertainty surrounding the ultimate effects of No Child Left Behind so vividly demonstrates, many of the policy decisions that most deeply affect people's lives are made within public bureaucracies. A **public bureaucracy** is an organization within the executive branch of government, whether at the federal, state, or local level. Such organizations run the gamut from the Federal Energy Regulatory Commission to the South Dakota Department of Game, Fish and Parks, to the Integrated Waste Management Department of Orange County, California.

As Figure 1.1 illustrates, the federal executive branch consists of dozens of public bureaucracies. Fifteen of these bureaucracies are **cabinet departments,** including the Department of Homeland Security, the first addition to the cabinet since 1989. Some noncabinet bureaucracies are referred to as **independent agencies,** as they are structured to operate with relative autonomy from White House authority. The Federal Reserve System is a prominent example of such an organization. Despite their designation, however, not all independent agencies actually enjoy such autonomy. For example, presidents of all political stripes closely monitor and influence the priorities and decisions of the Environmental Protection Agency (EPA).

The Food and Drug Administration (FDA), created in 1906, is one of many important agencies located within the Department of Health and Human Services. The FDA's primary responsibility is to ensure the safety of the nation's food, drugs, and cosmetics. The FDA also inspects blood banks and biologics manufacturing firms. In addition, the agency monitors the safety of medical devices through its Bureau of Medical Devices. Figure 1.2 provides an overview of the FDA's organization. An administrator appointed by the president and confirmed by the Senate heads the FDA, overseeing a workforce of approximately 10,000 employees and a budget of about $2 billion.[14] Approximately 1,100 employees are investigators or inspectors who inspect about 15,000 facilities per year. The FDA's workforce is better educated than most, with more than 2,000 scientists on staff.

Accountability and Performance in Public Bureaucracies

Because of the importance of their decisions, bureaucracies from the FDA to local school systems are accountable to a variety of individuals and organizations throughout government and society. These parties include political overseers, such as the president and city council members, as well as constituencies—parents, pharmaceutical users, and countless others—who are regulated or served by agencies.

Figure 1.1 The Government of the United States

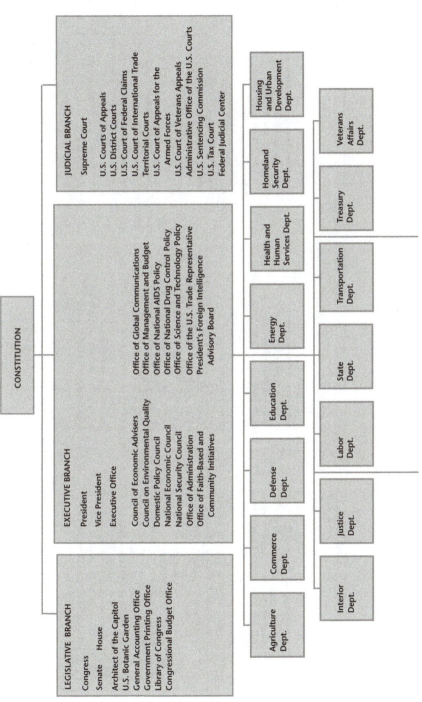

(Continued)

Figure 1.1 (Continued)

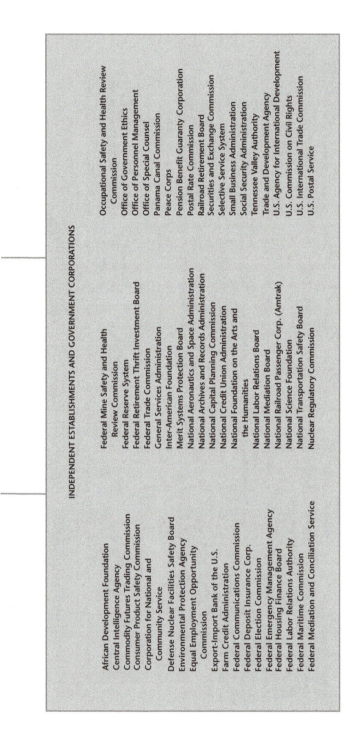

INDEPENDENT ESTABLISHMENTS AND GOVERNMENT CORPORATIONS

African Development Foundation
Central Intelligence Agency
Commodity Futures Trading Commission
Consumer Product Safety Commission
Corporation for National and
    Community Service
Defense Nuclear Facilities Safety Board
Environmental Protection Agency
Equal Employment Opportunity
    Commission
Export-Import Bank of the U.S.
Farm Credit Administration
Federal Communications Commission
Federal Deposit Insurance Corp.
Federal Election Commission
Federal Emergency Management Agency
Federal Housing Finance Board
Federal Labor Relations Authority
Federal Maritime Commission
Federal Mediation and Conciliation Service

Federal Mine Safety and Health
    Review Commission
Federal Reserve System
Federal Retirement Thrift Investment Board
Federal Trade Commission
General Services Administration
Inter-American Foundation
Merit Systems Protection Board
National Aeronautics and Space Administration
National Archives and Records Administration
National Capital Planning Commission
National Credit Union Administration
National Foundation on the Arts and
    the Humanities
National Labor Relations Board
National Mediation Board
National Railroad Passenger Corp. (Amtrak)
National Science Foundation
National Transportation Safety Board
Nuclear Regulatory Commission

Occupational Safety and Health Review
    Commission
Office of Government Ethics
Office of Personnel Management
Office of Special Counsel
Panama Canal Commission
Peace Corps
Pension Benefit Guaranty Corporation
Postal Rate Commission
Railroad Retirement Board
Securities and Exchange Commission
Selective Service System
Small Business Administration
Social Security Administration
Tennessee Valley Authority
Trade and Development Agency
U.S. Agency for International Development
U.S. Commission on Civil Rights
U.S. International Trade Commission
U.S. Postal Service

Source: Ben's Guide to U.S. Government, U.S. Government Printing Office, Washington, D.C., http://bensguide.gpo.gov/files/gov_chart.pdf (accessed July 25, 2011).

Figure 1.2 Organizational Chart of the Food and Drug Administration

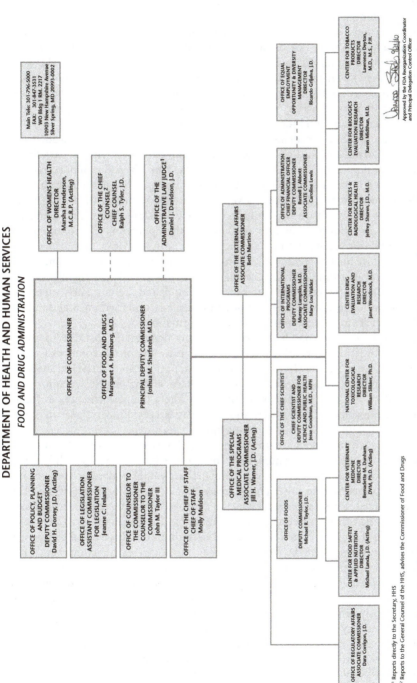

DEPARTMENT OF HEALTH AND HUMAN SERVICES

FOOD AND DRUG ADMINISTRATION

Main Tele: 301-796-5000
FAX: 301-847-3531
WO Bldg 1 RM. 2217
10903 New Hampshire Avenue
Silver Spring, MD 20993-0002

OFFICE OF COMMISSIONER

OFFICE OF WOMENS HEALTH
DIRECTOR
Marsha Henderson, M.C.R.P. (Acting)

OFFICE OF THE CHIEF COUNSEL[2]
CHIEF COUNSEL
Ralph S. Tyler, J.D.

OFFICE OF THE ADMINISTRATIVE LAW JUDGE[1]
Daniel J. Davidson, J.D.

OFFICE OF FOOD AND DRUGS
Margaret A. Hamburg, M.D.

PRINCIPAL DEPUTY COMMISSIONER
Joshua M. Sharfstein, M.D.

OFFICE OF POLICY, PLANNING AND BUDGET
DEPUTY COMMISSIONER
David H. Dorsey, J.D. (Acting)

OFFICE OF LEGISLATION
ASSISTANT COMMISSIONER FOR LEGISLATION
Jeanne C. Ireland

OFFICE OF COUNSELOR TO THE COMMISSIONER
COUNSELOR TO THE COMMISSIONER
John M. Taylor III

OFFICE OF THE CHIEF OF STAFF
CHIEF OF STAFF
Molly Muldoon

OFFICE OF THE SPECIAL MEDICAL PROGRAMS
ASSOCIATE COMMISSIONER
Jill H. Warner, J.D. (Acting)

OFFICE OF THE EXTERNAL AFFAIRS
ASSOCIATE COMMISSIONER
Beth Martino

OFFICE OF THE CHIEF SCIENTIST
CHIEF SCIENTIST AND DEPUTY COMMISSIONER FOR SCIENCE AND PUBLIC HEALTH
Jesse Goodman, M.D., MPH

OFFICE OF INTERNATIONAL PROGRAMS
DEPUTY COMMISSIONER
Murray Lumpkin, M.D
ASSOCIATE COMMISSIONER
Mary Lou Valdez

OFFICE OF ADMINISTRATION
CHIEF FINANCIAL OFFICER
DEPUTY COMMISSIONER
Russell J. Abbott
ASSOCIATE COMMISSIONER
Caroline Lewis

OFFICE OF EQUAL EMPLOYMENT OPPORTUNITY & DIVERSITY MANAGEMENT
DIRECTOR
Ricardo Grijalva, J.D.

OFFICE OF FOODS
DEPUTY COMMISSIONER
Michael R. Taylor, J.D.

CENTER FOR VETERINARY MEDICINE
DIRECTOR
Bernadette M. Dunham, DVM, Ph.D. (Acting)

NATIONAL CENTER FOR TOXICOLOGICAL RESEARCH
DIRECTOR
William Slikker, Ph.D.

CENTER DRUG EVALUATION AND RESEARCH
DIRECTOR
Janet Woodcock, M.D.

CENTER FOR DEVICES & RADIOLOGICAL HEALTH
DIRECTOR
Jeffrey Sharen, J.D., M.D.

CENTER FOR BIOLOGICS EVALUATION RESEARCH
DIRECTOR
Karen Midthun, M.D.

CENTER FOR TOBACCO PRODUCTS
DIRECTOR
Lawrence Deyton, M.D., M.S., P.H.

OFFICE OF REGULATORY AFFAIRS
ASSOCIATE COMMISSIONER
Dara Corrigon, J.D.

CENTER FOR FOOD SAFTEY & APPLIED NUTRITION
DIRECTOR
Michael Landa, J.D. (Acting)

[1] Reports directly to the Secretary, HHS

[2] Reports to the General Counsel of the HHS, advises the Commissioner of Food and Drugs

Approved by the FDA Reorganization Coordinator and Principal Delegation Control Officer

Source: Ben's Guide to U.S. Government, U.S. Government Printing Office, Washington, D.C., http://bensguide.gpo.gov/files/gov_chart.pdf (accessed July 25, 2011).

Public bureaucracies are not unique in this regard. Business firms, such as ExxonMobil and Home Depot, must also answer to supervisors and clients, including their boards of directors and shareholders. Likewise, nonprofit organizations, such as the American Red Cross and Ford Foundation, are held accountable to their boards of directors and to the beneficiaries of their services. Unlike these other organizations, however, government agencies also bear the burden of being institutions of American democracy. In democratic institutions, **accountability** to the American public and its elected representatives is a vital and unique concern. It would be troubling, in other words, if policy were made by officials with little or no connection to the public.

Accountability in democratic policymaking is often viewed through the lens of **fairness.** According to this viewpoint, all parties desiring to participate in particular decision-making processes should be given the opportunity to make their preferences known.[15] This principle is embodied in the **Administrative Procedure Act,** the statute governing the process through which agencies formulate many of their most important policy decisions. This statute generally requires agencies to allow interested parties the opportunity to comment on proposed courses of action.

Like democracy itself, this approach to bureaucratic policymaking often proves cumbersome and untidy. Many agency proposals are highly controversial, take an exceedingly long time to develop, and are ultimately met with vociferous opposition.[16] These difficulties raise a second fundamental standard that agencies are called upon to meet—performance.

As with accountability, performance in democratic institutions often means something very different from what it means in the context of other types of organizations. In the business world, performance is tracked through well-established indicators such as market shares and stock prices. Appropriate indicators also exist in the nonprofit sector, where the performances of foundations, hospitals, and colleges and universities are routinely measured and compared with those of similar institutions.

Yet such indicators are not always as useful as we would like them to be. As we have already highlighted, performance in education policy is difficult to assess, even with instruments such as report cards and standardized tests. Similar difficulties hold in other policy areas: How is the performance of the FDA to be judged? By the speed with which it approves new drug requests? But haste could be dangerous, or even deadly. By the care with which it reviews new drug requests? But unwarranted delays could harm both pharmaceutical companies and consumers. The FDA, like many other bureaucracies, has competing goals that are sometimes difficult to reconcile.[17] These difficulties, in turn, make it hard for politicians and others to judge the agency's performance. Furthermore, even if one agreed on the relative importance of agency goals, many goals are notoriously difficult to measure. For example, it typically takes years to determine the safety of products on the market. At what point is evidence of product safety "hard" enough to be reliable? Also, some products reduce the risk of one ailment while elevating the risk of another. Is a product "safe" if it reduces health risks for one disease more often than it increases health risks for something else? These are among the many challenges of performance measurement.

Although it may be tough to judge accountability and performance in public bureaucracies, this task is crucial given the vital role agencies play in the policymaking process. Equally important is the need to carry out this evaluation in a systematic manner. With these things in mind, we approach the bureaucracy from four distinct perspectives, which deal with the people who work inside executive branch agencies, the political actors who serve as the bureaucracy's supervisors, the clients whom agencies regulate and serve, and the conflict and cooperation that occur both within the bureaucracy and between agencies and other types of organizations. To better understand these facets of bureaucracy and their implications for accountability and performance, we draw on insights from four prominent social scientific frameworks—bounded rationality, principal-agent theory, interest group mobilization, and network theory. Before applying these frameworks to particular aspects of bureaucratic policymaking, we first lay out in greater detail what accountability and performance mean in the context of the executive branch so that the nature of the task at hand becomes fully apparent.

Accountability and Its Many Faces

Accountability, like peace and motherhood, is one of those wonderful words that instantly evoke all sorts of positive images. But what exactly does it mean? In thinking about accountability within the executive branch, it is useful to distinguish between the source of control over agencies—internal or external—and the degree of control over agency actions—high or low.[18] As Figure 1.3 illustrates, there are four possibilities: **bureaucratic accountability,** where effective control emanates from within the executive branch; **legal accountability,** where control from the outside is effective; **professional accountability,** where internal structures and processes produce low levels of control; and **political accountability,** where control is external and limited. These distinctions can be summed up in this way:

> Under the bureaucratic system, expectations are managed through a hierarchical arrangement based on supervisory relationships; the legal accountability system manages agency expectations through a contractual relationship; the professional system relies on deference to expertise; while the political accountability system promotes responsiveness to constituents as the central means of managing the multiple expectations.[19]

In practice, these distinctions are not always borne out. For example, political control via instruments such as legislative oversight is not necessarily less potent than legal control through statutory requirements.[20] In the early 1990s, in a not uncommon chain of events, the Health Care Financing Administration (now the Centers for Medicare and Medicaid Services) made significant changes to its rules on Medicare physician payments after its administrator was dressed down at a congressional committee hearing.[21] It is also not always the case that professional norms and standards exert less influence over agency

Figure 1.3 Forms of Executive Branch Accountability

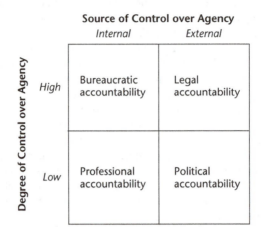

| | | Source of Control over Agency | |
		Internal	External
Degree of Control over Agency	High	Bureaucratic accountability	Legal accountability
	Low	Professional accountability	Political accountability

Source: Barbara Romzek and Melvin Dubnick, "Accountability in the Public Sector: Lessons from the *Challenger* Tragedy," *Public Administration Review* 47 (May/June 1987): 227–238. Used with permission.

behavior than does hierarchical supervision within the bureaucracy.[22] Over the past several decades, the influx of economists into the federal workforce has had a dramatic effect on how agencies assess the impact of their regulations, socially as well as economically.

Because of such complications, policymakers must think very carefully when promoting a particular form of accountability. A decision to emphasize one form of accountability over another can have significant consequences. At times it can even spell the difference between life and death. On January 28, 1986, the National Aeronautics and Space Administration (NASA) defied the views of engineers who warned that the space shuttle *Challenger* was not fit to be launched that day. Despite concerns that O-rings, or seals, would fail to function properly if temperatures were too low, the agency succumbed to political pressure to launch the vehicle more or less on schedule. The *Challenger* exploded not long after takeoff, and its seven-member crew, including schoolteacher Christa McAuliffe, perished in the accident. By substituting political accountability for professional accountability in a situation in which technical judgments were absolutely crucial, the agency made a fatal mistake.[23]

Another simpler way to think about accountability is to distinguish between **carrots** and **sticks**. The case for carrots, which reward bureaucrats for "good" behavior, is that they encourage superior performance without stigmatizing and penalizing those who fail to achieve it. The case for sticks, which punish bureaucrats for "bad" behavior, is that they send a strong message to bureaucrats who are set in their ways and who are not delivering services to the public as well as they should. Many heated debates over accountability hinge on this key choice between carrots and sticks.

But carrots and sticks are not always easy to distinguish. Consider, for example, the Obama administration's signature education initiative—the Race to the Top. Under this initiative, which encouraged states to be education innovators, the U.S. Department of Education awarded substantial sums to states that demonstrated a strong commitment to education reform. The Department of Education defined that commitment, in operational terms, as strong support for charter schools, performance pay for teachers, and tough strategies for turning around poorly performing schools (for example, firing principals). In response to that "carrot," many states altered their policies to promote charter schools and performance pay, even if they had reservations about one or both.[24] Especially in the midst of a major recession, it was difficult for states to resist the lure of substantial federal funding. For this reason, Michael Petrilli of the Fordham Institute has referred to the Race to the Top as "the carrot that feels like a stick."[25] Under some circumstances, a "voluntary" grant can be more irresistible than a nominal mandate.[26] As noted earlier, the Every Student Succeeds Act appears to bar the Department of Education from using "sticks" or carrots that feel like sticks in trying to shape state and local education policies. As a candidate for president, Donald Trump vowed to end the Common Core. To accomplish this goal, President Trump and Secretary DeVos would need to use either a big stick or a carrot that feels like a stick, contrary to the ESSA.

The Evolution of Accountability

During the latter half of the twentieth century, accountability emerged as a dominant concern among both policymakers and those outside government. Some bureaucracies, such as the now-defunct Interstate Commerce Commission, were viewed as runaway agencies, beyond the control of elected officials and ordinary citizens. In 1966, in response to such concerns, Congress passed the **Freedom of Information Act,** aimed at making the government's information more readily available to the public. Ten years later, the **Government in the Sunshine Act** specified that most federal commission meetings must be open to interested parties from outside government. Congress did not stop there. It also created inspectors general in most cabinet departments to serve as internal watchdogs over agency officials and passed "whistle-blower" legislation to protect federal employees who expose illegal or inappropriate behavior by others in the bureaucracy. While all of this was going on, congressional oversight of the executive branch was becoming more frequent and more intense.[27]

At the state level, similar developments were under way.[28] Many states passed their own freedom of information acts and sunshine laws. Across the country, states enacted legislation requiring the appointment of a public or consumer representative to occupational licensing boards. Most states created offices of consumer counsel to act as advocates for ratepayers in public utility commission proceedings. The overwhelming majority of states established a nursing home ombudsman's office to represent residents before governmental and nongovernmental organizations. Furthermore, many states enacted legislative veto provisions that facilitated political oversight of administrative rules and sunset laws that terminated relatively small agencies on a fixed date unless the legislature intervened.

The overall thrust of these reforms was to make the executive branch more accountable to politicians and to citizens or their surrogates. These reforms, in other words, emphasized external sources of control over bureaucratic and professional approaches. Whereas the Progressives had sought to insulate the bureaucracy from politics during the early days of the twentieth century, reformers in the 1960s, 1970s, and 1980s saw insulation as the problem to be solved. To put it differently, these three decades saw an era of "watchful eye" reforms aimed at curbing the bureaucracy.[29] Other reform movements, such as scientific management in the early twentieth century and liberation management in the 1990s, placed greater faith in bureaucratic discretion and internal sources of control.

Federal Agencies and Electoral Politics

Information disclosure is so closely related to accountability in contemporary American politics that there is considerable pressure on federal agencies to be transparent and to divulge as much information as possible about what they are doing and why they are doing it. But should this extend to an election campaign? Until the 2016 presidential election, the long-standing assumption about federal agency involvement in electoral politics was that it would not and should not occur. A well-established norm at the Justice Department, for example, was that DOJ should avoid commenting on an ongoing investigation, especially during the heat of a general election campaign.[30] The rationale was that an unsubstantiated assertion might carry disproportionate weight at a time when voters were trying to make up their minds, with possible political fallout effects for either or both candidates.

This norm became extremely important in the fall of 2016 when the FBI violated it, while the CIA did not. Hillary Clinton's use of a private e-mail account during her tenure as secretary of state triggered an FBI investigation that seemed to be resolved in the summer of 2016. In a public news conference on July 5, FBI director James Comey upbraided Clinton for being "extremely careless" but indicated that there were insufficient grounds to prosecute her. In Comey's words, "Our judgment is that no reasonable prosecutor would bring such a case."[31] In October, the FBI stumbled across additional e-mails in a parallel investigation, focusing on the sexting antics of former Congressman Anthony Weiner, who was married to top Clinton aide Huma Abedin. Contrary to advice from his DOJ superiors, Comey disclosed the existence of the new e-mails on October 28, less than two weeks before Election Day.[32] This damaged Clinton, who was surging in the polls, and gave Donald Trump new momentum in his presidential campaign. Although Comey later announced, two days before the election, that there were no new incriminating e-mails, the damage had been done.[33]

During the same time period, the CIA became increasingly concerned that the government of Russia was attempting to influence the U.S. presidential election. Evidence suggested that the Russians had hacked into the computers of Clinton campaign officials, including campaign chair John Podesta, as well as those of the Democratic National Committee. Many of these e-mails were provided to WikiLeaks, which released them to the public. As the presidential campaign continued, embarrassing leaks dogged and distracted the Clinton campaign. Later, after the election, the CIA announced that there was strong evidence connecting Russia to the leaks.[34] It was also revealed that the Russians had access to the Republican National Committee's e-mails but chose not to release them. This strongly suggested that the Russians were not only trying to undermine confidence in the U.S. electoral process but were actively trying to boost prospects for Trump being elected.[35]

These two cases raise some difficult questions for federal agencies that acquire sensitive information damaging to one or both candidates during a presidential election campaign. Should agencies adhere to the traditional norm that a general election campaign is not the right time to disclose incendiary information that does not have time to be properly sifted and winnowed? Or should they disclose information promptly, in the hope that the American people, with help from the news media, will be able to make sense of fragmentary information and reach a reasonable conclusion about its implications for the presidential campaign? In the fall of 2016, the FBI opted for disclosure, while the CIA did not. The FBI made its decision, despite strong admonitions—but no direct order—from top DOJ officials.[36] The CIA actually favored disclosure, but the White House declined to do so after Senate Republican leader Mitch McConnell, who knew about the CIA's evidence, threatened to lambast any preelection disclosure as partisan politics.[37] Together, the FBI's decision to go public and the CIA's decision not to go public enhanced the prospects for a Trump victory. Whether Hillary Clinton might otherwise have been elected, however, remains unclear.

A key question in all of this is whether agency officials should be accountable to their executive branch bosses or their congressional overseers, or both. And what if the two voiced different preferences? A related question is whether prompt public disclosure of developing information in an ongoing investigation is good or bad, in the middle of an election campaign or even in other, more quiescent times. These questions will undoubtedly trigger a good deal of soul-searching in the future.

The Limits of Accountability

Just as the quest for particular forms of accountability has ebbed and flowed over the years, it has also varied across agencies, depending especially on the complexity of the issues the agency must resolve. For agencies dealing with highly complex issues, both politicians and judges have been more willing to delegate authority and defer to the agency's technical expertise.[38] For instance, financial regulatory agencies, such as the Securities and Exchange Commission, often enjoy more autonomy than most agencies in part because of the arcane nature of their jurisdictions.

Such independence enables skilled, creative leaders to manage their agencies more effectively than would otherwise be possible. For example, during the 1990s, Alan Greenspan, then chair of the Federal Reserve Board, was widely credited with using his extraordinary influence over the nation's monetary policy to help propel the economy into one of its most robust periods of growth ever.[39] Although Greenspan's effectiveness was derived in no small part from his personal credibility and experience,[40] his agency's independence from Congress and the president enabled him to pursue his vision of sound monetary policy without interference and distraction.

Complexity alone does not account for the enormous power vested in some agencies. Political factors play a central role as well. The interests regulated by the Securities and Exchange Commission—brokerage firms, investment banks, mutual funds, and stock exchanges, to name a few—are quite diverse and generally at odds with one another.[41] Given this conflict, members of Congress find it desirable to empower the agency and, in the process, avoid the inevitable wrath of those parties that come out on the losing end of securities policy. If the agency's political environment were less contentious, then Congress might insist on a greater measure of political or legal, as opposed to professional, accountability.

A final factor to consider is the trade-off between accountability today and accountability in the future.[42] In democratic politics, the majority is never more than an election away from being banished to minority status. When such a shift occurs, the bureaucracy naturally falls under the domain of a new majority. Fearful that this shift will bring about a fundamental change in the political pressure exerted on the executive branch, the existing majority has an incentive to insulate agencies from outside sources of control. This incentive is especially strong when the existing majority has only a tenuous grip on the reins of power. During such times, great emphasis is placed on bureaucratic and professional accountability, and agencies are loaded with cumbersome structures and procedures. For example, some agencies are given restrictive mandates and are located within the executive branch in places relatively impervious to external influence.

Another example is known as **burrowing in.** Given that the White House regularly changes partisan hands, administrations have long sought to convert political appointees into career civil servants who will remain at their agencies indefinitely, carrying on the president's legacy in a new, potentially hostile administration. According to records of the Office of Personnel Management (OPM), 135 appointees moved into career positions during the Bush administration.[43] From 2010 to 2015, there were 69 such conversions of President Obama's appointees. In one instance, OPM concluded that the conversion process gave the appointee an "unfair advantage in the hiring process by manipulating the requirements of the career position to align with the appointee's background rather than with the position's classified duties."[44] Although burrowing in is not all that common a phenomenon, it can present accountability challenges for presidential administrations, especially those that do not share the partisan leanings of their predecessors. In the end, the lack of political and legal accountability decried by officials from across the ideological spectrum owes its existence not only to factors internal to the bureaucracy but to the dictates of electoral politics as well.

The Push for Performance

In the 1990s the concept of **performance** came to rival accountability as a standard for evaluating executive branch agencies. On its own merits, performance is important in democratic institutions, as the public is well served by government organizations that operate effectively and produce generally acceptable results. Performance is also of concern because it is intimately connected with accountability. To take one example, agencies subjected to particularly strict forms of political accountability may find it difficult to take sufficient advantage of their expertise and specialization. In recent years, scores of teachers have expressed deep dissatisfaction with an ongoing erosion of their classroom autonomy, arguing that this development stifles not only their instructional efforts but also the learning possibilities of many of their students.

Like accountability, performance can be defined and measured in a variety of ways. One approach is to focus on the activities, or **outputs,** over which agencies exert direct control. For an organization such as the EPA, outputs include the number of inspections conducted and the amount of monetary fines imposed. Another approach is to pay attention to the results, or **outcomes,** that agencies seek to bring about. Examples include cleaner air, lower poverty, safer workplaces, less disease, and more employment. A third approach is to focus on the effects of agency outputs on societal outcomes, controlling for other factors—economic growth, to name one—that play an important role in shaping such outcomes.

Managing for results is not an entirely new idea. The Wizard of Oz, for example, was an early believer in this managerial strategy. When Dorothy, the Scarecrow, the Tin Man, and the Cowardly Lion came to the Emerald City and submitted some very specific requests, the Wizard had some choices. He could have simply acceded to their requests on the spot, which would not have challenged these highly resourceful individuals to do their very best. Or he could have told them to compile statistics on how many miles they had traveled along the Yellow Brick Road. But instead he told them, "Bring me the broomstick of the Wicked Witch of the West!" In other words: Produce results, and I will grant your requests! Which they did, and which he did too.

Just as accountability is multidimensional, so too is performance. Consider, by way of example, the distinction between routine performance and behavior during a crisis. A given agency may do well when handling routine tasks but may stumble when called upon to confront a novel challenge or situation. Most observers acknowledge that the U.S. Postal Service is a remarkably efficient and productive organization.[45] In part, the agency's success derives from the nature of its fundamental task, which is unambiguous and easy for all to see. When it comes to delivering the mail under normal, relatively favorable conditions, letter carriers and clerks perform well.

But what about when the agency suddenly found itself confronting mail contaminated by potentially deadly anthrax spores? On October 15, 2001, a letter that had passed through a District of Columbia postal processing facility, on its way to the office of Sen. Tom Daschle, D-S.D., tested positive for anthrax. When postal workers expressed concern and asked whether they should take antibiotics, their supervisors told them antibiotics would not be necessary.[46] At a press conference, Postmaster General John Potter offered reassurances that the contaminated letter posed little, if any, threat to postal or congressional employees. Tragically, however, two postal workers died within a week, and many others found themselves potentially at risk.[47] In fairness to the postmaster general, he got much of his advice from the Centers for Disease Control and Prevention, whose scientists drew inappropriate conclusions from the limited evidence available to them. Regardless, the decision not to administer antibiotics proved to be a fatal error in a time of crisis for a normally effective organization.

A related distinction exists between **policymaking** and **implementation.** An agency such as the Social Security Administration (SSA) may perform well because its central task is routine—distributing checks to retirees and other program recipients. When performing roles such as this one, agencies implement policies established elsewhere in government. An agency can, without too much difficulty, develop procedures for effectively delivering resources to beneficiaries. If Congress specifies social security legislation in sufficient detail, the SSA need not fret about bigger, more difficult policy concerns.

Other agencies make policy all the time, a much harder task to perform well. For example, the EPA takes many important actions each year. In fiscal year 2006 alone the agency issued forty-two rules considered particularly significant.[48] These rules, which have the full force of law, ultimately determine the cleanliness of air, ground, and water, as well as who bears the costs of providing these public goods. Although the agency's enforcement practices have their own difficulties, it is generally easier to conduct an inspection or even to organize a cluster of inspections than to develop a rule from scratch.

Distinguishing between **efficiency** and **equity** as operational manifestations of performance is also important. For decades, state welfare agencies were free to set benefit levels but were not free to deny services to eligible clients. With the passage of the Personal Responsibility and Work Opportunity Reconciliation Act of 1996, these agencies were, for the first time, granted the discretion to decide who gets services and who does not. Such judgments, which determine how equitable welfare policies will be, require agency officials to make the tough decisions previously made by state legislators and other elected politicians. To further complicate matters, equity can be defined in many different ways. The distinction between equality of opportunity and equality in outcomes is just one dimension that must be considered. The end result of all of this is that it is tougher to measure equity than to gauge efficiency, and it is exceedingly difficult to reconcile competing views of how resources should be allocated across society. As this discussion implies, performance cannot be meaningfully separated from the values that make up the core of American democracy.

The Government Performance and Results Act

Given the centrality of performance in democratic policymaking, the federal government has for some time experimented with management reforms aimed at rationalizing the allocation of scarce resources. These experiments—with names such as "management by objectives" and "zero-base budgeting"—have been roundly criticized as fads long on symbolism and short on substance.[49] Despite these reforms, critics have contended, federal budgeting continues to be incremental in nature, with powerful interests blocking any significant departure from the status quo.

The enactment of the **Government Performance and Results Act** (GPRA) in 1993 struck some observers as a more promising development. Unlike other management reforms, put forth by the executive branch alone, GPRA was a law with bipartisan support from both the legislative and executive branches. GPRA also differed from previous reform efforts in that it allowed agencies several years to develop and implement strategic plans and performance measures and reports. After the initial incubation period, these documents were to be used by the executive and legislative branches in making budgetary decisions. According to one interpretation, agencies that performed poorly would get less, while agencies that performed well would get more. According to another interpretation, performance measures and reports would help policymakers redesign failing programs and learn from successful ones.

In implementing GPRA's early requirements, most agencies were successful in meeting congressional deadlines for producing various documents, but few were successful in actually measuring results. For example, the Department of Housing and Urban Development collected and reported data on uncollected rents but not on housing quality, thus severely limiting its ability to measure the performance of its public housing program. Other agencies, such as the Forest Service, struggled with conflicting goals (producing timber versus sustaining wildlife, for example), which made it difficult to measure overall success. Four years after GPRA's enactment, the General Accounting Office (GAO), which in July 2004 became the **Government Accountability Office,** characterized the law's implementation as "uneven."[50] Two years after this characterization, in 1999, the GAO concluded that "moderate" improvements had been made but that "key weaknesses" remained.[51] A few agencies, such as the Department of Transportation, Department of Education, and Department of Justice, had assembled credible performance information. But most agencies still struggled with conceptual and methodological issues. Despite GPRA's emphasis on shifting from outputs to outcomes, many agencies continued to measure outputs (for example, the number of clients enrolled in a program) rather than outcomes (the impact of enrollment on health, employment, or some other desired result). For example, the Medicaid program's goals for the Department of Health and Human Services include process measures (assisting states in conducting payment accuracy studies, participating with states in the Performance Measurement Partnership Project, improving the quality of nursing home surveys) and output measures (increases in child immunization rates, increases in State Children's Health Insurance Program enrollment rates, reducing the use of restraints in nursing homes) but only one outcome measure (reducing pressure ulcers in nursing homes).[52] Some of the biggest challenges confront agencies with significant intergovernmental relationships. This is because intergovernmental grant programs tend to be more flexible with respect to data gathering and outcome measurement than other government programs.[53] This flexibility makes it more difficult for the federal government to assess success. The EPA, for example, depends on states to implement numerous programs aimed at reducing water pollution. Because states measure water quality in many different ways, it is difficult for the agency to know how much progress has been made over time and across different areas of the country. Even within the same region, states use different sampling methods to determine water quality. Within New England, Rhode Island samples all of its waters every two years, while New Hampshire focuses its efforts on problematic waters. Other states sample one-fifth of all their waters annually.

Similarly, the Department of Health and Human Services relies upon states to measure progress in areas such as welfare reform, child support enforcement, and access to health care services. For such programs, the data the agency supplies to Congress are only as good as the data generated by the states. Definitional variations present problems here as well. For example, the Centers for Medicare and Medicaid Services allows states to define what constitutes "full immunization" for a two-year-old child when reporting such data to the federal government. Again, in New England, states differ from each other in how many shots each requires before children are considered fully immunized. As Table 1.1 illustrates, Vermont does not require two-year-olds to receive the hepatitis B vaccine, while Massachusetts, New Hampshire, and Rhode Island call for three such immunizations.

Although the GAO has criticized the executive branch for implementing GPRA in a poor and uneven fashion, the truth is that Congress deserves at least some of the blame. With few exceptions, legislators have ignored performance data, even from agencies that have produced relatively useful and complete information. In response to such criticisms, Congress passed the **GPRA Modernization Act** in 2010. The new law attempts to better integrate plans, programs, and performance information. Following the leads of our past three presidents (Bill Clinton, George W. Bush, and Barack Obama), it requires each agency to designate a chief performance officer. More significant, it requires quarterly reports to Congress, rather than annual reports.[54] The hope is that these quarterly reports will encourage both Congress and federal agencies to take GPRA's performance measures more seriously. An early assessment found that federal agencies used performance information more if they developed routines centered around the pursuit of cross-agency priority goals, the prioritization of a small number of agency goals, and data-driven reviews.[55] Whether GPRA improves government performance will also depend on Congress itself. If Congress continues to ignore GPRA, federal agencies will have few incentives to take it seriously.

The Program Assessment Rating Tool

More than most presidents, George W. Bush exhibited a keen interest in linking performance measures to budgetary decisions. His most important contribution to performance management within the federal government was the

Table 1.1 "Full Immunization" of Two-Year-Old Children, New England States

	Diphtheria, Tetanus, and Pertussis	Injectable or Oral Polio Vaccine	Mumps, Measles, and Rubella	Hemophilus Influenza Type B	Hepatitis B Vaccine	Varicella Zoster Vaccine
Connecticut	4	3	1	3	2	0
Maine	4	3	1	1	2	0
Massachusetts	4	3	1	1	3	0
New Hampshire	4	3	1	3	3	0
Rhode Island	4	3	1	4	3	0
Vermont	4	3	1	4	0	0

Sources: Centers for Medicare and Medicaid Services, "Government Performance and Results Act: Immunization of Medicaid Two-Year-Old Children" (Baltimore, Md.: CMS, July 2002). Also Karen Halverson, Vermont Department of Health, e-mail communication with Gormley, July 23, 2002.

Note: The numbers indicate how many shots or other forms of immunization are required for two-year-olds to satisfy the state's definition of what constitutes "full immunization."

creation of the **Program Assessment Rating Tool** (PART), administered by the **Office of Management and Budget** (OMB), which helps the president oversee the preparation of the federal budget and the making of executive branch regulations. Beginning in fiscal 2003, OMB annually rated a substantial number of federal programs as effective, moderately effective, adequate, ineffective, or "results not yet demonstrated." In putting together these ratings, OMB sought explicitly to incorporate performance measures into its budgetary decision making.[56] In principle, every major program was to be rated every five years.

Through PART, OMB examiners were able to encourage program managers to develop better measures of program success. In contrast with GPRA, there was much more emphasis on adopting authentic outcome measures.[57] Also in contrast with GPRA, there was a stronger commitment to a link between program assessments and budget decisions. Departments with a substantial proportion of programs rated "results not yet demonstrated" were told that their budgets might be reduced—a powerful incentive to develop appropriate measures of program success! As a result, the proportion of programs rated "results not yet demonstrated" declined over time.[58] Of graded programs, grades increased more often than they have decreased.[59] According to John Gilmour and David Lewis, PART scores had an impact on OMB's budget decisions. Specifically, programs with higher PART scores received larger budget increases. The impact seems to have been greater for small- and medium-sized programs than for large programs.[60] However, the "results" component of PART contributed less to budget decisions than did other elements of the total PART score. Also, some evidence suggests that PART scores mattered more for "traditionally Democratic departments" than for other departments.[61] If so, it would seem that PART was politicized to some degree. In short, PART enabled the executive branch of the federal government to link program assessments to budget decisions, but that link still needed improvement.

Though appreciative of PART, the Obama administration decided to try a somewhat different approach to improving performance management. Every cabinet-level department and eight other large agencies were instructed to develop three to eight "high-priority performance goals" that would guide the agency—and OMB. These goals should be ambitious—in the lexicon of the business community, **stretch targets** that would encourage agencies to focus on some really important objectives, even if there was no certainty of achieving them on schedule. The deputy secretary of each cabinet department (or someone comparable at the other agencies) would meet quarterly with top OMB officials to monitor progress toward designated goals. At budget time, agencies would be rewarded not for achieving certain goals but, less tangibly, for thinking clearly about problems and opportunities, for using evidence well, for staying on top of the management process, and for making smart adjustments.

Although it is too early to judge the success or failure of the Obama administration's approach to performance management, it does appear that several agencies redefined their goals significantly and reallocated resources to try to achieve those goals. For example, the Department of Housing and Urban Development (HUD) shifted its emphasis from home ownership to affordable rental housing as a goal. HUD established an ambitious goal—250,000 new affordable rental housing units in two years—and took steps to try to achieve it. Other agencies, including the Department of the Interior, the Department of Agriculture, the Food and Drug Administration, and the Centers for Disease Control, also embraced this more flexible approach to performance management with vigor and intelligence. As a top OMB official put it, "The old mind-set was, 'Tell me what I need to do!' The new mind-set is, 'We want you to really *think* about management.'"[62]

Agency Reputations in the Real World

Although the quest for systematic measures of performance has developed considerable momentum in recent years, perceptions of bureaucratic performance still depend in large part on soft judgments rather than hard data, on intuitions rather than indicators. To put it differently, a revolution in data generation does not guarantee a revolution in data utilization. Sometimes a vivid story matters more than a well-designed chart or graph. Sometimes a clever phrase or a lovable mascot proves more effective than a thick document chock full of statistics.

In a world where bureaucratic reputations are at times only loosely linked to actual performance, several points should be made about how agencies are perceived. First, perceptions vary dramatically. Those who must pay taxes have a rather different view of the Internal Revenue Service (IRS) than do those who prepare tax returns for a living. Among the latter, 61 percent believe the IRS does a good or excellent job. Among the former, only 40 percent give the IRS such a rating. To cite another example, 68 percent of environmental advocates believe the EPA does a good or excellent job. In contrast, only 41 percent of business managers give the agency such a rating.[63]

Second, perceptions change, sometimes very quickly. As Frank Sinatra sang, you can be "riding high in April, shot down in May." Consider the case of the Securities and Exchange Commission (SEC), once regarded as the crème de la crème of federal regulatory agencies.[64] In 2002, following accounting scandals at Enron and other corporations, some observers accused the SEC of being "asleep at the wheel."[65] They singled out its chair, Harvey Pitt, for meeting with corporate executives whose firms were being investigated for securities fraud and for requesting that the SEC be elevated to cabinet status. Congress rejected, and even President Bush disavowed, this request, which would have boosted Pitt's salary by nearly $30,000.[66] Not long after these episodes, Pitt stepped down as SEC chair under great pressure from an administration embarrassed by his missteps and bent on shoring up perceptions of its ability to manage the economy effectively. Unfortunately, Pitt's successor proved disappointing as well. Appointed by President Bush to head the SEC in 2005, Christopher Cox did little to prevent the unraveling of several of the nation's biggest investment banks, including Bear Stearns, which was borrowing $40 for every dollar of capital it held. In March 2008, the federal government provided an emergency "bailout" to keep Bear Stearns from going bankrupt. Largely ignored by its nominal regulator, Bear Stearns eventually collapsed during the financial disaster of 2008. The SEC also ignored numerous warnings that Bernard Madoff was engaged in massive securities fraud, through use of a Ponzi scheme. Eventually, Madoff's deceit cost investors an estimated $18 billion. The SEC also moved slowly to curb "short sellers" during the financial crisis—investors who borrow shares and make money when a stock's price drops. By the time President Obama took office in January 2009, the SEC's reputation was tattered and torn.

Bureaucratic reputations can also change for the better. In 2003, NASA was widely seen as an agency in disarray. Early that year, the space shuttle *Columbia* disintegrated during reentry, claiming the lives of all seven crew members and leaving the future of manned space exploration in doubt. Two years later, though, the agency's reputation began to turn around with the appointment of Michael D. Griffin as NASA administrator. One of Griffin's first moves was to replace the majority of NASA's top civil servants, a move that prompted one observer to state: "It's a rare moment when you get a housecleaning like this. It could presage a strong turnaround for an agency that's been adrift for years if not decades."[67] These internal changes were quickly followed by external evidence of success, most notably the return to flight of the shuttle fleet in the summer of 2005. In a broader sense, Griffin's "messianic vision" rekindled confidence in some quarters that NASA has the ability to spearhead human exploration of the moon, Mars, and the solar system beyond.[68]

Third, perceptions can be manipulated. Many agencies have their own publicity machines and work hard at generating both diffuse and specific support. A century ago, the Forest Service was particularly successful at generating political support. By mailing out more than nine million circulars annually, the Forest Service created a highly favorable image for itself in the public's mind.[69] The agency then helped sustain this image by conjuring up a marvelous "spokesman"—the legendary Smokey Bear, who is depicted in action in Figure 1.4. In similar fashion, state health agencies have recently generated popular support for the Children's Health Insurance Program by linking their programs to popular local symbols, such as the badger (Wisconsin) or the husky (Connecticut).

Fourth, perceptions matter. By winning the support of most Progressive magazines and newspapers, the Postal Service was able to convince Congress to establish a postal savings system in 1910.[70] For years the Federal Bureau of Investigation enjoyed a reputation for no-nonsense, vigorous law enforcement that enabled the agency to augment its budget and staff. Movies and television shows celebrating G-men and their crusade against gangsters such as Al Capone enabled the agency to fare well on Capitol Hill, even when times were tight. For example, J. Edgar Hoover received congressional authorization to establish a Division of Identification and Information in 1930, right in the heart of the Great Depression.[71] More recently, a positive image helped the FDA win passage of user-fee legislation, which requires pharmaceutical and biotechnology companies to pay the agency to review new drug applications.[72] As this example illustrates, perceptions are not wholly separate from actual performance, as the user fees collected by the FDA played a key role in helping the agency cut its average approval time nearly in half during the mid-1990s.

Figure 1.4 1956 Poster of Smokey Bear

Source: Forest Service, USDA. The name and character of Smokey Bear are the property of the United States, as provided by 16 U.S.C. 580p-1 and 18 U.S.C. 711, and are used with the permission of the Forest Service, U.S. Department of Agriculture.

Accountability and Performance: Theories and Applications

Thus far the discussion has emphasized that accountability and performance are multifaceted concepts of fundamental importance when it comes to evaluating the place of executive branch bureaucracies in the American democratic system. A number of questions remain, however: How are accountability and performance best judged, given their significance and complexity? Are there theories of politics and organizations that might provide particular insight into various aspects of accountability and performance? In the end, what general lessons can be learned about the determinants of both bureaucratic successes and failures? These questions motivate the chapters that follow.

Our basic orientation is to evaluate accountability and performance not through impressions and anecdotes, however telling these may sometimes be, but through systematic analysis. As summarized in Table 1.2 (and noted earlier in the chapter), we consider the bureaucracy from four different perspectives, in each instance drawing on a well-known social scientific theory especially well equipped to shed light on at least one facet of accountability and performance. We then apply the lessons learned from this exercise to case studies of particular agencies and issues to bring the implications of the disparate frameworks together in the context of actual agency experiences. We conclude by offering some general rules of thumb about the prospects for bureaucratic accountability and performance in light of the unique place occupied by administrative agencies in American democracy.

Chapter 2 focuses on the bureaucracy's people, from the secretaries who head cabinet departments to the teachers and other public servants with whom citizens have direct, sometimes daily, contact. We approach the behavior of these officials through the lens of **bounded rationality.** The basic premise holds that although individuals in organizations are rational, they do not comprehensively assess the benefits and costs of all, or even most, of their possible courses of action. Rather, decision makers seek to satisfice—that is, to arrive at outcomes that, while not necessarily ideal, are nonetheless quite satisfactory. Bounded rationality draws our attention to shortcuts, such as problem disaggregation and standard operating procedures, which are routinely a part of bureaucratic decision making.

Chapter 3 turns our attention to the bureaucracy's bosses, from the president all the way down to local officials. All of these actors routinely delegate policymaking authority to the bureaucracy. Delegation is essential, given the scope and complexity of contemporary government, yet it also raises the possibility that the agencies charged with making and implementing public decisions may serve their own interests rather than those of the citizenry and its elected representatives. According to **principal-agent theory,** the key for the bureaucracy's bosses is to design agencies wisely and to carefully monitor the behavior of executive branch actors. Although there are a variety of ways in which these tasks can be accomplished, no particular strategy is foolproof in limiting agency freedom.

Chapter 4 also focuses on actors external to the bureaucracy—the individuals and organizations that agencies regulate and protect. For these clients,

Table 1.2 Evaluating Bureaucratic Accountability and Performance

	Theoretical Framework			
	Bounded Rationality	*Principal-Agent Theory*	*Interest Group Mobilization*	*Network Theory*
Aspect of bureaucratic accountability and performance	The bureaucracy's people	Bureaucratic supervisors	Agency clients	Conflict and cooperation
Form of accountability emphasized	Bureaucratic and professional	Political and legal	Political	Bureaucratic
Key performance value	Problem solving	Policymaking and implementation	Responsiveness to constituents	Coordination and influence across organizations
Some important structures and processes	Specialization, standard operating procedures, authority, socialization	Institutional design, oversight, appropriations, appointments	Direct lobbying, grassroots, legislative support	Grants-in-aid, public-private partnerships, interagency meetings
Social science roots	Psychology, public administration	Economics, political science	Political science	Sociology, public administration

the consequences of bureaucratic policymaking vary over time and across issues. Importantly, the distribution of benefits and costs affects the mobilization of interest groups and the general public. At times, benefits accrue to small segments of society, such as specific businesses and industries, while costs are spread widely across the population. In these situations, organized interests, but not broad societal forces, are compelled to bring their influence to bear on government agencies through **interest group mobilization.** Although it is widely thought that the prevalence of such situations has declined in recent decades, interest groups certainly continue to play a central role in shaping public policy.

In Chapter 5 we return to the bureaucracy itself and consider how agencies interact with one another, and with other organizations, through a variety of **networks.** These networks include intergovernmental partnerships in areas such as environmental protection, collaborations between agencies and nongovernmental organizations, and interagency structures such as the president's cabinet. By linking network theory to what is sometimes known as the tools approach, we gain an understanding of how networks actually operate. In general, the use and efficacy of networks are topics of emerging importance for understanding accountability and performance in the executive branch.

Chapter 6 assesses the utility of the four theoretical perspectives by applying each of them to the management of three types of disasters—an unprecedented disaster (the September 11, 2001, terrorist attacks); a disaster with ample precedent (Hurricane Katrina, BP oil spill); and a disaster that has not yet taken place (an avian flu pandemic). Because these high-stakes cases are extremely challenging, both conceptually and logistically, they run the risk of portraying the bureaucracy in an unfavorable light. Nevertheless, these cases are undeniably important in evaluating bureaucratic accountability and performance. If the theoretical perspectives are useful, they ought to help us understand and analyze what went wrong, what went right, and (most important) why. They may also help us to do a better job of preparing for future disasters.

Finally, in Chapter 7 we consider the factors, including accountability, that account for variations in executive branch performance. In doing so, we rely on evaluations of dozens of federal agencies that have been carried out in recent years. These ratings are then used to support a series of general propositions regarding the root causes of bureaucratic successes and failures.

As we view bureaucratic accountability and performance from all of these perspectives, it will become apparent that the executive branch is a dynamic collection of organizations that perform, in some instances better than others, innumerable vital functions in the American political system. Along the way we will hear directly from four well-known public servants— Dan Glickman, Tom Ridge, Donna Shalala, and Christine Todd Whitman—who have run federal agencies under several presidential administrations. Through their stories, the bureaucracy will be brought to life in a way that complements our effort to think systematically about the internal and external workings of executive branch organizations.

Key Terms

Notes

1. William T. Gormley Jr., *The Critical Advantage: Developing Critical Thinking Skills in School* (Cambridge, Mass.: Harvard Education Press, 2017).

2. Thomas Dee and Brian Jacob, "The Impact of No Child Left Behind on Student Achievement," *Journal of Policy Analysis and Management* 30, no. 3 (2011): 418–446.

3. Sean Reardon et al., "Left Behind? The Effect of No Child Left Behind on Academic Achievement Gaps" (Palo Alto, Calif.: Center for Education Policy Analysis, Stanford University, August 12, 2013).

4. William Howell, "Results of President Obama's Race to the Top," *Education Next* 15, no. 4 (Fall 2015): 58–66.

5. Laura Hamilton, Mark Berends, and Brian Stecher, "Teachers' Responses to Standards-Based Accountability" (working paper WR 259-EDU, Santa Monica, Calif.: RAND Corporation, April 2005).

6. Elizabeth Harris, "20% of New York State Students Opted Out of Standardized Tests This Year," *New York Times,* August 12, 2015.

7. Valerie Strauss, "The Testing Opt-Out Movement Is Growing, Despite Government Efforts to Kill It," *Washington Post,* January 31, 2016.

8. Kate Taylor, "New York Regents Vote to Exclude State Tests in Teacher Evaluations," *New York Times,* December 14, 2015.

9. Valerie Strauss, "Diane Ravitch: Why All Parents Should Opt Their Kids Out of High-Stakes Standardized Tests," *Washington Post,* April 3, 2016.

10. Alyson Klein, "New Law, Fresh Challenges," *Education Week,* January 6, 2016, 10–12.

11. Ibid.

12. Kimberly Hefling and Benjamin Wermund, "Can DeVos Sell School Choice to America?" *Politico,* www.politico.com/story/2017/03/devos-becomes-saleswoman-in-chief-for-school-choice-236276 (accessed March 21, 2017).

13. Stephenie Johnson, Neil Campbell, Kami Spicklemire, and Lisette Partelow, "The Trump-DeVos Budget Would Dismantle Public Education, Hurting Vulnerable Kids, Working Families, and Teachers," https://www.americanprogress.org/issues/education/news/2017/03/17/428598/trump-devos-budget-dismantle-public-education-hurting-vulnerable-kids-working-families-teachers/ (accessed March 21, 2017).

14. U.S. Food and Drug Administration, Office of Management, Budget Formulation and Presentation, www.fda.gov/oc/oms/ofm/budget/documentation.htm (accessed May 2, 2007).

15. Robert Behn, *Rethinking Democratic Accountability* (Washington, D.C.: Brookings Institution Press, 2001).

16. Cornelius M. Kerwin, *Rulemaking: How Government Agencies Write Law and Make Policy,* 2nd ed. (Washington, D.C.: CQ Press, 1999).

17. David Frederickson and H. George Frederickson, *Measuring the Performance of the Hollow State* (Washington, D.C.: Georgetown University Press, 2006), 132–137; see also James Q. Wilson, *Bureaucracy* (New York: Basic Books, 1989).

18. Barbara Romzek and Melvin Dubnick, "Accountability in the Public Sector: Lessons from the *Challenger* Tragedy," *Public Administration Review* 47 (May/June 1987): 229.

19. Ibid., 230.

20. William Gormley Jr., *Taming the Bureaucracy: Muscles, Prayers, and Other Strategies* (Princeton, N.J.: Princeton University Press, 1989).

21. Steven J. Balla, "Administrative Procedures and Political Control of the Bureaucracy," *American Political Science Review* 92 (September 1998): 663–673.

22. John Brehm and Scott Gates, *Working, Shirking, and Sabotage* (Ann Arbor: University of Michigan Press, 1997).

23. Romzek and Dubnick, "Accountability in the Public Sector."

24. Sam Dillon, "States Skeptical about 'Race to Top' School Aid Contest," *New York Times,* April 4, 2010.

25. Michael Petrilli, "The Race to the Top: The Carrot That Feels Like a Stick," Flypaper blog, July 23, 2009, http://www.educationgadfly.net/flypaper/2009/07/the-race-to-the-top.

26. Gormley, *Taming the Bureaucracy.*

27. Joel D. Aberbach, *Keeping a Watchful Eye: The Politics of Congressional Oversight* (Washington, D.C.: Brookings Institution Press, 1990).

28. William Gormley Jr., "The Representation Revolution: Reforming State Government through Public Representation," *Administration and Society* 18 (August 1986): 179–196.

29. Paul C. Light, *The Tides of Reform: Making Government Work, 1945–1995* (New Haven, Conn.: Yale University Press, 1997).

30. Eric Holder, "Comey Is a Good Man, but He Made a Serious Mistake," *New York Times,* November 1, 2016, p. 17.

31. Mark Landler and Eric Lichtblau, "FBI Director James Comey Recommends No Charges for Hillary Clinton on Email," *New York Times,* July 5, 2016.

32. Josh Gerstein and Madeline Conway, "FBI Reviewing New Evidence in Clinton Email Probe," *Politico,* October 28, 2016; Jane Mayer, "James Comey Broke with Loretta Lynch and Justice Department Tradition," *New Yorker,* October 29, 2016; Matt Apuzzo et al., "Justice Department Strongly Discouraged Comey on Move in Clinton Email Case," *New York Times,* October 29, 2016.

33. Matt Apuzzo, Michael Schmidt, and Adam Goldman, "Emails Warrant No New Action against Hillary Clinton, FBI Director Says," *New York Times,* November 6, 2016.

34. Adam Entous, Ellen Nakashima, and Greg Miller, "CIA: Russia Favored Trump," *Washington Post,* December 10, 2016, p. 1.

35. David Sanger and Scott Shane, "Russian Hackers Acted to Aid Trump in Election, U.S. Says," *New York Times,* December 9, 2016.

36. Sari Horwitz, "Why Lunch Didn't Stop Comey Bombshell Letter on Clinton," *Washington Post,* December 23, 2016, p. 1.

37. Adam Entous, Ellen Nakashima, and Greg Miller, "CIA: Russia Favored Trump," *Washington Post,* December 10, 2016, p. 1.

38. Gormley, "Representation Revolution"; Kathleen Bawn, "Political Control versus Expertise: Congressional Choices about Administrative Procedures," *American Political Science Review* 89 (March 1995): 62–73; David Epstein and Sharyn O'Halloran, "Administrative Procedures, Information, and Agency Discretion," *American Journal of Political Science* 38 (August 1994): 697–722.

39. Bob Woodward, *Maestro: Greenspan's Fed and the American Boom* (New York: Touchstone Books, 2001).

40. John M. Berry, "Nervous Eyes on Greenspan's Big Shoes," *Washington Post,* August 7, 2002.

41. Anne M. Khademian, *The SEC and Capital Market Regulation: The Politics of Expertise* (Pittsburgh: University of Pittsburgh Press, 1997).

42. Terry M. Moe, "The Politics of Structural Choice: Toward a Theory of Public Bureaucracy," in *Organization Theory: From Chester Barnard to the Present and Beyond,* ed. Oliver E. Williamson (New York: Oxford University Press, 1990).

43. Dave Boyer, "GOP Warns against Obama Appointees 'Burrowing In' for Career Federal Jobs," *Washington Times,* November 27, 2016, http://www.washingtontimes.com/news/2016/nov/27/obama-appointees-burrowing-in-for-career-federal-j/ (accessed March 23, 2017).

44. Ibid.

45. Charles Goodsell, *The Case for Bureaucracy,* 3rd ed. (Chatham, N.J.: Chatham House, 1994).

46. Justin Blum, "Anthrax Cited in 2 D.C. Postal Deaths," *Washington Post,* October 23, 2001.

47. Ben White, "Postmaster General Lauded Despite Mixed Performance," *Washington Post,* October 25, 2001.

48. Office of Management and Budget, *2006 Report to Congress on the Costs and Benefits of Federal Regulations and Unfunded Mandates on State, Local, and Tribal Entities,* www.whitehouse.gov/omb/inforeg/2006_cb/2006_cb_final_report.pdf (accessed January 29, 2007).

49. Richard Nathan, introduction to *Quicker Better Cheaper? Managing Performance in American Government,* ed. Dall Forsythe (Albany, N.Y.: Rockefeller Institute Press, 2001).

50. U.S. General Accounting Office, *The Government Performance and Results Act: 1997 Government Wide Implementation Will Be Uneven* (Washington, D.C.: GAO, 1997), 9.

51. U.S. General Accounting Office, *Managing for Results: Opportunities for Continued Improvements in Agencies' Performance Plans* (Washington, D.C.: GAO, 1999), 3.

52. Frederickson and Frederickson, *Measuring the Performance of the Hollow State,* 78.

53. See Beryl Radin, *Challenging the Performance Movement: Accountability, Complexity, and Democratic Values* (Washington, D.C.: Georgetown University Press, 2006), 159–163; see also U.S. General Accounting Office, *Results-Oriented Government: GPRA Has Established a Solid Foundation for Achieving Greater Results,* Report no. 04-38 (Washington, D.C.: GAO, March 2004).

54. John Kamensky, "GPRA Modernization Act of 2010 Explained," IBM Center for the Business of Government, Washington, D.C., January 6, 2011, http://www.businessofgovernment.org/blog/business-government/gpra-modernization-act-2010-explained-part-1 (accessed March 23, 2017).

55. Donald Moynihan and Alexander Kroll, "Performance Management Routines That Work? An Early Assessment of the GPRA Modernization Act," *Public Administration Review* 76, no. 2 (2016): 314–323.

56. Office of Management and Budget and National Science Foundation, "Improving the Measurement of Program Effectiveness" (paper presented at the OMB/NSF workshop

"Strengthening Program Effectiveness Measurement of Federal Programs," Arlington, Va., May 21, 2002).

57. John Gilmour, *Implementing OMB's Program Assessment Rating Tool (PART): Meeting the Challenges of Integrating Budget and Performance* (Washington, D.C.: IBM Center for the Business of Government, 2006), 12.

58. Ibid.

59. Ibid., 13.

60. John Gilmour and David Lewis, "Assessing Performance Budgeting at OMB: The Influence of Politics, Performance, and Program Size," *Journal of Public Administration Research and Theory* 16 (April 2006): 169–186.

61. John Gilmour and David Lewis, "Does Performance Budgeting Work? An Examination of the Office of Management and Budget's PART Scores," *Public Administration Review* 66 (September/October 2006): 742–752.

62. Interview with Shelley Metzenbaum, Associate Director, OMB, February 10, 2011.

63. *Performance and Purpose: Constituents Rate Government Agencies* (Washington, D.C.: Pew Research Center for the People and the Press, April 2000).

64. Senate Governmental Affairs Committee, *Reports on the Study of Federal Regulation* (Washington, D.C.: Government Printing Office, January/February 1997).

65. Bloomberg News, "Spitzer Criticizes SEC, Pitt," *Newsday,* July 26, 2002, 56.

66. Kathleen Day, "Harvey Pitt Raises a Promotion Commotion," *Washington Post,* July 25, 2002.

67. Guy Gugliotta, "New Staff, New Directions for NASA; Shake-Up Is Part of Chief's Plan to Reach for the Moon (Again)," *Washington Post,* October 21, 2005.

68. Marc Kaufman, "NASA Looks to the Future with Eye on the Past," *Washington Post,* December 4, 2006.

69. Daniel P. Carpenter, *The Forging of Bureaucratic Autonomy: Reputations, Networks, and Policy Innovation in Executive Agencies, 1862–1928* (Princeton, N.J.: Princeton University Press, 2001).

70. Ibid.

71. Eugene Lewis, *Public Entrepreneurship: Toward a Theory of Bureaucratic Practice* (Bloomington: Indiana University Press, 1980), 109.

72. Carpenter, *Forging of Bureaucratic Autonomy.*

2 | Bureaucratic Reasoning

WHEN A STATE CHILD CARE INSPECTOR visits a day care center and finds some routine problems, it is relatively easy to know what to do. Consider, for example, the following hypothetical scenario presented to child care inspectors in Colorado, North Carolina, Oklahoma, and Pennsylvania.

> You visit the Little Flower Day Care Center for a renewal visit and discover that one of the toilets is overflowing onto the bathroom floor. The center director is already aware of the situation and has called a plumber. Before you leave, the plumber has arrived and fixed the problem.

A majority of inspectors in each of the four states would talk with the director; a majority in three of the four states would place a record in the center's file.[1] For this particular problem, there is strong consensus on how to proceed. Inspectors in all four states have developed similar **standard operating procedures** to follow when they encounter an isolated code violation that does not pose a serious threat to the health and safety of children.

Agencies of all kinds have developed standard operating procedures for dealing in a consistent way with situations regularly encountered. One goal in the use of such procedures is equitable treatment. The Baltimore City Department of Transportation follows a clearly articulated process for towing vehicles that are abandoned, parked illegally, or involved in an accident or police activity.[2] This process specifies the locations to which vehicles are towed, the information that is needed to retrieve vehicles, the forms of payment that are accepted, and the conditions under which individuals other than owners can claim vehicles. The resulting patterns of towing and retrieving are relatively predictable and affect Baltimore residents in a straightforward manner. But standard operating procedures, helpful in routine situations, may be of limited use when bureaucrats encounter unusual circumstances. Consider, for example, the following hypothetical scenario, also presented to child care inspectors in the same four states.

> You visit the Little Bo Peep Day Care Center after receiving a complaint that a staff member required an entire class of preschoolers to

stuff a sock in their mouths for two minutes as a disciplinary measure. Your investigation reveals that the incident did occur, that two
children vomited afterwards, and that the director refused to fire the
responsible staff member despite parental complaints. Your investigation further reveals sloppy record keeping, occasional lunches without
vegetables, and no field trips in recent memory. Although matters have
worsened since the center's last license renewal, the center has had
some serious problems in the past, including inadequate supervision
of children, infrequent washing of children's hands, and a malfunc-
tioning hot-water heater.[3]

Unlike in the previous example, inspectors would respond in strikingly
different ways to these provocations. Some inspectors would issue a monetary
fine, while others would not. Some inspectors would issue a provisional or
probationary license, while others would not. The percentage of inspectors
who would revoke the center's license (the ultimate sanction) ranged from 12
percent in Oklahoma to 32 percent in Colorado to 60 percent in Pennsylvania
to 64 percent in North Carolina.[4] Standard operating procedures, which prove
so helpful when inspectors encounter a minor code violation, are of little use
when inspectors consider a truly egregious day care center.

Standard operating procedures may also be of little guidance when personnel deal with unprecedented situations. Consider the protests that occurred on
the streets of Baltimore following the funeral of Freddie Gray, who had died a
few days earlier of spinal cord injuries suffered while in police custody. As the
protests turned violent, with cars burned and businesses looted, it became evident that Baltimore police officers were in desperate need of assistance in quell-
ing the tense and dangerous situation. Deployment of the Maryland National
Guard, however, did not occur immediately, a delay that allowed the volatile and
destructive environment to persist. As later explained by Maryland Governor
Larry Hogan, no deployment could be ordered until the state government had
received a formal request from the mayor's office. Although this revelation cast
city government officials, most notably Mayor Stephanie Rawlings-Blake, in
an unfavorable light, Governor Hogan emphasized the difficult nature of the
circumstances: "I don't want to second-guess the mayor's decision. I know she
was doing the best she could."[5]

Together, these examples illustrate important differences between the handling of routine problems and the managing of crisis situations. With routine
problems, reliance on standard operating procedures often serves both government officials and citizens reasonably well. When a crisis occurs, the existence
of standard operating procedures, while it may still prove helpful in certain
respects (city governments would certainly bristle at an uninvited deployment
of the state National Guard), it may ultimately not be enough to avoid poor
decisions and outcomes.

These cases also illustrate another important point. Bureaucratic decisions
are a function of both the task environment (e.g., the provocation or threat)
and the decision maker (e.g., civil servants such as child care inspectors). In
the Baltimore towing and first child care examples, the task environments

were simple, familiar, and determinative. In the Freddie Gray protest and second child care examples, the task environments were complex, unusual, and far from determinative. The Freddie Gray protest also reveals how decision makers—such as Baltimore police officers, other civil servants, and the mayor herself—may affect the outcome of events.

In sum, a full analysis of decision making requires that one pay attention to both the problem to be solved and the persons who have been asked to solve it. In this chapter, we take up this challenge by examining how individual bureaucrats reason, as well as how they behave within organizational and environmental settings. The *core questions* we explore are as follows:

- *HOW DO BUREAUCRATS MAKE DECISIONS?* We argue that bureaucrats employ a variety of strategies for simplifying decision-making problems. The use of such strategies implies that bureaucratic reasoning differs from other modes of decision making, such as **comprehensive rationality.**

- *DO BUREAUCRATS MANAGE TO APPROXIMATE RATIONAL BEHAVIOR?* We argue that bureaucrats can indeed mimic rational decision making. We highlight satisficing as a mechanism through which bureaucrats systematically, though not comprehensively, identify and select courses of action.

- *WHAT MOTIVATES BUREAUCRATS?* We view bureaucrats, as a general matter, as neither purely self-interested nor wholly public spirited. We consider the implications for bureaucratic decision making of elements such as empathy and commitment, attitudes toward risk, money, descriptive representation, and organizational advancement and cohesion.

In the end, what are the consequences of bureaucratic reasoning for government decisions and outcomes? Our aim is to understand how task environments and bureaucratic decision making influence the effectiveness of government organizations, from child care agencies to transportation departments to law enforcement offices, in solving problems that bureaucracies are asked to address on behalf of the American people.

Bounded Rationality

In this chapter, we adopt a perspective on bureaucratic reasoning originally championed by **Herbert Simon**, who won the Nobel Prize for his work on **bounded rationality.**[6] From a bounded rationality perspective, individuals who work within organizations, such as bureaucrats, face at least three difficulties. First, their knowledge of the consequences of possible choices is fragmentary. Given time constraints and the limits of the human mind, knowing all the consequences that will flow from a given choice is impossible. For example, if an inspector closes a poorly performing day care center, some children may be relocated to better centers, but others may be placed with relatives who really would prefer to be doing something else. Thus, the quality of care children receive may not ultimately improve. Second, values can be only imperfectly anticipated, as the experience of a value differs from the anticipation of that value. In other words, when we experience something (a vacation, a dessert, a public policy), the actual experience may cause us to rethink how valuable the goal was in the first place. If parents pay 20 percent more for a better day care center, they may or may not conclude that the additional expense was worthwhile. Third, only a few alternatives can be considered when making a decision. In the case of a bad day care center, an inspector might have the option of pursuing literally dozens of options. In practice, however, inspectors tend to zero in quickly on only a handful of options.

This perspective of bounded rationality is distinct from other notions of decision making, such as **incrementalism.**[7] In incrementalism, instead of working with a range of choices, decision makers begin with the status quo. Deviations from the status quo are then considered cautiously, ultimately yielding policies that differ only incrementally from previous iterations. Incremental outcomes are entirely possible under bounded rationality but are certainly not preordained. Incrementalism, in other words, is not the only way for boundedly rational decision makers to cope with limited time and information. Evidence suggests, in fact, that incrementalism is not the best way to describe bureaucratic decision making or the policymaking process in general.[8] Bounded rationality also stands in sharp contrast to the **rational choice model.** In its purest form, this comprehensive approach to rationality assumes that individuals making decisions know their values, are able to consider all possible alternatives, and can anticipate the full set of consequences that will flow from each alternative. In short, decision makers **optimize**—that is, they make the best decisions. Most versions of comprehensive rationality do not go quite so far as the pure model. Rational choice theorists, for example, commonly assume that decision makers lack complete, perfect information about alternatives and consequences.[9] The main implication of these assumptions is that the rational choice model ultimately portrays decision makers not as outright utility maximizers but rather as optimizers of **expected utility.**[10] Although decision makers make mistakes, they nevertheless make the best decisions possible given the limitations in the information they possess about the environment around them. Despite such limitations, by placing to the side elements such as decision maker uncertainty about values, the rational choice model suggests a much greater degree of optimization than is present in bounded rationality.

Under bounded rationality, decision makers such as bureaucrats make decisions through the use of **shortcuts** that help them to function effectively despite cognitive and situational limits. This process is known as **satisficing.** Satisficing implies that a bureaucrat considers options only until finding one that seems acceptable, given the bureaucrat's values and the probable consequences of the option. In Simon's words: "Because administrators satisfice rather than maximize, they can choose without first examining all possible behavior alternatives and without ascertaining that these are in fact all the alternatives."[11] Although satisficing sometimes leads to poor decisions, it is relatively quick and productive. Think of it this way: Would you rather devote an entire week to getting one decision exactly right or, instead, get one hundred decisions approximately right? The latter outcome might well be worth the risk of getting a few decisions wrong.

Applications of satisficing in bureaucratic decision making are plentiful. When urban planners in the San Francisco Bay area contemplated mass transit options in the 1950s and the 1960s, they considered a relatively narrow range of options. Planners for the five-county Bay Area Rapid Transit (BART) system considered only rail options, ignoring buses and automobiles as means of transportation. In nearby Oakland, planners for the two-county Alameda–Contra Costa Transit Authority (AC) gave initial consideration to a wider range of options, but only because they had inherited a multimodal system. Following a decision by the California Public Utilities Commission to allow the use of buses instead of trains, AC gave serious consideration to bus options only. The systems ultimately developed by these two sets of planners reflected these circumscribed alternatives: BART evolved as a rail system, while AC evolved as a bus system.[12]

The U.S. Customs and Border Protection's response to the problem of "port running" also illustrates satisficing behavior. Port running is a particularly bold form of smuggling in which the driver of a vehicle carrying illegal contraband proceeds brazenly to an inspection booth. If challenged by the inspector, the driver attempts to escape with little regard for life or property. When port running between Mexico and the United States became a serious problem in the mid-1990s, the Customs Service (as it was then known) actively considered approximately five solutions.[13] Eventually, the agency chose to arrange concrete barriers in a zigzag pattern just behind the inspection booths. Drivers leaving the inspection booth had to maneuver slowly through the barriers before they could drive away. If they tried to run, they could be stopped without putting other people at great risk. There is no way of knowing whether this was the best possible solution. For the Customs Service, it was sufficient that the policy seemed to reduce the number of port-running incidents and contributed to a substantial increase in the black-market price of running an illegal load (a good sign that smugglers regarded the new policy as an effective one!).

Although satisficing is predicated on limited information, bureaucracies do try to gather relevant information before making important decisions. Consider, for example, the steps that eventually led to the successful raid on Osama bin Laden's compound in Abbottabad, Pakistan, in May 2011. When U.S. intelligence officials learned in August 2010 that bin Laden's most important courier had been spotted in Abbottabad, they were surprised. The home of Pakistan's military academy (the rough equivalent of West Point), Abbottabad was teeming with soldiers who, in theory, were on the lookout for notorious terrorists. At first, it seemed highly unlikely that bin Laden himself would be hiding in a bustling metropolis, less than a mile from the Pakistani military's headquarters.

Slowly but surely, though, U.S. intelligence officers put the pieces of the jigsaw puzzle together. Local surveillance revealed a property with exceptionally high walls, barbed wire, and very tight security. The absence of telephone and Internet service at a $1 million home seemed unusual. The residents were so secretive that they did not leave to take out their trash, burning their garbage inside the compound instead. When neighborhood boys playing nearby lost a ball in the compound, they were paid to buy a new one rather than being allowed inside. When the courier left the compound to make a telephone call, he drove at least ninety minutes before even placing a battery in his cell phone. At times, spies observed a tall man pacing back and forth inside the compound—a man whose physical dimensions fit the description of bin Laden. Although U.S. officials could not be certain, considerable evidence suggested that bin Laden could be residing in Abbottabad, in plain sight. With that evidence in hand, President Barack Obama and his national security team devised a daring midnight raid on the compound that led to bin Laden's death on May 2, 2011. Although the encounter within the compound lasted about forty minutes, it had taken years to locate bin Laden and months to orchestrate his demise. As former CIA Director Michael Hayden put it, the path to bin Laden was built not brick by brick but "pebble by pebble."[14]

Simplified Problem Solving

Bureaucracies utilize a wide array of techniques to help solve difficult problems through boundedly rational decision making. These include problem disaggregation, the use of standard operating procedures, attention to sunk costs, the diffusion of policy innovations, and conducting simulations and tests. The purpose of these techniques is to simplify problems and the search for solutions. If these techniques work, satisficing bureaucracies can save time and money and make progress toward important goals.

Problem Disaggregation

Many problems are multifaceted or multidimensional. By breaking such problems down into their component parts—**problem disaggregation**—bureaucrats can transform daunting mega-problems into an assortment of soluble mini-problems. Efforts to solve the drug problem, for example, have yielded considerable progress following critical decisions on how to disaggregate the problem and then allocate scarce resources. The Department of Justice has distinguished between domestic and international cases, between major and minor cases, and between arrests (which generate favorable statistics in the short run) and breaking up drug cartels (arguably more important in the long run).

Consider, also, the problem of pollution. In 1970, the newly created Environmental Protection Agency (EPA) attacked the problem by breaking it down in several ways. First, the agency distinguished pollution by medium—air versus water versus land. Second, it distinguished between pollution from point sources (such as power plants) and pollution from nonpoint sources (such as runoff from farms). Third, the EPA distinguished between pollution in attainment areas (relatively good environmental quality) and pollution in nonattainment areas (relatively poor environmental quality).

With these distinctions in mind, and with considerable guidance from Congress and the federal courts, the EPA was able to zero in on problems based on several factors—severity, visibility, and tractability. Initially, the agency tackled air pollution from point sources, especially in nonattainment areas. Next, it focused on water pollution from point sources. In the first two decades of the agency's existence, the EPA made considerable progress in both areas. For example, the amount of lead in the atmosphere declined sharply (see Table 2.1),[15] and several major waterways became fishable and swimmable again. Other pollution problems, such as hazardous waste disposal, nonpoint pollution, and global climate change, proved more vexing and initially received little attention. But over time they, too, have become major EPA priorities. Had the EPA attempted to address all these problems at once, the outcome would probably have been much frenetic activity with few positive results. This is exactly what happened in the early years of the Occupational Safety and Health Administration (OSHA). Rather than disaggregate the complex landscape of occupational safety and health, OSHA (as mandated by law) acted immediately to issue thousands of regulations.[16] Many of these regulations turned out to be "trivial, absurd, or hopelessly complex."[17] In the end, not only did business interests oppose OSHA's rapid-fire approach, but even labor unions turned against an agency that they themselves had endorsed and helped to create.

Table 2.1 Changes in Air Quality and Emissions, 1986–1995

Pollutant	Air Quality Change	Emissions Change
Carbon monoxide	–37%	–16%
Lead	–78%	–32%
Nitrogen dioxide	–14%	–3%
Ozone	–6%	–9%
Particulate matter	–22%	–17%
Sulfur dioxide	–37%	–18%

Source: Clarence Davies and Jan Mazurek, Pollution Control in the United States (Washington, D.C.: Resources for the Future, 1998), 60.

Standard Operating Procedures

Habits and routines are excellent devices for coping with familiar problems. As Simon noted: "Habits and routines may not only serve their purposes effectively, but also conserve scarce and costly decision-making time and attention."[18] Within the bureaucracy, standard operating procedures are habits and routines designed to suit specific circumstances, available to organization members when situations resembling those circumstances occur. Standard operating procedures arise from many sources. When agency officials prepare an environmental impact statement before approving a major project, it is because they are required by law to do so. When welfare caseworkers insist on receiving a Social Security number before endorsing a welfare application, it is because they are required by law to do so. Many standard operating procedures originate with the political executives who run the bureaucracy. Some procedures, however, originate with bureaucrats on the front lines—**street-level bureaucrats**—such as teachers, police officers, and social services workers.[19]

A particularly interesting standard operating procedure emerged within the military during World War I. Much of the warfare in France and Belgium occurred in or near trenches, where opponents were pinned down in close proximity to one another. After a pitched battle, sentries patrolled each side's perimeter, placing themselves and their enemy counterparts at great risk. Remarkably, an unspoken agreement emerged over time that neither side would shoot at the other, giving everyone a breather from the stresses and strains of warfare. This live-and-let-live system evolved without the approval of higher authorities and persisted despite efforts to control it.[20] It is a good example of a standard operating procedure developed by street-level bureaucrats.

Though standard operating procedures tend to persist over time, they can be changed. For instance, a common approach to child care regulation is to visit all day care centers once a year, to make sure they are complying with state laws and regulations. This approach seems fair in that it treats all day care centers alike, but it is inefficient (and ultimately unfair) because it leaves insufficient time to address serious problems at really bad centers. For this reason, some state child care agencies have opted for **differential monitoring,** linking the frequency of inspections to past performance, giving more attention to worse facilities and less to better ones.[21] Differential monitoring is a form of **responsive regulation,** in which bureaucratic action (e.g., the frequency of inspection) is contingent upon the behavior of individuals and organizations under agency jurisdiction.[22]

Similar changes in standard operating procedures have occurred in child protection agencies. For example, Missouri's child protective services agency used to treat serious and nonserious cases alike. As a result of legislation passed in 1994, the agency developed a differential response system calibrating the agency's response to the severity of the provocation. More serious cases continued to trigger an investigation by child protection personnel and police, while less serious cases were referred to family assessment personnel, who provided assistance rather than punishment.[23] Other states followed Missouri's lead. By 2003, eleven states had established statewide differential monitoring systems for

Table 2.2 Workers' Compensation Claims, Maine

Year	Workers' Compensation Claims (Injuries with 1 Lost Workday or More)	Incidence Rates (Lost Workday Cases per 100 Full-Time Workers)
1991	8,923	49.43
1992	7,090	43.39
1993	5,808	37.43
1994	4,695	37.48

Source: Maine Area OSHA Office, "Annual Report on the Maine Top 200 Program, 1995." Data supplied by Dr. John Mendeloff, Graduate School of Public and International Affairs, University of Pittsburgh.

child protective services, while nine had pilot or local programs.[24] An evaluation of Minnesota's differential monitoring plan found that families randomly assigned to an alternative response track (counseling plus social services) were less likely to have a repeat report than families randomly assigned to the traditional investigative track.[25]

Occupational safety and health agencies have also embraced differential monitoring. In Maine, the OSHA regional office discovered that 200 firms were responsible for approximately 44 percent of the state's workplace injuries, illnesses, and deaths. OSHA gave each of the 200 firms a choice—conduct a comprehensive hazard assessment, correct all hazards identified, and develop an improvement plan for the future, or face a comprehensive inspection. An overwhelming majority of the firms opted for the former, and worker compensation claims dropped dramatically thereafter (see Table 2.2).[26]

Some cities, led by Baltimore, have tried to alter standard operating procedures across multiple agencies, through the use of **performance measures** on city agencies. When Martin O'Malley became mayor of Baltimore in 1999, he established **CitiStat,** which required agency officials to meet with the mayor and his team every two weeks in sessions highlighting worrisome trends in government and society. CitiStat was based on a crime-specific performance measurement system, **CompStat,** first introduced in New York City by Police Commissioner William Bratton. Although the data- and analytics-driven CitiStat encountered bureaucratic resistance at first, it helped to turn some agencies around and improve living conditions. For example, thanks to CitiStat, the mayor's office was able to reduce overtime payments at the Department of Public Works and city fire stations. The mayor's office was also able to reduce lead violations by 25 percent and increase the number of children tested for lead by 51 percent.[27] Other cities, such as Atlanta, Chattanooga, Providence, and San Francisco, have emulated Baltimore's CitiStat program.[28] O'Malley, who served as governor of Maryland from 2007 to 2015, sought to replicate Baltimore's successes at the state level by adopting a **StateStat** system. Like CitiStat, StateStat relies on data, analytics, and regular meetings with agency officials to ensure that the chief executive has an intimate grasp of trends in different regions, counties, cities, and neighborhoods. One of the more successful spin-offs of StateStat is **BayStat,** which uses GIS maps to track progress and decline in the Chesapeake Bay watershed.[29] Given its success, the Obama administration decided to use BayStat as the template for its own system of monitoring the Chesapeake Bay.

Baltimore's performance management system and its counterparts elsewhere are not without their risks. One danger is that such a system may encourage the chief executive to spend too much time in the "weeds" of management, instead of developing a broad vision for the future.[30] A related danger is that it may encourage "bean counting" at the expense of problem solving. By rewarding "good numbers" and punishing "bad numbers," chief executives and their political appointees may encourage a dysfunctional bureaucratic preoccupation with statistics. In an episode of *The Wire,* a gritty television drama based in Baltimore, the police commissioner and his deputy publicly berate police majors whose numbers fail to measure up. In desperation, Major Colvin legalizes drugs in one corner of west Baltimore, which becomes known as "Hamsterdam." The experiment yields a noticeable decline in crime, which impresses Colvin's bosses until they learn that he has legalized drug trafficking without their authorization. The moral of the story is debatable: Should we care more about drug sales or the corresponding crimes that accompany them? Once performance goals have been set by politicians, should bureaucrats be free to pursue these goals through any means necessary? Fortunately, it is possible to improve performance, as measured by statistical indicators, without violating the law. Nevertheless, this fictional case illustrates real-world dilemmas that are likely to arise with greater frequency as performance management continues its spreads.

Performance measures have undoubtedly been misused by public officials, and not just on television. In Baltimore, a police officer (who later became a college professor and wrote a book about his experiences) found that some officers used creative ways to boost their precinct's statistics—for example, by routinely locking up people who ride bicycles without a light late at night.[31] One officer's sergeant endorsed this practice, citing his lieutenant's reaction: "The lieutenant eats that shit up! . . . As long as the lieutenant likes them, I'm all for it."[32] At the same time, Baltimore police officers sometimes ignored more serious offenses, either to lower the reported crime rate or, more commonly, to avoid time-consuming paperwork.[33]

Baltimore is not the only city whose police officers care about their statistics. A few years ago, a New York City police officer tape-recorded conversations in which his superiors seemed to encourage the downgrading of certain crimes by insisting that a sergeant or lieutenant be present before the crime was classified for the record books. In New York City, at least, felony thefts are sometimes downgraded to misdemeanor thefts, robberies are sometimes downgraded to assaults, and assaults are sometimes downgraded to harassments, all in an effort to support the story line that serious crime is declining. In some instances, burglaries are not recorded at all unless the victim can produce receipts for the stolen goods.[34] Although it is difficult to know how widespread such practices are, they clearly subvert the purposes that performance measures are intended to serve.

Sunk Costs

Although procedural changes do occur, bureaucrats become invested in a certain way of doing things as any new strategy requires up-front costs that may turn out to be considerable. In Simon's words: "Activity very often results in 'sunk costs' of one sort or another that make persistence in the same direction advantageous."[35] In effect, **sunk costs** refer to the investment already made in a particular strategy that renders the pursuit of other strategies less attractive.

The phenomenon of sunk costs helps explain why it is so difficult to create a new agency or cabinet-level department. To bureaucrats, the status quo means established cubicles in familiar buildings at convenient subway stops, established relationships with familiar personnel whose quirks and foibles are well understood, and an established mission that flows from a familiar statute whose nuances are well known. Occasionally, the sunk-costs argument can be overcome. But it takes national emergencies (such as those that led to the Department of Energy and Department of Homeland Security) or strong constituencies (such as those involving the Department of Education and Department of Veterans Affairs) to do so.

Diffusion of Policy Innovations

In a federal system such as the United States, decision makers in different jurisdictions often confront similar problems and environments. For example, in the aftermath of the 2008–2009 global financial crisis, state and local governments across the country faced budgetary difficulties. In the summer of 2014, southwestern states faced a shared crisis when tens of thousands of women and children from El Salvador, Guatemala, and Honduras crossed the Rio Grande and turned themselves into the U.S. Border Patrol. For years, local governments have sought to restrict smoking in and around entrances to buildings.

Rather than create policy solutions to such problems from scratch, bureaucrats and other government officials can learn from and emulate the experiences of other jurisdictions that have already crafted policies and programs. In this way, bureaucrats do not need to explore all possible alternatives, but instead can direct their attention to courses of action that have already been implemented, as well as the consequences of these actions. Such learning and emulation facilitate the **diffusion of policy innovations** across government lines.[36]

The use of this form of bounded rationality varies by jurisdiction and across policy areas. Wealthy, urban states with highly professionalized state governments tend to be leaders in the creation of programs and policies.[37] That said, rural, less affluent states are under certain circumstances more likely to be leaders than followers. Consider restrictions on abortion, which have been mainly adopted in southern and midwestern states. As Figure 2.1 illustrates, no New England or West Coast states require ultrasounds to be performed prior to abortions.

Evidence suggests that successful policies are more likely to be emulated than poorly performing policies. The Children's Health Insurance Program (CHIP), which is administered separately in each state, provides health insurance coverage to children in low-income families. Early in the history of CHIP,

Figure 2.1 States Requiring Ultrasound before Abortion

States not requiring ultrasound
States requiring ultrasound before abortion

Source: Allison McCann, "Maps of Access to Abortion by State," http://
fivethirtyeight.com/datalab/maps-of-access-to-abortion-by-state/ (accessed
September 20, 2015).

states engaged in a variety of different approaches to implementation. Over
time, however, states gravitated toward specific approaches that had proven
particularly effective at addressing the needs of uninsured poor children.[38] This
diffusion of successful approaches demonstrates that bounded rationality can
under certain circumstances readily produce quality outcomes.

Historically, the diffusion of policy innovations proceeded largely along
geographic lines, with states emulating their immediate neighbors.[39] Regional
diffusion occurs to this day, as nearby states continue to encounter similar
problems (border states from Texas to California were especially impacted by
the influx of Central American women and children in the summer of 2014).
Nevertheless, there is now less of a need to turn to neighboring states than
in the past. Information and communication technologies, such as websites,
e-mail, and social media, make it easier for bureaucrats to learn about innovations occurring in distant places. In environmental regulatory enforcement, for
example, states are as likely to look to similar states (in terms of economic and
business profiles) for guidance as they are to look to neighboring states.[40]

Furthermore, recent decades have witnessed the proliferation of organizations specializing in the diffusion of policy innovations. The National
Association of Insurance Commissioners (NAIC), for example, consists of the
insurance commissioners of the fifty states, District of Columbia, and U.S.
territories. One of the NAIC's primary activities is crafting model laws and
regulations, which provide states with fully developed policies bearing the

organization's stamp of approval. Over the years, the NAIC has issued dozens of model acts, addressing issues ranging from annuities to supervision of insurers to workers' compensation.[41] Model acts are often adopted by large numbers of states, thereby promoting the diffusion of policy innovations. The Model HMO Act, for instance, has been adopted by more than thirty states.[42] Such mechanisms ensure that bureaucrats have no need to go it alone when satisficing through emulation and learning.

Simulations and Tests

When familiar problems arise, bureaucrats can rely on standard operating procedures. But what are they to do when unusual circumstances arise? This question has become especially pressing in recent times because new technological developments have accelerated the generation of new problems. For example, in the late 1990s government officials began to fret that massive computer failures would occur when the year 2000 arrived, as computers had been programmed with two-digit codes for the year (00–99), making them ill equipped to cope with the transition from 1999 to 2000. From a human point of view, the transition was a logical progression from one year to the next; from a computer's point of view, however, it was a backward shift of ninety-nine years. To a computer, 00 meant 1900, not 2000. Without appropriate corrections, this reading could result in enormous calculation errors, malfunctions, and shutdowns. Imagine, for instance, how someone's Social Security check might be deflated in keeping with a retroactive cost-of-living adjustment of nearly a century!

To anticipate the transition to the year 2000 (or Y2K), companies, agencies, and others ran **simulations,** or **tests,** to discover what might happen. The Chrysler Corporation, for instance, turned all of its clocks to December 31, 1999, at its Sterling Heights, Michigan, automobile assembly plant. The security system shut down and would not let anybody out. A Florence, Arizona, prison conducted a similar test and got the opposite result—the security system opened all its doors.[43] Not a good outcome for a prison! Fortunately, it was a test. Such simulations can be very helpful to bureaucrats and private employers as a way of confirming that real problems do exist. Eventually, government agencies were able to correct their computer problems. When Y2K arrived, few problems developed. A serious crisis was thus averted.

A dramatic example of the value of simulations occurred on May 2, 2011, when a highly trained team of twenty-five Navy SEALs killed Osama bin Laden during the raid on his compound in Abbottabad. For weeks, the SEALs had trained at a full-scale replica of the compound built for training purposes at a U.S. air force base near Kabul, Afghanistan.[44] By practicing repeatedly in a setting designed to mimic bin Laden's actual hiding place, the SEALs were better able to make split-second decisions that seemed familiar because they had experienced something similar before.

Simulations are useful and important, but only if they meet certain conditions. First, they must be conducted early enough so that mistakes, once identified, can be corrected. Second, when simulations reveal major problems, public officials must rethink their strategies, tactics, and timetables. Unfortunately, neither of these conditions fits the Obama administration's rollout of healthcare.gov—the website designed to serve American citizens wishing to sign up for health insurance coverage under the Affordable Care Act, otherwise known as Obamacare.

The Obama administration conducted a simulation of its website just a few days before the projected rollout of the website on October 1, 2013. The simulation, involving approximately 500 people, crashed the website.[45] This confirmed the fears of private contractors who believed that the Obama administration's deadline was unrealistic. It also confirmed the frustrations of White House and Department of Health and Human Services (HHS) officials who believed that the prime contractor, CGI Federal, was not up to the job.

Despite the simulation, the Obama administration stuck to its ambitious timetable, after tinkering with the system and adding staff to help manage it. Within hours after healthcare.gov went public, the website crashed. Thousands of Americans were unable to sign up for health insurance, and the Obama administration got a well-deserved black eye for promising more than it could deliver.

What exactly went wrong? In a nutshell, almost everything. As one computer expert involved with the project put it, "Almost everyone was at fault."[46] In retrospect, several troubling questions arise: Why was a simulation conducted so late in the game? Why was there no backup system if the website failed? Why was coordination between contractors, between government officials, and between contractors and government officials so poor? Why, despite abundant evidence that the website was not ready for prime time, did the Obama administration proceed on schedule?

These questions are difficult to answer. Haste, intense controversy, and a lack of good precedents and standard operating procedures were all to blame. The sheer enormity of the undertaking was breathtaking, which should have given key officials pause. And dwindling political support for Obamacare was a double-edged sword. On the one hand, it encouraged the Obama administration to move forward quickly rather than invite additional opposition. On the other hand, it should have sent flashing red lights to the White House and HHS. When political support for a program is weak, a major gaffe can only make matters worse.

Evidence-Based Research

In theory, an excellent way to enhance rationality in both legislative and bureaucratic decision making is through greater reliance on **evidence-based research.** If Congress adopts programs with good track records and eschews programs with poor track records, bureaucracies should find themselves administering more successful programs. If bureaucracies fund grant applications rooted in strong scientific evidence and decline to fund grant applications with little or no evidentiary support, then program benefits are more likely to exceed program costs. The Obama administration, building on performance-based efforts begun during the George W. Bush administration, promoted this strategy quite vigorously, especially in health care reform. [47] In the American Recovery and Reinvestment Act of 2009, otherwise known as the stimulus bill, as proposed by President Obama, Congress allocated $1.1 billion for health care **comparative effectiveness analysis,** aimed at identifying medical procedures that are more likely to improve patients' health. The following year, when it adopted President Obama's health care reform initiative, Congress included funds for comparative effectiveness research that quickly reached $500 million per year.

The Obama administration institutionalized evidence-based research in other policy domains as well. As noted in Table 2.3, significant applications of evidence-based policymaking can now be found at several federal agencies and in several policy domains. In two of these policy domains (teen pregnancy and home visiting), considerable rigorous evidence is available to guide public officials, while in others, systematic evidence on program impacts is much more limited.[48] However, in both types of policy domains, the Obama administration insisted on new evidence, using credible research techniques such as experiments or quasi-experimental designs, to gauge program impacts. As a result, research-based evidence should grow quickly over time and soon may inform judgments on which programs to keep, which programs to scrap, and which programs are ripe for improvement.

This new emphasis on evidence-based policymaking constitutes a significant departure from the status quo, which relied primarily on congressionally determined formulas to allocate funds to state and local governments. In contrast, 90 percent of the awards listed under the six programs in Table 2.3 are competitive.[49] State and local governments compete for these funds and receive funding if their application is deemed worthy. In effect, the new approach substitutes merit for pork as the key determinant for awarding scarce federal dollars to state and local governments.

To be sure, this new approach has not been without controversy, both inside and outside the bureaucracy. Inside the bureaucracy, the Department of Labor (DOL) expressed reservations about evidence-based policymaking, which required the agency to fundamentally alter standard operating procedures.[50] Eventually, however, DOL was able to adapt rather well to the new requirements and to calls for better management practices. Among other steps, it increased program evaluation resources by approximately 1200 percent![51] According to a Government Accountability Office report, DOL made significant improvements between 2007 and 2013 in its use of performance information to make decisions.[52]

Outside the bureaucracy, some critics questioned the judgments of Department of Education officials when making i3 (**Investing in Innovation**) awards. The charge was not partisanship (Republican and Democratic states fared equally well), but rather poor judgment. Others asked whether the Obama administration may have responded to congressional pressure to include some less than stellar programs among the pool of eligible applicants. Such pressure may have manifested itself when HHS decided to allow the Parents as Teachers program to be eligible for home visiting funds.[53]

Table 2.3 Obama Administration's Evidence-Based Initiatives

Evidence-Based Initiative	Initial Funding Source; Amount	Administering Agency	Evidence Requirement
Teen Pregnancy Prevention	$110 million; Consolidated Appropriations Act of 2010	Department of Health and Human Services	Program must be identified by HHS as evidence based (tier 1); about 75 percent of funds are for tier 1 programs.
Maternal, Infant, and Early Childhood Home Visiting	$1.5 billion; Patient Protection and Affordable Care Act of 2010	Department of Health and Human Services	Programs must be identified by HHS as evidence based; 75 percent of funds are for approved programs.
Investing in Innovation	$650 million; American Recovery and Reinvestment Act of 2009	Department of Education	There are three tiers of grants, reflecting the amount of evidence required.
Social Innovation Fund	$50 million; Consolidated Appropriations Act of 2010 (for first year; more money in subsequent years)	Corporation for National and Community Service	Evidence is incorporated into selection criteria; applicants must meet certain level of evidence by end of grant.
Trade Adjustment Assistance Community College and Career Training	$2 billion; Health Care and Education Reconciliation Act of 2010	Department of Labor, Department of Education	Points are given for evidence in selection process.
Workforce Innovation Fund	$125 million; the Department of Defense and Full-Year Continuing Appropriations Act, 2011	Department of Labor	There are three tiers of grants, reflecting the amount of evidence required; more money is awarded for higher levels of evidence.

Source: Adapted from Ron Haskins and Greg Margolis, *Show Me the Evidence: Obama's Fight for Rigor and Results in Social Policy* (Washington, D.C.: Brookings Institution Press, 2014).

In addition to its high-profile evidence-based policymaking initiatives, the Obama administration engineered more subtle reforms in individual departments, including departments responsible for foreign policymaking. For example, in 2011, then Secretary of State Hillary Clinton established an Office of Chief Economist. The head of the office has a small staff and reports to the Undersecretary of State for Economic Growth, Energy, and the Environment. The basic rationale for this office was to facilitate "economic statecraft" in a world where "security is shaped in boardrooms and on trading floors as well as battlefields."[54] Since its creation, the State Department's Office of Chief Economist has conducted economic analyses of refugee resettlements, international trade agreements, climate change policies, and other subjects.[55]

Despite some concerns, the Obama administration's push for evidence-based policymaking was, in most respects, deep, broad, and innovative. This development reflects a growing awareness by both Democrats and Republicans that public funds should be spent wisely and should not be wasted on programs that don't work. At the same time, it does not preclude useful experimentation on programs that have not yet been proven.

States have also taken steps to integrate evidence-based decision making into their policymaking processes. The Washington State Institute for Public Policy, under the leadership of Steve Aos, conducted cost-benefit analyses of numerous social programs that helped the state of Washington (and other states) to use scarce resources more wisely. Evidence-based analysis has also received some attention in the juvenile justice field. For example, Arizona and North Carolina have used an innovative approach to evidence-based practice, developed by Mark Lipsey of Vanderbilt University, to assign juveniles to different treatment programs by matching juveniles with certain characteristics to the programs that are likely to benefit them the most.[56]

Efforts to identify and support more successful medical and public policy interventions have sparked broad debates about the relative importance of efficiency versus other goals (e.g., equity, autonomy) in the policymaking process. For all of its merits, comparative effectiveness research, to the extent that it has the effect of limiting the consideration of patient values and physician training and experience in medical decision making, has been criticized as a pathway to rationing in the health care system.[57] Tony Coelho, a former member of Congress and disability rights activist, has argued that certain uses of comparative effectiveness research potentially limit access to health care for persons with disabilities, for whom demonstrating the efficacy of treatments can be difficult.[58]

As this example illustrates, it is not always easy to distinguish between successful and unsuccessful programs. In hearings before the House Ways and Means Committee's Income Security and Family Support Subcommittee, witnesses disagreed on whether a successful home visitation program requires professionals, as opposed to paraprofessionals, or registered nurses, as opposed to other professionals.[59] Without a consensus on such critical institutional design questions, policymakers might allocate funds to home visiting strategies that are either unnecessarily costly or ineffective. Despite these concerns, efforts to link legislative and bureaucratic decisions to evidence-based research are, by a variety of metrics, likely to enhance the success of government programs.

The Trump administration's approach to science and to evidence-based policy has been strikingly different from the Obama administration's, generally, and on specific issues like the environment and health care. For years, scientists have been warning that our nation's temperatures are rising steadily, that this poses an imminent threat to the planet, and that a key cause is a sharp rise in carbon dioxide emissions from power plants, automobiles, and heavy manufacturing.[60] These warnings have been substantiated by literally thousands of peer-reviewed journal articles.[61] On the broad causes and consequences of climate change, there is an unusually strong scientific consensus.[62]

Yet the head of the EPA, Scott Pruitt, announced shortly after taking office that he is a climate change skeptic, that we need more evidence before addressing climate change as a man-made phenomenon, and that we should not rush to judgment on this issue. In his own words: "I think that measuring with precision human activity on the climate is something very challenging to do and there's tremendous disagreement about the degree of impact, so no I would not agree that it is a primary contributor to the global warming that we see."[63] This point of view, contradicted by an abundance of scientific evidence, has the potential to retard promising efforts to address climate change by the U.S. EPA and to weaken international support for the 2015 Paris accords, which sought to reduce global emissions through voluntary actions by the world's leading contributors to global warming. President Trump emphatically reinforced Pruitt's climate change skepticism when he issued an executive order instructing the EPA to repeal and rewrite the Obama administration's Clean Power Plan, which sought to reduce greenhouse gas emissions.[64]

The Trump administration also demonstrated a weak commitment to empirical evidence by dismissing the nonpartisan Congressional Budget Office's analysis of the health care reform bill sponsored by House Speaker Paul Ryan, R-Wis. The CBO's report reached a shocking conclusion: that the Ryan bill was likely to cause 24 million Americans to lose their health insurance within ten years.[65] The CBO reached more sanguine conclusions on cost containment: that the Ryan bill was likely to reduce the deficit by $337 billion within ten years.[66] Even before the CBO report was released, White House spokesman Sean Spicer sought to discredit the report: "If you're looking to the CBO for accuracy, you're looking in the wrong place."[67] Following the report's release, HHS Secretary Tom Price denounced the report as "just not believable" while acknowledging that he had not actually read the report.[68] In fact, the CBO has long enjoyed a stellar reputation for hard-edged, rigorous, nonpartisan analysis of the fiscal impacts of congressional proposals.[69] Although it overestimated the number of people who would sign up for the ACA, that was due in part to the bungled rollout of Obamacare—something that would have been hard to predict. Overall, the CBO's projections over the years have been more objective and more accurate than those advanced by other groups.[70] By dismissing such analysis, the early days of the Trump administration demonstrated that the bipartisan "evidence agenda is at a crossroads," with nothing less than cost effectiveness, program improvement, and the resulting benefits to the American people in jeopardy.[71]

Implications for Policy Analysis

An important development in the history of bureaucratic decision making has been the creation of policy analysis bureaus within administrative agencies. The purpose of such bureaus is to provide cabinet secretaries and other agency officials with valuable information on the probable consequences of choices under active consideration. From the perspective of bounded rationality, policy analysis bureaus recognize important limits to individual and organizational decision making and seek to overcome these limitations.

If this perspective is correct, policy analysis within the bureaucracy differs from the rational choice model, which in its purest form assumes a world of complete and perfect information and unlimited time and cognition. According to this version of the rational choice model, decision makers specify their goals, consider a wide range of alternatives, gather evidence on the expected consequence of each alternative, and choose the alternative that maximizes the achievement of their specified goals.[72] Bounded rationality assures us that decision making in the real world cannot be so comprehensive.

At the same time, bounded rationality adheres to the notion that bureaucrats are trying to be rational. In a brief discussion of firefighting, for example, Simon suggests that the problem is not that some neighborhoods are whiter than others or more affluent than others or represented by a more powerful alderman than others. Rather, the fundamental difficulty is that bureaucrats cannot know the likelihood that a fire will break out in one section of the city as opposed to another.[73]

Other observers, by contrast, argue that policy analysis is inherently political.[74] Instead of clarifying their values, decision makers often disguise them. Alan Greenspan, the former head of the Federal Reserve Board, was known for his cryptic utterances. He once said before the Senate Banking Committee, "If I say something which you understand fully in this regard, I probably made a mistake."[75] The search for alternatives may therefore be less public spirited than implied by bounded rationality. Instead of a good-faith search for relevant alternatives, decision makers sometimes deliberately keep threatening alternatives from being considered.

In some respects, policy analysis within the bureaucracy tends to be inconsistent with both comprehensive rationality and bounded rationality. Some observers contend that policy analysis is usually not intended for a specific decision, that it rarely addresses a well-specified problem, and that it seldom is completed in time to have an impact. For example, an analysis of twelve papers prepared by Department of Energy policy analysts discovered that only one report could be clearly linked to a pending decision. Policy analysis may therefore not help to solve problems but rather produce interpretations of issues that assist policymakers in gaining a better understanding of the world around them.[76]

Despite these complications, some forms of policy analysis conducted by bureaucrats are strikingly consistent with bounded rationality. One such form is **cost-benefit analysis.** Cost-benefit analysis places a monetary value on both the costs and the benefits of proposed policy alternatives. To the extent that such valuation is credible, cost-benefit analysis helps to render bureaucratic decision making more rational by supplying decision makers with benefit-cost ratios that facilitate comparisons across policy options. For example, if a dam in Mississippi has a benefit-cost ratio of 6/1, while a dredging project in Louisiana has a benefit-cost ratio of 2/1, the Army Corps of Engineers ought to prefer the dam.

At first, it might appear that cost-benefit analysis is more consistent with comprehensive rationality than with bounded rationality. After all, the basic idea is to monetize all costs and benefits and produce a single number comparing these two quantities. In the real world, however, cost-benefit analysis suffers from incomplete and imperfect information. Benefits are notoriously difficult to measure, and discount rates, which convert future costs into current dollars, are controversial. Though animated by a vision of comprehensive rationality, cost-benefit analysis resembles bounded rationality in practice.

Going forward, cost-benefit may come to embody bounded rationality to an even greater extent. One criticism is that its "detailed monetization" and "complex quantification" renders cost-benefit analysis practically indecipherable.[77] Furthermore, much like other forms of policy analysis, cost-benefit analysis typically ignores the consideration of certain salient alternatives and is often not completed in time to affect an agency's choice between policy alternatives.[78]

One solution that has been proposed is a computationally simpler, timelier version of cost-benefit analysis, known as **"back-of-the-envelope" analysis** (BOTE). By eschewing the search for complete and perfect measurement, BOTE analysis offers the possibility of considering meaningful alternatives in an expeditious manner. As such, BOTE analysis represents an effort to bring bounded rationality principles such as satisficing to bear on an important and enduring form of policy analysis. BOTE sometimes serves as a prelude to a full-scale cost-benefit analysis. For example, EPA analyst Joel Schwartz conducted a two-day BOTE of a possible ban on lead additives in gasoline that yielded a rough benefit-cost ratio of 2/1. Based on that encouraging result, Schwartz's bosses invited him and a colleague to prepare a detailed cost-benefit analysis over a period of two months. That cost-benefit analysis, which yielded even more favorable results, helped to convince the EPA administrator, William Ruckelshaus, to adopt a rule reducing the amount of lead in gasoline.[79] Congress would later ban lead in gasoline altogether.

Motivation

In the rational choice model, self-interest motivates bureaucrats. In advancing their self-interest, bureaucrats seek to maximize expected utility. But does this perspective adequately characterize bureaucratic behavior? **Purposive incentives** (such as the pursuit of the public interest) and **solidary incentives** (such as the respect of one's peers) are potentially powerful motivating forces, at least for some bureaucrats.[80] Research suggests that although material incentives (good pay, job security) help to explain why individuals join the civil service and remain there, solidary and purposive incentives are highly important

Table 2.4 Types of Bureaucrats

Climbers consider power, income, and prestige as nearly all-important in their value structures.

Conservers consider convenience and security as nearly all-important. In contrast to climbers, conservers seek merely to retain the amount of power, income, and prestige they already have, rather than to maximize it.

Zealots are loyal to relatively narrow policies or concepts, such as the development of nuclear submarines. They seek power both for its own sake and to effect the policies to which they are loyal. We shall call these their sacred policies.

Advocates are loyal to a broader set of functions or to a broader organization than zealots. They also seek power because they want to have a significant influence upon policies and actions concerning those functions or organizations.

Statesmen are loyal to society as a whole, and they desire to obtain the power necessary to have a significant influence upon national policies and actions. They are altruistic to an important degree because their loyalty is to the "general welfare" as they see it. Therefore statesmen closely resemble the theoretical bureaucrats of public administration textbooks.

Source: Adapted from Anthony Downs, *Inside Bureaucracy* (originally published by Little, Brown & Co., Boston, Mass., 1967, p. 88). Copyright ©1967 RAND Corporation, Santa Monica, Calif. Reprinted with permission.

considerations as well.[81] Even proponents of rational choice theory acknowledge that many bureaucrats have "mixed motives," combining self-interest and altruistic support for certain values. The bureaucracy is populated not just by self-interested **climbers** and **conservers** but by **zealots, advocates,** and **statesmen** as well (see Table 2.4).[82] It is difficult to reduce the behavior of zealots, advocates, and statesmen to unadulterated self-interest.

Empathy and Commitment

Empathy represents one departure from pure self-interest. Some bureaucrats identify with disadvantaged constituents, such as the poor or disabled. Other bureaucrats identify with regulated firms, perhaps because they interact with industry representatives on a regular basis. Still other bureaucrats, due to their own demographic characteristics, identify with members of a particular gender, religious organization, racial or ethnic group, or some other economic or societal constituency.

Technically, empathy and self-interest can be reconciled. If a bureaucrat's concern for others directly affects that bureaucrat's own welfare as well, then such concern may in fact be a subtle manifestation of self-interest. As Amartya Sen notes, however, some people "commit" themselves to a principle that clashes with their own self-interest.[83] When a bureaucrat fights for a cause that puts at risk that bureaucrat's personal career, such **commitment** suggests that purposive incentives are at work. When a white bureaucrat fights prejudice against racial or ethnic minorities, the underlying motivation may well be commitment rather than empathy.

An analysis of bureaucratic motivation during the Reagan administration found considerable evidence of self-interested behavior, where bureaucrats complied with questionable directives for fear of losing their jobs. Such behavior was especially prevalent at the National Highway Traffic Safety Administration and the Food and Nutrition Service. In contrast, bureaucrats at the Civil Rights Division of the Department of Justice and the EPA were more willing to place their jobs at risk. A strong sense of professionalism motivated some rebellious bureaucrats, while others were driven by ideological aversion to President Ronald Reagan's policies.[84]

A similar phenomenon occurred at the outset of the Trump administration, but with a twenty-first-century twist. Some civil servants set up social media accounts to anonymously leak information about prospective changes in procedures and policies with which they disagree. A Twitter account—@Rogue_DoD—posted Defense Department documents on climate change, while @viralCDC became a repository for public health information that bureaucrats feared the new administration might remove from official websites.[85]

Self-interest and commitment as bureaucratic motivations were both evident in the protracted effort by the Obama administration to close the detention center at Guantánamo Bay. One of President Obama's first acts was to sign an executive order mandating the detention center's closure. For years, officials in the State Department used a variety of bureaucratic maneuvers to circumvent the president's order. These maneuvers included refusing to "provide photographs, complete medical records and other basic documentation to foreign governments willing to take detainees."[86] For some military officials, self-interest motivated their resistance. General John F. Kelly's son was killed fighting the Taliban in Afghanistan, a tragic and powerfully personal reason for his behavior in creating obstacles.[87] For others, commitment drove their behavior, even at the expense of self-interest. Secretary of Defense Chuck Hagel opposed closing the detention center on principle, a stance that was a contributing factor to his removal from office by President Obama.[88]

Empathy and commitment were evidenced at the highest levels of government in the early days of the Trump administration when acting Attorney General Sally Yates, an appointee of President Obama, instructed Justice Department lawyers not to defend the administration's travel ban for refugees and residents of seven predominantly Muslim countries.[89] President Trump promptly fired Yates, demonstrating once again the conflict that can arise between self-interest, on the one hand, and empathy and commitment, on the other hand.

Empathy and commitment also operate in state and local governments. Kim Davis was an obscure county clerk in Rowan County, Kentucky. That all changed after the U.S. Supreme Court legalized same-sex marriage and Davis refused to issue marriage licenses to same-sex couples.[90] This stance, which derived from a commitment to her religious beliefs, put her job and her freedom at risk. Indeed, a judge ordered Davis to jail, where she spent five days for contempt of court.[91] Upon her release, Davis, who vowed not to resign from her post, was ordered not to interfere with her deputies issuing marriage licenses to all legally eligible couples.[92]

Bureaucratic motivations can change over time. While training at the Baltimore police academy, more than 60 percent of recruits cited a desire to "help other people" as a major reason for becoming a police officer. A year after these officers had worked on the streets, the percentage declined to 40 percent.[93] Even bigger changes in motivation occurred as rookie officers became seasoned veterans. One Baltimore police officer, who began his career with enthusiasm and fearlessness, put it this way: "I guess when I first came out I was more gung-ho, jacking people up (stopping and searching people). But then I got shot at. It's a humbling experience. . . . Now my priority is to me. I'm going to go home to me and my family."[94]

Representative Bureaucracy

It is natural that bureaucrats empathize more with some groups than with others. Research on **representative bureaucracy** demonstrates that race and ethnicity are at times powerful shapers of bureaucratic attitudes and behavior. For example, school districts with a higher percentage of black teachers are less likely to suspend black students from school, assign black students to "educable mentally retarded" classes, or place black students in special education classes.[95] Teachers are more likely to perceive a student as disruptive or inattentive if the teacher does not share the student's racial or ethnic identification.[96] At the other end of the spectrum, studies have found a positive relationship between the percentage of teachers who are black and the percentage of students in gifted programs who are black.[97]

Representative bureaucracy also can affect outcomes beyond the primary mission of the organization. In Georgia public schools, for example, the presence of black teachers is associated with lower black teen pregnancy rates.[98] This association suggests that black teachers may act as role models for black students. One black teacher reported that some black students asked her about relationships, parenting, and premarital sex.[99]

Gender representation also matters, though more in some contexts than others. On the one hand, a study of child care inspectors found no gender differences in the propensity to be tough with child care providers who have violated state rules and regulations.[100] On the other hand, a study of local police forces found that rapes were more likely to be reported in jurisdictions with a higher percentage of females on the force. Of course, this difference might be a function of rape victims' perceptions that female officers would be more responsive or more sensitive than male officers rather than the actual attitudes or behavior of police officers themselves. However, arrests for rape are also more likely in jurisdictions with a higher percentage of females on the force, which suggests that female police officers are more proactive in pursuing rapists.[101]

On the campaign trail, Bill Clinton promised to assemble a cabinet that "looks like America," an explicit nod to the notion of representative bureaucracy.[102] As president-elect, Clinton nominated seven white men, four women, four African Americans (one of whom was a woman), and two Latinos.[103] Although more representative than President George H. W. Bush's cabinet, President Clinton's appointments were far less representative than the appointments made by President Obama sixteen years later. Among all appointments requiring Senate confirmation, President Obama placed women and minorities in 53.5 percent of these positions.[104] As one senior White House adviser put it, President Obama made a "very deliberate effort to be inclusive in the diversity of his administration at all levels."[105] According to a Democratic operative, this effort has "settled the fact that diversity is a permanent part of the federal government."[106]

Cabinet-level appointments at the outset of the Trump administration suggest that such a conclusion may be premature. President Trump's initial cabinet contained fewer women and nonwhites than those of his four immediate predecessors, prompting one observer to state that "Donald Trump is rolling back the clock on diversity in the cabinet."[107] All of the so-called inner cabinet positions—the attorney general and the secretaries of defense, state, and the Treasury—were filled with white men.

Money as a Motivator

Although purposive and solidary incentives are powerful bureaucratic motivators, material incentives are also important. Whether the hiring organization is public, private, or nonprofit, salaries matter, and bonuses may matter as well. When President Obama proposed a two-year pay freeze for most federal employees, reactions from many federal workers were understandably negative. Some federal workers, however, took the position that budget cuts were necessary, that shared sacrifice was appropriate, and that a pay freeze was preferable to layoffs.

It is well established that government employees are compensated less generously than their private sector counterparts. In 2014, for example, the public–private sector pay gap was 35.2 percent.[108] This gap widened in recent years.[109] One reason for this gap is politics. The president of the American Federation of Government Employees had this to say about the Obama administration's hesitance to raise the pay of government workers: "The excuses keep piling up. They are scared of the reaction of House Republicans. They are scared that the public won't understand what they're doing. They are scared to find out what might happen if they actually do something positive for federal employees, worried that anti-government extremists will somehow hurt them."[110]

Some of the biggest battles over compensation in recent years have focused on public school teachers. Although teacher recruitment and retention depend on many factors, teacher pay is one of them. According to one careful study, teacher pay is a key factor in explaining low retention rates for science teachers.[111] A Texas study found that a 1 percent increase in teacher pay reduces turnover by 1.4 percent.[112] In Oklahoma, where teacher pay now ranks forty-ninth out of fifty states, frustrated teachers have migrated to other states or other jobs. In Tulsa, Oklahoma, a survey found that 52 percent of departing teachers cited low pay as their top reason for leaving.[113]

Given the well-established pattern for "better" teachers to prefer "better" students, some school districts have decided to offer higher salaries to teachers who agree to work in schools with more disadvantaged students. This additional compensation, in some jurisdictions (for example, Guilford County, North Carolina), has been effective in attracting more highly qualified teachers to schools that desperately need the help.

In recent years, some school districts have experimented with more radical reforms, restructuring their teacher compensation systems to reward teachers who have been most successful in improving their students' standardized test scores. Such compensation systems substitute performance and results for seniority and credentials as the key criteria for determining teacher pay. Washington, D.C., Baltimore, and Denver are among the jurisdictions that have experimented with this approach. Thus far, the results of these experiments have been mixed. In Nashville, a randomized control trial found that teachers were no more successful in raising their students' test scores if they received higher pay for performance (the treatment group) than if they did not (the control group).[114] In contrast, a study of Washington, D.C.'s IMPACT teacher assessment system, based in part on value-added models that predict student test scores, found that it provided incentives for stronger teachers to stay while encouraging weaker teachers to leave.[115]

Whatever the merits of teacher performance pay systems, they have proven highly controversial. Washington, D.C.'s experiment with strong teacher accountability measures, including performance pay, was dealt a setback in September 2010, when voters defeated incumbent mayor Adrian Fenty, whose school chancellor, Michelle Rhee, had generated strong opposition from teacher unions to her education reforms.[116]

Kaya Henderson, who succeeded Rhee, revamped the IMPACT merit pay system, to put more emphasis on classroom observations and less emphasis on students' test scores, when determining each teacher's rating. Other school systems seem eager to strike a balance between being fair to teachers, who perform such difficult, important work, while at the same time holding them accountable for the extent of student progress toward educational goals.

Attitudes toward Risk

Observers often assert that bureaucrats are **risk averse.** In fact, most people are risk averse most of the time. Most of us wear seatbelts when we drive, don't smoke, stay home during a bad snowstorm, and avoid crime-ridden neighborhoods after dark. Once the dangers of Pinto fuel tanks were exposed, consumers switched to other cars; once the dangers of Firestone tires became apparent, consumers switched to other tires. Our national investment in homeland security after September 11, 2001, suggests a collective aversion to risk. Thus, the question is not whether bureaucrats are risk averse but whether they are more risk averse than the rest of us.

Foreign Service officers, within the State Department, are at times depicted as unusually risk averse. Specifically, some observers claim the officers are more cautious and timid than the political appointees who run the department. Chester Bowles, who served as a diplomat and ambassador under multiple presidents, argued that Foreign Service officers, being less prepared to take risks and less likely to think creatively, make poor candidates for top positions at the State Department.[117]

Not everyone agrees with this assessment. Charles Bohlen, who served as U.S. ambassador to the Soviet Union during the 1950s, argued that Foreign Service officers "were just as willing, in fact more so, to stick their neck out than were political appointees."[118] More broadly, it appears that while attitudinal differences between bureaucrats and politicians do exist, they are less striking in the United States than in other countries.[119]

The 2014 **Flint, Michigan, water crisis** demonstrates that risk taking, while sometimes desirable, can lead to disastrous consequences. On the verge of bankruptcy, the city of Flint was operating under the control of a state-appointed emergency manager. In an effort to save millions of dollars, state and city officials ended Flint's long-standing practice of purchasing treated Lake Huron water from Detroit. As a temporary measure, until the completion of its own Lake Huron pipeline, the city began using water from the Flint River.[120] The move occurred even though the Michigan Department of Environmental Quality warned that Flint River water could put the public's health at risk.[121] Sure enough, residents immediately began complaining about the smell and color of the new water. Before long, boil water advisories were in place, and bacteria, disinfectant by-products, and lead were all detected in Flint's water.[122] Research indicates that the number of children with elevated levels of lead in their blood, a serious health and developmental condition, may have doubled as a result of the risky change in water supply.[123]

If bureaucrats are so averse to risk, then how can one explain the willingness of Michigan's environmental bureaucracy to expose the residents of Flint to elevated lead levels in their drinking water? One answer to this question is that the culpable state officials were political appointees, who downplayed the risks and allowed the problem to worsen until it reached crisis proportions. But why would they do that? Perhaps because there were competing risks—the risks of insolvency (Flint was in danger of going bankrupt and was being run by a state-appointed emergency manager) versus the public health risks associated with switching from a safe water supply (Lake Huron water, routed from Detroit) to an uncertain water supply (Flint River water, whose levels of contamination had not been properly assessed).[124] In difficult financial times, key public officials made the decision to cut costs and hope for the best.

In thinking about risk, bureaucrats and politicians alike seem to be guided by what cognitive psychologists call the **availability heuristic.** Rather than considering all existing examples of some phenomenon and then reaching a conclusion, people tend to judge a situation based on the most readily available case, oftentimes the most recent occurrence.[125] In the wake of an accident or a disaster, we become more cautious, more risk averse because that accident or disaster is more readily available to us, more easily called to mind. The availability heuristic helps to explain why bureaucrats and politicians reacted with strong rhetoric and tough policies to the Three Mile Island accident of 1979, near Harrisburg, Pennsylvania, which threatened the possibility of a meltdown of a nuclear power plant reactor core. Although this kind of bounded rationality might seem perverse, it has its advantages. In addition to saving time and effort, it takes into account the psychological costs of certain choices. In Charles Perrow's words, the availability heuristic recognizes that "the public's fears must be treated with respect, and a way found to bring them into policy considerations."[126]

A limitation of the availability heuristic is that it can lead bureaucrats to behave in ways that, while expedient, do not promote effective solutions to the problems at hand. In the aftermath of the April 20, 2010, explosion and oil spill in the Gulf of Mexico, which resulted in eleven deaths and an unprecedented environmental catastrophe, the pressure was on the Obama administration to take decisive action. One of the administration's primary responses was dividing the Minerals Management Service (MMS) into a number of separate organizations. As Secretary of the Department of the Interior Ken Salazar pointed out, the MMS was responsible both for collecting oil and gas exploration revenues and ensuring the safety and environmental integrity of this exploration.[127] In Salazar's judgment, this dual, conflicting responsibility had impeded the MMS's ability to see unambiguously the warning signs in the Gulf and thus prevent the disaster from happening. Bureaucratic restructuring is a common response to disasters (e.g., the Department of Homeland Security was created in the aftermath of the September 11, 2001, terrorist attacks), and thus was an available heuristic for an Obama administration eager to act swiftly and publicly. Research suggests, however, that the MMS's internal conflicts among its multiple missions were overblown as reasons for the organization's regulatory failures in the years, months, and days prior to the oil spill.[128] More important in this regard were presidential, congressional, and public pressures placed on the MMS to favor energy exploration over environmental protection.[129]

The availability heuristic may therefore have caused the Obama administration to take steps that, while pleasing to the public in the immediate aftermath of the oil spill, did little to address the underlying pathologies that have long been pervasive in oil and gas exploration.

Organizational Advancement

For many bureaucrats, the welfare of the agency itself comes to rival individual welfare in importance. Bureaucracy's defenders and critics alike have observed a striking tendency for bureaucrats to identify with their organization and its mission. As Simon puts it, "The common claim that economic self-interest is the only important human motivation in the workings of a society is simply false, for it is an easily observable fact that, within organizations, organizational identification requires at least equal billing with self interest."[130]

A key advantage of **organizational identification** is that it enables the bureaucracy to socialize its members to pursue organizational goals that have been duly authorized by elected officials. In this sense, organizational identification promotes legal accountability. By ensuring that civil servants and political executives promote the same goals, organizational identification also promotes bureaucratic accountability.

But what if political executives or politicians sacrifice organizational goals for political self-promotion? A potential disadvantage of organizational identification is that bureaucrats who simply do what their bosses command may lose sight of the broader goals of the organization. If the bureaucracy veers substantially from its legitimate goals, individual bureaucrats may veer with it (exercising **loyalty**), rather than challenging the organization from within (articulating **voice**) or resigning in public protest (opting for **exit**).[131]

Promoting Organizational Cohesion

How do bureaucracies and their political appointees promote the kind of **organizational cohesion** Simon and others have applauded? One strategy is to train bureaucrats so that they know exactly what is expected of them. When a new recruit arrives, it is customary to have a probationary period, during which the new arrival learns the ropes from a mentor or a cluster of mentors. At some agencies, the probationary period is relatively long and the training process relatively rigorous. Police departments, for example, rely on police academies to ensure the learning of proper techniques.

A second strategy is to ensure that information flows up and down the organization. Regular meetings offer one opportunity for superiors and subordinates to exchange information and ideas. Organizers hope that by the meeting's end, all personnel will be on the same wavelength. Memos are also important tools for guidance from above and feedback from below.

A third strategy is to rely upon professions to socialize individuals and to certify values and skills. By hiring members of a profession whose tenets and norms match its own, a bureaucracy can save itself a good deal of time and effort. A classic study of the Forest Service demonstrated how bureaucrats used this technique to counter centrifugal tendencies inherent in an agency whose employees work, for the most part, in remote locations and with limited supervision. By hiring professional foresters for numerous jobs, including personnel management, administrative management, and budgeting positions that actually could have been filled by persons with different credentials, the Forest Service helped to ensure a common outlook that lessened the need for close supervision.[132] By rotating these professionals on a regular basis, the Forest Service also ameliorated tendencies toward **capture** and **localism.** Capture occurs when regulatory agencies adopt the thinking of the interests they are supposed to be regulating (e.g., the Interstate Commerce Commission, created to regulate railroad and trucking companies, served these companies' needs by restricting the entrance of competing businesses). Localism occurs when clientele agencies adopt the thinking of local clients (e.g., Department of Agriculture extension agents, whose responsibility is to train local farmers, may advance the interests of favored farmers at the expense of the community as a whole).

Although some agencies rely heavily on one profession, as the Forest Service does, most recruit individuals with diverse professional backgrounds. Such practices help agencies to perform varied and complex tasks by taking advantage of people with different professional norms and skills. For better and for worse, these professionals are like the tiger whose stripes remain well after being placed in a zoo.

Consider, for example, the Federal Trade Commission (FTC), which has recruited both lawyers and economists to handle antitrust matters. The lawyers, with a relatively short time frame and a penchant for litigation, prefer to pursue lots of antitrust cases, including small ones. The economists, with a longer time frame and a preference for restructuring industries, prefer to wait for a blockbuster case to come along.[133] While conflicts between lawyers and economists may require agency managers to spend time arbitrating disputes, such conflicts can also be constructive in terms of both process and outcomes. Along these lines, the FTC pursues a good mix of easy and difficult cases, thanks to the combined input of lawyers and economists.

Consequences of Bounded Rationality

Is bounded rationality a virtue, a vice, or a practical necessity? Simon's perspective is clear. Although bounded rationality underscores the limits of organizational decision making, individuals have the ability to adapt to formidable challenges through satisficing and other shortcuts. Furthermore, organizations can help individuals to make decisions roughly consistent not only with their personal preferences but also with their organizations' most important goals. In Simon's words, "The rational individual is, and must be, an organized and institutionalized individual. If the severe limits imposed by human psychology are to be relaxed, the individual must in his decisions be subject to the influence of the organizational group in which he participates."[134] In short, Simon was optimistic about bounded rationality.

Is such optimism justified? To answer this question, it is useful to reconsider some of the essential elements of bounded rationality: a narrow search, problem disaggregation, approximations, and standard operating procedures.

A Narrow Search

A hallmark of bounded rationality is an explicit willingness to limit the decision-making process to a relatively narrow range of options. We saw earlier in this chapter that planners for the BART system limited their choices to rail initiatives, while planners for the nearby AC system limited their choices to bus routes. One can imagine that these pragmatic decisions, understandable in the short run, might prove disastrous in the long run. Yet careful analysis reveals quite the opposite. Thanks to a circumscribed range of options, the two mass transit systems developed independently as **parallel systems,** or organizations with similar goals but very different strengths and weaknesses. When strikes afflict one system, the other absorbs the sudden spike in demand. When bad management plagues one system, the other keeps running smoothly. When technical breakdowns undermine one system, the other helps out. The result, though serendipitous, is far better than two blended systems would have been: As Jonathan Bendor concluded, "Taken together, AC and BART form a more flexible response to long-term problems than does either one taken separately."[135] Satisficing, at least in this instance, resulted in outcomes that are more than satisfactory.

Inside Bureaucracy with	Christine Todd Whitman
	EPA Administrator
	(2001–2003)

"One of the first things I tried to do was to move to appoint someone whose name had come to us as an expert in air to put them in water and take the person who was the expert in water and put them in air. It's really important for them to understand that those two things were not separate. Action in one affected the other. But I was overruled by the White House. So I couldn't make that move. But I wanted to do that from the very beginning. Because I do believe there is too much the mentality that this is the only way to do things. . . . I fought back for a little bit but I lost. Ultimately you're not the decider. The White House is the decider. You as an appointed official were not elected anything. You work for them. At the end of the day, you give them your best advice and you push back as much as you think you can but at the end of the day it's their decision."

Problem Disaggregation

Anne Lamott, a novelist and nonfiction writer, describes a childhood scene etched in her memory. Her brother, a procrastinator, had put off writing a lengthy report on birds until the night before it was due. Frustration led to fear, then to panic. How could he possibly finish the assignment on time? Their father, calm and reassuring, put his arm around his son's shoulder and shared one of the secrets of writing (and problem solving): "Bird by bird, buddy. Just take it bird by bird."[136]

Like Lamott's brother, bureaucratic decision makers have learned that they need to break big problems down into digestible chunks. That is how NASA put a man on the moon. That is how Robert Moses, one of the nation's most well-known city planners, transformed the landscape of New York City over a period of decades. That is how Jaime Escalante, a Bolivian immigrant and educator, enabled disadvantaged students from a Los Angeles barrio to excel in mathematics and pass the Advanced Placement calculus exam. And that is how environmental bureaucrats have combated pollution.

Yet the bird-by-bird approach has a down side. In the case of environmental protection, the EPA's decision to tackle pollution medium by medium has been reinforced by structural arrangements that mimic this approach. The EPA has an Air and Radiation Division, a Water Division, and a Solid Waste and Emergency Response Division, among others (see Figure 2.2). Because the Air and Radiation Division focuses on air pollution, it pays limited attention to water and land impacts. Similarly, the Water Division, with its emphasis on water pollution, pays limited attention to air and waste impacts. Given that most pollution transcends a single medium, a **stovepipe mentality,** in which problems are disaggregated and compartmentalized, may inhibit a more **holistic perspective.** EPA Administrator Stephen Johnson emphasized the importance of this latter perspective when he said, "Addressing the multi-dimensional environmental challenges of the 21st century requires a more holistic mindset, one that looks beyond today and toward achieving truly sustainable solutions for tomorrow."[137] Although the EPA has in recent years taken steps to overcome its stovepipe mentality, a systems approach in which environmental protection is truly integrated across land, air, water, and toxins remains an implementation challenge for decision makers at the agency.[138]

Approximations

Another feature of bounded rationality is a willingness to settle for approximately correct answers rather than insisting on precise solutions. Perhaps it is this sort of thinking that gave us the Leaning Tower of Pisa! But in most instances, approximations serve us rather well.

Consider the problem of tips earned by waiters and waitresses at restaurants and similar establishments. Because tips are often cash transactions, employees have incentives to underreport earnings, thus failing to meet their tax obligations and imposing a burden on the rest of us. Instead of counting

Figure 2.2 EPA Organizational Structure

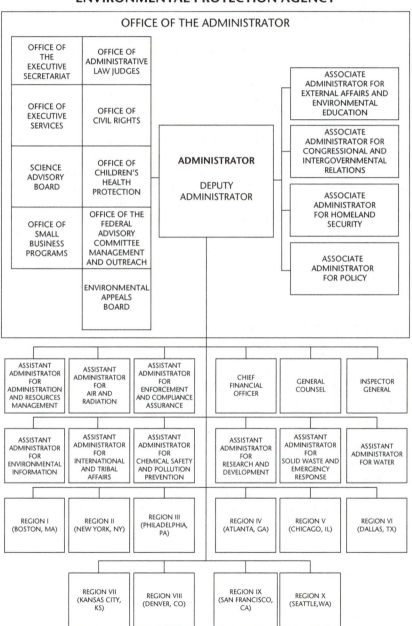

ENVIRONMENTAL PROTECTION AGENCY

Source: *The United States Government Manual 2016,* Office of the Federal Register, National Archives and Records Administration, https://www.gpo.gov/fdsys/pkg/GOVMAN-2016-12-16/pdf/GOVMAN-2016-12-16.pdf, p. 1343 (accessed March 16, 2017).

tips at every restaurant in the United States—a herculean task—the Internal Revenue Service (IRS) decided in 1994 to calculate probable tip revenue based on business volume. By the end of 1996 the IRS had introduced this system at more than 22,000 establishments, and reported tip income had increased by more than $2 billion.[139] Estimates of tip revenue were sufficiently conservative that no one, or almost no one, paid more than was actually owed.

For reasons discussed earlier, cost-benefit analysis, an instrument of comprehensive rationality, produces answers that are at best approximations of actual benefit-cost ratios. In some instances, such approximations result in bad decisions. For example, in evaluating the Dickey-Lincoln School hydroelectric power project in Maine, the Army Corps of Engineers estimated the benefit-cost ratio to be 2/1, when in fact the ratio was more like 0.8/1 or 0.9/1.[140] Fortunately, this mistake was discovered, and Congress terminated funding for the project. Despite this example, cost-benefit calculations most of the time fall well beyond the boundary of 1.0, thus reducing the policy implications of calculation errors. A cost-benefit analysis of the EPA's proposal to reduce the amount of lead in gasoline yielded a benefit-cost ratio higher than 10/1, although it was impossible to measure all the benefits.[141] In this instance, the policy implications were clear. Even if the true benefit-cost ratio was 11/1 or 12/1—or even 9/1—the EPA was justified on analytical grounds in proceeding with its lead reduction plan.

Standard Operating Procedures

In a wonderful set of mysteries featuring park ranger Anna Pigeon, Nevada Barr has written about situations that may require departures from standard operating procedures. In case after case, Anna deviates from well-established rules and norms to gain evidence, catch criminals, and save lives. In *Blind Descent,* for example, Anna returns to a dangerous and fragile cave in order to rescue an abandoned colleague, without securing her boss's permission.[142] Anna, a pragmatist, justifies her behavior by arguing that you shouldn't go by the book when lives are at stake.[143]

It is possible to identify cases where standard operating procedures, designed to rationalize bureaucratic decision making, produce questionable results. Regulatory inspectors who always go by the book sometimes behave unreasonably.[144] Policy analysts who become preoccupied with routines sometimes waste time and lose sight of broader goals.[145] Adherence to standard operating procedures does not always prevent accidents from occurring.[146] Standard operating procedures may be useless in a novel situation.

The aftermath of a devastating tornado in Joplin, Missouri, in May 2011 illustrates some of the drawbacks of standard operating procedures, especially in a crisis situation. Unable to identify more than 100 dead bodies, local officials placed the remains in a temporary morgue just outside Joplin. Understandably, families of missing persons migrated to this site, to identify their loved ones. Because many of the bodies were, in a word, "gruesome," local officials decided to adhere to federal protocols, which required DNA or dental record matches for victim identification. This process seemed unduly bureaucratic to grieving family members seeking closure. Under pressure, local officials relented in some cases. But in one instance, family members incorrectly identified their son—an error that was not detected until the viewing at the funeral home. Stunned by this mistake, local officials reverted to a modified version of the federal protocol, allowing exceptions in certain situations, such as where tattoos might quickly lead to positive identification. They also sought to expedite the process of DNA matching.[147]

Another tornado that occurred in May 2013 in Moore, Oklahoma, demonstrates the utility of throwing standard operating procedures out the window and responding instinctively to an extraordinary crisis. As deadly 200-mile-per-hour winds bore down on Plaza Towers Elementary School, sixth-grade teacher Rhonda Crosswhite used her body as a shield for fourth grader Damian Britton and other students in a bathroom stall. As Damian later recalled, "She was covering me and my friend Zachary. I told her we were fine because we were holding on to something, and then she went over to my friend Antonio and covered him, so she saved our lives."[148]

Despite their drawbacks, standard operating procedures help street-level bureaucrats to process cases and resolve routine problems quickly. These procedures also allow managers to control those street-level bureaucrats. In addition, standard operating procedures can prevent police officers from abusing suspects, inspectors from playing favorites, and IRS auditors from targeting individuals for political reasons. Furthermore, they enable bureaucracies to devote more resources to novel problems because bureaucrats need not reinvent the wheel when a familiar problem appears.

One of the simplest, but most compelling, examples of a standard operating procedure that works well is the emergency response calling system. Over time, most adults and even some young children have learned that in an emergency they should dial 911. This arrangement has saved an untold number of lives. The 911 system is particularly interesting because it involves a standard operating procedure for nonroutine situations. Even in the middle of a crisis, standard operating procedures can be extremely helpful.

Still, it is in crisis situations that strict reliance on standard operating procedures is most controversial. During the financial crisis of 2008, Treasury Secretary Henry Paulson, Federal Reserve Board Chair Ben Bernanke, and Federal Reserve Bank of New York President Timothy Geithner shared a rough consensus that they should do "whatever it takes" to avert a collapse of the financial industry, including its leading institutions.[149] Sheila Bair, chair of the Federal Deposit Insurance Corporation (FDIC), argued instead that some banks and investment banks should be allowed to fail, if existing law did not justify a heroic intervention. When Wachovia Bank, the nation's fourth-largest bank, stood on the brink of collapse in September 2008, Geithner and others strongly urged Bair to use her deposit insurance fund to guarantee a potential buyer against failure. At first, Bair refused, noting that the relevant statute authorized this response only in extremely unusual situations. Bair also believed that a major bank failure could discourage overly risky investments in the future. Geithner pressed hard, arguing strenuously that the FDIC's fund would be worthless if the economy were in a shambles. Eventually, Bair agreed to a guarantee, though a last-minute change in Wachovia's purchaser, from Citicorp to Wells Fargo, enabled her to protect the deposit insurance fund from depletion.[150] The same dispute played out again later in 2008, when top government officials persuaded a reluctant Bair to help bail out Citicorp, a leading investment bank. This time, the FDIC did surrender $10 billion of its fund, despite Bair's misgivings.[151] In retrospect, it is difficult to say who was right and who was wrong in these extremely complicated high-wire negotiations. Clearly, standard operating procedures, if followed faithfully, do not always lead to desired outcomes in financial markets. On the other hand, precedent-shattering decisions may reward or encourage bad behavior by reckless firms and investors.

Conclusion

Bounded rationality is a useful starting point for an in-depth discussion of bureaucratic politics because it is more realistic than a rational choice or incremental perspective. With limited information, limited alternatives, and limited time, real bureaucrats make decisions as best they can without necessarily being constrained by the status quo. They learn from experience, relying on standard operating procedures to make their tasks more manageable. They simplify problems by disaggregating them, or breaking them into bite-size chunks. In Simon's words, they satisfice because they cannot optimize.

Despite its strengths, bounded rationality is not the only useful way to think about bureaucratic decision making. In a sense, the world of bounded rationality resembles a planet populated by *Star Trek*'s Vulcans, beings such as Spock, known for his iron logic, his capacity for independent thought, and his incorruptibility. What is missing from Spock, and from bounded rationality, is not just emotion but politics. In the real world, pressure from legislators, chief executives, judges, interest groups, journalists, and citizens constrains bureaucratic decision making.

In our next chapter, we focus on some of these actors—the politicians and judges authorized to tell bureaucrats what to do. We introduce an alternative theoretical perspective, known as principal-agent theory, which pays much closer attention to the bureaucracy's sovereigns. Bureaucrats do not make decisions in a vacuum, as bounded rationality sometimes implies. Yet, as we shall see, the bureaucracy's principals experience many of the same limitations that bureaucrats do. As they seek to control the bureaucracy, politicians and judges are constrained by limited information, limited options, and limited time.

Key Terms

Notes

1. William Gormley Jr., "Regulatory Enforcement: Accommodation and Conflict in Four States," *Public Administration Review* 57 (July/August 1997): 285–293.

2. Baltimore City of Transportation, "Vehicle Towing," http://transportation.baltimorecity.gov/towing (accessed March 16, 2017).

3. Gormley, "Regulatory Enforcement," 289.

4. Ibid.

5. Elizabeth Chuck, "Baltimore Mayor Stephanie Rawlings-Blake under Fire for 'Space' to Destroy Comment," NBC News, http://www.nbcnews.com/storyline/baltimore-unrest/mayor-stephanie-rawlings-blake-under-fire-giving-space-destroy-baltimore-n349656 (accessed March 16, 2017).

6. Herbert Simon, *Administrative Behavior,* 4th ed. (New York: Free Press, 1997).

7. Charles Edward Lindblom, "The Science of 'Muddling Through,'" *Public Administration Review* 29 (Spring 1959): 79–88.

8. Bryan Jones, *Politics and the Architecture of Choice: Bounded Rationality and Governance* (Chicago: University of Chicago Press, 2001); John Kingdon, *Agendas, Alternatives, and Public Policies* (Boston: Little, Brown, 1995); Bryan Jones, Frank Baumgartner, and James True, "Policy Punctuation: U.S. Budget Authority, 1947–1995," *Journal of Politics* 60 (February 1998): 1–33.

9. George Akerlof, "The Market for Lemons," *Quarterly Journal of Economics* 84 (August 1970): 488–500; Burton Weisbrod, *The Nonprofit Economy* (Cambridge, Mass.: Harvard University Press, 1988).

10. Donald P. Green and Ian Shapiro, *Pathologies of Rational Choice Theory: A Critique of Applications in Political Science* (New Haven, CT: Yale University Press, 1994).

11. Simon, *Administrative Behavior,* 119.

12. Jonathan Bendor, *Parallel Systems: Redundancy in Government* (Berkeley: University of California Press, 1985), 85–118, 209–215.

13. Malcolm Sparrow, *The Regulatory Craft* (Washington, D.C.: Brookings Institution Press, 2000), 127.

14. Quoted in Peter Finn, Ian Shapira, and Marc Fisher, "A Victory Built on Lessons Learned from the Enemy," *Washington Post,* May 6, 2011. See also Greg Miller, "Safe House Was Key to Bringing bin Laden Down," *Washington Post,* May 6, 2011; Karin Bruilliard and Karen DeYoung, "Site of Hideout Raises Questions about Complicity," *Washington Post,* May 3, 2011; Scott Wilson and Anne Kornblut, "Obama: 'The World Is Safer . . . because of the Death of Osama bin Laden,' SM." *Washington Post,* May 3, 2011; Bob Woodward, "Trail to bin Laden Began with One Call," *Washington Post,* May 7, 2011; Elisabeth Bumiller, Carlotta Gall, and Salman Masood, "Bin Laden's Secret Life in a Shrunken World," *New York Times,* May 8, 2011.

15. J. Clarence Davies and Jan Mazurek, *Pollution Control in the United States* (Washington, D.C.: Resources for the Future, 1998), 59–63.

16. Terry M. Moe, "The Politics of Bureaucratic Structure," in *Can the Government Govern?,* ed. John E. Chubb and Paul E. Peterson (Washington, D.C.: Brookings Institution Press, 1989).

17. Ibid, 302.

18. Simon, *Administrative Behavior,* 89.

19. Michael Lipsky, *Street-Level Bureaucracy* (New York: Russell Sage Foundation, 1980).

20. Robert Axelrod, *The Evolution of Cooperation* (New York: Basic Books, 1984), 73–87.

21. William Gormley Jr., *Everybody's Children: Child Care as a Public Problem* (Washington, D.C.: Brookings Institution Press, 1995), 113–117.

22. Ian Ayres and John Braithwaite, *Responsive Regulation: Transcending the Deregulation Debate* (Oxford, UK: Oxford University Press, 1992).

23. Jane Waldfogel, *The Future of Child Protection: How to Break the Cycle of Abuse and Neglect* (Cambridge, Mass.: Harvard University Press, 1998), 148–151.

24. Jane Waldfogel, "The Future of Child Protection Revisited," in *Child Welfare Research,* ed. Duncan Lindsey and Aron Shlonsky (New York: Oxford University Press, 2008).

25. Ibid.

26. Sparrow, *Regulatory Craft,* 86–87.

27. Marsha Schachtel, "CitiStat and the Baltimore Neighborhood Indicators Alliance: Using Information to Improve Communication and Community," *National Civic Review* (Fall 2001): 253–265.

28. Robert Behn, "The Varieties of CitiStat," *Public Administration Review* 66 (May/June 2006): 332–340.

29. Chad Vander Veen, "Governor O'Malley Uses StateStat to Transform Maryland," *Government Technology,* August 4, 2009, http://www.govtech.com/featured/102492329.html (accessed March 16, 2017).

30. Aaron Davis, "'Never Off Work': O'Malley Has Governed Maryland with an Obsession for Detail, but Some Wonder if He Misses the Bigger Picture," *Washington Post,* October 20, 2010.

31. Peter Moskos, *Cop in the Hood: My Year Policing Baltimore's Eastern District* (Princeton, N.J.: Princeton University Press, 2008), 140.

32. Ibid., 141.

33. Ibid., 52.

34. Graham Rayman, "The NYPD Tapes: Inside Bed-Stuy's 81st Precinct," *Village Voice,* May 4, 2010.

35. Simon, *Administrative Behavior,* 105.

36. Jack L. Walker, "The Diffusion of Innovations across the American States," *American Political Science Review* 63, no. 3 (September 1969): 880–899.

37. Ibid.

38. Craig Volden, "States as Policy Laboratories: Emulating Success in the Children's Health Insurance Program," *American Journal of Political Science* 50, no. 2 (April 2006): 294–312.

39. Walker, "The Diffusion of Innovations across the American States"; Frances Stokes Berry and William D. Berry, "State Lottery Adoptions as Policy Innovations: An Event History Analysis," *American Political Science Review* 84, no. 2 (June 1990): 395–415.

40. David Konisky, "Regulatory Competition and Environmental Enforcement: Is There a Race to the Bottom?" *American Journal of Political Science* 51, no. 4 (October 2007): 853–872.

41. National Association of Insurance Commissioners, "Model Categories Index," http://www.naic.org/committees_index_model_description.htm (accessed September 20, 2015).

42. Steven J. Balla, "Interstate Professional Associations and the Diffusion of Policy Innovations," *American Politics Research* 29, no. 3 (May 2001): 221–245.

43. Charles Perrow, *Normal Accidents: Living with High-Risk Technologies* (Princeton, N.J.: Princeton University Press, 1999), 403.

44. Damien McElroy, "Osama bin Laden Dead: U.S. Built Replica of bin Laden Compound after Building Complete Intelligence Picture," *Telegraph,* May 3, 2011.

45. Eric Lipton, Ian Austen, and Sharon LaFraniere, "Tensions and Flaws before Health Website Crash," *Washington Post,* November 22, 2013, p. 1.

46. Ibid.

47. Robert Doar and Andrew Feldman, "Trump Should Support Bipartisan 'Evidence Based' Revolution," http://www.realclearpolicy.com/articles/2017/02/22/trump_should_support_bipartisan_evidence_based_revolution_110171.html (accessed March 21, 2017).

48. Ron Haskins and Greg Margolis, *Show Me the Evidence: Obama's Fight for Rigor and Results in Social Policy* (Washington, D.C.: Brookings Institution Press, 2015), 26–30.

49. Ibid.

50. Ibid.

51. Seth Harris, Former Deputy Secretary of Labor, Remarks at Workshop on Performance, Accountability, Evidence, and Improvement (Washington, D.C.: National Academy of Public Administration, October 5, 2016).

52. "Managing for Results: Agencies' Trends in the Use of Performance Information to Make Decisions," Report no. GAO-14-747 (Washington, D.C.: U.S. Government Accountability Office, September 2014).

53. William Gormley Jr., *Voices for Children: Rhetoric and Public Policy* (Washington, D.C.: Brookings Institution Press, 2012), 137–138.

54. U.S. Department of State, Office of the Chief Economist, http://www.state.gov/e/oce (accessed October 28, 2016).

55. Interview with Rodney Ludema, Associate Professor of Economics, Georgetown University, and former Chief Economist, State Department, September 26, 2016.

56. Mark Lipsey, James Howell, Marion Kelly, Gabrielle Chapman, and Darin Carver, "Improving the Effectiveness of Juvenile Justice Programs: A New Perspective on Evidence-Based Practice" (PowerPoint presentation at the Conference on Evidence-Based Practice in Juvenile Justice, Center for Juvenile Justice Reform, Georgetown University, Washington, D.C., December 3, 2010).

57. Kathryn Nix, "Comparative Effectiveness Research under Obamacare: A Slippery Slope to Health Care Rationing," http://www.heritage.org/research/reports/2012/04/comparative-effectiveness-research-under-obamacare-a-slippery-slope-to-health-care-rationing (accessed August 29, 2016).

58. Tony Coelho, "Policymakers Should Choose Patient Empowerment over Paternalism," http://www.huffingtonpost.com/tony-coelho/policymakers-should-choos_b_9774328.html (accessed August 29, 2016).

59. House Committee on Ways and Means, Subcommittee on Income Security and Family Support, Hearing on Proposals to Provide Federal Funding for Early Childhood Home Visitation Programs, 111th Cong., 1st sess., June 9, 2009.

60. Nicholas Stern, *The Economics of Climate Change: The Stern Review* (Cambridge, UK: Cambridge University Press, 2007).

61. Peter Doran and Maggie Zimmerman, "Examining the Scientific Consensus on Climate Change," *Eos* 90, no. 3 (2009): 22–23; John Cook et al., "Quantifying the Consensus on Anthropogenic Global Warming in the Scientific Literature," *Environmental Research Letters* 8, no. 2 (2013): 1–7.

62. Cary Funk and Brian Kennedy, *Public Views on Climate Change and Climate Scientists* (Washington, D.C.: Pew Research Center, October 4, 2016).

63. Chris Mooney and Brady Dennis, "EPA's Leader Dismisses Climate-Change Science," *Washington Post,* March 10, 2017, p. 8.

64. Juliet Eilperin and Brady Dennis, "Trump Acts to Erase Obama's Climate Legacy," *Washington Post,* March 28, 2017, p. 1.

65. Amy Goldstein et al., "ACA Revision Would Reduce Insured Numbers by 24 Million, CBO Reports," *Washington Post,* March 14, 2017.

66. Ibid.

67. Linda Qiu, "Fact Check: Spicer's Pre-emptive Attack on the Nonpartisan CBO," *New York Times,* March 9, 2017.

68. "Read the Report, Republicans," editorial, *Washington Post,* March 15, 2017, p. 14.

69. Philip Joyce, *The Congressional Budget Office* (Washington, D.C.: Georgetown University Press, 2011).

70. Linda Qiu, op. cit.; Philip Joyce, op. cit.

71. Robert Doar and Andrew Feldman, "Trump Should Support Bipartisan 'Evidence Based' Revolution," http://www.realclearpolicy.com/articles/2017/02/22/trump_should_support_bipartisan_evidence_based_revolution_110171.html (accessed March 21, 2017).

72. Deborah Stone, *Policy Paradox: The Art of Political Decision Making* (New York: W. W. Norton, 2002), 256.

73. Simon, *Administrative Behavior,* 94.

74. Stone, *Policy Paradox,* 375.

75. Greenspan, quoted in ibid., 244.

76. Martha Feldman, *Order without Design: Information Production and Policy Making* (Stanford, Calif.: Stanford University Press, 1989), 81, 106–114.

77. Christopher Carrigan and Stuart Shapiro, "What's Wrong with the Back of the Envelope? A Call for Simple (and Timely) Benefit-Cost Analysis," *Regulation & Governance,* http://onlinelibrary.wiley.com/doi/10.1111/rego.12120/full (accessed August 30, 2016).

78. Ibid.

79. David Weimer and Aidan Vining, *Policy Analysis: Concepts and Practice,* 5th ed. (New York: Longman, 2011), 424–447.

80. Peter Clark and James Q. Wilson, "Incentive Systems: A Theory of Organizations," *Administrative Science Quarterly* 6 (September 1961): 129–166.

81. John Brehm and Scott Gates, *Working, Shirking, and Sabotage: Bureaucratic Response to a Democratic Public* (Ann Arbor: University of Michigan Press, 1997): 80–83.

82. Anthony Downs, *Inside Bureaucracy* (Boston: Little, Brown, 1967), 88.

83. Amartya K. Sen, "Rational Fools: A Critique of the Behavioral Foundations of Economic Theory," *Philosophy & Public Affairs* 6, no. 4 (Summer 1977): 317–344.

84. Marissa Golden, *What Motivates Bureaucrats? Politics and Administration during the Reagan Years* (New York: Columbia University Press, 2000), 154–168.

85. Juliet Eilperin, Lisa Rein, and Marc Fisher, "Resistance from Within: Federal Workers Push Back against Trump," https://www.washingtonpost.com/politics/resistance-from-within-federal-workers-push-back-against-trump/2017/01/31/c65b110e-e7cb-11e6-b82f-687d6e6a3e7c_story.html?utm_term=.d36a0f6bedde (accessed March 22, 2017).

86. Charles Levinson and David Rohde, "Special Report: Pentagon Thwarts Obama's Effort to Close Guantanamo," http://www.reuters.com/article/us-usa-gitmo-release-special-report-idUSKBN0UB1B020151229 (accessed August 30, 2016).

87. Ibid.

88. Ibid.

89. Evan Perez and Jeremy Diamond, "Trump Fires Acting AG after She Declines to Defend Travel Ban," www.cnn.com/2017/01/30/politics/donald-trump-immigration-order-department-of-justice/ (accessed March 22, 2017).

90. Mariano Castillo and Kevin Conlon, "Kim Davis Stands Ground, but Same-Sex Couple Gets Marriage License," http://www.cnn.com/2015/09/14/politics/kim-davis-same-sex-marriage-kentucky/ (accessed August 30, 2016).

91. Ed Payne and Catherine E. Shoichet, "Kim Davis Released, but Judge Bars Her from Withholding Marriage Licenses," http://www.cnn.com/2015/09/08/politics/kim-davis-same-sex-marriage-kentucky/ (accessed August 30, 2016).

92. Ibid.

93. Moskos, *Cop in the Hood*, 46.

94. Ibid., 143.

95. Kenneth Meier, "Teachers, Students, and Discrimination: The Policy Impact of Black Representation," *Journal of Politics* 46 (February 1984): 252–263.

96. Thomas Dee, "A Teacher Like Me: Does Race, Ethnicity, or Gender Matter?" *American Economic Review* 95 (May 2005): 158–165.

97. Jason Grissom, Emily Kern, and Luis Rodriguez, "The 'Representative Bureaucracy' in Education: Educator Workforce Diversity, Policy Outputs, and Outcomes for Disadvantaged Students," *Educational Researcher* 44, no. 3 (April 2015): 185–192.

98. Danielle N. Atkins and Vicky M. Wilkins, "Schools That Employ More Minority Teachers Have Lower Minority Teenage Pregnancy Rates," http://blogs.lse.ac.uk/usappblog/2013/10/17/minority-teachers-lower-teen-pregnancy-rates/ (accessed August 30, 2016).

99. Ibid.

100. Gormley, "Regulatory Enforcement."

101. Kenneth Meier and Jill Nicholson-Crotty, "Gender, Representative Bureaucracy, and Law Enforcement: The Case of Sexual Assault," *Public Administration Review* 66 (November/December 2006): 850–860.

102. Thomas L. Friedman, "Clinton's Cabinet Choices Put Him at Center, Balancing Competing Factions," http://www.nytimes.com/1992/12/27/us/transition-clinton-s-cabinet-choices-put-him-center-balancing-competing-factions.html?pagewanted=all (accessed August 31, 2016).

103. "Looks Like America," http://www.nytimes.com/1992/12/25/opinion/looks-like-america.html (accessed August 31, 2016).

104. Juliet Eilperin, "Obama Has Propelled Diversity at Top Levels," *Washington Post*, September 21, 2015, p. 4.

105. Ibid.

106. Ibid.

107. Jasmine C. Lee, "Trump's Cabinet So Far Is More White and Male Than Any First Cabinet Since Reagan's," https://www.nytimes.com/interactive/2017/01/13/us/politics/trump-cabinet-women-minorities.html?_r=0 (accessed March 22, 2017).

108. Kellie Lunney, "Public–Private Sector Pay Gap Remains at 35 Percent," http://www.govexec.com/pay-benefits/2014/10/public-private-sector-pay-gap-remains-35-percent/96830/ (accessed August 31, 2016).

109. Ibid.

110. Ibid.

111. Richard Ingersoll and Henry May, "The Magnitude, Destinations, and Determinants of Mathematics and Science Teacher Turnover," *Educational Evaluation and Policy Analysis* 34 (2012): 435–464.

112. Matthew Hendricks, "Does It Pay to Pay Teachers More? Evidence from Texas," *Journal of Public Economics* 109 (2014): 50–63.

113. Arianna Pickard, "Teacher Survey: See the Top Reasons Tulsa Public Schools Teachers Say They're Leaving," *Tulsa World*, February 28, 2017.

114. Nick Anderson, "Study Undercuts Teacher Bonuses," *Washington Post,* September 22, 2010; Matthew Springer et al., "Teacher Pay for Performance: Experimental Evidence from the Project on Incentives in Teaching," National Center on Performance Incentives at Vanderbilt University, Nashville, September 21, 2010.

115. Thomas S. Dee and James Wycoff, "Incentives, Selection, and Teacher Performance: Evidence from IMPACT," *Journal of Policy Analysis and Public Management* 34, no. 2 (Spring 2015): 267–297.

116. Tim Craig and Bill Turque, "Rhee to Resign as Schools Chancellor," *Washington Post,* October 13, 2010; Richard Whitmire, *The Bee Eater: Michelle Rhee Takes on the Nation's Worst School District* (San Francisco: Jossey-Bass, 2011).

117. Barry Rubin, *Secrets of State: The State Department and the Struggle over U.S. Foreign Policy* (New York: Oxford University Press, 1985), 124–129.

118. Ibid., 127.

119. Joel Aberbach, Robert Putnam, and Bert Rockman, *Bureaucrats and Politicians in Western Democracies* (Cambridge, Mass.: Harvard University Press, 1981), 84–112.

120. Merritt Kennedy, "Lead-Laced Water in Flint: A Step-by-Step Look at the Makings of a Crisis," http://www.npr.org/sections/thetwo-way/2016/04/20/465545378/lead-laced-water-in-flint-a-step-by-step-look-at-the-makings-of-a-crisis (accessed August 31, 2016).

121. Gary Ridley, "Flint Water Switch Approved Despite DEQ Health Warnings a Year Earlier," http://www.mlive.com/news/flint/index.ssf/2016/02/deq_official_warned_of_flint_r.html (accessed August 31, 2016).

122. Kennedy, "Lead-Laced Water in Flint."

123. Mona Hanna-Attisha, Jenny LaChance, Richard Casey Sadler, and Allison Champney Schnepp, "Elevated Blood Lead Levels in Children Associated with the Flint Drinking Water Crisis: A Spatial Analysis of Risk and Public Health Response," *American Journal of Public Health* 106, no. 2 (December 21, 2015): 283–290.

124. Julie Bosman et al., "As Water Problems Grew, Officials Belittled Complaints from Flint," *New York Times,* January 20, 2016.

125. Amos Tversky and Daniel Kahneman, "Availability: A Heuristic for Judging Frequency and Probability," *Cognitive Psychology* 5 (1973): 207–232.

126. Perrow, *Normal Accidents,* 321.

127. "Salazar Divides MMS's Three Conflicting Missions," https://www.doi.gov/news/pressreleases/Salazar-Divides-MMSs-Three-Conflicting-Missions (accessed August 31, 2016).

128. Christopher Carrigan, *Structured to Fail? Explaining Regulatory Performance under Competing Mandates* (New York: Cambridge University Press, 2017); Christopher Carrigan, "Captured by Disaster? Reinterpreting Regulatory Behavior in the Shadow of the Gulf Oil Spill," in *Preventing Capture: Special Interest Influence, and How to Limit It,* ed. Daniel Carpenter and David A. Moss (New York: Cambridge University Press, 2014), 239–291.

129. In Norman J. Vig and Michael E. Kraft, *Environmental Policy: new Directions for the Twenty-First Century.* 4th edition. CQ Press 2006. Washington, DC. A Myrick Freeman III, "Economics, Incentives, and Environmental Policy." 193–214.

130. Herbert Simon, "Why Public Administration?" *Journal of Public Administration Research and Theory* 8 (January 1998): 10.

131. Albert Hirschman, *Exit, Voice, and Loyalty* (Cambridge, Mass.: Harvard University Press, 1970).

132. Herbert Kaufman, *The Forest Ranger* (Baltimore: Johns Hopkins University Press, 1960), 214–215.

133. Robert Katzmann, *Regulatory Bureaucracy: The Federal Trade Commission and Antitrust Policy* (Cambridge, Mass.: MIT Press, 1980).

134. Simon, *Administrative Behavior,* 111.

135. Bendor, *Parallel Systems,* 117.

136. Anne Lamott, *Bird by Bird: Some Instructions on Writing and Life* (New York: Anchor Books, 1994), 18–19.

137. Stephen L. Johnson, U.S. EPA Administrator, RFF Policy Leadership Forum, http://www.rff.org/events/event/2007-04/stephen-l-johnson-us-epa-administrator-rff-policy-leadership-forum (accessed August 31, 2016).

138. Alan D. Hecht and William H. Sanders III, "Rejoinder: How EPA Research, Policies, and Programs Can Advance Urban Sustainability," https://sspp.proquest.com/rejoinder-how-epa-research-policies-and-programs-can-advance-urban-sustainability-539c8de519f2#.ymnps3kyn (accessed August 31, 2016).

139. Sparrow, *Regulatory Craft,* 123–124.

140. Myrick Freeman III, "Economic Incentives and Environmental Regulation," in Norman J. Vig and Michael E. Kraft, eds., *Environmental Policy: New Directions for the Twenty-first Century,* 4th ed. (Washington, D.C.: CQ Press, 2006), 193–214.

141. Ibid., 191.

142. Nevada Barr, *Blind Descent* (New York: Putnam, 1998).

143. For more on the ethical implications of these choices, see William T. Gormley Jr., "Moralists, Pragmatists, and Rogues: Bureaucrats in Modern Mysteries," *Public Administration Review* 61 (March/April 2001): 184–193.

144. Eugene Bardach and Robert Kagan, *Going by the Book: The Problem of Regulatory Unreasonableness* (Philadelphia: Temple University Press, 1982).

145. Feldman, *Order without Design.*

146. Perrow, *Normal Accidents,* 170–231.

147. Eliot Spitzer, "In the Arena," *CNN Reports,* interview with Mark Bridges, coroner, Newton County, Mo., May 26, 2011.

148. Scott Stump, "Okla. School Survivor: Teacher Threw Herself over Us and 'Saved Our Lives,'" http://www.today.com/news/okla-school-survivor-teacher-threw-herself-over-us-saved-our-6C9996716 (accessed August 31, 2016).

149. David Wessel, *In Fed We Trust: Ben Bernanke's War on the Great Panic* (New York: Crown Business, 2009).

150. Henry Paulson Jr., *On the Brink* (New York: Business Plus, 2010); Ryan Lizza, "The Contrarian: Sheila Bair and the White House Financial Debate," *New Yorker,* July 6 and 13, 2009, 30–37; Wessel, ibid.

151. Paulson, ibid., 402–415.

3 | The Bureaucracy's Bosses

In SEPTEMBER 2011, President Barack Obama stunned observers by rejecting a proposed Environmental Protection Agency (EPA) regulation on air pollution. The landmark regulation would have significantly reduced emissions of ground-level ozone, a smog-producing chemical that has been linked to asthma and other lung diseases.[1] The regulation was a top priority of EPA Administrator Lisa Jackson, who had staked a strong claim that existing ozone standards were appreciably weaker than those recommended by the agency's science advisers and therefore "not legally defensible."[2] Despite such claims and years of EPA effort, the regulation was quickly and unceremoniously scuttled during the course of a single White House meeting.

In a statement issued after the tense meeting, President Obama provided a rationale for his decision: "I have continued to underscore the importance of reducing regulatory burdens and regulatory uncertainty, particularly as our economy continues to recover."[3] According to EPA estimates, the ozone regulation would have imposed billions of dollars in annual costs on industries and local governments.[4] Such costs, and accompanying job losses, would have hit especially hard in the Midwest and Great Plains, regions that are major sources of ozone pollution.[5] Although the White House denied that political considerations informed the president's decision, the Midwest and Great Plains also loomed large as battlegrounds in the 2012 presidential election, which was just over a year away.

Regardless of the president's motivations, the ozone regulation withdrawal illustrates the power that policymakers outside the bureaucracy can wield over an agency. They usually exercise this power more subtly, however. Efforts by legislators to influence bureaucracies often take, for example, the form of informal staff communications and requirements that agencies give advance notice of their intended actions.

Despite the ubiquity of such efforts, bureaucracies retain considerable autonomy over policymaking, even in the face of direct instructions from elsewhere in government. In 2010, President Obama with great fanfare signed into law the **Dodd-Frank Wall Street Reform and Consumer Protection Act.** This massive law fundamentally overhauled the operation and supervision of the nation's financial system, in an effort to prevent a recurrence of the 2008 global financial crisis, the most significant economic downturn since the Great Depression. The law delegated to agencies such as the Federal Reserve (Fed) and Securities and Exchange Commission (SEC) the authority to write hundreds of regulations that were to collectively serve as the foundation of the government's management of financial practices and institutions.[6] As a means of expediting bureaucratic action, the law required that many of these regulations be promulgated by specified deadlines. Over the next several years, however, agencies missed more than 50 percent of these **statutory deadlines.**[7] It is certainly no small task to issue hundreds of complex, controversial regulations in short order, and some observers emphasize that the agencies in question have "actually done quite a bit."[8] Nevertheless, the implementation of Dodd-Frank demonstrates that agencies at times make decisions in a manner that explicitly deviates from the intent of Congress and the president.

Contentious episodes such as the battles over ozone emissions and financial reform are commonplace in the American political system. They are also vitally important. The interactions of agencies with their external political environments determine which public decisions will be made in bureaucracies and which will be made in other institutions of government. Put differently, the outcomes of these interactions establish the very **boundaries of bureaucratic authority.**[9]

As illustrated by the ozone and financial reform examples, these boundaries are sometimes, but not always, set with an eye to democratic principles such as accountability and performance. President Obama took away EPA's authority to make ozone policy, at least until after the upcoming presidential election—a particularly blunt imposition of political accountability. In the case of the Dodd-Frank Act, it is not clear that the promulgation of regulations in accordance with statutory deadlines is effective in bringing about the outcomes—a secure and prosperous financial system—desired by policymakers and their constituents. In the end, the boundaries of bureaucratic authority are best understood as manifestations of the ongoing contest between government agencies and their political supervisors for control over the policymaking process.

With these issues in mind, this chapter provides a detailed examination of the relationship between agencies and the outside political world. It is organized around the following *core questions:*

- *UNDER WHAT CONDITIONS IS POLICYMAKING RESPONSIBILITY DELEGATED TO THE BUREAUCRACY?* In general, President Obama entrusted EPA with the authority to make environmental policy, only to severely limit this authority when the dictates of electoral politics trumped ordinary policymaking considerations.

- *IN WHAT WAYS DO OTHER GOVERNMENT ACTORS SEEK TO INFLUENCE THE MANNER IN WHICH AGENCIES EXERCISE THEIR RESPONSIBILITIES?* The Dodd-Frank Act not only gave agencies such as the Fed and SEC the authority to write regulations but also attached strict timetables to this authority, thereby limiting agency flexibility in making and implementing financial policy.

- *TO WHAT EXTENT ARE EFFORTS AT POLITICAL CONTROL SUCCESSFUL, IN LIGHT OF THE FACT THAT AGENCIES CAN, AND DO, TAKE STEPS TO PRESERVE AND EXTEND THEIR AUTHORITY?* In contrast to the White House meeting that resulted in the withdrawal of the ozone regulation, a 2013 meeting between President Obama and financial regulators failed to bring about increased agency compliance with the Dodd-Frank Act's statutory deadlines.[10] These contrasting results suggest that political control of agency decision making varies widely across political and policy contexts.

The chapter approaches these core questions primarily from the perspective of principal-agent theory, an approach widely used to understand the origins and implications of delegated authority. It is particularly appropriate in that it places bureaucratic policymaking in its broader context. Agencies do not operate in a vacuum but rather in an environment in which public decisions can be, and often are, made in alternative venues. As will become apparent, this environmental reality has fundamental consequences for both bureaucratic accountability and performance.

Delegation, Adverse Selection, and Moral Hazard

Delegation is a common feature of modern life. Clients grant attorneys the authority to provide legal representation, patients rely on doctors to treat illnesses, and employers hire workers to perform tasks of all sorts. These types of relationships share fundamental characteristics. Clients, patients, and employers all face difficulties in choosing and monitoring those to whom they delegate authority. Principal-agent theory is an approach to understanding the causes and consequences of these difficulties.[11]

A **principal** is an actor who enters into a contractual relationship with another actor, an **agent.** The agent is entrusted to take actions that lead to outcomes specified by the principal. For example, doctors act as agents when they prescribe medicines and perform procedures to enhance the duration and quality of the lives of their patients (that is, principals), and lawyers act as agents for persons accused of a crime. These arrangements arise when principals lack the ability to achieve their goals by themselves. Self-representation is not advisable, in most cases, for defendants seeking to minimize the likelihood of a guilty verdict!

A key assumption of principal-agent theory is that **self-interest** primarily motivates both principals and agents. These actors, in other words, are considered to be rational decision makers. In general, principals and agents face **divergent incentives,** and this divergence means that purely self-interested behavior on the part of agents may not produce the outcomes desired by principals. For instance, the owners of business firms are concerned first and foremost with maximizing profits. Although rank-and-file employees certainly share a stake in company performance, their subordinate status shapes their actions in important ways. The workers on assembly lines may have little reason to work at top speed if the benefits of their efforts accrue solely to corporate executives and shareholders.

Principals face two specific difficulties when dealing with agents. The first is known as **adverse selection.** This difficulty arises when principals cannot directly observe important characteristics of agents but must rely on rough indicators. Defendants cannot easily discern the true motivations and skills of attorneys and therefore must select legal representation on the basis of factors such as reputations and caseloads. Although such proxies may have merit, they are not foolproof. In the end, principals run the risk of hiring agents not ideally suited for the task at hand.

The second difficulty is known as **moral hazard.** This difficulty stems from the fact that agents, once selected, cannot be readily evaluated in their work environments. As a result, principals must make inferences about the degree to which agents are effectively securing the outcomes they were hired to bring about. Potential patients often judge doctors who perform laser eye surgeries by their success rates. Such measures, however, prove to be far from perfect. It may be hard to discern the individual performance of a doctor who works as part of a team of laser eye surgeons. To further complicate matters, the outcomes of surgeries are affected not only by the doctors' actions but also by the patients' pre-surgery eyesight conditions (such as how nearsighted or farsighted they were). Because of these uncertainties, agents may find it possible to shirk their duties, or even to undermine the goals sought by principals, without being detected.

Can principals overcome the difficulties caused by adverse selection and moral hazard? One of the main lessons of principal-agent theory is that delegation almost invariably leads to **agency loss.** Agency loss occurs when the behavior of agents leaves principals unable to achieve their goals in an efficient manner or realize them at all. Agency loss, however, can be limited under the right circumstances. For principals, then, the key task is to take steps that help bring such circumstances about.[12]

For years, researchers have cited police departments as among the agencies that are most difficult for supervisors to control.[13] That is because their behavior is so difficult for supervisors to observe.[14] Yet there is growing evidence that police supervisors can reshape the behavior of front-line officers in profound ways if they have compelling reasons to do so. A good example would be New York City's stop-and-frisk policies, which came under fire because critics believed that police officers were using such interactions to harass and intimidate African American and Hispanic males. In March 2013, New York City Police Commissioner James Hall issued a memo requiring officers who stop someone suspected of possessing a weapon to write up the details (already required) *and* share the notes with their supervisor (a new requirement). This seemingly modest procedural requirement had a sudden and dramatic effect on police behavior. Following the memo, there was a 40 percent decline in stops for criminal possession of a weapon (CPW).[15] At the same time, the percentage of weapons stops that produced an actual weapon increased. In short, principals were successfully controlling agents.

One reason why this intervention succeeded is because police departments are under much closer scrutiny for their interactions with persons of color and they are also more visible because of the rise of body cameras and cell phone videos of police–client interactions. Thus, the old premise that police officer interactions with suspects are unobservable is no longer correct. This makes accountability measures easier to implement successfully.

Perhaps the most common way to mitigate the agency loss associated with adverse selection is the use of **screening mechanisms.** Basically, principals induce agents to reveal their motivations and skills before hiring them. For example, employers routinely judge the qualifications of applicants through apprenticeships and examinations. The problem of moral hazard can be ameliorated in two distinct ways. The first is **institutional design.** Here, principals place agents in situations in which they find it in their self-interest to work toward outcomes favored by their principals. Corporations, for instance, commonly provide workers with a financial stake in company performance through devices such as stock options. The second approach is **oversight** of agent actions. By monitoring agents at work, principals aim to identify and redirect behavior inconsistent with their objectives. Principals can also use oversight as a deterrent. The mere possibility of being monitored may compel agents to forgo activities that do not serve principals well.

Principal-agent theory can readily be applied to policymaking in the bureaucracy. Administrative agencies are agents to whom policymaking authority is delegated. This authority originates with principals such as chief executives, legislatures, and judiciaries. The act of delegation brings each of these principals face to face with particular manifestations of adverse selection and moral hazard. For example, legislators have relatively little influence over the selection of agency officials, as personnel matters fall largely under the domain of the chief executive and the civil service system. Given such difficulties, why do principals empower agencies in the first place? Put differently, what are the benefits of policymaking in the bureaucracy?

Why Bureaucracy?

One obvious rationale for bureaucracy is the scope of modern government. Early in its history, the federal government performed only a handful of functions, such as setting duties on foreign goods. Figure 3.1 illustrates that as the government's reach extended, the **size of the bureaucracy** grew as well. Between the New Deal and Great Society, two of the most ambitious expansions of government power in American history, the number of employees in the executive branch grew from less than half a million to more than two million. On the other hand, the size of the federal bureaucracy declined noticeably during the Clinton administration, after peaking in 1990. It has been roughly stable since that time, although expectations are that that will change over the course of President Donald Trump's administration.

On March 13, 2017, President Trump signed the Comprehensive Plan for Reorganizing the Executive Branch, part of his effort to make good on his campaign pledge to "drain the swamp."[16] The plan, in seeking to reduce "duplication and redundancy," has the potential to significantly shrink the size of the federal workforce.[17] Early in his administration, President Trump also touted

Figure 3.1 Size of the Federal Bureaucracy, 1820–2014

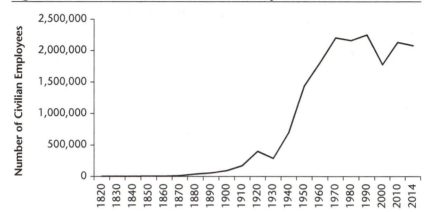

Sources: U.S. Census Bureau, *Bicentennial Edition: Historical Statistics of the United States, Colonial Times to 1970,* https://fraser.stlouisfed.org/docs/publications/histstatus/hstat1970_cen_1975_v2.pdf (accessed July 7, 2015); U.S. Office of Personnel Management, "Executive Branch Civilian Employment Since 1940," https://www.opm.gov/policy-data-oversight/data-analysis-documentation/federal-employment-reports/historical-tables/executive-branch-civilian-employment-since-1940/ (accessed July 7, 2015). All numbers exclude U.S. Postal Service employees.

the fact that he was purposefully leaving a number of appointed posts unfilled: "I look at some of the jobs and it's people over people over people. I say, 'What do all these people do?' You don't need all those jobs."[18]

Such efforts, on top of a hiring freeze instituted on President Trump's first full day in office, appear to have produced results in short order.[19] According to the Bureau of Labor Statistics, the Washington, D.C., area lost 2,700 federal jobs in early 2017.[20] One projection estimated that President Trump's initial budget, were it to be enacted as written, would lead to a loss of at least 20,000 federal jobs in the nation's capital alone.[21] Presidential budgets are, of course, subject to political negotiations with Congress, and economic projections are subject to all kinds of uncertainties. Nevertheless, the Trump administration aspires to "deconstruct the administrative state," and one intended result is a historic reduction in the size of the federal bureaucracy.[22]

A different indicator of the bureaucracy's growth is the number of pages the **Federal Register** (the executive branch's official daily publication) consumes. The documents published in the *Federal Register* include agency regulations and proposed rules, as well as executive orders and other presidential materials. As indicated in Table 3.1, the size of the *Federal Register* has grown more than sevenfold since 1960.

Contemporary government addresses issues that are not only wide ranging but often quite complex. In formulating the ozone regulation, EPA had to synthesize knowledge from fields as diverse as chemistry, economics, engineering, medicine, and meteorology. Policymaking efforts such as this one are simply

Table 3.1 Number of Pages in the *Federal Register*, 1950–2013

Year	Number of Pages
1950	9,745
1955	17,989
1960	22,877
1965	34,783
1970	54,834
1975	71,224
1980	102,195
1985	105,935
1990	126,893
1995	138,186
2000	138,049
2005	151,973
2010	165,494
2013	175,496

Source: George Washington University Regulatory Studies Center, "Pages in the *Federal Register*, 1936–2013," http://regulatorystudies.columbian.gwu.edu/reg-stats#Pages%20in%20the%20Federal%20Register%20%281936%20-%202013%29/ (accessed July 7, 2015).

beyond the existing capabilities of other government institutions. Congress, even with hundreds of members and thousands of staffers, possesses a mere fraction of the specialized expertise found in the bureaucracy.

Bureaucracies are also valuable to government actors pursuing specific, self-interested goals. Legislators build their cases for reelection in part by helping constituents overcome bureaucratic "**red tape.**"[23] A classic example of such **casework** is the assistance commonly offered to retirees whose Social Security checks have been lost in the mail. On a broader scale, elected officials can use agencies to avoid the blame that comes with controversial or difficult decisions.[24] By placing responsibility for management of the financial system in the hands of agencies such as the Fed and SEC, Congress distanced itself from culpability in the event of a catastrophic economic breakdown.

Importantly, the motivation behind the delegation of authority to the bureaucracy cannot be meaningfully separated from agency effectiveness. For example, agencies called upon to perform contradictory tasks may find it particularly difficult to succeed. Despite the Dodd-Frank Act's emphasis on

Dan Glickman
Secretary of Agriculture
(1995–2001)

"On farm issues, I heard from members of Congress all the time. It was part of the historic operation of the government. Congress had so much interplay on traditional farm and commodity issues that they would always be in contact with the department on the implementation of farm rules and farm programs. Less so in food and nutrition, and food safety and research. I would hear quite a bit. I used to kid the North Dakota senators that there was a door in my office that was 'reserved for North Dakota problems' because [Senators Byron] Dorgan and [Kent] Conrad would inundate me with problems. When I say inundate, I would get twenty to thirty calls a week directly from members of Congress about specific farm issues. It could be dairy, it could be wheat, it could be livestock, it could be disaster-related. The secretary of agriculture has to be very, very accessible to constituencies because there are lots of them out there."

consumer protection, Congress still expects financial regulators to promote the profitability of Wall Street institutions. In a similar vein, EPA's mission—to protect human health and the environment—does not mention consideration of the costs imposed on businesses, even though it is central to the agency's often contentious decision-making processes.[25] In general, the efficacy of agencies as institutions of democratic policymaking is in part a product of the politics surrounding the bureaucracy's supervisors.

Why Delegation Varies

Although delegation to the bureaucracy is widespread, it nevertheless varies considerably across issue areas, as laid out in Figure 3.2. When issues are low in **salience,** politicians are more likely to delegate authority to the bureaucracy. Occupational licensing and child care regulation usually fall into this category. When issues are high in salience, as is the case with civil rights disputes and environmental policy, delegation is less viable because citizens and organized interests expect elected officials to act decisively.[26] **Complexity** also matters, especially for highly salient issues. When issues are high in salience and low in complexity, politicians often seek to control the bureaucracy by specifying the substance of policy in great detail. Antidiscrimination edicts exemplify this approach. When issues are high in both salience and complexity, elected officials are more likely to exert leverage over policymaking through procedural instruments, such as the requirement that agencies conduct environmental impact assessments before adopting rules likely to have major ecological effects.[27]

Figure 3.2 Explaining Variation in Delegation

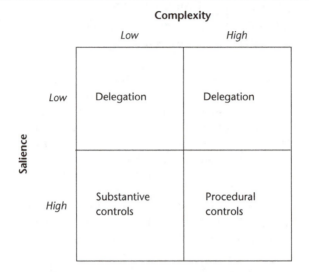

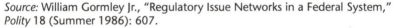

Source: William Gormley Jr., "Regulatory Issue Networks in a Federal System," *Polity* 18 (Summer 1986): 607.

For similar reasons, delegation also varies within issue areas. It is thought that congressional control of the making and implementing of health policy is greatest when both legislative preferences and capabilities are strong, as when issues are high in salience and low in complexity. Among the key provisions of the Patient Protection and Affordable Care Act (ACA) (i.e., Obamacare), those pertaining to dependent coverage expansion certainly fit this description. Historically, employer-based health insurance plans have covered dependent children until age nineteen or college graduation. The ACA extended dependent benefits through the age of twenty-six. This provision of the ACA was highly salient (expanding dependent coverage was bipartisan and popular), as well as low in complexity. On the latter score, the dependent coverage provision took up a grand total of 152 words, a drop in the bucket of the ACA, which altogether consumed more than 900 pages.[28] Furthermore, implementation of the dependent coverage expansion was straightforward and consistent with statutory intent. In fact, many insurance companies began enrolling older eligible dependents almost immediately after President Obama signed the ACA into law, before the provision officially took effect.[29]

When congressional preferences and capabilities are not as well developed, Congress is less apt to provide such precise instructions. The ACA called for a variety of changes in the manner in which doctors, hospitals, and other health care providers are paid for their services. To implement these highly complex changes, the ACA delegated to the Department of Health and Human Services (HHS) the authority to write the necessary regulations. In the years following passage of the ACA, HHS promulgated in excess of a dozen regulations, some of which took up hundreds of pages in the *Federal Register*.[30] These regulations may well be rewritten by HHS Secretary Tom Price, in an effort to reduce regulatory burdens on health care insurers and providers. One key strategy could be to eliminate requirements to provide certain benefits. For example, in congressional testimony, Price expressed reservations about requiring health care companies to provide maternity and newborn care, substance abuse and mental health treatment, and free contraceptives.[31] In this instance, as in many others, the rulemaking process provides federal agencies with an opportunity to make policy when Congress is unable or unwilling to do so.

Issue characteristics alone do not determine whether delegation occurs and what form it takes. Characteristics of the delegating body are also significant determinants of bureaucratic authority. Consider the capacity of state legislatures. Some legislatures, such as the New York State Assembly, closely resemble Congress in their professionalism. The New York legislature meets throughout the year, employs thousands of staff members, and compensates elected representatives handsomely.[32] In contrast, the legislature in Mississippi is in session for three months, has a permanent staff of 164, and pays legislators a base salary of $10,000.

As one might expect, **legislative professionalism** is closely linked to delegation. As capacity increases, legislators who might like to limit bureaucratic power are in fact more inclined to craft detailed statutes that delegate little policymaking authority.[33] During the 1990s states all across the country sought to create managed care programs as a way of containing the skyrocketing costs of Medicaid, which provides health care to low-income and other needy residents. However, individual states approached this task in different ways. In crafting its Medicaid managed care statute, the Texas legislature spelled out specific details regarding numerous aspects of the program, including eligibility requirements, continuity of care, and competition among public and private providers.[34] By contrast, the Medicaid managed care statute enacted in Idaho reads in its entirety:

> The Department of Health and Welfare is hereby directed to develop and implement, as soon as possible, a new health care delivery system for those clients on Medicaid, utilizing a managed care concept.[35]

The Idaho legislature—comprising "'citizen' legislators, not career politicians"—delegated significantly more authority to the bureaucracy in the area of Medicaid managed care policy than did its more professional Texas counterpart.[36]

Partisan control of the legislative and executive branches affects delegation as well. When **divided government** exists—with one party controlling at least one chamber in the legislature and the other the office of chief executive—delegation becomes less likely.[37] Understandably, Democratic legislators are less trusting of bureaucracies headed by Republicans, and Republican legislators less trusting of bureaucracies run by Democrats. The history of major trade legislation illustrates these tendencies quite vividly. In the postwar period, it has been a virtual certainty for Congress to increase bureaucratic discretion over tariff rates in times of unified government and decrease this discretion when divided government is in place.[38]

In the end, political principals evaluate policymaking in the bureaucracy against its alternatives. The critical question is: Would these principals be better served by making policy themselves or by delegating authority to bureaucratic agents? As we have seen, principals sometimes eschew delegation altogether. The benefits of delegation, however, often prove too irresistible to pass up. For principals, then, the trick is to capture these benefits without being unduly harmed by the actions of self-interested agents.

Implementing Child Care Legislation

To more fully appreciate the politics of the delegation decision and the boundaries of bureaucratic authority, consider the implementation of a pair of federal child care laws passed in 1990 and 1996. In both instances, Congress approved child care subsidies to be distributed by state governments to families with relatively low incomes. The first law created the Child Care and Development Block Grant, while the second consolidated a number of different funding streams, including the block grant, under the rubric of the Child Care and Development Fund.

As Table 3.2 indicates, the 1990 legislation, sometimes known as the ABC bill, delegated considerable discretion to the Department of Health and Human Services. In addition to appropriating a certain amount of money for the program, thereby placing a ceiling on how much could be spent, Congress stressed the importance of parental choice, indicating that it wanted children to be enrolled with the provider preferred by parents "to the maximum extent practicable." In interpreting this provision, the agency specified that a state could not exclude certain categories of care (such as family child care), certain types of providers (such as church-based centers), or "significant numbers of providers" in any category or type of care. As for payment rates, Congress specified that the agency must take the costs of different settings and age groups into account and that there should be separate rates for children with special needs. But Congress left it up to the agency to determine whether states should be free to pay providers more for delivering higher-quality services. After wrestling with this issue, the agency decided to allow such differentials but to limit these differences to 10 percent. In effect, Congress established basic guidelines for administration of the block grant but left a lot of the specific operational decisions to the agency.

When revisiting the program in 1996, Congress decided to reiterate its strong commitment to parental choice and payment rates that would promote equal access. For its part, however, the agency decided to lift the 10 percent ceiling on rate differences within a category of care. In addition, for the first time the agency decided to recommend that states imposing a copayment requirement on parents restrict that copayment to 10 percent of the total fee. Table 3.3 provides a summary of these new provisions.

Table 3.2 Implementation of the 1990 Child Care Law

Issue	Provision of the Law	Agency Implementation
Parental choice	The child will be enrolled with the eligible provider selected by the parent "to the maximum extent practicable."	State and local rules cannot have the effect of excluding certain categories of care, certain types of providers, or "significant numbers of providers" in any category or type of care.
Payment rates	Payment rates must take into account variations in the costs of providing child care in different settings, for different age groups, and for children with special needs.	States may distinguish between higher-quality and lower-quality providers within a category of care in setting payment rates, but such rate differentials may not exceed 10 percent.
Administrative expenses	States must spend 75 percent of their child care allotments to improve the quality and availability of child care, and a "preponderance" of the 75 percent must be spent on child care services.	For the first two years at least 85 percent of the 75 percent share must be spent on child care services, as opposed to administrative expenses.

Source: Adapted from House Ways and Means Committee, Subcommittee on Human Resources, "Regulations Issued by the Department of Health and Human Services on Child Care Programs Authorized by Public Law 101-508" (Washington, D.C.: Government Printing Office, September 13, 1991).

A comparison of these decisions helps clarify both the constraints that legislation imposes on the bureaucracy and the discretion that agencies can use to promote their own policy preferences. The Department of Health and Human Services (HHS) under President George H. W. Bush, headed by Louis Sullivan, imposed limits on state child care agencies to promote parental choice and keep costs down. In contrast, the HHS under President Bill Clinton, headed by Donna Shalala, sought to foster improvements in child care quality and limit the financial contributions parents would have to pay. Together these episodes demonstrate that the preferences of elected officials fundamentally shape bureaucratic decisions and that the influence of these political principals is invariably limited when policymaking authority is delegated.

Table 3.3 Implementation of the 1996 Child Care Law

Issue	Provision of the Law	Agency Implementation
Copayments	Rates should be designed in a way that facilitates parental choice.	It is recommended that no state require a copayment greater than 10 percent; copayments, if required, can be waived for children in protective services or for families with incomes at or below the poverty level.
Payment rates	Rates should be designed in a way that promotes equal access.	States should be free to set differential payment levels within categories of care, to reward providers who offer higher quality; a prior limit of 10 percent for differential payment levels within a category is rescinded.
Market rate survey	Payment rates established by states should be comparable to those paid by families who are not eligible for subsidies.	States must conduct a biennial market rate survey to ensure that payment rates reflect changing market conditions.

Source: Adapted from U.S. Department of Health and Human Services, Administration for Children and Families, "Child Care and Development Fund; Final Rule," *Federal Register*, July 24, 1998, 39935–39998.

Managing Delegation

Given the persistence of agency loss, political principals not only make delegation decisions with an eye to strategic considerations but also think carefully about managing the authority vested in agencies. Principals differ in the tools they can call upon as they set about this exceedingly difficult task. Some principals find themselves better equipped to cope with adverse selection issues than with moral hazard concerns, while others find the reverse to be true.

Presidential Power

When cataloging the efforts of principals to limit agency loss, a logical place to start is with the president, the formal head of the federal bureaucracy. The presidency is a unique institution in American politics. Only the president has a national constituency and a strong desire to build a legacy that will be remembered fondly in history. For these reasons, the president, more so than others in government, has an incentive to bring the bureaucracy under **coordinated control.**[39] A bureaucracy that functions well as a unit, rather than as an uncoordinated batch of agencies, would be a valuable asset for a president seeking grand policy achievements. But does the president possess the capabilities necessary to bring about such coordination?

Unilateral Actions. The ambiguity of Article II of the Constitution is widely viewed as important in determining the president's ability to command the bureaucracy. Historically, the relative dearth of enumerated powers has been taken as a sign of presidential weakness. With little formal authority, presidents must generally rely on their interpersonal skills to persuade other policymakers to go along with White House initiatives.[40] This lack of authority holds even within the executive branch, where the president is "chief" in name only.[41]

Recently, Article II's ambiguity has come to be seen by some analysts in a fundamentally different light.[42] Throughout history, presidents have taken **unilateral actions** not explicitly permitted by the Constitution. Famous examples include the Louisiana Purchase, the Emancipation Proclamation, and the creation of the EPA. Such actions are unilateral in that they are not subject to congressional or judicial approval. In fact, it is difficult for Congress and the courts to stand in the way of presidential unilateralism, even when such behavior expands and consolidates the power of the White House. The ability of the president to control the nation's policymaking apparatus, including the federal bureaucracy, has therefore accumulated over time and continues to accumulate to this day.

Examples from recent presidencies illuminate the potency of unilateral action as well as the boundaries of this approach to policymaking. During the course of the Obama administration, Congress became increasingly Republican in its composition. In the first two years of the Obama presidency, both the Senate and House of Representatives were controlled by the Democratic Party. This situation was completely reversed by the last two years of the administration, with Republican majorities in both chambers. Facing an increasingly hostile Congress, President Obama turned to **executive orders** and **presidential memoranda** as means of steering the bureaucracy and influencing public policy. Executive orders and presidential memoranda are declarations issued by the president that carry the full force of law without requiring the assent of Congress.[43] In 2014, President Obama issued more such unilateral actions than during the first three years of his presidency combined.[44]

Many of these actions instituted significant, and sometimes controversial, policy changes, such as making millions more American workers eligible for overtime pay, permitting families to make private ransom payments for relatives kidnapped overseas, and installing solar panels on federally subsidized housing developments.[45] In both quantity and scope, President Obama's use of unilateral actions resembled that of the closing years of the Clinton presidency. Facing Republican majorities in both the Senate and House of Representatives, President Clinton frequently turned to executive orders to achieve such policy aims as revising the food labeling system and banning discrimination against homosexuals in federal hiring practices.[46] As Paul Begala, one of President Clinton's advisers, put it, "Stroke of the pen, law of the land. Kind of cool."[47]

Although Presidents Clinton and Obama projected far-reaching authority through executive orders, their powers of unilateral action were not without limitation. The Clinton administration's executive order barring federal contractors from hiring permanent striker replacements was struck down in court. In addition, strident opposition from the nation's governors compelled the administration to suspend an executive order on federalism it had issued just three months earlier.[48] In 2014, President Obama issued executive orders on immigration that prompted responses on the part of both legislators and the courts. Among other actions, President Obama expanded amnesty and protection for immigrants brought to the United States illegally as children, as well as undocumented immigrants who are parents of U.S. citizens and permanent residents.[49] Twenty-six states filed a lawsuit against these actions, claiming they violate the Constitution. Shortly thereafter, a judge in Texas issued an injunction placing the actions on hold, and the 5th Circuit Court of Appeals ruled against the Obama administration, triggering a showdown in the U.S. Supreme Court.[50] A deadlocked Supreme Court, missing one judge following the death of Justice Antonin Scalia, overturned the Obama administration's deportation policy in a 4–4 vote that effectively sustained the lower court decision without setting a precedent.[51] Following that decision, President Obama announced that deportation would not be a high priority, except for criminals.[52] However, the fundamental issues remained unresolved.

President George W. Bush also experienced both the utility and constraints of unilateral action as a means of steering the bureaucracy. Shortly after the September 11, 2001, terrorist attacks, the Bush administration instituted a program of monitoring, without first obtaining warrants, the international communications of individuals inside the United States when either the individual or the interlocutor was suspected of having ties to al-Qaida or other terrorist organizations.[53] This program placed surveillance authority in the hands of the National Security Agency (NSA), an organization that has traditionally focused on foreign communications, not domestic ones.

For four years, the program operated without any public disclosure. Knowledge of the program was limited to a handful of key policymakers.[54] Although some of these insiders, including Sen. John D. Rockefeller IV, D-W.Va., privately expressed concerns about the legality and constitutionality of eavesdropping inside the United States without a warrant, the program was never abandoned or modified in a substantial way.[55] The Bush administration's actions were a stark manifestation of the use of unilateral power as a tool for managing policymaking in the bureaucracy.

Even in this instance, however, the limitations of unilateral action were ultimately put on display. In 2006, after the *New York Times* exposed the program, both Congress and the courts took steps to limit the NSA's discretion. Committees in both the House and the Senate held hearings on the program and heard testimony from administration officials such as Attorney General Alberto R. Gonzales.[56] Legislation to modify the program, either at the margins or more fundamentally, was introduced but never enacted into law.[57]

In the meantime, organizations such as the American Civil Liberties Union filed lawsuits against the program in federal courts throughout the country. In Detroit, a federal district judge ruled the program unconstitutional.[58] Perhaps in response to these accumulated efforts as well as to the midterm elections that delivered to Democrats control of Congress, the Bush administration agreed, in January 2007, to subject the program to court supervision, a move it had publicly resisted for more than a year.[59]

Six years later, NSA surveillance garnered unwanted worldwide attention again when former Central Intelligence Agency contractor Edward Snowden leaked documents showing that the NSA was, among other activities, collecting the phone records of Americans and tracking online communications through the servers of Yahoo, Google, Facebook, and Microsoft.[60] In the aftermath of the Snowden revelations, President Obama took unilateral actions that, while retaining such practices, placed procedural limits on the NSA's conduct of domestic surveillance.[61] The president also worked with Congress to enact legislation phasing out the bulk collection of phone records, a particularly unpopular program opposed by a strong majority of Americans.[62]

In the end, unilateral actions that do not clearly derive from formal presidential authority provide presidents with opportunities to exert powerful influence over the bureaucracy, opportunities that recent presidents have utilized frequently. That said, other policymaking institutions and the American public can check these opportunities when the conditions are "right," as they eventually were in the area of terrorism communications and NSA surveillance of Americans at home.

Two statements from President Obama neatly summarize the promise and perils of executive orders as instruments of presidential power. In 2014, the president—raring for a fight with Republicans on Capitol Hill—extolled the virtues of unilateralism: "I've got a pen to take executive actions where Congress won't, and I've got a telephone to rally folks around the country on this mission."[63] Two years later, the outgoing president, perhaps chastened by his experiences with unilateral action, had this advice to give President-elect Trump: "My suggestion to the president-elect is, you know, going through the legislative process is always better, in part because it's harder to undo."[64]

Despite this admonition, the president-elect vowed to issue executive orders, beginning on Inauguration Day, to start the process of repealing Obamacare and undoing other policies enacted under his predecessor.[65] As a candidate, Trump promised to "eliminate every unconstitutional executive order" issued during the Obama administration.[66] Although he walked back on this promise in the extreme after Election Day,[67] it is nonetheless the case that erasing unilateral actions in areas such as immigration, climate change, Syrian refugees, transgender bathrooms, and the closing of the detention center at Guantánamo Bay remain high priorities for the Trump administration and represent prime pathways for limiting the policy legacy of the Obama presidency.[68]

The Budget. At the beginning of every year, the president proposes a budget, drafted by OMB, with input from federal agencies. That proposal begins a long, protracted negotiation process between the legislative and executive branches of the federal government. Ultimately, Congress decides which programs to expand and which programs to cut, but the White House frames the debate. By tradition, cabinet secretaries and other agency heads are expected to present a united front and accept budget cuts for their agency gracefully, regardless of their private views.

When the Trump administration presented its first budget in March 2017, it shocked many observers by proposing deep cuts in key federal agency budgets. If approved by Congress, the EPA would experience a 31 percent cut and the State Department would experience a 29 percent cut.[69] A number of agencies would be eliminated altogether, including the Corporation for Public Broadcasting, the National Endowment for the Humanities, the National Endowment for the Arts, and the Woodrow Wilson Center for International Scholars. These and other proposed cuts lent credence to White House policy adviser Steve Bannon's warning that the Trump administration meant to eviscerate the "administrative state."[70]

Deep cuts in federal agency budgets are controversial not simply because they weaken agencies but, more important, because they make it difficult for agencies to provide vital services to citizens. For example, the Trump administration's proposed elimination of federal funding for the Chesapeake Bay clean-up project could abruptly stall efforts to improve the bay's fishing and recreational opportunities, with important consequences for regional economic development.[71] Proposed cuts in the budget of the Internal Revenue Service illustrate the same point. According to the Government Accountability Office, the IRS fails to collect $385 billion in tax revenue annually, mainly because of underpayments and overstated deductions.[72] Cuts in the IRS budget, which constrain enforcement, have contributed to such shortfalls. Studies show that every dollar spent on the IRS yields $4 in tax revenues and as much as $10 in tax revenues when invested in enforcement.[73] Additional cuts in the IRS budget would make it more difficult for the federal government to pay its bills and reduce annual spending deficits.

Although the president's proposal frames the budget debate and carries substantial weight, it is typically not determinative of ultimate outcomes across the board. Early reactions demonstrated that President Trump's initial proposal is likely to face some resistance from Congress. According to Sen. John McCain, R-Ariz., "It is clear that this budget proposed today cannot pass the Senate."[74] Members of Congress whose constituents benefit from particular agencies and the services they provide objected to specific proposed cuts. Rep. Hal Rogers, R-Ky., protested cuts to the Appalachian Regional Commission, which assists communities in his district, as "draconian, careless and counterproductive."[75] In the end, the president's budget, while a powerful tool for signaling broad priorities, is subject to negotiation and dependent on congressional action.

Appointments. In terms of formal authority, the president is relatively well equipped to address the problem of adverse selection. Presidents have the power to appoint cabinet secretaries, regulatory commissioners, administrators of independent agencies, and a host of subordinates to these top-ranking officials. All in all, political appointees fill approximately 3,000 positions in the executive branch bureaucracy.[76]

What factors do administrations consider when filling agency vacancies? Although observers generally agree that substantive knowledge and administrative competence are attributes that would serve any appointee well, there is no escaping the centrality of politics in the nomination process.[77] The politics of each presidency is somewhat distinctive, with the Reagan administration, for example, valuing loyalty to the conservative movement. George H. W. Bush put a premium on individuals who had served in previous positions with the president.[78] As a candidate, Barack Obama stated the aspiration of assembling a Lincolnesque "team of rivals." As president, however, he surrounded himself, a few notable exceptions aside, with a cabinet of loyalists.[79]

To increase its leverage over the bureaucracy, the Trump White House was loath to allow cabinet secretaries to appoint key subordinates, often known as subcabinet officials. For example, Secretary of State Rex Tillerson wanted Elliott Abrams to be deputy secretary of state. The White House said no, apparently because Abrams had been critical of Trump during the presidential campaign.[80] Similarly, Secretary of Defense James Mattis proposed to name Anne Patterson as the fourth-highest-ranking individual in the Defense Department. The White House said no, apparently because of Patterson's close ties to deposed Egyptian president Mohamed Morsi and the Muslim Brotherhood, which has been accused of supporting terrorist groups.[81] By scrutinizing subcabinet appointments with unusual vigilance, the White House sought to ensure that agency officials would be accountable to the president and not to the head of their department.

Inside Bureaucracy with	Christine Todd Whitman
	EPA Administrator
	(2001–2003)

"At the very beginning the Energy Task Force was put in place and every time I went in and talked with the President [George W. Bush] we were in the same place. He wanted not just no net loss of wetlands, he wanted to have more wetlands. That wasn't the issue. But the Vice President [Dick Cheney] was in a different place on a lot of those issues. Right at the beginning there was the Energy Task Force—because of the rolling brownouts in California and from the get-go of that the focus was on EPA regulations, that they were the ones that were causing the problem. Particularly the Clean Air Act. They wanted to take some parts of that away to be enforced by the Department of Energy. I fought back and actually won that one."

Another reason for the White House to consider politics when making presidential appointments to the executive branch is that many such appointments require **Senate confirmation** before they can take effect. At first glance, the Senate—which approves almost every nominee offered by the president—does not act as much of a hurdle, but, as one expert has stated, "that is the wrong conclusion drawn from the wrong evidence."[82] Presidents strategically anticipate Senate reactions to their nominees and routinely put forth individuals likely to pass muster at confirmation. In addition, the Senate flexes its constitutional muscles in ways other than outright rejection, through tactics such as delay in considering and voting on nominations. In recent years, the Senate confirmation process has gotten somewhat slower, and the White House vetting process may have gotten slower as well. At the end of their respective first years in office, 80 percent of President George Herbert Walker Bush's executive branch vacancies were filled, as opposed to 64 percent of President Obama's.[83] Increasingly, presidential nominations to top executive branch positions and the federal judiciary are being defeated without a formal vote.[84] Delay is particularly prevalent during periods of divided government and ideological polarization in the Senate, suggesting that even the most well-qualified individuals can run into trouble if the nomination is ill timed.[85] For example, Sen. Mary Landrieu, D-La., placed a **hold** on President Obama's nomination of Jacob (Jack) Lew to head the Office of Management and Budget, stating publicly that she would not lift the hold until the Obama administration lifted its freeze on deepwater oil and gas drilling. The Obama administration lifted the moratorium in October 2010, Landrieu lifted her hold, and Lew was confirmed the following month, four months after being nominated.[86] Similarly, in 2015, President Obama's nomination of Loretta Lynch as attorney general was not confirmed by the Senate for nearly six months, held up due to opposition on the part of some senators to the president's unilateral actions on immigration reform.[87]

The politics of confirmation underscore that appointments can be powerful instruments for influencing the scope and content of bureaucratic policymaking. For example, priorities and outputs in agencies ranging from the Food and Drug Administration (FDA) to the Equal Employment Opportunity Commission (EEOC) have shifted noticeably as a direct response to changes in leadership. Product seizures by the FDA declined by more than 50 percent after the Reagan White House tapped Arthur Hull Hayes—a champion of regulatory relief for business—to lead the agency.[88] Under the leadership of commissioners who had mainly been appointed by President Obama, the EEOC issued enforcement guidelines regarding the use by employers of criminal background checks during the hiring process.[89] These guidelines were subsequently used to pursue actions (not always successfully) against companies whose background checks, according to the agency, discriminated against minority populations, such as African American males, who are disproportionately incarcerated in the criminal justice system.[90]

Despite such influences, appointees face a variety of constraints when seeking to shape bureaucratic decisions. The tenure of the average agency head is less than three years.[91] With such a short time horizon, appointees must move quickly if they want to leave a significant mark on their organization. The fact

Christine Todd Whitman

EPA Administrator
(2001–2003)

"The vice president [Dick Cheney] and I were just not on the same page on a lot of environmental issues. I had fairly good flexibility in being able to push back and it was tolerated for a while, and then it would reach a point where it was: 'No, sorry, this is the way it's gonna be, so move on.' That's when I left. . . . I resigned over the definitions within the Clean Air Act of 'routine maintenance repair and replacement.' I'd been arguing with the White House about that for about two years. The vice president was the one who really put the EPA in a place that I could not support. He wanted where the definition was set at a place where we at the agency couldn't run numbers that made it real and could justify it. As a governor I had joined an amicus to go after the other states—the ones that were really gaming the system. There were companies and states that were truly gaming the system. But there were others that were dead honest in it. They were doing routine maintenance repair and replacement. Where the White House was going (their check point on the definition) was actually to let off the hook the bad actors. At the very end of the Clinton administration there had been a sudden rethink of how you define 'routine.' The problem was when you've got ten regions the regions were acting pretty independently. Congress did not define 'routine' when they put that language in. It had been left to the agency. And the agency had really left that to the various regions. It had been an uneven application of the criteria. This made it very difficult for utilities, particularly those that had utilities in a number of different states. The fact that we needed to define it better and needed to find the actual checkpoint, if you will, made absolute sense to me. It was where you put that that the argument came in. And that was what I argued for when I was there. I finally got called in. A lot of language went down. . . . I had several long conversations with the vice president just discussing how you would do this. Where and why and how we were running the numbers. Then there was the decision that there was no point discussing this any further. This was where it was going to be. That was their decision to make, not mine. I wasn't elected anything. So, anyway, that's when I decided that they had a right obviously to set that number and they had a right to have an administrator who could implement that in good faith. And I couldn't. So, time to step down."

that most appointees are not personal associates of the president and therefore do not enjoy open access to the White House and its resources makes this task all the more difficult. Hence, appointees are largely left to their own devices in dealing with their subordinates, the vast majority of whom were at the agency long before the current administration came to power and will continue in their positions well after the presidency has again changed hands. In this difficult environment, it is not uncommon for appointees to **go native.**[92] Rather than act as advocates for the administration, such appointees seek to advance the positions of civil servants inside the bureaucracy, those professionals with whom they interact regularly. The utility of appointments as a way of managing delegated authority is best viewed as highly variable across administrations, agencies, and appointees themselves.

What separates effective leaders from appointees who run into difficulties in dealing with their agencies and the administration? Instructive is the case of Paul O'Neill, President George W. Bush's first secretary of the Treasury. Less than two years into his tenure, O'Neill became the first cabinet member to leave the administration. Several months of criticism about his handling of an economy in the midst of a prolonged slump preceded O'Neill's departure.

Despite his experience as chair and chief executive officer of aluminum giant Alcoa, O'Neill did not enjoy the confidence of Wall Street, an absolutely critical constituency for any Treasury secretary. In addition, O'Neill did not demonstrate the flair for publicity that successful appointees so often bring to their positions. Even on a made-for-TV trip to Africa, alongside rock star Bono, O'Neill came off as a wooden leader who did not fully understand and appreciate the plight of debt-ridden countries in the developing world.[93] In the end, O'Neill did not possess the combination of personal and professional skills necessary to be an effective appointee for President Bush.

By contrast, Ray LaHood proved to be a surprisingly effective secretary of transportation under President Obama. LaHood, a Republican, became a public champion of mass transit, high-speed rail, bicycle paths, and other infrastructure improvements. During his first two years in office, he helped to steer transportation grants to high-speed rail projects in California, Washington state, and elsewhere.[94] During his next two years, LaHood established pilot programs to curb distracted driving and encouraged states to adopt laws banning texting while driving, which causes many accidents and deaths.[95] When LaHood retired in July 2013, forty-one states had such laws in place, thanks in part to LaHood's jawboning.[96] As for LaHood's efforts to improve high-speed rail, Federal Railroad Administrator Joseph Szabo put it this way: "When the history books are written on the success of the high-speed and intercity rail program, Ray LaHood is going to be one of the stars."[97]

The most prominent of President Obama's cabinet secretaries was, of course, Hillary Clinton. While serving as secretary of state, she drew praise for traveling to over 100 countries, for her strong condemnations of North Korea (for refusing to relinquish nuclear weapons) and Iran (for attempting to develop nuclear weapons), and for helping to convince the Russians not to sell military hardware to Iran.[98] She also became a strong champion of "civil society" throughout the world and forged ties between the State Department and nonprofit organizations in other countries.[99] On the other hand, she drew criticism for the deaths of U.S. Ambassador to Libya J. Christopher Stevens and three other Americans who were killed by a mob of Libyan militants in Benghazi on September 11, 2012. Although a congressional report found no evidence of wrongdoing by Clinton, the deaths occurred on her watch, after pleas for more security went unheeded.[100] Clinton also received harsh criticism from the FBI for using a private e-mail server to send and receive some classified information. Although the FBI decided not to prosecute Clinton for her behavior, FBI Director James Comey publicly criticized her and her colleagues for being "extremely careless."[101]

Firings. Although the most common transitions from office for political appointees are either voluntary resignations or departures by mutual consent, some appointees are fired outright, especially when they become embroiled in controversy. Several firings occurred in 2007, during President George W. Bush's second term, when it came to light that recovering Iraq war veterans were receiving substandard medical care at the Walter Reed Army Medical Center in Washington, D.C. As congressional and public protests escalated, three top officials lost their jobs, including Secretary of the Army Francis Harvey, Maj. Gen. George Weightman (commander of Walter Reed), and Lt. Gen. Kevin Kiley (surgeon general of the army).[102] These dismissals helped the White House and Defense Department assert that those responsible for the problem were being held accountable.

Perhaps most dramatically, President Obama fired Gen. Stanley McChrystal as the top military officer in Afghanistan on June 23, 2010, after the release of an inflammatory article in *Rolling Stone* magazine that hinted strongly at insubordination.[103] In that article, McChrystal and his staff made disparaging remarks about the administration's civilian leaders—including Vice President Joe Biden and Obama himself.[104] "I welcome debate among my team, but I won't tolerate division," Obama said in announcing McChrystal's dismissal.[105]

Presidential decisions to fire an agency head can be extremely controversial, as President Trump discovered when he fired FBI Director James Comey on May 9, 2017, apparently because of an ongoing investigation into possible collusion between Trump associates and Russians who tried to interfere with the 2016 presidential election. Originally, the White House claimed that Trump fired Comey because Attorney General Jeff Sessions and Deputy Attorney General Rod Rosenstein urged him to do so. However, Trump himself demolished that claim in an interview with NBC's Lester Holt: "I was going to fire Comey—my decision. I was going to fire regardless of recommendation."[106] To some observers, Trump's firing of Comey was reminiscent of President Richard Nixon's firing of Archibald Cox, the independent counsel assigned to investigate the Watergate burglary. Both dismissals were desperate efforts to halt or disrupt an ongoing investigation into illegal acts committed by persons close to the President.[107] No one doubts that the president has the legal authority to fire the director of the FBI. But many politicians, journalists, and citizens object when a firing seems intended to prevent evidence of wrongdoing from being disclosed. Following Comey's firing, congressional pressure grew to hand the Russia investigation over to a special counsel. On May 17 Deputy Attorney General Rosenstein appointed Robert Mueller, former head of the FBI, as special counsel to investigate the Russia scandal—a move that won praise from both Democratic and Republican lawmakers.[108]

At all levels of government, it is relatively hard to fire civil servants, even if they turn out to be incompetent. Laws and union contracts aimed at protecting employees from arbitrary dismissal for political reasons also sometimes protect employees who are not doing a good job. In recent years, the teaching profession has emerged as a key battleground for such disputes. Even change-oriented school superintendents have trouble sacking teachers for poor performance. Between 2008 and 2010, Joel Klein, then chancellor of New York City public schools, was able to fire only three teachers for incompetence.[109] During her three-year-plus tenure as chancellor of D.C. Public Schools, Michelle Rhee fired dozens of teachers whose performance was judged to be weak. But such actions infuriated teachers and their supporters and ultimately led to Rhee's resignation.[110] Under unusual circumstances, a local school superintendent can fire large numbers of teachers. In Rhode Island, the superintendent of the Central Falls School District fired all seventy-seven teachers and other personnel at Central Falls High School after failing to reach agreement with the local teachers' union on a plan for teachers to spend more time helping students to improve their test scores.[111] The teachers were later rehired and the school has since made some progress from this ignominious low point, boosting its graduation rate from a miserable 52 percent to a more respectable but still far from excellent 70 percent.[112] In short, even when they occur, teacher firings may be reversed.

Although it is very difficult to fire civil servants, it is relatively easy to redeploy them, by transferring them to less desirable functions, offices, or locations. It is also possible to intimidate civil servants through veiled threats. The Trump transition team did this, intentionally or unintentionally, in December 2016, when it submitted a list of seventy-four questions to the Energy Department, asking agency officials to identify employees and contractors who have actively worked on or promoted climate change initiatives. For example, one question asked for a list of department employees or contractors who attended interagency meetings on the "social cost of carbon," a way of calculating the consequences of greenhouse gas emissions.[113] Scientists and Democratic members of Congress strongly objected to the questionnaire. Rep. Elijah Cummings, D-Md., put it this way: "I am sure there are a lot of career scientists and others who see this as a terrible message of fear and intimidation—'either ignore the science or we will come after you.'"[114] After receiving considerable negative feedback from employees and others, the Department of Energy rejected the request. A Department of Energy official announced that DOE would provide a good deal of information to the Trump team but not any individual names.[115] The Trump transition later disavowed the information request, saying it was not authorized.[116] Still, the episode raised questions as to whether climate change scientists and other civil servants within DOE would be free to continue their work on climate change reduction without political interference.

Civil Service Reform. Through much of the nation's history, presidents have sought to enhance their control over the bureaucracy by reforming the rules that govern civil servants, those executive branch officials not subject to presidential appointment and Senate confirmation. In 1905, President Theodore

Roosevelt formed the **Keep Committee** to investigate ways of improving the organization and effectiveness of the federal government.[117] Franklin Roosevelt oversaw passage of the **Reorganization Act** of 1939, establishing the **Executive Office of the President,** which provides the White House with an apparatus for directing and coordinating policy in areas particularly central to the president's agenda. The Council of Economic Advisers and the National Security Council have both been a part of the Executive Office for many years. Under President Obama, the staff supporting the National Security Council—a body focused on foreign policy matters—was merged with the staff supporting the Homeland Security Council, an organization created by President George W. Bush in the aftermath of the September 11, 2001, terrorist attacks.[118] As Gen. James L. Jones, the president's national security adviser, put it, "The idea that somehow counterterrorism is a homeland security issue doesn't make sense when you recognize the fact that terror around the world doesn't recognize borders."[119] As this example illustrates, presidents value the executive branch organization as an instrument for shaping their influence over policy priorities and implementation.

In 1978, the **Civil Service Reform Act** brought significant changes to the personnel system of the executive branch. For example, the act established the **Senior Executive Service** (SES), a group of top-level civil servants with less job security than their colleagues but more of an opportunity to earn bonuses based on productivity and other performance measures. The idea behind this reform was to create a senior management system under the president that could meaningfully compete with the private sector in recruiting and retaining individuals of exceptional talent. Decades later, in announcing a series of updates to the SES, President Obama noted that its ideals had not yet been achieved. The president called his initiative a "step toward fulfilling the vision of the Senior Executive Service and developing senior civil servants with critical skill sets such as leading change, building coalitions, working across government to solve problems and performance management."[120]

At first glance, career bureaucrats—who number in the millions—would seem unlikely to be very responsive to presidents and politics more generally.[121] Consider, however, that rather than remain loyal to supervisors in the face of changing presidents and administrative tasks, thousands of senior executives instead exited the federal bureaucracy altogether in the years following passage of the Civil Service Reform Act.[122] From the early 1970s to the early 1990s—a period during which Republicans controlled the White House for all but four years—top-level civil servants became increasingly conservative and Republican as a group.[123] In 1970, President Richard Nixon faced a civil service leadership that favored Democrats by a three-to-one margin. By the first Bush administration, Republicans enjoyed an 11 percent edge among these officials.

The potency of personnel management is illustrated by the debate over the creation of the Department of Homeland Security.[124] In 2002, President Bush proposed merging twenty-two agencies and 170,000 employees into a single organization aimed at protecting the American homeland from terrorist threats. The president's proposal ran into difficulty in the Senate, then under Democratic control. The key stumbling block was presidential prerogatives in managing the department's civil servants. Bush requested the authority to hire, demote, and transfer employees for national security reasons. A majority of senators opposed this request on the grounds that it represented too significant an erosion in the collective bargaining rights usually held by federal employees. Not until Republicans gained control of the Senate following the November 2002 elections did the administration muster the congressional support necessary to secure a personnel system with the flexibility and control President Bush sought.

The implementation of this system proved challenging for the Bush administration. In early 2005, four labor unions filed suit to block the Department of Homeland Security from adopting its rules, several years in the making, for strengthening the link between employee pay and performance on the job.[125] A series of court decisions upheld the unions' complaint, compelling the agency to redraft its rules, a cumbersome and time-consuming process.[126]

Regulatory Review. As the scope and complexity of bureaucratic policy-making have grown, presidents have taken steps to enhance their ability to observe and evaluate agency decisions. One way in which recent presidents have coped with the problem of moral hazard is by systematically reviewing agency regulations. Established in 1981 by President Ronald Reagan in Executive Order 12291, **regulatory review** is widely considered one of the most important developments in the executive branch during the past several decades.[127] Under regulatory review, agencies are required to submit drafts of prospective actions to the **Office of Information and Regulatory Affairs** (OIRA), an organization located in the White House's Office of Management and Budget (OMB). Only after OIRA clears an agency submission can the rule be published in the *Federal Register* and become law.

Inside Bureaucracy with	Donna Shalala *Secretary of Health and Human Services* *(1993–2001)*

"You always negotiate with OMB. Everything with OMB is a negotiation. OMB would say that they influenced the privacy regulations, and they did, around the edges. But OMB normally acts as an honest broker. Also remember that the political side of the White House is going to weigh in. It doesn't mean they will win, but sometimes they weigh in on an issue. For example, OMB got involved in the question of whether a police officer would have unfettered access to read records without going to a judge. Justice said yes. We said absolutely not! OMB resolved it one way, and then I got them to resolve it the other way. There are advantages to being around for a while!"

OIRA, a bureaucracy in itself, serves as a kind of **counterbureaucracy,** overseeing executive branch agencies to ensure that regulations will not be unnecessarily costly or deviate too significantly from presidential priorities.[128] Given its desire for a bureaucracy operating under coordinated control, the White House more than other institutions of government is concerned about the costs and benefits of the regulatory system as a whole. Individual agencies, by contrast, naturally emphasize the specific advantages of their regulatory actions without paying much regard to more general policy or political considerations.

Given such divergent incentives, regulatory review has been controversial from its inception. Supporters of OIRA argue that White House clearance promotes consistency and overarching standards in an otherwise uncoordinated regulatory system.[129] In this view, bureaucratic decision making is strengthened by passing through an array of economic, scientific, and technical checkpoints and by possessing the political and constitutional legitimacy of presidential approval. Critics claim that centralized clearance provides industry interests and ideological opponents of regulation with a way of undermining efforts to protect health, safety, and the environment. OIRA review, according to this perspective, is grounded in ideas, such as cost-benefit analysis, that are inherently antiregulatory in their orientation.[130]

Although such criticisms might be expected to be most prevalent during Republican administrations, Democratic presidents have found themselves facing similar complaints. During President Obama's first term, prominent legal scholar Cass Sunstein, a close friend of the president's, served as OIRA administrator. It was during Sunstein's tenure that the EPA's proposed ozone regulation was stopped dead in its tracks. Actions such as this, as well as Sunstein's unwavering support for the application of cost-benefit analysis in the regulatory process, led one disaffected observer to remark: "He's acting as if it was George W. Bush's administration."[131] Lisa Heinzerling, who served as a senior EPA staffer during the first two years of the Obama administration, characterized OIRA as "aggressive" in promoting cost-benefit analysis: "Certainly for a Democratic administration it's notably aggressive. . . . You need to show bigger benefits than costs, and if you don't, except in exceptional circumstances, that rule won't issue."[132]

President Obama's utilization of OIRA as an instrument for considering regulatory costs was also evident in the administration's **regulatory look-back** initiative. Under OIRA's direction, agencies were instructed to revisit their existing stock of regulations and identify those that might be modified or eliminated altogether.[133] According to the administration, the first round of eliminations produced billions of dollars in cost savings for businesses and citizens.[134] When he stepped down as OIRA administrator near the end of President Obama's first term, Sunstein attributed $91 billion in net benefits to OIRA's review under his stewardship.[135]

Within days of winning the 2016 presidential election, Donald Trump called for regulatory look-back of a different sort: "for every one new regulation, two old regulations must be eliminated."[136] Similar requirements have been in place in Australia, Canada, the Netherlands, and the United Kingdom.[137] Shortly after his inauguration, President Trump made good on his promise, signing a "two-for-one" executive order on January 30, 2017.[138] Both

Figure 3.3 OIRA Rejection and Alteration of Agency Rules

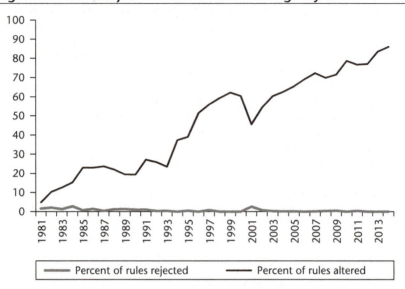

Source: Data gathered by authors from website produced by the Office of Management and Budget and General Services Administration: http://www .reginfo.gov/public/do/eoCountsSearchInit?action=init (accessed April 3, 2017).

supporters and critics questioned the workability of such a system, with one remarking, "It is not a trivial undertaking at all" and another stating, "It's extraordinary. That's all I can say."[139] Several weeks later, the administration issued a follow-up executive order requiring each agency to designate a Regulatory Reform Officer, a position charged with implementing presidential initiatives, including the two-for-one system.[140] OIRA also issued a guidance document instructing agencies about the details of two-for-one implementation, demonstrating the organization's ongoing centrality in reviewing regulations in a changing political landscape.[141]

Information presented in Figure 3.3 leaves no doubt that OIRA has had a profound effect on regulatory processes and outcomes. Although OIRA rarely rejects agency rules altogether, it alters the content of a significant proportion of actions each year. During the Reagan administration, OIRA grew increasingly tough on agencies. In 1981, OIRA required modifications in only 5 percent of the rules it reviewed. By 1988, this percentage had grown to 22 percent.

President Clinton brought important changes to regulatory review shortly after taking office. **Executive Order 12866,** issued on September 30, 1993, limited OIRA's jurisdiction to rules designated as significant and with an annual impact on the economy of at least $100 million. Because of this limitation, and as illustrated in Figure 3.4, the number of rules reviewed by OIRA dropped noticeably from 1994 forward. With this smaller portfolio, OIRA now requires agencies to alter the vast majority of their submissions before granting approval.

Figure 3.4 Number of Rules Reviewed by OIRA

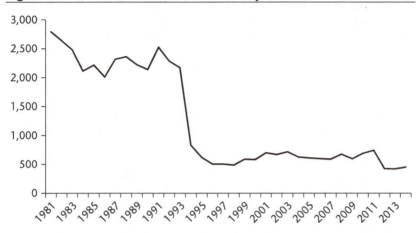

Source: Data gathered by authors from website produced by the Office of Management and Budget and General Services Administration: http://www .reginfo.gov/public/do/eoCountsSearchInit?action=init (accessed April 3, 2017).

How effective is regulatory review as a way for presidents to mitigate the agency loss that follows from moral hazard? OIRA is charged not only with pursuing presidential priorities but also with increasing the role of economic analysis in the regulatory process. At times, these dual missions point OIRA in the same direction. But what happens when political imperatives and economic considerations are at odds? Here, the evidence suggests that accountability to the president trumps fealty to analytical ideals.[142]

During Clinton's administration, only sixteen rules were prevented from taking effect. During the administration of George W. Bush, who emphasized a strong response to the threat of terrorism, OIRA did not reject a single rule addressing homeland security, even though such regulations often had ill-defined benefits and high costs.[143] Although President Obama rarely rejected agency rules, OIRA did substantially affect the regulatory process in a different, yet important way during his administration. Historically, OIRA completes regulatory reviews on average in under 60 days.[144] In 2012, the average review time increased to 79 days, and then ballooned dramatically to 140 days the following year.[145] With a substantial number of reviews consuming more than one year's time, OIRA greatly impacted the allocation of costs and benefits across businesses and citizens that invariably accompanies government regulations. In the end, regulatory review provides presidents with an institutionalized mechanism for competing with other principals for influence over the content and timing of bureaucratic decisions. A recent study shows that OIRA reviews rules more quickly when the rule coincides with a high presidential priority.[146] This is a useful reminder of the special connection between OIRA and the White House.

Midnight Regulations. In the days and months leading up to the inauguration of President George W. Bush, agencies—still operating under the Clinton administration—issued tens of thousands of pages of rules.[147] These so-called **midnight regulations** represented a 51 percent increase in regulatory activity when compared with the same period during the three previous years.[148] Once in office, the Bush administration responded by releasing what became known as the **Card memorandum** (named after President Bush's chief of staff, Andrew Card). The Card memo called for agencies to "postpone the effective date of [recently issued but not yet effective] regulations for 60 days."[149] This postponement provided the incoming administration with an opportunity to review the regulatory output that had occurred since Election Day. Although the vast majority of rules were eventually allowed to take effect, a number of regulations did not survive the partisan shift in administrations.[150]

A battle over midnight regulations also occurred during the transition from the Bush presidency to the Obama administration. On May 9, 2008, President Bush's chief of staff, Joshua Bolton, issued a memo ordering agencies to issue all proposed rules by June 1 and promulgate all final rules by November 1.[151] Bolton justified these deadlines as a "principled approach to regulation as we sprint to the finish, and resist the historical tendencies of administrations to increase regulatory activities in their final months."[152] Despite this effort, regulatory activity spiked dramatically in the waning months of the Bush administration.[153] On January 20, 2009, with this spike in mind, President Obama's chief of staff, Rahm Emanuel, instructed agencies to "stop all pending regulations until a legal and policy review can be conducted by the Obama administration."[154]

One obvious explanation for midnight regulations is that a burst of rulemaking offers the outgoing administration one last opportunity to leave its mark on the executive branch and bolster its policymaking legacy. While not denying the centrality of this political motivation, there are also bureaucratic reasons for finishing regulations before the change in administrations. As Susan Dudley, who served as OIRA administrator during President Bush's midnight period, put it: "Initially, there was broad support for avoiding the midnight crunch, but . . . we faced strong objections . . . not only from political appointees [but] career employees who had worked hard on many of the regulations, were disappointed when they did not get them across the finish line before the end . . . many . . . had been through presidential transitions before . . . [and] did not relish having to break in a new crew of political appointees before completing their projects."[155]

Underscoring the political and bureaucratic dimensions of midnight regulations, the transition from President Obama to President Trump was marked by significant regulatory activity in areas—such as environmental policy—characterized by the incoming administration's hostility toward the work of its predecessor. EPA Administrator Gina McCarthy signaled this action on the day after Donald Trump won the presidential election. Writing to agency employees, McCarthy encouraged a vigorous pace of work during the midnight period: "As I've mentioned to you before, we're running—not walking—through the finish line of President Obama's presidency. Thank you for taking that run with me."[156]

Congressional Control of the Bureaucracy

Owing to its orientation as a lawmaking and investigatory body, Congress is naturally equipped to manage the bureaucracy through institutional design and oversight. Congress enacts, usually with presidential approval, the statutes that create and assign tasks to executive branch agencies. These statutes provide legislators with opportunities to place structural and procedural constraints on bureaucratic policymaking. When Congress established the Consumer Product Safety Commission in 1972, for example, it allowed the agency to issue regulations but limited this authority to standards that had been offered by industry interests, representatives of the general public, and other parties from outside government.[157]

Congress also bears responsibility for keeping a watchful eye on the policies and programs formulated and operated within the executive branch. It carries out these responsibilities through channels such as **oversight hearings** and investigations into allegations of waste, fraud, and abuse. Many of these monitoring activities are routine and attract little outside attention, but occasionally oversight becomes front-page news and transforms bureaucratic organizations, as happened in the late 1990s, when Senate hearings exposed widespread mistreatment of taxpayers by officials in the Internal Revenue Service.[158] Oversight also generates publicity when overseers try to intimidate or embarrass a prominent witness. In May 2011, for example, Rep. Patrick McHenry, R-N.C., chairing a congressional oversight subcommittee hearing, came very close to calling Elizabeth Warren, the primary architect of the new Consumer Financial Protection Bureau, a liar.[159] This testy exchange led to demands for an apology, which did not happen.[160]

Toward what ends do legislators usually make use of instruments of institutional design and oversight? Because hundreds of different constituencies are enfranchised in the Senate and the House of Representatives, congressional control of the bureaucracy is fundamentally uncoordinated in its orientation.[161] Specific committees and subcommittees may influence what goes on in particular agencies, but the bureaucracy as a whole does not operate under the direction of Congress as an institution. In the end, no matter how potent Congress and its members may be, the control exercised by the legislative branch is particularistic rather than aimed at furthering general societal and political interests.

Politics of Bureaucratic Structure. At times, agencies seem designed to fail, or at least to operate in ways not even their most ardent supporters can appreciate and understand. Consider again the Consumer Product Safety Commission (CPSC). The CPSC is an independent regulatory body charged with reducing the risk of injury and death associated with consumer products. Reluctant to champion the burgeoning consumer movement, the Nixon administration originally proposed placing the CPSC within the Department of Health, Education, and Welfare, where it would have had relatively little power and could have been easily monitored by the White House.[162] Congress, however, rejected this proposal and structured the CPSC so that it would be well insulated from presidential control. Importantly, this insulation was not complete because the commission was forced to rely on the Justice Department to carry out most legal actions against violators of safety standards. Over time such requirements have served to weigh the CPSC down and inhibit its ability to carry out its mission effectively.

Critics have argued that the Consumer Financial Protection Bureau (CFPB), whose creation was authorized in the Dodd-Frank Act, has structural elements that limit the ability of political principals to bring accountability to bear on the agency.[163] The director of the CFPB can be removed only under a limited set of circumstances, which do not include poor performance.[164] Congress does not have the authority to appropriate money to the CFPB or exercise oversight of the agency's spending practices. The Dodd-Frank Act instructed the courts to defer to the CFPB on its interpretations of consumer financial laws. Five years after the creation of the CFPB, Elizabeth Warren defended such structures, arguing that the agency "should remain free of political influence."[165]

Why do legislators structure agencies in ways that all too often undermine bureaucratic accountability and performance? Two features of the democratic process are particularly salient when considering these structural choices.[166] The first is **political uncertainty.** Thanks to periodic elections, powerful politicians and their favored constituencies cannot count on controlling the institutions of government into the indefinite future. Inevitably, opposing ideological and partisan forces will take over the reins of power. This uncertainty has important implications for bureaucratic design, as agency benefactors have incentives to protect their creations from meddling by unkind political authorities. In the case of the CPSC, such protection came through the appointment of commissioners to fixed, staggered, seven-year terms, thus effectively distancing the commission from presidential control, even from administrations with consumerist sentiments. The CFPB receives its appropriations directly from the Federal Reserve, effectively removing from legislators an important avenue of influence over agency priorities and actions. In the end, political uncertainty leads agency supporters to "purposely create structures that even they cannot control."[167]

The second key feature of the democratic process is **political compromise.** Under the separation of powers system, opponents of legislative action are usually granted concessions. At times, these concessions prove to be of great consequence, severely limiting the ability of legislative advocates to achieve their objectives. The creation of the CPSC was not a total loss for business interests. In addition to the **offeror process** (whereby the CPSC invites outside parties to propose a suitable safety standard) and Justice Department enforcement, these interests secured the right to judicial review of CPSC decisions and a guarantee that the agency would come up for reauthorization in the short span of three years. In other words, Congress gave business and other CPSC foes the leverage necessary to immediately set about the task of undermining the agency and abolishing it completely before it became too entrenched in the executive branch. By contrast, unified Democratic control of the White House and both chambers of Congress meant that Republicans had relatively little say in the passage of the Dodd-Frank Act and the subsequent creation of the CFPB. Despite this contrary example, the dictates of political compromise generally imply that agencies are designed "in no small measure by participants who explicitly want them to fail."[168] The lessons of political uncertainty and political compromise, taken together, reveal that if Congress has difficulty managing delegated authority, this difficulty springs not only from bureaucratic behavior but also from the nature of the legislative process.

Administrative Procedures. Within the constraints imposed by bureaucratic structure, Congress can influence what the executive branch does by manipulating the **administrative procedures** under which agencies operate. Administrative procedures specify the steps agencies must follow when making

Inside Bureaucracy with	Donna Shalala
	Secretary of Health and Human Services
	(1993–2001)

"Members of Congress would call and ask us to see people. We tried to be accommodating as long as it wasn't illegal. We made sure it was legal. Members of the Congress intervened most often on waivers. They would say, 'We hope you'll approve the waiver.' Usually, they wouldn't have a clue what it was about! When we got a waiver request, if we were giving them flexibility, we wanted to be sure that they were protecting certain groups, such as the disabled. We wanted to make sure they were expanding services and improving quality."

decisions and formulating policies. These steps typically include gathering certain types of information and consulting with stakeholders in particular ways. The **National Environmental Policy Act** requires agencies to prepare **environmental impact statements** for rules with potentially significant ecological consequences, as when the Federal Energy Regulatory Commission considers whether to approve the construction of a hydroelectric facility.[169] Such assessments lay out the likely effects of the rule—harm to a fishery, for example—and the steps the agency will take to minimize prospective environmental damage.[170]

Administrative procedures sometimes target specific agencies or decisions. For example, a statute requires the Federal Railroad Administration (FRA) to hold public hearings during all of its rulemakings.[171] These hearings provide interested parties with opportunities to address agency officials in person, often without having to leave their communities. When seeking to modify its regulations on the power braking systems used in nonpassenger trains, the FRA convened hearings not only in Washington, D.C., but also in Chicago, Newark, and Sacramento.[172]

In what ways do administrative procedures potentially enhance congressional control over the bureaucracy? Administrative procedures can create bureaucratic environments that **mirror** the politics that occurred in Congress when it delegated authority to the agency.[173] In 1996, Congress amended the Safe Drinking Water Act. While they were working on the amendments, legislators heard from three distinct types of stakeholders—utilities and other water producer interests, state and local regulators, and environmental and consumer organizations.[174] The amendments delegated great authority to the EPA to set standards for contaminants, such as arsenic, that pose a threat to drinking water. The amendments also specified very carefully the composition of the National Drinking Water Advisory Council, a stakeholder organization with which the agency consults when crafting drinking water regulations. Specifically, the advisory council must be composed of an equal number of water producers, state and local government officials, and representatives of the general public. This membership requirement means that the agency can expect to hear from the interests that participated in the congressional debate over the amendments. In other words, the pattern of participation in drinking water rulemakings is likely to resemble closely the participatory environment that had characterized the lawmaking process.

Administrative procedures can also **stack the deck** in favor of particular constituencies. Over time, the National Environmental Policy Act has brought ecological considerations more to the fore than they would otherwise have been in agency proceedings. For example, environmentalists have used the act to stop construction projects initially endorsed by the Army Corps of Engineers. These successes have led to a noticeable change in the types of projects the corps is willing to propose.[175] Similarly, the Federal Energy Regulatory Commission became substantially more inclined to render proenvironment licensing decisions in the years following passage of the act.[176]

Finally, administrative procedures can place bureaucratic policymaking on **autopilot**. In other words, as the preferences of enfranchised constituencies change, agency decisions change correspondingly. During the 1970s the cable television industry emerged as a powerful political force in Congress. Shortly thereafter, the industry became the beneficiary of a major deregulation effort by the Federal Communications Commission. This deregulation occurred without any direct congressional intervention but came about through changes in the set of interests represented in commission proceedings.[177] In general, well-designed administrative procedures obviate the need for constant legislative attention to agency behavior.

Administrative procedures, it is important to recognize, vary in the leverage they give members of Congress over the management of delegated authority. Some administrative procedures, such as the requirement that the FRA hold public hearings, serve to place hurdles in front of agencies.[178] These hurdles increase the costs to agencies of doing their day-to-day business. The FRA for years deferred acting on power braking systems as a result of hostile and contradictory testimony delivered at its rulemaking hearings.[179] Other administrative procedures, by contrast, increase the costs of taking *particular courses* of action. The National Environmental Policy Act makes it difficult for agencies to give short shrift to the environment in cases where the ecological stakes are relatively pronounced. With this variation in mind, it is difficult to make blanket claims about the efficacy of administrative procedures in promoting congressional control of the bureaucracy.

Appropriations. As suggested by the examples of the CFPB, the **power of the purse** is of critical importance to Congress's success in influencing the bureaucracy. Without appropriations, most laws cannot be implemented. Without adequate appropriations, most laws cannot be implemented effectively. These realities give legislators who sit on appropriations committees extraordinary political clout. If stingy, they can starve an agency to death; if generous, they can help an agency to flourish. Congressional Republicans obviously appreciated this fact when they proposed a nearly 10 percent cut in the EPA's appropriations for the 2016 fiscal year.[180] Such a sharp cut in agency funding would have severely constrained the EPA's ability to enforce sometimes unpopular environmental laws.

The power of the purse was demonstrated on a much broader scale in 2011, when Congress enacted the **Budget Control Act.** The law specified that if Congress was not able to produce a deficit reduction bill with at least $1.2 trillion in spending cuts, then across-the-board reductions would automatically occur. Such compulsory reductions are known as **sequestration.** Sequestration was viewed at the time as a universally unpalatable outcome, so the common assumption was that Congress and the White House and Republicans and Democrats would together find a way to avoid walking over such a steep fiscal cliff.[181] In 2013, however, no deficit reduction deal had been signed and sequestration went into effect. The subsequent effects of sequestration have been the subject of widespread public debate, with some warning of massive job losses and others claiming minimal effects on employment.[182]

According to the U.S. Government Accountability Office, sequestration caused agencies to reduce or delay the provision of certain services, while taking steps to limit the effects of the spending cuts.[183] For example, public housing authorities provided less rental assistance to low-income households than prior to sequestration. U.S. Customs and Border Protection reported increased wait times for passengers arriving in the United States on international flights. The Department of Defense scaled back its military training and readiness activities. Air Force Secretary Deborah James was not alone in worrying about the impacts of such cutbacks: "I believe sequestration is going to place American lives at greater risk both at home and abroad."[184]

Uncertainty over appropriations decisions can sometimes have as big an impact on administrative agencies as appropriations decisions do themselves. In the months leading up to the passage of the Budget Control Act, Congress passed a series of short-term continuing resolutions keeping federal agencies funded at current levels. Although this device averted a government shutdown, it nevertheless had profound effects on federal agency decisions. Unsure of where things stood, numerous federal agencies froze hiring, canceled projects, delayed contracts, curbed training, and reduced travel.[185] The Social Security Administration suspended plans to open eight new offices to cope with a backlog of appeals from people denied disability benefits, and the SEC delayed work on a major information technology project that would help the agency detect and correct securities law violations. Head Start programs across the country told parents they could not assure them that slots would be available in coming months. A new federal prison in New Hampshire, with enough space for 1,280 inmates, was unable to open because of uncertain funding.[186] These examples remind us how utterly dependent administrative agencies are on congressional appropriations.

Oversight. Legislators possess the ability to reduce their moral hazard problem through oversight of the bureaucracy. Oversight occurs in a variety of forms, including committee hearings and scandal-induced investigations.[187] For a long time, observers maintained that members of Congress tend to neglect oversight in favor of other functions, such as bringing federal projects and other forms of "bacon" home to their constituents.[188] Thus, in practice, oversight has not been viewed as an especially important tool of congressional control.

This assessment has come under critical scrutiny, as evidence suggests a significant increase in the volume of oversight activity in the 1970s and 1980s.[189] On average, congressional committees collectively spent fewer than 200 days per year conducting oversight during the decade of the 1960s. By 1983, this level of activity had grown substantially, to 587 days. In relative terms, oversight as a percentage of total committee activity increased from 9.1 percent in 1971 to 25.2 percent in 1983. Oversight, then, emerged as an integral part of the surveillance system used by members of Congress to monitor the bureaucracy's exercise of delegated authority.

Why did legislators become more interested during these years in actively overseeing executive branch agencies? Internally, the congressional reforms of the early 1970s, such as the proliferation of subcommittees and staff resources, enhanced the ease with which most members could carry out meaningful oversight. Externally, increases in the size and complexity of government made bureaucratic accountability and performance more valuable commodities than

| Inside Bureaucracy with | Tom Ridge
Secretary of Homeland Security
(2003–2005) |

"I believe my three successors would probably share the same point of view. All of us believe in congressional oversight—an important part of how we govern ourselves—but the oversight was, I believe, dysfunctional because it was disparate. . . . We were accountable, and overseen, by over 100 committees and subcommittees in the House and the Senate. And so no smaller group in the legislative branch ever understood the kind of integrative initiatives we were undertaking. My thought has been (and I think all my successors would say) the best oversight would have been and continues, even today as you are still trying to integrate this massive enterprise, to be to have far fewer members of the House and Senate become more completely aware, not of individual functions, but the operational integration of the department, rather than the siloed approach that a lot of these committees took. So it required an enormous amount of time and I think would have been for me helpful in helping to create a more effective and more closely integrated operational platform if at the same time as building the department they narrowed the committees of jurisdictions. I was on the Hill twelve years. I understand the role, the importance, and the criticality of congressional oversight. But when you're running helter skelter from this committee to the next and this group is more interested in these two agencies, you don't have an unlimited budget, so you have to set priorities. It's understandable. Committee chairmen and committees may deem that their particular focus on that particular part of the department deserves their attention and their priorities should be elevated to the highest among all. But I think it created appropriations problems. The process could have been more helpful in slowly integrating the capabilities that we had."

in previous eras of policymaking.[190] Together with divided government, these internal and external changes made it exceedingly difficult to create new legislation and therefore put a premium on influencing policy by overseeing already existing programs.

High, sustained levels of oversight are still not a given, even under the favorable environmental conditions of the postreform Congress. It is well established that the business of governance, including oversight, was not a strong suit of congressional Republicans when, in 1995, they returned to a bicameral majority for the first time in four decades.[191] Congressional oversight of the George W. Bush administration was also noticeably weaker in 2003–2004 than it was of the Clinton administration in 1993–1994.[192] Democrats promised—and delivered—a revival of oversight when they regained full control of Congress in 2007. Within two months after assuming control of Congress, Democratic legislators conducted a total of eighty-one hearings on the Iraq war.[193] Congressional Democrats also held high-profile hearings on security leaks (the outing of Central Intelligence Agency undercover employee Valerie Plame), the quality of medical care at Walter Reed Army Medical Center, and other controversial subjects.

When Rep. Darrell Issa, R-Calif., became chair of the House Committee on Oversight and Government Reform in January 2011, he vowed to be a tough and aggressive overseer. He had already signaled that he would be a partisan overseer, calling President Obama "one of the most corrupt presidents in modern times."[194] During the course of his tenure, Issa investigated the Benghazi attacks and conducted contempt of Congress proceedings against Attorney General Eric Holder.[195] During a hearing on the IRS, Issa cut off the microphone of fellow committee member Elijah Cummings, D-Md.[196] Given his style, Issa received predictably partisan reviews from other members of Congress. While one Republican praised him for hitting a number of "singles" and "doubles," Democrats decried excessive partisanship and a lack of focus.[197]

When engaging in oversight of the executive branch, members of Congress can pursue one of two basic strategies. The first is **police patrol oversight.** In police patrols, legislators search for bureaucratic actions that fail to conform to congressional expectations, much in the way that officers on the beat seek to ferret out criminal activity. In contrast, **fire alarm oversight** places much of the burden of monitoring the bureaucracy on citizens and organized interests, through instruments such as the **Freedom of Information Act** and Government in the Sunshine Act. Like firefighters, legislators swing into action after an alarm is sounded, using their policymaking apparatus to bring recalcitrant agencies under control. Given that police patrols require a relatively significant investment of congressional time and resources, it is widely presumed that the fire alarm approach dominates oversight.[198]

This presumption is not necessarily accurate, however. According to research, committee hearings—over time, across policy areas, and in both chambers—more often than not prove to be police patrol in their orientation.[199] In 1995, for example, 86.1 percent of the House Judiciary Committee's hearings consisted of routine, ongoing legislative activities, not reactions to crises and other types of galvanizing events. These activities included consideration of the reauthorization of the **Administrative Conference of the United States** (ACUS), an organization charged with studying agency processes and making recommendations to Congress regarding how to improve these processes. Several months after this hearing, Congress voted to terminate the agency's funding and ACUS ceased to exist until it was reestablished fifteen years later. All of this occurred with very little outside involvement or even awareness. Rather, Congress's oversight of ACUS took place within the context of the agency's regularly scheduled reauthorization process.

Also, recent research suggests that federal agencies can and sometimes do limit opportunities for fire-alarm oversight—for example, by limiting the length of the public comment period or by bypassing the notice and comment process altogether. In Rachel Potter's words: "Agencies are more likely to close the participation valve when the complaints of activated interest groups are likely to fall on sympathetic congressional ears."[200]

In all forms, oversight is inherently limited in its ability to constrain agency behavior. Once legislators have identified transgressions, they must have the incentive and capacity to sanction and redirect agencies. Each set of tools that might be used for such purposes—appointments, budgets, and legislative actions—is problematic in important respects.[201] Congress, with its dispersion of authority across chambers and committees, has difficulty passing legislation of any kind. Even if Congress enacts legislation targeting an agency, there is no guarantee that the new law will succeed where previous efforts failed in bringing about compliant behavior. Although oversight occasionally produces dramatic results, more often than not it is most useful as a way of deterring agencies from running too far afoul of legislators and their preferred policies.

Congressional Review Act. In the waning days of the Clinton presidency, the Occupational Safety and Health Administration (OSHA) issued a rule designed to protect workers against injuries caused by repetitive motion. This rule was a major policy action in that hundreds of thousands of Americans, in settings as diverse as corporate offices, meat-cutting plants, and medical facilities, miss work each year because of "ergonomics-related" injuries. The rule was also highly controversial. Analysts projected that collectively businesses would incur costs in the billions of dollars to comply with OSHA's requirements, which included reviewing employee complaints, redesigning problematic workstations, and providing compensation for disabilities.

Shortly after George W. Bush assumed the presidency, in 2001, the controversy surrounding the **ergonomics rule** erupted on Capitol Hill. Most Republican legislators, as well as some Democrats, vehemently opposed the rule, preferring either a less expansive approach or no regulation at all. Seeking to overturn OSHA's action, these lawmakers resorted to an obscure parliamentary maneuver. Under the **Congressional Review Act** (CRA) of 1996, agency rules can be nullified within sixty legislative days of promulgation if both chambers of Congress enact a **resolution of disapproval.** Because it is relatively difficult to subject such resolutions to committee hearings, extensive debate, and other standard features of the lawmaking process, they are easier to pass than normal legislation. On March 21, 2001, barely two months after the ergonomics rule took effect, it became the first agency action ever to have been repealed in this way when President Bush signed into law a resolution disapproving the standards established by OSHA.[202]

The CRA has been called the "nuclear bomb" of congressional oversight of the executive branch, and with good reason.[203] Not only does the CRA eliminate a regulation in its entirety, it also prevents the agency from subsequently issuing a rule that is "substantially the same" without express authorization from Congress.[204] Perhaps for this reason, the CRA lay dormant for many years after the ergonomics regulation was disapproved.

This all changed in 2016 after the election of Donald Trump and Republican majorities in both the Senate and House of Representatives. Sensing a "stars align" opportunity to scuttle regulations issued at the end of the Obama administration, Republicans revived the CRA, using it like never before.[205] By the end of March 2017, seven midnight regulations had been nullified, with another half-dozen heading to the White House or awaiting the president's signature.[206] These targeted regulations included a Department of Education rule setting standards for teacher preparation programs, a Department of the Interior rule limiting coal mining in the vicinity of streams, and a Department of Health and Human Services rule preventing states from denying funds to Planned Parenthood and other organizations that provide abortions.[207] The latter rule was nullified in the Senate after a 50–50 tie vote that was broken by Vice President Mike Pence. The broad scope of these disapprovals demonstrates the blunt, immediate, and lasting power of the CRA that, although untapped for sixteen years, served Republicans well during the early months of the Trump administration.

Judicial Review

The judicial system, like the presidency and Congress, is appropriately viewed as a principal to the bureaucracy's agents. Judges routinely oversee and review the work of executive branch agencies. In this vein, one of the most common judicial tasks is verifying that bureaucrats act in accordance with the law. A somewhat less common task is ensuring that bureaucratic actions are consistent with the Constitution. If an agency takes steps deemed illegal or unconstitutional, then its work can be overturned in the judiciary. When this happens, the court in question will often remand the action to the bureaucracy, with specific instructions as to how the agency's legal or constitutional mistakes might be rectified. How, then, do the courts go about dealing with their moral hazard difficulties?

Judges versus Politicians. **Judicial review** has several characteristics that distinguish it from instruments of presidential and congressional control. First, whereas politicians can engage in either police patrol or fire alarm oversight, the latter alone is available to judges. Courts can hear only those cases brought to their doorsteps by plaintiffs. Put differently, judges must wait for individuals or organizations to pull a fire alarm indicating that they have been injured or aggrieved by some agency action. Thus, in its basic orientation toward the bureaucracy, the judiciary is more passive than either the executive or the legislative branch.

Second, judges place greater emphasis than do politicians on procedural fairness and irregularities. One of the hallmarks of judicial review is an acute awareness of the requirements the **Administrative Procedure Act** and other relevant laws impose on agencies. The courts sometimes overturn bureaucratic actions because agencies have failed to provide adequate notice of a proposed rulemaking. Likewise, an agency that fails to provide interested parties with an adequate opportunity to comment on a proposed rule or fails to adequately explain the reasoning behind a final rule may find itself prohibited from completing or implementing the action at hand.

Third, because the judiciary is subject to numerous legal and operational constraints, interactions between judges and agencies tend to be more formal and less frequent than those between politicians and agencies. The nature of these interactions can lead to both negative and positive results. On the one hand, formal, infrequent interactions discourage flexible problem solving by agencies and stifle negotiations between judges and bureaucrats. On the other hand, these arrangements make it somewhat more difficult for agencies to shirk judicial orders. Unlike politicians, who express themselves through laws, hearings, executive orders, informal meetings, telephone conversations, and other mechanisms, judges essentially express themselves through official decisions and decrees. Agencies can at times deflect pressure from one politician by contending that demands from elsewhere impose obligations to the contrary. Pressure from judges is far more visible, much easier to document, and ultimately more difficult to resist.

These characteristics can be observed in the reactions of federal agencies to Supreme Court decisions that reversed or remanded executive branch actions. Over the decades, there have been hundreds of such decisions. According to research, these decisions have provoked a significant response on the part of the bureaucracy. Major policy change occurred after 72.7 percent of the decisions, while moderate and minor alterations followed 14.1 and 5.9 percent of them, respectively. Only 7.3 percent resulted in a complete absence of policy change.[208] As these episodes indicate, the coercive power of the Supreme Court and other judicial bodies is rather potent on those occasions when it is imposed. What remains an open question is whether this coercion serves to enhance bureaucratic performance as well as accountability.

Circuit Courts and Administrative Law. Within the federal judiciary, most lawsuits challenging agency decisions originate in district or trial courts. By law, however, some agency decisions may be appealed directly to a circuit court of appeals. Regardless of where a case originates, circuit courts of appeals are particularly important in the field of administrative law. Prominent among them is the U.S. Court of Appeals for the District of Columbia—or the D.C. Circuit—because a disproportionate number of appeals are filed in the city, where most agencies are headquartered. Indeed, legal analysts sometimes refer to the D.C. Circuit as the second most important court in the land, behind only the Supreme Court.[209] Whether or not that assessment is true, it is indisputable that the D.C. Circuit "enjoys an unmatched reputation as a leader in determining the substance and content of administrative law."[210] As a general rule, circuit courts of appeals affirm decisions made by executive branch agencies. During the 1970s circuit courts affirmed, on average, more than 60 percent of all agency decisions subjected to challenges. During the 1980s this affirmation rate rose to more than 70 percent. The D.C. Circuit, however, has been consistently less deferential than other circuit courts. During the 1970s and 1980s the D.C. Circuit sustained agencies only 57 and 56 percent of the time, respectively.[211]

The greater judicial activism of the D.C. Circuit can be traced back to the 1970s, especially to the thinking of Judge Harold Leventhal. In *Greater Boston Television Corp. v. Federal Communications Commission,* Leventhal first articulated the **hard look doctrine** of judicial review, which called for judges to take their supervisory responsibilities seriously. In that decision, Leventhal wrote that a court must intervene if it "becomes aware, especially from a combination of danger signals, that the agency has not really taken a 'hard look' at the salient problems, and has not genuinely engaged in reasoned decision-making."[212] In a series of subsequent decisions, Leventhal and other judges on the D.C. Circuit struck down a variety of major bureaucratic actions after tough scrutiny of the agencies' substantive reasoning in complex cases. For example, in *International Harvester Co. v. Ruckelshaus,* the D.C. Circuit invalidated the EPA's emission standards under the Clean Air Act by challenging the agency's underlying methodology.[213]

Another prominent D.C. Circuit judge, David Bazelon, supported Leventhal's call for tough scrutiny but preferred strong procedural review over strong substantive review. In the *International Harvester* case, for example, Bazelon argued that the agency's refusal to grant a one-year suspension of its 1975 emission standards was procedurally flawed because the agency had not allowed the petitioners a general right of cross-examination during the rulemaking proceedings.[214] Ultimately, in the *Vermont Yankee* case in 1978 the Supreme Court curbed the D.C. Circuit's penchant for strong procedural review when it held that a federal court may not impose procedural requirements on an agency above and beyond those specified in the Administrative Procedure Act.[215] Importantly, this decision left strong substantive review untouched and may have even encouraged it.[216]

Although the D.C. Circuit enjoys considerable prestige, the Supreme Court does not automatically defer to it or any other court. The *Vermont Yankee* decision aptly illustrates this point. In 2001, the Supreme Court overruled a 1999 decision by the D.C. Circuit that had overturned a soot and smog rule adopted by the EPA. In *American Trucking Associations v. EPA,* the D.C. Circuit had reversed the agency's rule by reviving a moribund tenet of administrative law known as the **nondelegation doctrine.** This doctrine states that Congress may not delegate legislative authority to the executive branch of the government. In effect, the doctrine implies that congressional standards must have some teeth, some specificity. In *American Trucking,* the Supreme Court unanimously upheld the agency's authority to set new and tougher clean air standards without first considering the potential economic impact of these standards on the trucking industry. The Supreme Court also explicitly declined to invoke the nondelegation doctrine, thus repudiating the D.C. Circuit.[217]

In perhaps the most important case in modern administrative law, *Chevron v. Natural Resources Defense Council,* the Supreme Court constrained judicial review by articulating the doctrine of **administrative deference.**[218] In short, the justices upheld the authority of the EPA to define sources of air pollution under the Clean Air Act of 1977. More generally, this ruling means that judges must defer to agency interpretations of executive branch authority when the statute granting this authority is ambiguous and the agency's interpretation of the underlying ambiguity is reasonable. In 2017, at his Supreme Court confirmation hearing, Neil Gorsuch was questioned by senators such as Al Franken, D-Minn., about an opinion he had issued as a circuit court of appeals judge in which he characterized *Chevron* deference as allowing "executive bureaucracies to swallow huge amounts of core judicial and legislative power."[219] Gorsuch's opinion, and the Senate's interest in his prospective behavior as a Supreme Court justice in deferring to agency interpretations, demonstrates the high stakes of judicial doctrine in determining the boundaries of the administrative state.

Supreme Court. In light of existing decisions and doctrines, it is not surprising that, like circuit courts of appeal, the Supreme Court is more likely to defer to agencies than to overturn them.[220] While the outcome of any Supreme Court case depends on many factors—the legal merits of the case, the skills of the attorneys, and so forth—political ideology also plays a role in the Court's decision making. The more liberal Warren Court (1953–1969) supported liberal agency decisions 85.7 percent of the time, while the more conservative Burger Court (1969–1986) supported liberal agency decisions only 69.1 percent of the time. Similarly, the Warren Court supported conservative agency decisions 63.4 percent of the time, a rate nearly 20 percent lower than that of the Burger Court. Although the Supreme Court, and courts more generally, often hesitate to rule against agencies, this does not mean judicial review is ineffectual. Agencies undoubtedly craft decisions with an eye to the possibility that their procedures and substantive reasoning may at some point be subjected to judicial scrutiny.

Also, it is possible to exaggerate the importance of the *Chevron* decision. As William Eskridge and Lauren Baer have noted, the Supreme Court is more likely to engage in ad hoc judicial reasoning than to simply invoke *Chevron* as the rationale for deferring to administrative agency decisions.[221] In fact, the Court's reactions to administrative decisions fall along a "continuum of deference," with deference at one end of the spectrum and support at the other end. Many Supreme Court decisions fall somewhere in between these two extremes. Furthermore, overall patterns can obscure important exceptions. Although the Court, under Chief Justice John G. Roberts, has deferred to administrative agencies in some instances, it has sometimes overturned significant administrative agency decisions.[222] While the overall pattern continues to be that administrative agencies win before the Supreme Court more often than not, administrative agencies cannot take judicial review for granted.

Principal-Agent Theory and the Bureaucracy's Clients

Consistent with principal-agent theory, chief executives, legislatures, and judiciaries all find themselves in positions where they can limit the loss associated with the delegation of policymaking authority to the bureaucracy. None of these political principals, however, can completely eliminate the problems raised by adverse selection and moral hazard. When setting about the task of managing delegation, each principal faces unique difficulties, from the judiciary's inherently reactive nature to the president's ambitious desire for coordinated control of a sprawling bureaucracy.

An approach common to all of these principals is enlisting the help of third parties in the use of screening mechanisms, institutional design, and oversight. For many years the White House has relied on organized interests to put forth and evaluate presidential appointees. In fact, President George W. Bush stoked a mild controversy when he broke from precedent by declining to consider the recommendations of the American Bar Association in filling federal judgeship vacancies. In Congress, the essence of fire alarm oversight is the empowerment of citizens and groups to keep a watchful eye on agency proceedings and decisions. To keep their dockets full, the courts rely on litigants to press claims about the illegality and unconstitutionality of bureaucratic actions.

All of this raises the question of whether principal-agent theory can provide insight into the role and influence of agency clients in bureaucratic policymaking. Strictly speaking, clients are not bureaucratic principals, as they are neither the hierarchical supervisors of agencies nor the wellsprings of delegated authority. As a result, clients are only as potent as the public officials whose backing they enjoy.

For such backing to materialize, clients must possess attributes of significant value to political principals. For example, members of Congress have a never-ending need for information about the views of their constituents, the predispositions of their colleagues on pending legislation, and the outcomes likely to follow from their policy choices.[223] Clients who can meet these information needs are naturally advantaged in the lawmaking process. These advantages carry over into the bureaucracy when legislators structure agencies, design administrative procedures, and conduct oversight in ways targeted to ensure that policymaking in the executive branch does not stray too far from deals struck in Congress.

Who then are the clients best positioned to serve as powerful third parties in the principal-agent hierarchy? The key consideration here is mobilization. For some time it has been clear that not all parties with a stake in government activity organize in pursuit of their policy preferences.[224] Likewise, the extensiveness of client mobilization varies greatly across the issues that fall under the domain of the executive branch. In the end, principal-agent theory points not only to the unique position of clients in the policymaking hierarchy but also to the need for a close examination of the factors affecting the mobilization of both the beneficiaries and targets of agency actions.

Principals and Principles

As this chapter has demonstrated, the bureaucracy has no shortage of bosses. At times these bosses exercise extraordinary influence over what agencies can and cannot do. In one meeting President Obama set aside the EPA's ozone regulation, a major policy action years in the making. Such highly visible cases aside, the bureaucracy's bosses usually exercise their authority, if at all, in much subtler and more conditional ways. Years after the passage of the Dodd-Frank Act, many regulations necessary to the implementation of financial reforms had not yet been completed, a state of affairs President Obama found himself unable to immediately resolve.

If the power of those who serve as the bureaucracy's principals is conditional, then what specific conditions determine the contours of agency discretion? Part of this story deals with the tools principals possess, and do not possess, to combat adverse selection and moral hazard. Although the Constitution provides the presidency with few formal advantages vis-à-vis the bureaucracy, presidents are powerful in ways difficult to measure. When the president puts the full authority and prestige of the White House behind an initiative, it is often difficult for other policymakers, including bureaucrats, to resist. Yet from the perspective of these policymakers, presidential agendas are usually rather limited in scope. As a result the president exercises power only on an occasional basis. The judiciary is also a potent principal that gets involved in agency decision making under a limited set of circumstances. For most agencies most of the time, judicial review undoubtedly represents an unpleasant prospect, but one they experience only occasionally. The same cannot be said when it comes to legislative principals. Legislators have their hands on everything from agency design to oversight of the bureaucracy. Although these instruments give Congress and other such principals strong leverage over the problem of moral hazard, this leverage by no means eradicates agency loss, as the following example illustrates.

The Resource Conservation and Recovery Act of 1976 empowers the EPA to issue standards for the treatment, storage, and disposal of hazardous wastes.[225] The act requires the agency to adhere to a variety of analytical, disclosure, and participation procedures when setting these standards. Importantly, the agency has found a way to get around these requirements when it so desires. In cases where it wishes to evade congressional scrutiny, the EPA eschews the issuance of formal rules and makes policy instead through **guidance documents.** Although guidance documents (statements agencies produce to flesh out their stances on particular issues) lack the full force of law, regulated firms routinely comply with them. Thus, despite Congress's efforts, hazardous waste policy is often made beyond the reach of the tools legislators normally use to limit bureaucratic discretion.

To put it differently, part of the story of the boundaries of bureaucratic authority concerns the willingness of agency officials to respond to their bosses' cues. In the broadest sense, the bureaucracy's bosses include not only chief executives, legislatures, and judiciaries but the public—the very society within which agencies operate—as well. With this in mind, many bureaucrats try to represent the public interest as best they can determine it. When viewed in this way, agencies appear to be populated for the most part with officials who are **principled agents.**[226] That is, agency officials are hard workers who are highly professional, devoted to the mission of their organizations, and only rarely driven to shirk or sabotage the policy aims of their bosses. In the end, control of the bureaucracy emanates not only from political principals but also from other sources inside and outside of agencies.

Key Terms

Notes

1. Environmental Protection Agency, "Ground Level Ozone," https://www.epa.gov/ozone-pollution/ozone-basics#what where how (accessed March 27, 2017).

2. Gabriel Nelson, "Bush Ozone Standards Are 'Not Legally Defensible'—EPA Chief," *New York Times,* July 14, 2011, http://www.nytimes.com/gwire/2011/07/14/14greenwire-bush-ozone-standards-are-not-legally-defensibl-19743.html (accessed March 27, 2017).

3. The White House, Office of the Press Secretary, "Statement by the President on the Ozone National Ambient Air Quality Standards," https://obamawhitehouse.archives .gov/the-press-office/2011/09/02/statement-president-ozone-national-ambient-air-quality-standards (accessed March 27, 2017).

4. Juliet Eilperin, "Obama Pulls Back Proposed Smog Standards in Victory for Business," *Washington Post,* September 2, 2011, http://www.washingtonpost.com/national/health-science/obama-pulls-back-proposed-smog-standards-in-victory-for-business/2011/09/02/gIQAisTiwJ_story.html (accessed March 27, 2017).

5. John M. Border, "Obama Administration Abandons Stricter Air-Quality Rules," *New York Times,* September 2, 2011, http://www.nytimes.com/2011/09/03/science/earth/03air.html?_r=0 (accessed March 27, 2017).

6. Vipal Monga, "Nearly Half of Dodd-Frank Rules Still Unwritten," *Wall Street Journal,* April 8, 2014, http://blogs.wsj.com/cfo/2014/04/08/nearly-half-of-dodd-frank-rules-still-unwritten/ (accessed March 27, 2017).

7. Patrick Brennan, "Obama Admin Has Missed over 60 Percent of Dodd-Frank Deadlines," *National Review,* August 20, 2013, http://www.nationalreview.com/corner/356262/obama-admin-has-missed-over-60-percent-dodd-frank-deadlines-patrick-brennan (accessed March 27, 2017).

8. Vipal Monga, "Nearly Half of Dodd-Frank Rules Still Unwritten," *Wall Street Journal,* April 8, 2014, http://blogs.wsj.com/cfo/2014/04/08/nearly-half-of-dodd-frank-rules-still-unwritten/ (accessed March 27, 2017).

9. David Epstein and Sharyn O'Halloran, *Delegating Powers: A Transaction Cost Politics Approach to Policy Making under Separate Powers* (New York: Cambridge University Press, 1999).

10. Emily Stephenson, "Obama Asks Regulators to Speed Up Wall Street Reforms," Reuters, August 19, 2013, http://www.reuters.com/article/2013/08/19/us-financial-regulation-obama-idUSBRE97I0TV20130819 (accessed March 27, 2017).

11. Terry M. Moe, "The New Economics of Organization," *American Journal of Political Science* 28 (November 1984): 739–777; John D. Huber and Charles R. Shipan, "The Costs of Control: Legislators, Agencies, and Transaction Costs," *Legislative Studies Quarterly* 25 (February 2000): 25–52.

12. D. Roderick Kiewiet and Mathew D. McCubbins, *The Logic of Delegation: Congressional Parties and the Appropriations Process* (Chicago: University of Chicago Press, 1991).

13. John Brehm and Scott Gates, *Working, Shirking, and Sabotage* (Ann Arbor: University of Michigan Press, 1999).

14. James Q. Wilson, *Varieties of Police Behavior* (Cambridge, Mass.: Harvard University Press, 1968).

15. Jonathan Mummolo, "Modern Police Tactics," presentation at McCourt School of Public Policy, Georgetown University, October 19, 2016.

16. Jack Davis, "Trump Signs Order to Reduce the Size of the Federal Bureaucracy," http://www.westernjournalism.com/trump-signs-order-reduce-size-federal-bureaucracy/ (accessed March 29, 2017).

17. Ibid.

18. Ibid.

19. Juliet Eilperin, "Trump Freezes Hiring of Many Federal Workers," *Washington Post,* January 23, 2017, https://www.washingtonpost.com/powerpost/trump-freezes-hiring-of-federal-workers/2017/01/23/f14d8180-e190-11e6-ba11-63c4b4fb5a63_story.html?utm_term=.96ede88a98c2 (accessed March 29, 2017).

20. Aaron Gregg, "Trump's War on the Federal Bureaucracy May Already Be Hurting D.C.'s Economy," *Washington Post,* March 24, 2017, https://www.washingtonpost.com/news/capital-business/wp/2017/03/24/trumps-war-on-the-federal-bureaucracy-may-already-be-hurting-d-c-s-economy/?utm_term=.9aede6f6db74 (accessed March 29, 2017).

21. Ibid.

22. Philip Rucker and Robert Costa, "Bannon Vows a Daily Fight for 'Deconstruction of the Administrative State,'" *Washington Post,* February 23, 2017, https://

www.washingtonpost.com/politics/top-wh-strategist-vows-a-daily-fight-for-deconstruction-of-the-administrative-state/2017/02/23/03f6b8da-f9ea-11e6-bf01-d47f8cf9b643_story.html?utm_term=.624b24e29ad6 (accessed March 29, 2017).

23. Morris P. Fiorina, *Congress: Keystone of the Washington Establishment*, 2nd ed. (New Haven, CT: Yale University Press, 1989).

24. R. Douglas Arnold, *The Logic of Congressional Action* (New Haven, CT: Yale University Press, 1990).

25. Environmental Protection Agency, "About EPA," https://www.epa.gov/aboutepa (accessed March 27, 2017).

26. William Gormley Jr., "Regulatory Issue Networks in a Federal System," *Polity* 18 (Summer 1986): 595–620.

27. Ibid.

28. The Patient Protection and Affordable Care Act, https://democrats.senate.gov/pdfs/reform/patient-protection-affordable-care-act-as-passed.pdf (accessed July 8, 2015).

29. T. R. Goldman, "Progress Report: The Affordable Care Act's Extended Dependent Coverage Provision," http://healthaffairs.org/blog/2013/12/16/progress-report-the-affordable-care-acts-extended-dependent-coverage-provision/ (accessed July 8, 2015).

30. Regulation Rodeo, http://regrodeo.com/?year[0]=2007&year[1]=2008&year[2]=2009&year[3]=2010&year[4]=2011&year[5]=2012&year[6]=2013&year[7]=2014&year[8]=2015&topic[0]=tag_1 (accessed July 8, 2015).

31. Juliet Eilperin and Mike DeBonis, "Trump Administration Still Plans to Undo Parts of the ACA, Tom Price Testifies," *Washington Post*, March 29, 2017.

32. The National Conference of State Legislatures provides information about session calendars, staff size, legislator compensation, and other salient characteristics on its website, http://www.ncsl.org/research/about-state-legislatures.aspx (accessed July 8, 2015).

33. John D. Huber and Charles R. Shipan, *Deliberate Discretion? The Institutional Foundations of Bureaucratic Autonomy* (New York: Cambridge University Press, 2002).

34. Ibid., 7.

35. Ibid., 6.

36. State of Idaho Legislature, www.legislature.idaho.gov/about/citizenlegislature.htm (accessed January 21, 2007).

37. Epstein and O'Halloran, *Delegating Powers*.

38. Ibid.

39. Morris P. Fiorina, "Congressional Control of the Bureaucracy: A Mismatch of Incentives and Capabilities," in *Congress Reconsidered*, 2nd ed., ed. Lawrence C. Dodd and Bruce I. Oppenheimer (Washington, D.C.: CQ Press, 1981).

40. Richard E. Neustadt, *Presidential Power and the Modern Presidents: The Politics of Leadership from Roosevelt to Reagan* (New York: Free Press, 1990).

41. Fiorina, "Congressional Control of the Bureaucracy."

42. Terry M. Moe, "The Presidency and the Bureaucracy: The Presidential Advantage," in *The Presidency and the Political System*, 4th ed., ed. Michael Nelson (Washington, D.C.: CQ Press, 1995); Terry M. Moe and William G. Howell, "The Presidential Power of Unilateral Action," *Journal of Law, Economics, and Organization* 15 (March 1999): 132–179. For a much earlier yet similar argument, see Edward S. Corwin and Louis W. Koenig, *The Presidency Today* (New York: New York University Press, 1956).

43. Gregory Korte, "Obama Issues 'Executive Orders by Another Name,'" *USA Today*, December 16, 2014, http://www.usatoday.com/story/news/politics/2014/12/16/obama-presidential-memoranda-executive-orders/20191805/ (accessed July 9, 2015).

44. Rachel Stolzfoos, "Obama's Issuing Executive Orders at Fastest Pace of Presidency," *Daily Caller*, April 23, 2015, http://dailycaller.com/2015/04/23/obamas-issuing-executive-orders-at-fastest-pace-of-presidency/ (accessed July 9, 2015).

45. Noam Scheiber, "Obama Makes Millions More Americans Eligible for Overtime," *New York Times*, June 30, 2015, http://www.nytimes.com/2015/06/30/business/obama-plan-would-make-more-americans-eligible-for-overtime.html (accessed July 9, 2015); David

Jackson and Kevin Johnson, "Obama Order Clears Ways for Private Ransom Payments," *New York Times,* June 30, 2015, http://www.nytimes.com/2015/06/30/business/obama-plan-would-make-more-americans-eligible-for-overtime.html (accessed July 9, 2015); Michael Bastasch, "Obama Issues 'Executive Actions' to Put Solar Panels on Federally Subsidized Housing," *Daily Caller,* July 7, 2015, http://dailycaller.com/2015/07/07/obama-issues-executive-actions-to-put-solar-panels-on-federally-subsidized-housing/ (accessed July 9, 2015).

46. Frank J. Murray, "Clinton's Executive Orders Still Are Packing a Punch; Other Presidents Issued More, but Many of His Are Sweeping," *Washington Times,* August 23, 1999.

47. Quoted in ibid.

48. William J. Olson and Alan Woll, "Executive Orders and National Emergencies: How Presidents Have Come to 'Run the Country' by Usurping Legislative Power," *Policy Analysis,* October 28, 1999.

49. Lydia Wheeler, "Fifth Circuit to Weigh Hold on Obama's Immigration Orders," *The Hill,* July 7, 2015, http://thehill.com/regulation/court-battles/247052-fifth-circuit-to-weigh-hold-on-obamas-immigration-orders (accessed July 9, 2015).

50. Matt Ford, "A Ruling against the Obama Administration on Immigration," *The Atlantic* (November 10, 2015).

51. Robert Barnes, "Supreme Court Won't Revive Obama Plan to Shield Illegal Immigrants from Deportation," *Washington Post,* June 23, 2016.

52. Sarah Wheaton and Nick Gass, "Obama Slams 'Frustrating,' 'Heartbreaking' Supreme Court Immigration Decision," *Politico,* June 23, 2016.

53. James Risen and Eric Lichtblau, "Bush Lets U.S. Spy on Callers without Courts," *New York Times,* December 15, 2005.

54. Ibid.; Carol D. Leonnig, "Secret Court's Judges Were Warned about NSA Spy Data; Program May Have Led Improperly to Warrants," *Washington Post,* February 9, 2006.

55. Eric Lichtblau and David E. Sanger, "Administration Cites War Vote in Spying Case," *New York Times,* December 19, 2005.

56. David S. Broder, "Bucking Bush on Spying," *Washington Post,* February 9, 2006; Charles Babington, "White House Working to Avoid Wiretap Probe; But Some Republicans Say Bush Must Be More Open about Eavesdropping Program," *Washington Post,* February 20, 2006.

57. Jonathan Weisman and Carol D. Leonnig, "No Compromise on Wiretap Bill; Focus Now on House Version," *Washington Post,* September 27, 2006.

58. Dan Eggen and Dafna Linzer, "Judge Rules against Wiretaps; NSA Program Called Unconstitutional," *Washington Post,* August 18, 2006.

59. Dan Eggen, "Court Will Oversee Wiretap Program; Change Does Not Settle Qualms about Privacy," *Washington Post,* January 18, 2007.

60. British Broadcasting Corporation, "Eric Snowden: Leaks That Exposed US Spy Programme," BBC News, January 17, 2014, http://www.bbc.com/news/world-us-canada-23123964 (accessed March 27, 2017).

61. Matt Sledge and Sabrina Siddiqui, "Obama NSA Reform Speech Promises Modest Changes," *Huffington Post,* January 17, 2014, http://www.huffingtonpost.com/2014/01/17/obama-nsa-reform_n_4612108.html (accessed July 9, 2015).

62. "Obama Signs Bill to Resume, Overhaul NSA Surveillance," Fox News, http://www.foxnews.com/politics/2015/06/02/legislation-to-resume-overhaul-nsa-surveillance-clears-key-senate-hurdle.html (accessed March 31, 2017) ; Sean Sullivan and Scott Clement, "The 4 Numbers You Need to Know for President Obama's NSA Speech," *Huffington Post,* January 17, 2014, http://www.huffingtonpost.com/2014/01/17/obama-nsa-reform_n_4612108.html (accessed July 9, 2015).

63. Mark Hensch, "RNC Official: Obama Lecturing Trump on Executive Orders 'Ironic'" (accessed January 12, 2017). http://thehill.com/homenews/administration/311386-rnc-official-obama-lecturing-trump-on-executive-orders-ironic (accessed March 31, 2017).

64. Ibid.

65. Matt Vespa, "Reports: President-Elect Trump to Issue Executive Orders That Will Help Roll Back Obamacare on Day One," Townhall, January 4, 2017, http://townhall.com/

tipsheet/mattvespa/2017/01/04/reports-presidentelect-trump-to-issue-executive-order-rolling-back-obamacare-on-day-one-n2267112 (accessed January 12, 2017).

66. Josh Israel, "Trump's Campaign Vowed to Undo All of Obama's Executive Orders. What Would Happen?" ThinkProgress, December 19, 2016, https://thinkprogress.org/trumps-campaign-vowed-to-undo-all-of-obama-s-executive-orders-what-would-happen-313e743e3219#.7rhpbqwit (accessed January 12, 2017).

67. Blake Neff, "Trump: I May Not Rescind Every Obama Executive Order," *Daily Caller*, December 1, 2016, http://dailycaller.com/2016/12/01/trump-i-may-not-rescind-every-obama-executive-order/ (accessed January 12, 2017).

68. NBC News, "President-Elect Trump Could Undo President Obama's Executive Orders," NBC News, http://www.nbcnews.com/nightly-news/video/president-elect-trump-could-undo-president-obama-s-executive-orders-850370627629 (accessed January 12, 2017).

69. Damian Paletta and Steven Mufson, "Trump Seeks Deep Federal Cuts," *Washington Post*, March 16, 2017, p. 1.

70. Jeremy Peters, "Steve Bannon Reassures Conservatives Uneasy about Trump," *New York Times*, February 23, 2017.

71. Brady Dennis and Juliet Eilperin, "Trump's Budget Takes a Sledgehammer to the EPA," *Washington Post*, March 16.

72. Carten Cordell, "4 Ways GAO Says the Government Can Save Money," *Federal Times*, April 13, 2016.

73. Dennis Ventry Jr., "Why Steven Mnuchin Wants a Stronger I.R.S.," *New York Times*, March 27, 2017.

74. Edmund Demarche, "Trump's First Budget Faces Early Republican Resistance," Fox News, March 16, 2017, http://www.foxnews.com/politics/2017/03/16/trumps-first-budget-faces-early-republican-resistance.html (accessed March 30, 2017).

75. Hal Rogers, "Congressman Rogers' Statement on President Trump's Budget Proposal," https://halrogers.house.gov/press-releases?ID=24250FDA-5BF7-4A2D-BD7C-8D4579A5AA1A (accessed March 30, 2017).

76. James Pfiffner, *The Modern Presidency* (New York: St. Martin's Press, 1994); James Pfiffner, "Presidential Appointments and Managing the Executive Branch," http://www.politicalappointeeproject.org/commentary/appointments-and-managing-executive-branch (accessed July 9, 2015).

77. G. Calvin Mackenzie, *The Politics of Presidential Appointments* (New York: Free Press, 1981).

78. Pfiffner, *The Modern Presidency*.

79. Todd Purdum, "Team of Mascots," *Vanity Fair* (July 2012), http://www.vanityfair.com/news/2012/07/obama-cabinet-team-rivals-lincoln (accessed July 9, 2015).

80. Anne Gearan, "Trump Rejects Veteran GOP Foreign Policy Aide Elliott Abrams for State Dept. Job," *Washington Post*, February 10, 2017.

81. Karen De Young, "Defense Secretary Mattis Withdraws Patterson as Choice for Undersecretary for Policy," *Washington Post*, March 14, 2015.

82. G. Calvin Mackenzie, *The Politics of Presidential Appointments* (New York: Free Press, 1981), 174.

83. Partnership for Public Service, *Government Disservice: Overcoming Washington Dysfunction to Improve Congressional Stewardship of the Executive Branch*, September 16, 2015, p. 28.

84. Jon Bond, Richard Fleisher, and Glen Krutz, "The Presumption of Success on Presidential Appointments Reconsidered: How Delay Has Become the Primary Method of Defeating Nominees" (paper presented at the annual meeting of the Midwest Political Science Association, Chicago, Ill., April 20–23, 2006).

85. Nolan McCarty and Rose Razaghian, "Advice and Consent: Senate Responses to Executive Branch Nominations, 1885–1996," *American Journal of Political Science* 43 (October 1999): 1122–1143.

86. Jonathan Tilove, "Senator Mary Landrieu Lifts Hold, Barack Obama's Budget Nominee Confirmed," *New Orleans Times-Picayune*, November 19, 2010.

87. Michael Walsh, "Obama: GOP Has Delayed Loretta Lynch Vote Longer Than 7 Previous Attorneys General Combined," http://news.yahoo.com/barack-obama-loretta-lynch-u-s-attorney-general-congress-senate-131109200.html (accessed July 9, 2015).

88. B. Dan Wood and Richard W. Waterman, "The Dynamics of Political Control of the Bureaucracy," *American Political Science Review* 85 (September 1991): 801–828.

89. EEOC Enforcement Guidance, http://www.eeoc.gov/laws/guidance/upload/arrest_conviction.pdf (accessed July 9, 2015).

90. Todd Lebowitz, "Courts Remind EEOC Again: Background Checks Don't Equal Racism," *The Hill*, March 13, 2015, http://thehill.com/blogs/congress-blog/labor/235568-courts-remind-eeoc-again-background-checks-dont-equal-racism (accessed July 9, 2015).

91. Linda L. Fisher, "Fifty Years of Presidential Appointments," in *The In-and-Outers: Presidential Appointees and Transient Government in Washington,* ed. G. Calvin Mackenzie (Baltimore: Johns Hopkins University Press, 1987); Matthew Dull, et al., "Appointee Confirmation and Tenure: The Succession of U.S. Federal Agency Appointees, 1989–2009," *Public Administration Review* 72, no. 6 (November/December 2012): 902–913.

92. Patricia W. Ingraham and Carolyn R. Ban, "Models of Public Management: Are They Useful to Federal Managers in the 1980s?" *Public Administration Review* 46 (March 1986): 152–160. See also Hugh Heclo, *A Government of Strangers: Executive Politics in Washington* (Washington, D.C.: Brookings Institution Press, 1977).

93. Paul Blustein, "Treasury Bonds with Bono; Secretary and Rock Star Join in a Seriously Strange Tour of African Poverty," *Washington Post*, June 4, 2002.

94. U.S. Department of Transportation, "U.S. Department of Transportation Redirects $1.195 Billion in High-Speed Rail Funds," Washington, D.C., December 9, 2010.

95. Matt Richtel, "LaHood Says Companies Must Wake Up to Distracted Driving," *New York Times*, July 24, 2013.

96. Sarah Rich, "Have All States Banned Texting While Driving?" GovTech, July 30, 2013, http://www.govtech.com/public-safety/Have-All-States-Banned-Texting-While-Driving.html (accessed October 29, 2016).

97. Tanya Snyder, "How Will the Next Transpo Secretary Build on Ray LaHood's Legacy?" Streetsblog USA, January 30, 2013, http://usa.streetsblog.org/2013/01/30/what-is-obama-looking-for-in-a-new-transportation-secretary/ (accessed October 29, 2016).

98. Jonathan Alter, "Woman of the World," *Vanity Fair* (June 2011): 140–201; Hillary Rodham Clinton, interview on *Meet the Press*, NBC News, July 26, 2009.

99. Alter, "Woman of the World," 119.

100. David Herszenhorn, "House Benghazi Report Finds No New Evidence of Wrongdoing by Hillary Clinton," *New York Times*, June 28, 2016.

101. Mark Landler and Eric Lichtblau, "FBI Director James Comey Recommends No Charges for Hillary Clinton on E-mail," *New York Times*, July 5, 2016, p. 1.

102. Michael Abramowitz and Steve Vogel, "Army Chiefs Plead Ignorance, but Lawmakers Are Skeptical," *Washington Post*, March 6, 2007; Pauline Jelinek, "Army's Kiley Ousted in Walter Reed Furor," *Washington Post*, March 13, 2007.

103. Helene Cooper and David Sanger, "Obama Says Afghan Policy Won't Change after Dismissal," *New York Times*, June 23, 2010.

104. Michael Hastings, "The Runaway General," *Rolling Stone*, July 8–22, 2010.

105. David Sanger, "In Week of Tests, Obama Asserts His Authority," *New York Times*, June 25, 2010.

106. Peter Baker and Michael Shear, "Trump Shifts Rationale for Firing Comey, Calling Him a 'Showboat,'" New York Times, May 11, 2017.

107. Marc Fisher and Karen De Young, "The Immediate Echo: Saturday Night Massacre," Washington Post, May 10, 2017, p. 1; Ken Gormley, Archibald Cox: Conscience of a Nation. Reading, Mass.: Addison-Wesley, 1997.

108. Paul Singer, Eliza Collins, and Erin Kelly, "Rare Bipartisan Moment: Both Sides Embrace Robert Mueller as Special Counsel," USA Today, May 17, 2017.

109. Richard Whitmire, *The Bee Eater: Michelle Rhee Takes on the Nation's Worst School District* (San Francisco: Jossey-Bass, 2011), 124.

110. Ibid.

111. Randi Kaye, "All Teachers Fired at Rhode Island School," CNN, February 24, 2010, http://www.cnn.com/2010/US/02/24/rhode.island.teachers (accessed July 27, 2015).

112. Elisabeth Harrison, "Central Falls High School, Three Years after a Mass Firing," Rhode Island NPR, December 31, 2013, http://ripr.org/post/central-falls-high-school-three-years-after-mass-firing (accessed July 27, 2015).

113. Steven Mufson and Juliet Eilperin, "Trump Transition Team for Energy Department Seeks Names of Employees Involved in Climate Meetings," *Washington Post,* December 9, 2016.

114. Joe Davidson, "Energy Department Rejects Trump's Request to Name Climate-Change Workers, Who Remain Worried," *Washington Post,* December 13, 2016.

115. Ibid.

116. Chris Mooney and Juliet Eilperin, "Trump Transition Says Request for Names of Climate Scientists Was Not Authorized," *Washington Post,* December 14, 2016.

117. Ronald N. Johnson and Gary D. Libecap, *The Federal Civil Service System and the Problem of Bureaucracy: The Economics and Politics of Institutional Change* (Chicago: University of Chicago Press, 1994).

118. Helene Cooper, "In Security Shuffle, White House Merges Staffs," *New York Times,* May 27, 2009, http://www.nytimes.com/2009/05/27/us/27homeland.html (accessed July 23, 2015).

119. Ibid.

120. Eric Katz, "Obama Announces Plans to Reform and Modernize the Senior Executive Service," *Government Executive,* December 9, 2014, http://www.govexec.com/management/2014/12/obama-announces-plans-reform-and-modernize-senior-executive-service/100818/ (accessed July 23, 2015).

121. Paul C. Light, *The True Size of Government* (Washington, D.C.: Brookings Institution Press, 1999).

122. Patricia W. Ingraham, "Building Bridges or Burning Them? The President, the Appointees, and the Bureaucracy," *Public Administration Review* 47 (September–October 1987): 425–435.

123. Joel D. Aberbach and Bert A. Rockman, *In the Web of Politics: Three Decades of the U.S. Federal Executive* (Washington, D.C.: Brookings Institution Press, 2000).

124. "Division on Homeland Security Department; Labor Rights Issue Still a Stumbling Block," CNN.com: Inside Politics, November 12, 2002, www.cnn.com/2002/ALLPOLITICS/11/11/homeland.security.

125. Robert Pear, "4 Unions Challenge Homeland Security Personnel Policies," *New York Times,* January 27, 2005.

126. Stephen Barr, "A Personnel Challenge at DHS," *Washington Post,* January 15, 2007; Eric M. Weiss, "Appeals Court Vetoes Bush Plan to Alter U.S. Personnel Rules," *Washington Post,* June 28, 2006.

127. Richard H. Pildes and Cass R. Sunstein, "Reinventing the Regulatory State," *University of Chicago Law Review* 62 (Winter 1995): 1–129; William F. West, "The Institutionalization of Regulatory Review: Organizational Stability and Responsive Competence at OIRA," *Presidential Studies Quarterly* 35 (March 2005): 76–93.

128. William Gormley Jr., "Counterbureaucracies in Theory and Practice," *Administration and Society* 28 (November 1986): 275–298.

129. Steven Croley, "White House Review of Agency Rulemaking: An Empirical Investigation," *University of Chicago Law Review* 70 (Summer 2003): 821–885; Christopher C. DeMuth and Douglas H. Ginsburg, "White House Review of Agency Rulemaking," *Harvard Law Review* 99 (March 1986): 1075–1088; Pildes and Sunstein, "Reinventing the Regulatory State"; Mark Seidenfeld, "A Big Picture Approach to Presidential Influence on Agency Policy-Making," *Iowa Law Review* 80 (October 1994): 1–50.

130. E. Donald Elliott, "TQM-ing OMB: Or Why Regulatory Review under Executive Order 12,291 Works Poorly and What President Clinton Should Do about It," *Law and Contemporary Problems* 57 (Spring 1994): 167–184; Pildes and Sunstein, "Reinventing the Regulatory State."

131. Dan Froomkin, "Cass Sunstein: The Obama Administration's Ambivalent Regulator," *Huffington Post*, June 13, 2011, http://www.huffingtonpost.com/2011/06/13/cass-sunstein-obama-ambivalent-regulator-czar_n_874530.html (accessed July 23, 2015).

132. Kate Sheppard, "Former EPA Climate Adviser Rips Obama over Environmental Regulations," *Mother Jones*, April 4, 2013, http://www.motherjones.com/print/220641 (accessed July 27, 2015).

133. The White House, "Executive Order—Identifying and Reducing Regulatory Burdens," https://www.whitehouse.gov/the-press-office/2012/05/10/executive-order-identifying-and-reducing-regulatory-burdens (accessed July 23, 2015).

134. The White House, 2012 State of the Union Address, https://www.whitehouse.gov/the-press-office/2012/01/24/remarks-president-state-union-address (accessed July 23, 2015).

135. John Broder, "Powerful Shaper of U.S. Rules Quits, with Critics in Wake," *New York Times*, August 3, 2012.

136. Susan E. Dudley, "President-Elect Trump's Two-for-One Plan to Reduce Regulatory Accumulation," *Forbes*, http://www.forbes.com/sites/susandudley/2016/11/23/president-elect-trumps-two-for-one-plan-to-reduce-regulatory-accumulation/#161675367b81 (accessed January 12, 2017).

137. Ibid.

138. Steven Mufson, "Trump Wants to Scrap Two Regulations for Each New One Adopted," *Washington Post*, January 30, 2017, https://www.washingtonpost.com/news/energy-environment/wp/2017/01/30/trump-wants-to-cut-two-regulations-on-businesses-for-every-new-one-imposed/?utm_term=.bad65c8706b7 (accessed March 30, 2017).

139. Ibid.

140. Griffin Davis, "Making Regulatory Reform a Reality," http://www.regblog.org/2017/03/30/davis-making-regulatory-reform-a-reality/ (accessed March 30, 2017).

141. The White House, Office of Information and Regulatory Affairs, "Memorandum: Interim Guidance Implementing Section 2 of the Executive Order of January 30, 2017, Titled 'Reducing Regulation and Controlling Regulatory Costs,'" https://www.whitehouse.gov/the-press-office/2017/02/02/interim-guidance-implementing-section-2-executive-order-january-30-2017 (accessed March 30, 2017).

142. Thomas O. McGarity, *Reinventing Rationality: The Role of Regulatory Analysis in the Federal Bureaucracy* (New York: Cambridge University Press, 1991); Stuart Shapiro, "Politics and Regulatory Policy Analysis," *Regulation* 29 (Summer 2006): 40–45.

143. Office of Management and Budget, *2006 Report to Congress on the Costs and Benefits of Federal Regulations and Unfunded Mandates on State, Local, and Tribal Entities*, www.whitehouse.gov/omb/inforeg/2006_cb/2006_cb_final_report.pdf (accessed January 29, 2007).

144. Curtis W. Copeland, "Length of Rule Reviews by the Office of Information and Regulatory Affairs," https://blackboard.gwu.edu/bbcswebdav/pid-5657735-dt-content-rid-6395103_2/courses/93447_201401/Draft%20OIRA%20Report%20120213.pdf (accessed July 23, 2015).

145. Ibid.

146. Alex Bolton, Rachel Augustine Potter, and Sharece Thrower, "The Limits of Political Control: How Organizational Capacity Influences Regulatory Review" (working paper, Princeton University, Department of Politics, August 20, 2014).

147. Susan E. Dudley, "Reversing Midnight Regulations," *Regulation* 24 (Spring 2001): 9.

148. Ibid.

149. Ibid.

150. Veronique de Rugy, "Bush's Midnight Regulations," *Reason*, January 14, 2009, http://reason.com/archives/2009/01/14/bushs-midnight-regulations (accessed September 21, 2016).

151. Cindy Skrzycki, "Bush Wants Sun to Set on Midnight Regulations," *Washington Post*, June 2, 2008, http://www.washingtonpost.com/wp-dyn/content/article/2008/06/02/AR2008060202893.html (accessed September 21, 2016).

152. Ibid.

153. Veronique de Rugy, "Bush's Midnight Regulations," *Reason*, January 14, 2009, http://reason.com/archives/2009/01/14/bushs-midnight-regulations (accessed September 21, 2016).

154. "White House Stops Pending Bush Regulations for Review," Reuters, January 20, 2009.

155. Susan E. Dudley, "Observations on OIRA's Thirtieth Anniversary," *Administrative Law Review* 63 (special edition).

156. Bob King and Nick Juliano, "Obama's Agencies Push Flurry of 'Midnight Actions,'" *Politico*, November 27, 2016, http://www.politico.com/story/2016/11/obama-regulations-231820 (accessed January 12, 2017).

157. Judith A. Hermanson, "Regulatory Reform by Statute: The Implications of the Consumer Product Safety Commission's 'Offeror System,'" *Public Administration Review* 38 (March/April 1978): 151–155; Mathew D. McCubbins, Roger G. Noll, and Barry R. Weingast, "Administrative Procedures as Instruments of Political Control," *Journal of Law, Economics, and Organization* 3 (Fall 1987): 243–277.

158. William V. Roth Jr. and William H. Nixon, *The Power to Destroy* (New York: Atlantic Monthly Press, 1999).

159. Barbara Barrett, "Rep. McHenry Blasted over Treatment of Consumer Advocate Warren," *Miami Herald*, May 25, 2011.

160. "McHenry Wrong to Verbally Abuse Warren," editorial, *Charlotte Observer*, May 28, 2011.

161. Fiorina, "Congressional Control of the Bureaucracy."

162. Terry M. Moe, "The Politics of Bureaucratic Structure," in *Can the Government Govern?* ed. John E. Chubb and Paul E. Peterson (Washington, D.C.: Brookings Institution Press, 1989).

163. Chad Reese and Todd Zywicki, "The Consumer Financial Protection Bureau: Designed to Fail?" Mercatus Center, George Mason University, http://mercatus.org/sites/default/files/CFPB-Summary_0.pdf (accessed July 24, 2015).

164. United States House of Representatives, Committee on Financial Services, "CFPB Lacks Oversight and Accountability," http://financialservices.house.gov/news/documentsingle.aspx?DocumentID=339512 (accessed July 24, 2015).

165. Eric Garcia, "Elizabeth Warren Strikes Back against New GOP Efforts to Weaken Dodd-Frank," *National Journal*, http://www.nationaljournal.com/congress/elizabeth-warren-strikes-back-against-new-gop-efforts-to-weaken-dodd-frank-20150318 (accessed July 24, 2015).

166. Terry M. Moe, "The Politics of Structural Choice: Toward a Theory of Public Bureaucracy," in *Organization Theory: From Chester Barnard to the Present and Beyond*, ed. Oliver E. Williamson (New York: Oxford University Press, 1990).

167. Ibid., 125.

168. Ibid., 326.

169. David B. Spence, "Managing Delegation Ex Ante: Using Law to Steer Administrative Agencies," *Journal of Legal Studies* 28 (June 1999): 413–459.

170. Cornelius M. Kerwin, *Rulemaking: How Government Agencies Write Law and Make Policy*, 2nd ed. (Washington, D.C.: CQ Press, 1999).

171. Mark H. Tessler, Federal Railroad Administration, interview by author, March 11, 2002.

172. Steven J. Balla, "Between Commenting and Negotiation: The Contours of Public Participation in Agency Rulemaking," *I/S: A Journal of Law and Policy* 1 (Winter 2005): 59–94.

173. Mathew D. McCubbins, Roger G. Noll, and Barry R. Weingast, "Structure and Process, Politics and Policy: Administrative Arrangements and the Political Control of Agencies," *Virginia Law Review* 75 (March 1989): 431–482.

174. Steven J. Balla and John R. Wright, "Interest Groups, Advisory Committees, and Congressional Control of the Bureaucracy," *American Journal of Political Science* 45 (October 2001): 799–812.

175. McCubbins, Noll, and Weingast, "Administrative Procedures."

176. David B. Spence, "Managing Delegation Ex Ante: Using Law to Steer Administrative Agencies," *Journal of Legal Studies* 28 (June 1999): 413–459.

177. McCubbins, Noll, and Weingast, "Administrative Procedures."

178. David B. Spence, "Agency Policy Making and Political Control: Modeling Away the Delegation Problem," *Journal of Public Administration Research and Theory* 7 (April 1997): 199–219.

179. Balla, "Between Commenting and Negotiation."

180. Timothy Cama, "EPA Head Slams GOP Budget Cuts," *The Hill*, July 7, 2015, http://thehill.com/policy/energy-environment/247064-epa-head-slams-gop-budget-cuts (accessed March 27, 2017).

181. Bob Woodward, *The Price of Politics* (New York: Simon and Schuster, 2012).

182. Stephanie McNeal, "Despite Doomsday Predictions, Report Finds Only 1 Layoff from Sequester Cuts," Fox News, May 8, 2014, http://www.foxnews.com/politics/2014/05/07/despite-doomsday-predictions-sequester-cuts-only-led-to-1-layoff-in-2013/ (accessed July 24, 2015).

183. U.S. Government Accountability Office, "2013 Sequestration: Selected Federal Agencies Reduced Some Services and Investments, While Taking Short-Term Actions to Mitigate Effects," http://www.gao.gov/assets/670/663620.pdf (accessed July 24, 2015).

184. Jacqueline Klimas, "Sequestration Will Put American Lives in Danger, Military Chiefs Warn," *Washington Times*, March 17, 2015, http://www.washingtontimes.com/news/2015/mar/17/sequestration-puts-lives-danger-military-chiefs/?page=all (accessed July 24, 2015).

185. Robert Pear, "Budget Stalemate Leaves Chaos at Many Agencies," *New York Times*, March 14, 2011.

186. Ibid.

187. Morris S. Ogul and Bert A. Rockman, "Overseeing Oversight: New Departures and Old Problems," *Legislative Studies Quarterly* 15 (February 1990): 5–24.

188. John F. Bibby, "Oversight and the Need for Congressional Reform," in *Republican Papers*, ed. Melvin R. Laird (Garden City, N.Y.: Anchor Books, 1968).

189. Joel D. Aberbach, *Keeping a Watchful Eye: The Politics of Legislative Oversight* (Washington, D.C.: Brookings Institution Press, 1990).

190. Ibid.

191. Richard F. Fenno Jr., *Learning to Govern: An Institutional View of the 104th Congress* (Washington, D.C.: Brookings Institution Press, 1997).

192. Norman Ornstein and Thomas Mann, "When Congress Checks Out," *Foreign Affairs* (November/December 2006).

193. Carol Leonnig and Amy Goldstein, "Libby Guilty on 4 of 5 Counts," *Washington Post*, March 7, 2007.

194. Ruth Marcus, "Which Darrell Issa Would Run House Oversight Panel?" *Washington Post*, October 27, 2010.

195. Cristina Marcos, "Chaffetz Succeeds Issa on Oversight," *The Hill*, November 18, 2014, http://thehill.com/homenews/house/224605-chaffetz-succeeds-issa-as-oversight-chief (accessed July 24, 2015).

196. Ibid.

197. Ben Pershing, "Six Months into Chairmanship, Issa Isn't What Either Side Expected," *Washington Post*, July 11, 2011.

198. Mathew D. McCubbins and Thomas Schwartz, "Congressional Oversight Overlooked: Police Patrols versus Fire Alarms," *American Journal of Political Science* 28 (February 1984): 165–179.

199. Steven J. Balla and Christopher J. Deering, "Police Patrols and Fire Alarms: An Empirical Examination of the Legislative Preference for Oversight," *Congress & the Presidency* 40 (February 2013): 27–40.

200. Rachel Augustine Potter, "Disabling the Alarm? The Politics of Participation in Rulemaking" (working paper, University of Virginia, Department of Politics, 2016), p. 2.

201. Terry M. Moe, "An Assessment of the Positive Theory of 'Congressional Dominance,'" *Legislative Studies Quarterly* 12 (November 1987): 475–520.

202. Ibid.

203. Ed Yong, "How Trump Could Wage a War in Scientific Expertise," *The Atlantic*, December 2, 2016, http://www.theatlantic.com/science/archive/2016/12/how-trump-could-wage-a-war-on-scientific-expertise/509378/ (accessed January 12, 2017).

204. Ibid.

205. Daren Bakst and James L. Gattuso, "Stars Align for the Congressional Review Act," The Heritage Foundation, December 16, 2016, http://www.heritage.org/research/reports/2016/12/stars-align-for-the-congressional-review-act (accessed January 12, 2017).

206. George Washington Regulatory Studies Center, "Congressional Review Act Tracker," https://regulatorystudies.columbian.gwu.edu/sites/regulatorystudies.columbian.gwu.edu/files/downloads/CRA%20Tracker%2003-30-2017-(1).pdf (accessed March 31, 2017).

207. Ibid.

208. James F. Spriggs II, "The Supreme Court and Federal Administrative Agencies: A Resource-Based Theory and Analysis of Judicial Impact," *American Journal of Political Science* 40 (November 1996): 1122–1151.

209. Christopher Banks, *Judicial Politics in the D.C. Circuit Court* (Baltimore: Johns Hopkins University Press, 1999).

210. Ibid., 42.

211. Ibid., 45, 82.

212. *Greater Boston Television Corp. v. Federal Communications Commission,* 444 F. 2d 841 (D.C. Cir. 1970).

213. *International Harvester Co. v. Ruckelshaus,* 478 F. 2d 615 (D.C. Cir. 1973).

214. Banks, *Judicial Politics,* 44.

215. *Vermont Yankee Nuclear Power Corp. v. Natural Resources Defense Council, Inc.,* 435 U.S. 519 (1978).

216. See, for example, *Motor Vehicle Manufacturers Association of the U.S. v. State Farm Mutual Automobile Insurance Co.* et al., 463 U.S. 29 (1983).

217. Charles Lane, "Clean-Air Authority of EPA Is Upheld," *Washington Post,* February 28, 2001; *EPA v. American Trucking Associations, Inc.* et al., 531 U.S. 457 (2001).

218. *Chevron U.S.A., Inc. v. Natural Resources Defense Council, Inc.,* 467 U.S. 837 (1984).

219. Jonathan H. Adler, "Should *Chevron* Be Reconsidered? A Federal Judge Thinks So," *Washington Post,* August 24, 2016, https://www.washingtonpost.com/news/volokh-conspiracy/wp/2016/08/24/should-chevron-be-reconsidered-a-federal-judge-thinks-so/?utm_term=.24c64c9ece09 (accessed March 31, 2017).

220. Reginald Sheehan, "Administrative Agencies and the Court: A Reexamination of the Impact of Agency Type on Decisional Outcomes," *Western Political Quarterly* 43 (December 1990): 875–885.

221. William Eskridge and Lauren Baer, "The Continuum of Deference: Supreme Court Treatment of Agency Statutory Interpretations from *Chevron* to *Hamdan*," *Georgetown Law Journal* (April 2008): 1083–1226.

222. *Gonzales v. Oregon,* 546 U.S. 243 (2006); *Hamdan v. Rumsfeld,* 548 U.S. 557 (2006).

223. John R. Wright, *Interest Groups and Congress: Lobbying, Contributions, and Influence* (Boston: Allyn and Bacon, 1996).

224. Mancur Olson, *The Logic of Collective Action: Public Goods and the Theory of Groups* (Cambridge, Mass.: Harvard University Press, 1965).

225. James T. Hamilton and Christopher H. Schroeder, "Strategic Regulators and the Choice of Rulemaking Procedures: The Selection of Formal vs. Informal Rules in Regulating Hazardous Waste," *Law and Contemporary Problems* 57 (Spring 1994): 111–160.

226. John Brehm and Scott Gates, *Working, Shirking, and Sabotage: Bureaucratic Response to a Democratic Public* (Ann Arbor: University of Michigan Press, 1997).

4 | The Bureaucracy's Clients

On June 17, 2015, Secretary of the Treasury Jacob Lew announced plans for a scheduled redesign of the $10 bill, a process that ordinarily attracts little attention from citizens and organizations. This redesign, however, was to be historic, in that the new $10 note would be the "first bill in more than a century to feature the portrait of a woman."[1] The timing of the redesign was fitting, as the new $10 bill would enter into circulation in 2020, the hundredth anniversary of the Nineteenth Amendment granting women the right to vote.

Secretary Lew's well-intentioned plan sparked an unexpected national debate that lasted nearly a year. By the time it was over, the debate had inspired the participation of ordinary citizens, women's rights organizations, and, most surprisingly, the cast and fans of a hit Broadway musical.

Several months prior to Secretary Lew's announcement, an organization called Women on 20s launched an **online campaign** to remove Andrew Jackson from the $20 bill and replace his image with the portrait of a woman.[2] At about the same time, Sen. Jeanne Shaheen, D-N.H., introduced a bill, the Women on the Twenty Act, directing the secretary of the Treasury to convene a citizen panel to recommend a woman to feature on the $20 bill.[3] Such efforts were met with disappointment when Secretary Lew selected the $10 bill as the denomination to be redesigned with a woman on the front. This disappointment stemmed in part from the fact that the $20 bill, as the primary currency of ATM machines, is far more widely circulated than the $10 bill, and thus would provide greater prominence for the featured woman. In addition, Andrew Jackson's involvement in the slave trade and forceful relocation of Native Americans made the nation's seventh president a particularly ripe target for replacement, more so than the "exemplary" Alexander Hamilton, whose image has long been enshrined on the $10 bill.[4]

Opposition to Secretary Lew's proposed removal of Alexander Hamilton was also fueled by the roaring success of the Broadway musical *Hamilton*. Winner of eleven Tony awards, including Best Musical, *Hamilton* blends hip-hop and history in telling the story of the life of Alexander Hamilton, from his youth as an orphan in the Caribbean to his death during a duel with Aaron Burr.[5] After taking in a performance, Secretary Lew met backstage with Lin-Manuel Miranda, the creator and star of *Hamilton*, who urged the secretary not to remove the musical's namesake from the front of the $10 bill.[6]

The controversy surrounding the redesign of the $10 bill placed the Department of the Treasury in a difficult, yet not uncommon, position. Currency redesign is primarily aimed at thwarting counterfeiting, and the department's Advanced Counterfeit Deterrence program had recommended updating the $10 bill in short order to ameliorate its particularly prevalent security threats.[7] As Secretary Lew noted, however, currency redesign fulfills another, more symbolic purpose: "America's currency is a way for our nation to make a statement about who we are and what we stand for."[8] These multiple objectives mean that the agency must find a way to circulate currency that is both difficult to counterfeit and reflective of American democracy.

For months after Secretary Lew's announcement, the Department of the Treasury was inundated with feedback at **roundtables** and **town halls,** as well as through more than a million comments submitted via mail, e-mail, and social media posts.[9] In response to all of this feedback, Secretary Lew did something that, according to an observer, is "fairly unusual, at least by Washington standards: He changed his mind."[10] In a bow to Hamiltonians, the redesigned $10 bill will retain Alexander Hamilton's image on the front, with heroes of women's suffrage placed on the reverse side.

Secretary Lew also ordered that the redesign timetable for the $20 and $5 bills, the next two notes up in the counterfeit protection program's sequence, be accelerated to the extent possible from their original 2030 circulation plan. The new $20 bill will feature abolitionist Harriet Tubman front and center, with Andrew Jackson's image moved to the back. The updated $5 note will continue to feature Abraham Lincoln, with historic events that have occurred at the Lincoln Memorial—such as Martin Luther King's "I Have a Dream" speech—commemorated on the back of the bill.[11]

The public's participation in the currency redesign process illustrates just how important, and difficult, it is for agencies to cultivate their constituencies. Citizens and organizations regularly wield enormous influence over policymaking in the bureaucracy. This power, however, does not necessarily direct agencies toward effective and noncontroversial decisions. Indeed, Secretary Lew's decision to remake the images on not just the $10 bill, but the $20 and $5 notes as well, although widely popular, did not meet with universal acclaim. In an open letter to Secretary Lew, several dozen prominent women—including Katie Couric, Geena Davis, Ellen DeGeneres, Gabrielle Giffords, Annie Leibovitz, Cokie Roberts, Gloria Steinem, and Abby Wambach—bemoaned the fact that by not removing Alexander Hamilton from the $10 bill, it might not be until 2030 that a woman will appear on the front of United States currency.[12]

This chapter focuses on the bureaucracy's **clients,** those interests in society that agencies are charged to regulate and protect. It is organized around three *core questions:*

- *WHAT TYPES OF CLIENTS ARE MOST ACTIVE IN BUREAUCRATIC POLICYMAKING?* Although counterfeit experts, women's rights advocates, and theater aficionados all made their voices heard during the currency redesign debate, it is often the case that important clients remain silent on matters being weighed by agencies.

- *THROUGH WHAT VENUES DO CLIENTS PARTICIPATE IN AGENCY POLICYMAKING?* Organizations and citizens access the bureaucracy in a multitude of ways. The Department of the Treasury offered interested parties opportunities to weigh in through written comments as well as attendance at roundtables and town halls. Some individuals and organizations, such as Katie Couric and Women on 20s, exerted pressure through alternative venues—open letters and online campaigns—not established and carried out by the relevant agency.

- *HOW MUCH INFLUENCE DO CLIENTS EXERT OVER AGENCY DECISIONS?* In the end, Secretary Lew was swayed not only by the argument to preserve Alexander Hamilton's place of honor on the $10 bill, but also by the notion that America's currency should celebrate a wide array of "champion(s) for our inclusive democracy."[13] Agencies, however, are not always responsive to clients and are sometimes accused of being out of control.

It may sound as if the politics of currency redesign are not indicative of agency–client relations in general. In fact, the theoretical perspective adopted in this chapter—**interest group mobilization**—is based on the notion that client activism and influence vary systematically across time and policy areas. Characteristics of the issues at hand have important implications, in ways described in the next section, for both the behavior of clients and agency accountability and performance.

The Benefits, Costs, and Politics of Public Policy

Public policies affect citizens, organized interests, and society itself in a plethora of ways. For example, the Federal Highway Administration allocates funds for road construction that benefit virtually all Americans, the Social Security Administration oversees the transfer of income from workers to retirees, and the Environmental Protection Agency (EPA) regulates the operation of firms that discharge pollutants into the air, ground, and water. One common feature of these policies, and all others, is that they deliver **benefits** and impose **costs**. The way in which these benefits and costs are distributed across agency clients varies, however.[14]

Benefits and costs can be concentrated or diffuse in their effects. **Concentrated effects** occur when benefits or costs accrue to specific segments of society, such as individuals with certain characteristics (for example, retirees) or firms doing business in particular industries. Effects are **diffuse** when broad swaths of the population feel the benefits or costs (for example, highway drivers).

Importantly, the benefits and costs of policies affect the mobilization of societal interests and ultimately the politics of the bureaucracy. Figure 4.1 summarizes these effects. When benefits are concentrated and costs diffuse, **client politics** characterize policies. Specific constituencies mobilized by the prospect of reaping significant rewards dominate such issues. Society in general subsidizes the rewards. With costs so widely spread, little incentive exists for broad public involvement in the policymaking process.

Figure 4.1 The Benefits, Costs, and Politics of Public Policies

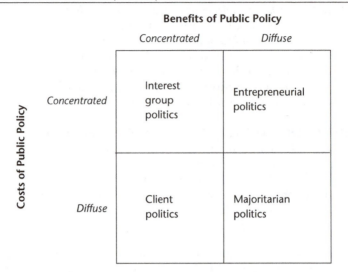

Benefits of Public Policy

	Concentrated	Diffuse
Concentrated	Interest group politics	Entrepreneurial politics
Diffuse	Client politics	Majoritarian politics

(left axis label: **Costs of Public Policy**)

Source: Adapted from James Q. Wilson, *Bureaucracy: What Government Agencies Do and Why They Do It* (New York: Basic Books, 1989). Copyright © 1989 by Basic Books, Inc. Reprinted by permission of Basic Books, a member of Perseus Books, LLC.

Nuclear power policy in the middle of the twentieth century offers a classic example of client politics.[15] At that time public utility companies and other economic interests pressed the Atomic Energy Commission to promote the production of nuclear power by readily approving the construction and operation of plants throughout the country. These efforts proved successful in part because they faced little opposition. The economic costs of building up the nuclear power industry were distributed widely across society, and the environmental consequences were not yet publicly apparent (the Three Mile Island accident and Chernobyl disaster lay well in the future).

When both the benefits and the costs of policies are concentrated, however, the mobilization of societal interests is not so one-sided. **Interest group politics** characterize such policies. Once again the general public is not actively engaged in, or perhaps even aware of, the contest over the direction of policy. Rather, this contest is fought among specific constituencies whose interests are at odds with one another. Early in the twentieth century, the trucking industry emerged as a serious competitor to railroads as a way of moving goods and services around the country. In the decades that followed, each set of interests continually lobbied the Interstate Commerce Commission for regulations that would profit its mode of transportation and cripple the other. Over time this battle became a mismatch as the agency went from being accommodating to railroads to being controlled by motor carrier organizations such as the American Trucking Association.[16]

Interest groups do not dominate the political process when the benefits of policies are diffuse. The combination of diffuse benefits and concentrated costs instead produces **entrepreneurial politics. Policy entrepreneurs** are individuals, from inside and outside government, who take on organized interests in the name of the general public. In 1965, public interest advocate Ralph Nader published *Unsafe at Any Speed*, a book about the dangers of cars as they were then designed. This book, and Nader's efforts in general, galvanized the consumer movement and ultimately provided the impetus for the adoption of many automotive safety features, such as air bags and antilock brakes, that Americans now take for granted.[17]

Finally, when both the benefits and the costs of policies are diffuse, **majoritarian politics** result. With little stake in the policymaking process, specific interests and organizations do not mobilize in support of, or opposition to, government actions. Rather, the political debate centers on broad, often ideological, considerations that cut across society, such as the proper role of government in economic and social matters. Some of the most significant policies in U.S. history fall into this category, including the Sherman Antitrust Act of 1890, a seminal moment in the trust-busting movement. At that stage of the industrial revolution, public sentiment was turning against large corporations and the power they increasingly wielded over the lives of each and every American. The Sherman Act, however, did not target specific firms and industries but rather aimed to check monopolistic practices in general. As a result, opposition to the act was diffuse and grounded in the constitutional argument that the federal government has no authority to break up industrial trusts or, more broadly, to foster economic competition.[18]

To sum up, the theoretical perspective adopted in this chapter suggests that organized interests can dominate policymaking in the bureaucracy, but only under certain conditions. A key question then becomes, How often do these conditions materialize? Interestingly, the answer to this question has changed quite a bit over the past five decades.

Inside Bureaucracy with	**Donna Shalala** *Secretary of Health and Human Services (1993–2001)*

"There are iron triangles in government today. You see it in education, where you have powerful education interests. You see it less in HHS. Interest groups get access because they contributed to the campaign. We had to be careful all the time. If we saw an interest group that contributed to the presidential campaign, we scheduled a meeting with the opponent. And we never let anyone into a room with me without a civil service notetaker. We had no private meetings. It sure didn't endear us to the White House, but it kept us clean! We heard the most from hospitals, nursing homes, and home health agencies. They were all helpful. They behaved badly in the process, but it was always important to know what their positions were. It was particularly important to know where powerful interests stood."

The Rise and Fall of Iron Triangles

A favorite pastime of journalists and pundits is bemoaning client politics, decrying the fact that organized interests, especially business and industry, have captured the U.S. government. In the years leading up to the global financial crisis, housing giants Fannie Mae and Freddie Mac convinced government officials to significantly ease capital reserve requirements in the mortgage industry. Similarly, large investment banks successfully lobbied the Securities and Exchange Commission to ease regulatory stipulations and permit the accumulation of historically large amounts of debt.[19] Such actions are portrayed in the documentary *Inside Job* as demonstrating the "systemic corruption of the United States by the financial services industry and the consequences of that systemic corruption."[20]

To be sure, interest groups have historically played a fundamental, and at times dominating, role in the political process. Researchers have developed a systematic account, called **capture theory,** to explain such domination. According to capture theory, elected officials and bureaucrats, seeking to maximize support for their decisions, are often captured by powerful firms and industries whose behavior they are commissioned to police and constrain. The end result is that policymaking processes and outcomes serve special interests at the expense of the general public.[21]

Consistent with capture theory, in the middle of the twentieth century it was widely observed that public policy was frequently the handiwork of **iron triangles.**[22] Figure 4.2 summarizes the essence of this observation. Iron triangles are issue-specific coalitions that consist of (1) the congressional committee of jurisdiction, (2) the relevant executive branch agency, and (3) those interests most directly affected by government actions in the area. These three parties jointly control policymaking by determining what issues make it onto

Figure 4.2 The "Iron Triangle" of Politics

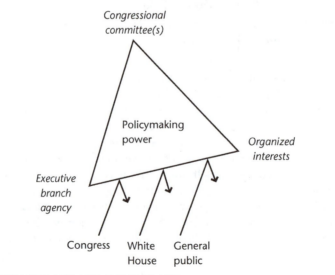

the political agenda and how these issues will be resolved. Put differently, other interested parties, such as Congress as a whole, the White House, and the general public, are afforded very little influence over the scope and content of public policy. A prime example is agriculture policy. Legislators from farming areas secure seats on Congress's agriculture committees and work closely with the Department of Agriculture (USDA) and organized representatives of farming interests, such as the National Farmers Union, to produce pro-farmer policies. Largely shut out of this process are the tens of millions of Americans who consume agricultural products, as well as their elected representatives.

The grip of iron triangles over policymaking began to loosen in the 1960s for two principal reasons. One is that the number and nature of interest groups active in the political process underwent a dramatic transformation. As a result, it has become more difficult over time for firms and industries to capture government officials and organizations.

In 1960, there were 523 advocacy organizations with offices in Washington, D.C. By 1980, this number had grown more than tenfold, to 5,769.[23] A significant part of this growth came in the form of **public interest groups,** organizations promoting broad societal causes rather than the material gain of their members. Examples include environmental groups such as the World Wildlife Fund, founded in 1961, and consumer groups such as Public Citizen, which got its start a decade later. Currently, there are well in excess of 10,000 registered lobbyists plying their trade in the nation's capital.[24] These lobbyists represent a wide range of interests, including Caesars Entertainment, the Teamsters Union, the Tax Reform Coalition, and the Gila River Indian Community, a Native American reservation located to the south of Phoenix.[25]

Inside Bureaucracy with	Dan Glickman *Secretary of Agriculture (1995–2001)*

"Traditionally, agriculture and commodity policy is an area where Congress probably exerted as much, or more, influence than [in any other] policy area involving the federal government. Direct policy interest. What programs actually looked like. What the wheat loan program looked like, how the soybean program was created. When it came to agriculture, interest groups would work with Congress to design the programs legislatively or put a lot of pressure on the Department of Agriculture to set up the programs to meet certain economic needs. True of the cotton and sugar programs, for example. In traditional agriculture and commodity policy, interest groups and commodity groups, coupled with the Congress, had such power over the decision-making process that I suppose you came as close to the iron triangle as you might have seen. Maybe in the Defense Department you see something like this. But on issues like forestry policy or food stamps or food safety, no, I didn't feel there was an iron triangle."

The diversification of interest groups in and of itself was not enough to overcome the entrenched presence of iron triangles. One reason iron triangles are often successful in protecting their political turf is that they take great care to envelop themselves in positive **policy images.**[26] For decades the nuclear power industry promoted itself as a clean, cheap source of energy.

As time went by, however, this positive policy image gave way to a far more negative one. Environmental groups and other opponents of nuclear power emphasized the dangers posed by mishaps at reactors and the difficulties associated with the storage of waste. Figure 4.3 illustrates that these tactics, no doubt strengthened by catastrophic and near-catastrophic events in the nuclear industry, proved largely successful. Media coverage of nuclear power went from overwhelmingly positive through the 1950s to decidedly negative in later decades. Just as telling is the fact that no new nuclear power plants have become operational since the Three Mile Island accident. In the twenty-first century, both

Figure 4.3 Positive and Negative Images in Media Coverage of Nuclear Power

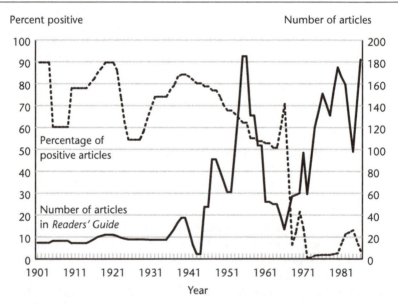

Source: Comparative Agendas Project (formerly Policy Agendas Project), http://www.comparativeagendas.net/. The data used here were originally collected by Frank R. Baumgartner and Bryan D. Jones, with the support of National Science Foundation grant numbers SBR 9320922 and 0111611, and are distributed through the Department of Government at the University of Texas at Austin. Neither NSF nor the original collectors of the data bear any responsibility for the analysis reported here.

Note: The lines provide information about (1) the number of articles in the *Readers' Guide to Periodical Literature* on nuclear power, and (2) the percentage of these articles that conveyed positive policy images.

Congress and Presidents George W. Bush and Barack Obama offered the nuclear power industry assistance in the form of loan guarantees designed to jump-start refurbishment and construction projects and, more broadly, reduce the nation's reliance on fossil fuels as a source of energy.[27] Although five reactors are currently being built, four others have closed down or are on the verge of shuttering operations.[28] In addition to facing stiff competition from the natural gas industry, nuclear power continues to be bedeviled by negative health, safety, and environmental images. Such images were dramatically reinforced by the tsunami-induced disaster at the power plant in Fukushima, Japan, the world's most significant nuclear accident in decades. Today most Americans favor increased reliance on wind, solar power, and renewable energy sources and reduced reliance on oil and coal, with nuclear power and natural gas falling somewhere in between.[29]

The shift in the locus of power in the area of nuclear energy is not unusual in that iron triangles of all sorts have lost their political monopolies. Today policymaking is often the domain of what are called **sloppy hexagons**[30] or, less colorfully, **issue networks.**[31] A constant flow of participants in and out of the decision-making arena, rather than limited access, characterizes issue networks. Some of these participants are traditional power brokers, such as business and industry, while others include public interest advocates, economic and technical experts, and representatives of state and local governments. Because of this diversity, high levels of conflict among participants, rather than strict agreement, typify these networks. Such conflicts encompass not only the question of how best to resolve policy problems but also more fundamental questions such as: What is the nature of the problem? Is there a problem at all?

A great example of an iron triangle giving way to an issue network comes from the area of embryonic and fetal research, one of the most controversial areas of public policy in the early twenty-first century.[32] When it first came onto the national agenda in the 1970s, this issue was dominated by a small set of actors, most notably the scientific community. Researchers in universities and medical schools worked closely with the National Institutes of Health to establish a positive policy image grounded in the benefits of scientific autonomy and progress. Ultimately, the aim was to ensure a constant flow of government funding for research that many scientists believe holds the key to unlocking the mysteries of many of the world's most painful and deadliest diseases. Today this image, and the iron triangle it helped sustain, does not enjoy the monopoly it once did. Embryonic and fetal research raises fundamental moral concerns, such as the value of different forms of human life and the role of medical science in creating, enhancing, and destroying such life. These concerns continue to be debated vigorously by ethicists, religious authorities, members of Congress, and activists on both sides of the abortion issue. Executive branch officials all the way up to Presidents Bush and Obama have been involved in making decisions that generally serve to heighten, rather than diminish, the level of disagreement embodied in this issue network.[33]

The rise and fall of iron triangles illustrates three central points with respect to the benefit-cost approach to understanding societal mobilization and bureaucratic politics. The first is that the benefits and costs of policies vary not only across issues but over time as well. A closely related lesson is that perceived, as well as actual, benefits and costs play a critical role in determining the nature of the politics surrounding a policy area. Although the benefits and costs associated with nuclear power and embryonic and fetal research have undoubtedly evolved over the years, the demise of these long-standing iron triangles was in no small part a product of seismic shifts in the images through which potentially contentious issues were appraised and acted upon. Finally, such developments suggest there are now fewer instances of client politics, and perhaps even interest group politics, than in years past. Although powerful interests and organizations still can, and do, exert extraordinary influence over the political process, the exercise of this power is not nearly as unchallenged as it once was.

The Venues of Client Participation

Thus far, this chapter has focused on the types of clients who are generally most active in bureaucratic policymaking, as well as on how patterns of client activism have changed over the past half-century. Little has yet been said about the specific venues through which clients make their views known to agency officials. These venues run the gamut from commenting on proposed agency policies to prevailing upon politicians to intervene in bureaucratic proceedings. As will become apparent, venues are distinct in terms of the resources clients must bring to bear if they wish to participate regularly and effectively through particular channels.

The Notice and Comment Process

One of the central ways in which agencies make policy is through **rulemaking,** the bureaucratic equivalent of legislative lawmaking.[34] When engaged in rulemaking, agencies craft decisions that allocate governmental resources, redistribute income and wealth across society, and regulate the behavior of economic actors. As an example, on September 14, 2016, the Food and Drug Administration updated its animal drug regulations and the Department of Housing and Urban Development (HUD) promulgated standards to be used in investigating and adjudicating allegations of discriminatory housing practices. These actions were two of twenty-one rules issued on that day by federal agencies. Over the course of a typical year, agencies promulgate thousands of regulations, a clear-cut metric of just how common rulemaking is within the executive branch.[35]

Not only is rulemaking common, it is also one of the primary means through which the federal government makes its most important policy decisions. Two of the most important, and controversial, legislative enactments of recent times—the Patient Protection and Affordable Care Act and Dodd-Frank Wall Street Reform and Consumer Protection Act—required the writing of tens of thousands of pages of rules to become operational. Agencies such as the Department of Health and Human Services and Internal Revenue Service issued 112 regulations in the years following the passage of the Affordable Care Act, a number exceeded by the 137 rules promulgated by nine different agencies in response to the Dodd-Frank Act.[36]

For more than sixty years, rulemaking at the federal level has been governed by the **Administrative Procedure Act** of 1946 (APA).[37] The APA generally requires agencies to provide public notice of their intention to take action by publishing a proposed rule in the *Federal Register.* Military and foreign affairs functions are not covered by this requirement, nor are actions where the agency, for good cause, finds prior notice to be "impracticable, unnecessary, or contrary to the public interest." In practice, about half of all agency regulations are not preceded by a **notice of proposed rulemaking.**[38]

The APA also instructs agencies to offer interested parties the opportunity to comment on proposals. The **notice and comment process,** as this participation venue is known, is one of the most common ways in which clients come into contact with agency decision makers.[39] HUD received sixty-three comments on its proposed rule on discriminatory housing practices. These comments were submitted by government agencies, housing providers, tenants, and civil rights and fair housing advocates.[40]

The number of comments submitted in response to proposed rules is for the most part rather modest. This modesty is a reflection of a broader tendency for interest groups to intervene in lawmaking rather than in the administrative process. Although a substantial level of interest group lobbying of the bureaucracy occurs, this level lags behind lobbying of the legislative branch.[41] Research shows that 85 percent of U.S. advocacy groups active at the federal level arrange interviews with members of Congress or their staffs. By contrast, 28 percent of these organizations arrange meetings with administrative agency officials.[42] Fewer groups—11 percent—submit written comments in response to notices of proposed rulemaking.[43]

Even important administrative decisions often attract limited attention. During the summer of 2016, federal agencies issued seventy-seven rules deemed to be "significant."[44] **Significant rules** are actions projected to have particularly pronounced consequences, such as annual effects on the economy of at least $100 million.[45] Despite their elevated significance, many of these seventy-seven actions generated small numbers of comments. For example, on August 30, 2016, the Animal and Plant Health Inspection Service promulgated a rule pertaining to the packaging and labeling of veterinary biological products. The agency received only six comments during the course of this rulemaking, even though its action affects nearly 2,000 products produced by approximately 100 veterinary biological establishments.[46]

On occasion, agencies are inundated with comments on their proposed rules. In 1995, the Food and Drug Administration stirred up great public controversy by proposing to regulate the advertising, labeling, and sale of tobacco products to juveniles. This proposal precipitated the submission of about 700,000 comments, a volume that is only occasionally approached or exceeded by other rulemakings.[47] One such rulemaking is the Federal Communications Commission's 2014 net neutrality proposal, which generated in excess of three million comments, an agency record.[48]

Oftentimes, rulemakings that result in the submission of large numbers of comments are characterized by concentrated costs and diffuse benefits. Over a period of three years, a trio of rules issued by the Department of Transportation generated far more comments than any of the agency's other notices.[49] These rules imposed costs on three industries—trucking companies, automobile manufacturers, and helicopter tourism operators. As expected under entrepreneurial politics, industry efforts to lighten their regulatory loads were countered by the mobilization of environmentalists and other advocates of broad societal interests. Organizations representing such interests served as policy entrepreneurs, instigating mass comment campaigns that drew in large numbers of participants who do not ordinarily comment on proposed rules.

Who are the clients that participate on a regular basis in notice and comment rulemaking? It has long been established that business and industry interests are at times more likely to submit comments on proposed rules than are representatives of other segments of society.[50] For example, when the EPA proposed new hazardous waste regulations, 45 of the 60 comments it received came from corporations.[51] This kind of business domination, however, does not inevitably manifest itself in the commenting process. When the Department of Housing and Urban Development crafted a rule pertaining to public housing for the elderly and disabled, only one comment, out of 268, was submitted by a corporation.[52] Similarly, when the USDA proposed to establish national standards for labeling organic products, it received thousands of comments, most of which were sent by consumers and small organic farmers.[53]

The interest group mobilization perspective provides a means of understanding variation in participation across different types of proposed rules. When the benefits of prospective regulations are concentrated, the number of comments is likely to be correspondingly small. When, however, the benefits are spread across large numbers of individuals and organizations, comment volume has the potential to rise into the thousands or millions, particularly if policy entrepreneurs mobilize **mass comment campaigns.**

To what extent do client comments have an impact on the actions agencies ultimately take when promulgating policy through rulemaking? It is widely acknowledged that agencies carefully consider the viewpoints expressed in comments.[54] In some instances, such consideration precipitates significant change in the content on regulations. For example, the comments submitted in response to the USDA's proposed standards for labeling organic products were overwhelmingly negative in tone.[55] In announcing a fundamental makeover of the proposal, the secretary of agriculture explicitly acknowledged the weight of the collective criticism: "If organic farmers and consumers reject our standards, we have failed."[56]

Despite the responsiveness of the USDA in this particular instance, it is often the case that proposed rules are altered very little in response to information provided by clients.[57] As one observer has put it, "Changes are made frequently enough during the comment phase of rulemaking, but they tend to be small and painful, and they are often subtractive rather than innovative or additive."[58]

Under what conditions are comments likely to matter the most? Research suggests that consensus among participants is an important determinant of responsiveness to comments, in that agencies are typically more inclined to revise proposed rules when presented with a unified constituent front.[59] As highlighted by the interest group mobilization perspective, consensus varies systematically across types of policies. Client politics, but not interest group politics, are characterized by mobilization on the part of constituencies whose preferences are in close alignment. Similarly, entrepreneurial politics can produce a consensus of large numbers, particularly if participation by broad societal interests overwhelms businesses and industries seeking to avoid the imposition of concentrated costs.

Although the notice and comment process provides a solid foundation for client participation, it has limitations as a means of fostering accountability and performance. In Executive Order 12866, President Bill Clinton instructed agencies to offer comment periods of sixty days under ordinary circumstances, an expectation maintained by subsequent presidents.[60] Given ample time, interested parties can marshal the resources necessary to produce informed, well-articulated comments.[61] In practice, however, comment periods often do not stay open for periods of sixty days. Research shows that one-third of comment periods last for thirty days, while 10 percent are closed within two weeks.[62] Agency officials argue that brief comment periods are useful when there is good reason to forego the notice and comment process altogether, in that interested parties are afforded opportunities to quickly alert decision makers of unexpected objections.[63]

In spite of the relatively short duration of comment periods, rules sometimes take years to come to fruition.[64] Although deliberate decision making offers accountability and due process for opponents and targets of regulations, unnecessary delays postpone the realization of the intended benefits of rules, which often include the prevention of illness and injury and the saving of lives.[65] Performance difficulties such as these are traceable in part to the inherently adversarial nature of notice and comment rulemaking. Under the APA, clients never come into direct contact with one another, but participate by submitting comments to agency officials. This lack of contact prevents clients from developing working relationships, shared understandings, and other connections that are useful in tamping down conflicts. Furthermore, client comments tend to stake out extreme positions and focus on pointing out flaws in agency proposals rather than identifying solutions to difficult rulemaking problems.[66] With these limitations in mind, there has been a movement over the past three decades to augment the notice and comment process with a variety of collaborative approaches to client participation.

Advisory Committees and Other Venues of Collaboration

On September 6, 2016, the Administration for Children and Families (ACF), an organization within the Department of Health and Human Services, promulgated a rule updating performance standards for the Head Start program. Head Start provides education, health, and nutrition services to children from low-income families who have not yet entered kindergarten. In crafting the rule, the ACF solicited public feedback and received approximately 1,000 comments.[67]

The ACF also consulted with the Advisory Committee on Head Start Research and Evaluation, a congressionally mandated panel of experts charged with assisting the agency in bringing evidence to bear in the rulemaking process.[68] The advisory committee consisted of "researchers with expertise in child development, early childhood education and development programs, research and evaluation, and methodology."[69] In assessing evaluations of Head Start, the advisory committee recommended, and the ACF incorporated into its performance standards, reforms such as increasing the dosage of the program received by children and improving instructional quality as ways of building upon established successes in enhancing school readiness among at-risk populations.[70] Studies show that disadvantaged children benefit from longer exposure to high-quality preschool programs.[71]

The Head Start reform process is not unusual, in that **advisory committees** are frequently called upon to assist agencies in the making of public policy. At any given moment, approximately 1,000 advisory committees are operating within the federal executive branch, across a wide range of policy areas.[72] Examples of advisory committees include the Advisory Committee on Family Residential Centers (Immigration and Customs Enforcement), Commercial Space Transportation Advisory Committee (Federal Aviation Administration), and Vaccines and Related Biological Products Advisory Committee (Food and Drug Administration). Some advisory committees are created by Congress or the president, while others are established by agencies themselves.[73] The tasks performed by advisory committees vary substantially, from helping agencies set their policymaking agendas to drafting reports on specific issues that arise during rulemakings and commenting jointly on agency proposals.

Inside Bureaucracy with	Christine Todd Whitman
	EPA Administrator
	(2001–2003)

"I had no qualms about putting someone on the Science Advisory Board who came from the industry. You didn't overload it with those people. But they have a perspective that no one else has. They have access to facts and figures and on-the-ground implementation challenges that again the environmentalists and others who work in labs don't have. They need to be heard."

The **Federal Advisory Committee Act** of 1972 (FACA) governs the operation of advisory committees. Under this statute, client representation on advisory committees must be balanced.[74] In other words, advisory committee members must consist of a representative cross section of clients with a stake in the policy area under committee jurisdiction. The balance requirement aims at preventing a single constituency, such as business interests, from dominating advisory committee processes and outcomes. Emblematic of this balance is the National Drinking Water Advisory Council. NDWAC consists of fifteen members, five from utilities and other water producers, five from state and local governments, and five from environmental, consumer, and other public interest groups.

Not all advisory committees, however, operate in a manner consistent with FACA requirements. For a time, the National Advisory Committee on Meat and Poultry Inspection did not have a single member affiliated with a consumer organization. Membership was dominated by industry interests such as the U.S. Meat Exporters Federation, American Association of Meat Processors, Veribest Cattle Feeders, and George A. Hormel and Company.[75] Other advisory committees have skirted client participation requirements by holding meetings in the State Department, Executive Office Building, and other restricted locations.[76]

Closed meetings, to be sure, can foster candid discussions and protect proprietary and national security information. Such reasonable exceptions from FACA, however, are at times subject to manipulation on the part of executive branch officials. In the aftermath of the December 14, 2012, shooting at Sandy Hook Elementary School in Newtown, Connecticut, the Obama administration labeled participants on a gun control task force as "consultants" rather than "members." This linguistic maneuver enabled the administration to keep participant names and meeting records secret.[77]

At times, there is vigorous debate regarding whether advisory bodies are subject to the dictates of FACA at all. In 2010, Freedom Watch sued the Obama administration on the grounds that meetings held during the formulation of the president's health care reform plan were not disclosed as required under FACA.[78] Three years later, a federal judge dismissed the lawsuit, arguing that attendance varied significantly across meetings and there was no effort to obtain "collective advice or collaborative work."[79] The meetings, in other words, could not reasonably be construed as the work of an advisory committee, as defined under federal law.

On occasion, advisory committees are used to facilitate a particular form of collaboration known as **negotiated rulemaking.** In negotiated rulemaking, an advisory committee is charged with the specific task of developing a notice of proposed rulemaking on behalf of an agency.[80] Why would an agency cede its policymaking authority to a committee composed mainly of individuals from outside of government? Given the adversarial nature of the notice and comment process, agencies at times find it difficult to issue in a timely manner rules that engender widespread client compliance. One solution to such impasses is empowering clients themselves to negotiate mutually acceptable courses of action. According to the theory of negotiated rulemaking, rules that are developed in this way ought to be promulgated quickly and enjoy high levels of client support.[81]

Experts acknowledge that the benefits of negotiated rulemaking are readily attainable only under certain circumstances.[82] For example, bargaining sessions are most likely to produce consensus when the number of clients is limited. To put it differently, an auditorium full of people will naturally experience difficulty engaging in meaningful negotiations. Negotiated rulemaking, therefore, is most likely to be utilized under the limited mobilization conditions of client politics and interest group politics.

For such reasons negotiated rulemaking has historically been used on a relatively limited basis. From 1983 to 1996, federal agencies undertook 67 negotiated rulemakings.[83] Of the 204 major regulations issued by agencies between March 1996 and June 1999, 4 were developed via negotiated rulemaking.[84] During the Bush and Obama administrations, the number of negotiated rulemaking committees in operation at any given moment could ordinarily be counted with the fingers on one hand.[85] Over the course of three years of the Obama administration, from January 2011 through December 2013, agencies conducted a total of 8 negotiated rulemakings.

Does negotiated rulemaking, on those occasions when it is used, have the effect of reducing delay and bringing about other desirable outcomes in bureaucratic policymaking? On the one hand, there have been instances in which negotiated rulemaking has made a positive difference. Participants in several EPA negotiated rulemakings have reported greater levels of satisfaction with the substance of the regulations ultimately adopted than have their counterparts in comparable rulemakings where negotiations were not an integral part of the process.[86] On the other hand, negotiated rulemaking has not generally proven faster and less contentious than notice and comment rulemaking, thus suggesting the limited applicability of advisory committees as consensus-building instruments.[87]

Advisory committees and negotiated rulemakings are not the only venues of collaborative participation. Agencies regularly hold **public meetings** and **public hearings,** during which clients have the opportunity to testify and perhaps rebut one another's arguments in front of executive branch officials. From March to May of 2000, the Federal Railroad Administration (FRA) held a series of ten hearings at locations around the country.[88] These hearings addressed the use of locomotive horns at highway-rail grade crossings. This issue is important from a public safety point of view in that trains collide with highway vehicles about 4,000 times during a typical year. In an effort to reduce property damage and personal injuries, the FRA proposed to require that locomotive horns be sounded as trains approach and enter highway-rail grade crossings.[89] During the hearings on this proposal, the FRA discovered that there is also a significant downside to the sounding of warning whistles, especially in the vicinity of communities normally characterized by peace and quiet. Tearful testimony was provided by residents linking sleep deprivation, and even the loss of livelihood, to horn blowing by trains passing nearby in the dark of night. Railroad conductors, too, recounted tales of personal trauma. One stated simply, "My ears have been harmed from too many train whistles."[90] The FRA responded to this vivid input and provided for exceptions to its whistle-blowing requirements, for example, in areas designated as "quiet zones."[91] In general, public hearings and meetings, and collaborative instruments overall, can under certain circumstances be useful venues for clients seeking to do more than submit written comments on agency proposals.

Political Intervention

Another way in which clients seek to influence bureaucratic policymaking is by securing **political interventions** by prominent politicians. Such interventions, often dubbed "**casework**," have enabled Florida developers and business groups, for instance, to win concessions in environmental policy from federal, state, and local agencies. A key battleground in this area has been the Florida Everglades, an assortment of swamps and forests vital to southern Florida's water supply and home to many endangered species, including the greatly revered Florida panther.

In the early 1990s, when a prominent Florida developer, Ben Hill Griffin III, proposed the construction of a new institution of higher education—Florida Gulf Coast University—on 760 acres of donated land, biologists at the Fish and Wildlife Service expressed strong reservations. Griffin's plan, scientists warned, would trigger "unprecedented" development for miles around the proposed campus, demolishing precious wetlands in the process.[92]

In the face of this warning, a Griffin lobbyist persuaded Sen. Bob Graham, D-Fla., to intervene on the developer's behalf. After a meeting between this lobbyist and Fish and Wildlife Service officials in Atlanta, the agency backed down from the confrontation. Next, Griffin supporters won the allegiance of Florida's other senator, Republican Connie Mack. Mack contacted the Florida commander of the Army Corps of Engineers, urging the agency to approve a permit so that the project could proceed expeditiously. Despite their reservations, Corps officials issued the permit, and the university, an "ecological disaster" according to critics, admitted its first student—Mariana Coto—in 1997.[93]

The story of Florida Gulf Coast University is not unique. Clients of all types make their views known to executive branch officials via legislators and other politicians. For example, firms located in districts represented on House committees with jurisdiction over the Federal Trade Commission are less likely to be sanctioned by the agency than firms lacking such representation.[94] Business and industry groups, it can be assumed, apply pressure on particularly influential members of Congress, who in turn communicate their constituents' preferences to the agency.

It would be a mistake to assume that business organizations are the only clients engaged in what might be called political meddling. Regulated firms face tougher enforcement by the Occupational Safety and Health Administration, as well as its state-level counterparts, in locations represented by congressional delegations sympathetic to labor interests.[95] Unions and other labor organizations facilitate this linkage by urging like-minded legislators to insist the agency be vigilant when enforcing worker safety laws, at least within specific geographic jurisdictions.

In 2015, Congress unanimously supported and President Obama signed the **Land Management Workforce Flexibility Act.** This law mandates that seasonal workers, such as federal firefighters, be permitted to count time served in temporary positions when applying for permanent jobs. The legislation's intent was to offer career advancement opportunities for workers who return to the same jobs, year after year, without immediate prospects for pay raises.[96] The Office of Personnel Management, however, issued regulations limiting time served benefits to the worker's agency of current employment, as opposed to opening up opportunities across the government as is customary for federal employees.[97]

Greatly disappointed by this development, the National Federation of Federal Employees lobbied Congress to intervene on behalf of seasonal workers. In responding to this intervention, Rep. Jason Chaffetz, R-Utah, had this to say: "This is, I think, a misread by OPM. These are people fighting fires. They're hired as seasonal workers, my goodness, and they can't even apply for a job? It really is quite amazing and ridiculous."[98] The House Oversight and Government Reform Committee, chaired by Chaffetz, advanced a bill to explicitly permit seasonal workers to apply for jobs across the federal government.[99] As demonstrated by this and the preceding examples, casework, when instigated by constituencies important to reelection-oriented politicians, can be a powerful instrument for opening bureaucratic decision making up to the influences of public opinion.

Political Protest

Another tactic available to groups opposed to an administrative agency decision or proposal is **political protest.** Marches, rallies, and demonstrations can be a dramatic way to put the spotlight on an issue, to generate favorable publicity, and to pressure public officials to rethink their position. The **Standing Rock Sioux Indian tribe** used this tactic successfully in the fall of 2016 when members objected to a 1,170-mile-long oil pipeline that would move crude oil from North Dakota to Illinois. The project, promoted by the Texas-based Energy Transfer Partners company, would cross federally regulated waters, including the Missouri River and Lake Oahe, a source of the tribe's drinking water, and come close to sacred burial grounds nearby.[100]

After an unsuccessful lawsuit that sought to stop the Dakota Access Pipeline, as it was called, tribal leaders, environmental activists and, somewhat surprisingly, combat veterans staged a sit-in on federal land, erecting makeshift dwellings and relocating mobile homes to the site. At rallies, they sought to convince the Army Corps of Engineers to reroute the project so it would not cross or threaten tribal lands or waters. The Corps had already made some concessions to the tribe, but they were not considered enough. Between August and November, more than 500 protesters were arrested by authorities. As tensions escalated, more than a dozen Native Americans who had previously served in the Obama administration sent a letter to President Obama asking him to block the $3.8 billion project. Although President Obama did not tell the Corps to halt the project, he did state publicly that he thought there was a way to "reroute" it.[101]

Early in December 2016, the Corps announced that it was going to deny an easement required for the project to cross federally regulated waters, to permit additional consultation with affected tribes. However, in January 2017 President Trump signaled his intent to reverse the Obama administration's policy by ordering an expedited review of the pipeline. Two weeks later, the Secretary of the Army Robert Speer announced that the pipeline would be approved. This episode illustrates both the strengths and weaknesses of political protests as a tactic for influencing bureaucratic policymaking. Depending on who controls the presidency, the bureaucracy will be more or less receptive to political protests by Indian tribes and other marginalized groups.[102]

Client Participation and the Internet

In 2013, the Consumer Financial Protection Board (CFPB) initiated a rule-making regarding consumer debt collection practices, an area of great concern to consumers, financial institutions, and debt collection firms. The aim of the CFPB's prospective action was to protect consumers from unclear and unscrupulous behavior on the part of creditors. As CFPB director Richard Cordray put it: "For decades, many consumers have reported various unacceptable practices in the debt collection industry. Today's action will allow us to hear from the public as we consider what rules are needed. We want to ensure that all players in the industry are working with correct information, that consumers are fully informed, and that consumers are treated fairly and with dignity."[103]

In soliciting feedback on its plan, the CFPB not only published a notice of proposed rulemaking in the *Federal Register,* it also encouraged interested parties to become involved via the website **Regulation Room** (http://regulationroom .org/).[104] A project of the Cornell e-Rulemaking Initiative, Regulation Room is an online platform designed to enhance stakeholder understanding of and participation in the rulemaking process. Regulation Room uses website design and social media, as well as human mediation, as instruments for ameliorating two interrelated difficulties in public commenting: (1) stakeholder ignorance of the opportunity to offer input on salient issues and (2) rulemaking documents characterized by excessive length and complexity.[105]

In the context of the consumer debt collection practices rulemaking, Regulation Room hosted a moderated discussion of the CFPB's prospective action. More than 1,200 comments were submitted to the Regulation Room website during the discussion period.[106] These comments addressed issues such as consumers disputing debts, unlawful collection practices, and the use of e-mail, texting, and social media in debt collection. In one exchange, a participant argued that debt collectors should use social media to locate targets but not to communicate with them, an assertion that was the subject of follow-up questioning from Regulation Room moderators.[107]

At the conclusion of the discussion period, the moderators wrote up a draft summary, which was circulated for public feedback. Once the summary was finalized, the document was submitted to the CFPB as a stand-alone comment on the agency's notice of proposed rulemaking.[108] In this way, CFPB decision makers working to complete the action were able to draw upon information generated during a collaborative discussion that occurred over the Internet.

All across government, bureaucracies such as the CFPB are turning to the Internet and other innovations in information technology for help in achieving their missions. Such innovations can be divided into two main categories. The first category is innovations that digitize existing paper-based processes. An example of **digitization,** explored below, occurs when agencies accept public comments on proposed rules via the Internet (in addition to, or in place of, comments sent by mail and fax). The second category is innovations that transform the structures and processes through which agencies engage their clients and make policy decisions.[109] Regulation Room, for example, goes beyond digitization of notice and comment by bringing interested parties into direct (virtual) contact with one another in a collaborative environment. The wide-ranging application of the Internet to agency structures and processes raises a pair of salient questions regarding clients and their participation in bureaucratic policymaking:

- Does the Internet attract new participants or simply provide established actors, such as iron triangles, with additional ways of making their views known?
- Does information technology increase the quality of client participation, by, for example, increasing the accessibility of information and offering opportunities for collaboration?

There are three basic schools of thought when it comes to addressing such questions. A first possibility is that the Internet "changes everything" for the better.[110] For example, if information technology facilitates broad-based client involvement in bureaucratic decisions, then it has the potential to enhance the democratic nature of policymaking in the executive branch. A second possibility is that digital technology is associated with "politics as usual." For most individuals, life online—shopping, hobbies, working, entertainment—closely resembles life in the "real world."[111] That is to say, citizens who are not involved in public affairs offline are unlikely to be activists when it comes to the Internet. A third possibility is that the effects of information technology are conditional.[112] In this account, some innovations transform agency processes and client behavior, while others simply replicate already existing structures and practices.

A prime example of digitization is **agency websites.** It has been common practice for many years for agencies of all types to operate websites as first points of contact for the public.[113] USA.gov provides links to the websites of hundreds of organizations, from the AbilityOne Commission (which serves people with disabilities) to the government of Wyoming.[114] With the proliferation of government websites, client interactions that historically occurred over the telephone, through the mail, and in person now in large part take place over the Internet.

The most visited government website is operated by the Internal Revenue Service.[115] During tax season, the IRS's "Where's My Refund?" tracking tool is especially popular.[116] Other high-traffic websites include the National Weather Service, Social Security Administration, and Department of Health and Human Services. In the information age, activities such as checking the weather forecast, obtaining retirement benefits, and signing up for health insurance have been digitized for clients who have the requisite access and ability.

In addition to websites, government organizations of all types have developed apps for phones, tablets, and other mobile devices. The MyTSA app, for example, allows travelers to check what they can and cannot bring onto flights, as well as any weather-related delays they might encounter. Ask Karen, an app run by the Department of Agriculture, provides access to information about food safety, such as how long food in the refrigerator is good after the power goes out. The White House's app provides press releases and live streams to the president's speeches.[117]

Government organizations have embraced social media instruments such as blogs, Facebook, Twitter, and Instagram as means of directly interacting with clients. The Department of Education, for example, uses the hashtag #AskFAFSA to answer questions about financial aid for college students.[118] Similarly, the Department of Veterans Affairs has organizations such as the American Legion share information on social media as part of its #VetQ campaign. The White House uses its blog (wh.gov/blog) for a specifically defined purpose: "The blog is the place for longer form content that really dives into the specifics of an issue. It doesn't receive the amount of visibility that, for example, a Facebook post or a Tweet might, but it's for people who want more than that."[119] One issue with social media is the relationship between such platforms and other digital instruments. The Department of the Interior addresses this issue by requiring that all information posted to third-party social media platforms must also be available on the agency's website.[120]

What are the hallmarks of government organizations that have effectively digitized their information and services? One essential feature is plain language that removes the need for clients to understand acronyms, jargon, and complex terminology. The Utah.gov portal, for example, features an "I want to" prompt that allows visitors to enter a description of what they want to accomplish.[121] Other best practices include designing websites and apps for mobile users, who scroll through content very differently than clients sitting in front of desktop computers.[122]

One persistent concern accompanying the government's embrace of information technology is the **digital divide.** Although 85 percent of adult Americans use the Internet, variation exists across segments of the population.[123] Senior citizens are less likely to use the Internet than younger adults. Internet use also varies by education, income, and race and ethnicity. People living in rural areas use the Internet at lower rates than residents of cities and suburbs. Furthermore, the quality of the devices and data plans used to access the Internet varies across clients. As a result, it is incumbent upon government organizations to design websites that are accessible to low-bandwidth users. The Sacramento County, California, website, for example, offers a button that allows visitors to readily switch from an image-laden version to a text-only presentation.[124]

In 1998, the Department of Transportation (DOT) made history when it became the first agency to move its entire docket system to the Internet. **Dockets** are repositories that contain, on a rule-by-rule basis, detailed records of agency and client activities, including notices of proposed rulemaking, final rules, cost-benefit analyses, and comments and other forms of public participation. By moving its docket system online, DOT enhanced the ease with which information about its rulemakings could be submitted, stored, and retrieved, thus saving the agency more than a million dollars annually in administrative costs.[125]

This digitization also prompted expectations of a great outburst of client participation in DOT rulemakings. On rare occasions, this expectation has been borne out. For example, the DOT received more than 65,000 comments on its proposed corporate average fuel economy standards for light trucks.[126] For the most part, however, comparisons of online processes with prior levels of paper-based commenting show that overall patterns of commenting have been remarkably stable since the introduction of the online docket system. Figure 4.4 illustrates that clients submitted 100 or more comments in only about 10 percent of the rulemakings before and after online docketing. In addition, about half of the rulemakings in both periods generated between 10 and 99 comments, the most common volume of client activity. This evidence suggests that established actors continue to be most active in participating in bureaucratic decision making, despite the promise of online dockets in mobilizing new constituencies.

In the years since the DOT launched its online docket, agencies from across the government have embraced this form of digitization. Today, **regulations.gov** serves as a single website where hundreds of agencies post documents and receive comments. As illustrated in Figure 4.5, at any given moment, visitors to regulations.gov are presented with hundreds of opportunities to comment on prospective agency actions.

Regulations.gov also allows interested parties to view comments that have been submitted by other individuals and organizations. Giving clients

Figure 4.4 Client Commenting before and after Online Docketing at the DOT

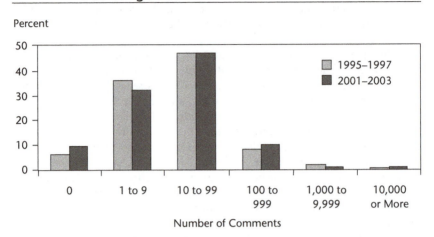

Percent

Number of Comments

Legend: 1995–1997, 2001–2003

Source: Steven J. Balla and Benjamin M. Daniels, "Information Technology and Public Commenting on Agency Regulations," *Regulation and Governance* 1 (March 2007): 46–67.

Note: Each bar represents the percentage of rulemakings in the period that fall into a particular category of comment activity.

Figure 4.5 Regulations.gov Website

Source: Regulations.gov. Screenshot taken on January 18, 2017.

the chance to respond to information that has previously been submitted is a mechanism for making participation more collaborative. Such a transformation can only occur, however, if comments are posted well before submission deadlines, so that other stakeholders have ample opportunity to read and react to what others have said. One limiting factor in this regard is that the most common day for participants to submit comments is on the day that feedback periods close, thereby shielding their input from the scrutiny of opposing interests.[127] Another barrier to collaboration is that agencies do not always post submitted comments in short order. Although the DOT has a standard operating procedure of posting comments within eight hours of submission, this deadline is not always met, especially during times of high comment volume.[128] At the Environmental Protection Agency, it takes an average of thirty-eight days for comments to be posted to regulations.gov.[129]

An early effort at using information technology to transform bureaucratic decision making occurred in 2007, when the Patent and Trademark Office (PTO) launched a pilot project hailed as "revolutionary."[130] Under the **Peer to Patent project,** patent examiners at the PTO used a Web-based system to access information about applications that would have been beyond their fingertips under traditional review methods. The system was oriented around the idea of community peer review. It incorporated open editing features similar to Wikipedia, as well as a rating system allowing users to evaluate one another's contributions (think eBay and Amazon). The idea was to use **crowdsourcing** to enhance both the openness and expertise of the patent review process. Although patent examiners continue to be the ultimate decision makers, their decisions are informed as never before by agency clients, especially those participants deemed by their peers to be particularly insightful.

A community-based review system is a far cry from the way patent examiners have historically gone about their jobs. At times, PTO officials have been prohibited from using the Internet, lest they inadvertently reveal proprietary secrets during the course of online searches.[131] Why, then, did the PTO become willing to move past such concerns and embrace the use of digital technology? In 2006, some 4,000 examiners handled a record 332,000 patent applications, thus limiting the PTO's ability to conduct thorough reviews.[132] The aim was to improve the PTO's performance in the face of such a massive workload, as well as to make the patent process more accountable to the agency's expert client community.

An evaluation of the pilot project concluded that, despite logistical difficulties, Peer to Patent ought to be expanded beyond its initial trial.[133] Although a temporary expansion did occur, the project never transformed the patent examination process in a permanent, across-the-board manner.[134] In this regard, Peer to Patent is similar to Regulation Room, which has to this point been used in the development of a total of six regulations.[135]

In general, there have been relatively few instances of agencies using the Internet to transform client participation. Most applications, such as electronic docket systems, have instead entailed the digitization of existing practices. Why have agencies been hesitant to embrace transformational modes of engagement? Generally speaking, information technology does not act solely as an agent of societal change and innovation. Technology itself is fundamentally shaped by existing institutions and power holders, including government agencies, thereby limiting the scope and speed of transformation.[136] The impact of the Internet on the accountability and performance of public bureaucracies is determined in no small part by decisions made inside the executive branch.

Client Influence on Bureaucratic Policymaking

The popular image of clients, particularly organized interests, is that they are enormously resourceful and extraordinarily influential.[137] The overall accuracy of these perceptions, however, may be questioned for a number of reasons. First, interest groups differ dramatically in size, finances, membership, expertise, and credibility. All interest groups are not created equal! Lists of the most powerful organized interests in America typically include the AARP, American Medical Association, Chamber of Commerce, and National Rifle Association.[138] Many thousands of organizations fall well short of these lobbies in terms of personnel and budgetary resources, as well as political clout.

Second, interest groups may be more effective in some settings than others. Whereas Congress is designed to be highly porous and accessible, the bureaucracy, despite a multiplicity of participatory venues, is not fundamentally an institution of representative government. This means that resources such as campaign contributions and grassroots mobilization may not be directly useful to clients seeking influence over executive branch policymaking. As one bureaucrat put it, "It's not a plebiscite. We're not doing rulemaking by vote."[139] Instead, economic, legal, scientific, and other forms of specialized information may be most relevant in affecting the course of agency decision making.

Third, interest groups are far more prominent in some policy debates than others. To reiterate a central theme of the chapter, the significance of organized interests depends in part on whether the costs and benefits of policies are concentrated or distributed.[140] Fourth, interest group power ebbs and flows over time. Evidence suggests that organizational influence in the federal bureaucracy declined from the early 1970s to the mid-1980s, then rebounded somewhat.[141] Fifth, the influence of particular types of interest groups changes systematically over time. Republican administrations tend to be more responsive to business organizations and conservative advocacy groups, while Democratic administrations tend to be more influenced by labor unions and advocacy groups with a liberal bent.

Despite all of these qualifications, there is considerable evidence that interest groups exert highly regular influence over bureaucratic decision making. Although no cabinet secretary today would come right out and say, "What's good for General Motors is good for the United States," business groups undoubtedly command the attention of executive branch officials. In a variety of policy areas, including the environment and consumer protection, public interest groups have become increasingly powerful in recent decades. State and local governments have also taken on the role of organized lobbyists, as when the National Governors Association seeks to shape welfare reform decisions that emanate from federal offices.

Business Organizations

The role of business in the policymaking process is uniquely important. As has long been acknowledged, "Businessmen generally and corporate executives in particular take on a privileged role in government that is, it seems reasonable to say, unmatched by any leadership group other than government officials themselves."[142] Because maintaining low unemployment and strong economic growth are high priorities for governments of all stripes, keen sensitivity to business interests is apparent throughout the world. It is especially striking, however, in the United States, where the private sector accounts for a relatively large percentage of the nation's economic productivity.

Research on federal agencies demonstrates that business groups are very influential in shaping administrative rulemaking decisions. Across a range of issues and agencies, proposed rules are more likely to be adjusted in the direction of less government intervention when business intervention is high.[143] According to researchers, it is the high number of businesses commenting rather than the quality of their inputs that explains the disproportionate influence of the business community.[144]

Business influence over the executive branch manifests in both Republican and Democratic administrations. Bloomberg Businessweek called President Obama the "anti-business president who's been good for business."[145] Regulatory reform advocates described the administration's courting of business in less glowing terms: "The problem is that they're wasting time trying to make the political move to the center to placate industry—talking about the 'terrible cost of regulation' and the 'burdens of regulation'—and in the meantime they've got important regulations waiting to go out, and they're pulling back on them."[146]

The so-called **revolving door** between government agencies and the private sector offers an important source of business power. Officials at the Federal Communications Commission (FCC) who used to work in the broadcast industry are more likely to vote in support of the industry when such issues

Inside Bureaucracy with	Dan Glickman *Secretary of Agriculture* *(1995–2001)*

"A lot of top-level bureaucrats at the USDA had been there many years. Some had worked in these commodity groups. It's kind of a small, incestuous community. Everybody knew each other."

come before the agency.[147] Even agency officials who have not previously worked in a particular industry may behave favorably toward it if they hope one day to secure a job in that industry.

Direct lobbying is another tactic that has been gainfully employed by business interests. In 1998, lobbyists from the sugar industry helped to persuade the Army Corps of Engineers to reconsider its water storage plans in the vicinity of Florida's Lake Okeechobee. Instead of building a large reservoir on sugar lands, as originally intended, the agency agreed to build underground storage systems, as proposed by sugar interests.[148] In exercising this influence "the sugar companies not only survived the battle over Everglades restoration; they guaranteed their future water supply."[149]

Similar conclusions have been reached for other agencies and policy arenas. Consider, for example, the EPA's authority, granted by the Federal Insecticide, Fungicide, and Rodenticide Act, to approve or cancel the registration of specific pesticides. Over a fifteen-year period, the agency was less likely to cancel a pesticide's registration if a grower group intervened in the decision-making process than if there were no intervention.[150] A decision not to cancel a registration permits growers to use the pesticide despite any environmental concerns.

Business organizations influence not only the federal government but state agencies as well. A study of public utility commissions in twelve states found that utility companies were moderately influential in one state and very influential in the other eleven.[151] Similarly, research has shown that water pollution standards are relatively weak in states in which the mining industry accounts for a particularly substantial share of economic activity.[152]

In general, business organizations, as common participants in iron triangles, fare better on issues where the glare of publicity is relatively dim. High issue salience works to the advantage of groups that can make broad appeals to the general public. Low issue salience, in contrast, favors economic interests with narrow constituencies. The actions of the mass media, which both react to and promote high issue salience, help to explain this pattern. The role of the press, it has been said, is to "afflict the comfortable and comfort the afflicted."[153] In performing this role, journalists and other media officials draw attention to policy arrangements that benefit small numbers of producers at the expense of large numbers of consumers. In the end, however, although the influence of business organizations is mitigated by media coverage and other factors, this influence remains pervasive across agencies and levels of government.

Public Interest Groups

At first glance the bureaucracy would not seem to be fertile territory for public interest groups—organizations such as Common Cause, the Consumers Union, and the Natural Resources Defense Council. Although bureaucratic decision making is surprisingly transparent, it is nonetheless more opaque than decision making in legislatures. This opacity enhances the difficulty for wide audiences seeking to participate in, and exercise influence over, agency proceedings. Moreover, issues addressed in bureaucratic settings tend to be more technical, more abstruse, and more remote than those resolved by legislatures. Such circumstances naturally favor experts, including agency personnel and the kinds of professionals public interest groups often cannot afford to maintain.

Despite these handicaps, public interest groups enjoy advantages today that they did not possess in previous generations. The Freedom of Information Act and the Government in the Sunshine Act make it easier for public interest groups, as well as other interested parties, to obtain important agency documents and attend meetings where vital policy decisions are being considered. In addition, the National Environmental Policy Act and other statutes have created opportunities for public interest groups to challenge bureaucratic decisions in the courts.

The long saga of the spotted owl illustrates public interest groups' ability to shape bureaucratic decisions with a combination of direct lobbying and indirect intervention through the judiciary. In 1986, a small Massachusetts-based environmental group, GreenWorld, asked the Fish and Wildlife Service to list the spotted owl as an endangered species. When the agency failed to do so, the Sierra Club Legal Defense Fund initiated litigation against the government. In 1989, a federal district court judge issued the first of a series of rulings that would ultimately compel the agency to designate the spotted owl as endangered. Subsequent interventions by environmental groups resulted in decisions sharply curtailing the ability of the government to sell timber in the Northwest's old-growth forests, particularly in the vicinity of spotted owl habitats.[154]

Environmental groups have been particularly influential participants in bureaucratic policymaking. In addition to restrictions on timber sales, they have used their power to promote reductions in livestock grazing and recreational use of national forests. It has been demonstrated that during the late 1980s and early

Inside Bureaucracy with	Dan Glickman *Secretary of Agriculture* *(1995–2001)*

"Some people believe that the Forest Service for years was so closely tied to timber interests that you had an iron triangle between Western-based senators, the timber industry, and the Forest Service bureaucracy. But during the Clinton administration that wasn't true. The Clinton Forest Service policy was very much more habitat protection oriented and species protection oriented. The environmental community was extremely active and was an equal match for the timber community. Frankly, it was one of the healthier areas of public policy because there was genuine debate, not only over legislative but also over regulatory issues. There was a kind of equality of engagement that you certainly did not see in farm policy, for example."

1990s, an "amenity coalition" of environmental groups and sympathetic government officials was more effective than a "commodity coalition" of ranchers and timber companies in shaping Forest Service planning decisions.[155] In 2015, the EPA promulgated rules designed to reduce greenhouse gas emissions. These rules, hailed by environmentalists as the "most important regulations on climate change ever issued by the U.S.," were issued over the vehement objections of coal companies, energy corporations, and their elected representatives.[156]

Ultimately, the influence of public interest groups depends a good deal on the policy preferences of the bureaucracies whose behavior they are trying to shape. Some agencies are widely regarded as liberal in their preferences, while others are viewed as having conservative orientations. Agencies with liberal reputations include the EPA, Department of Housing and Urban Development, and Commission on Civil Rights. On the conservative side are organizations such as the Department of Defense, National Security Council, and Small Business Administration.[157]

Agency preferences, it is important to note, can change over time. Take, for example, the making of child care policy at the Department of Health and Human Services (HHS). The Children's Defense Fund and other child advocacy groups fared better in shaping the child care policies of the Clinton administration than in influencing comparable policies during the preceding Bush administration.[158] Olivia Golden, the head of HHS's Administration for Children, Youth, and Families under President Clinton, was a former senior staffer at the fund, demonstrating that the revolving door can at times work to the advantage of public interest groups. In addition, Donna Shalala, the secretary of the Department of Health and Human Services, was very sympathetic to the fund and its aims. To top it off, First Lady Hillary Rodham Clinton had once been a fund board member. Interestingly, though these institutional linkages did not exist before President Clinton took office, child advocacy groups had won some modest victories during the administration of George H. W. Bush.[159] Many years later, during the Obama administration, early childhood education causes enjoyed strong support from the federal bureaucracy. For example, in May 2011 the Department of Education and Department of Health and Human Services announced a competition to allocate $500 million to states that propose innovative ideas for child care and early childhood education reform.[160] These victories, under both Democratic and Republican administrations, testify to the power that public interest groups can now bring to bear on the policymaking process, regardless of the political climate.

State and Local Governments

Governments themselves rank among the bureaucracy's most effective clients. Federal agencies hear all the time from state governments, local governments, and **professional associations,** such as the National Conference of State Legislatures, Association of State Drinking Water Administrators, and National League of Cities. State and local governments enjoy special deference in the policymaking process because they authoritatively represent citizens in particular parts of the country. This deference is heightened when state and local officials work together, through organizations that allow them to speak with one voice.[161] The National Governors Association, to take one example, has been a particularly powerful force under recent presidents, several of whom had been governors themselves.

It is important to note that state and local governments often target Congress and the White House rather than executive branch agencies. Even working alone, many governors enjoy the stature and prestige necessary to arrange audiences with key members of Congress and the president's closest aides. From the perspective of such officials, why bother with the bureaucracy when you can confer with the bureaucracy's bosses?

Inside Bureaucracy with	Tom Ridge *Secretary of Homeland Security* *(2003–2005)*

"State and local officials had significant input at our request. We built a national response plan after almost a year's engagement with state and local political officials, emergency management officials. Those associations represented political figures and institutions that I made it a priority for the department to be connected to in order to exchange information because it was precisely the state and locals who may be called upon by the president or by me to ratchet up security based on information we had in order to protect the country or a region or a city. The political interest groups were targeted specifically by me to build relationships so that there was communication going in both directions simply because the manpower burden and occasionally the financial burden and the psychological burden always fell on state and local governments if we asked them to ramp up their security given a particular threat environment. They were very helpful. Take the Urban Area Security Initiatives (UASI) grants. We finally worked with them to develop a formula so there was appropriate distribution and accountability. By and large our interactions with the politically related interest groups was very, very positive for the department. My mindset says you can't secure the country inside the Beltway; you need to have relationships with the state and locals, including the police. As a former DA I've got a great appreciation for the men and women in blue or whatever they're wearing these days (you've got 700,000 of them on the streets). We tried to stay in touch with these kinds of constituencies involving the people who potentially at any given time we would call into the service to secure either community location or nationwide security. So we stayed in pretty close contact with them."

State and local governments are in regular communication, however, with officials inside the bureaucracy. The rulemaking process is a common target for such interventions. For example, state and local governments file more than 1,000 comments per year in EPA rulemakings deemed to be "major" or "significant."[162] Furthermore, in occupying well over 100 membership spots on EPA advisory committees, states and localities constitute one of the best represented clientele groups in the agency's advisory system.[163]

In recent decades, state and local governments have repeatedly pressed federal agencies for **waivers** from rules and regulations. In the area of health care, states pursued waivers allowing them to substitute managed care for fee-for-service medicine in their Medicaid programs. In education, state governments and local school districts requested waivers enhancing their flexibility in administering education programs. In one year alone, the federal government received 174 waiver applications from states and local education agencies. Nearly a thousand such applications were submitted over the course of a decade that spanned the Clinton and Bush administrations.[164]

In responding to waiver requests, the federal government has generally accommodated states and localities while satisfying its own legal and political concerns. The Clinton administration was rather receptive to waiver requests.[165] When President Clinton took office, only one state—Arizona—had received the authority to create a statewide research and demonstration project under Medicaid. By the end of the Clinton administration, eighteen states were operating under such waivers. The administration of George W. Bush also looked favorably on waiver applications. In 2001, the Department of Education granted eighty-five of the ninety-nine requests it received. In all, during President Bush's first term, the administration approved about 70 percent of the education waivers sought by state and local governments.[166] Under the Obama administration, states seeking flexibility when implementing the requirements of the No Child Left Behind Act were almost unanimously granted waivers.[167]

As these data indicate, federal agencies occasionally deny state and local requests for waivers. In some instances the federal government denies such requests because it lacks the statutory authority to grant particular waivers. In other instances it denies requests because of expressed opposition. For example, the Clinton administration terminated New Mexico's managed care program for mental health after receiving extensive negative commentary from the Bazelon Center for Mental Health Law, a public interest group that enjoyed considerable credibility within the administration. This decision was reversed under President George W. Bush, whose administration was responsive to a different set of mental health interests.[168]

Direct intervention in a federal agency's deliberations is often accompanied by other approaches, such as expanding the **scope of conflict.**[169] In 2002, for example, Democratic South Carolina governor Jim Hodges used a variety of strategies in opposing a Department of Energy (DOE) decision to ship plutonium from Colorado to his state. Hodges pleaded with Energy Secretary Spencer Abraham to stop the shipment and also asked Tom Ridge, director of Homeland Security, to intervene on South Carolina's behalf. When these efforts bore no fruit, Hodges ratcheted up the level of controversy by taking DOE to court and generating considerable mass media attention. He even threatened to lie down in front of any truck attempting to carry a plutonium shipment across South Carolina's border! Ultimately, Hodges was forced to acquiesce when a federal appeals court ordered him not to interfere with the plutonium shipment.[170] He won an important concession along the way, however. In a written letter, Abraham promised to seek legislation guaranteeing the removal of the plutonium if it could not be processed.[171]

Clients and the Institutions of Government

The squabble between South Carolina and the federal government reinforces one of the central lessons of this, as well as the preceding, chapter. Client participation in bureaucratic policymaking does not occur in an institutional vacuum but through various arrangements, such as the court system, established and maintained by political principals. As third-party intermediaries, individuals and organizations play a crucial role in determining the degree to which principals are well equipped to address issues of adverse selection and moral hazard, and ultimately to mitigate the agency loss associated with the delegation of authority.

Principal-agent theory, however, does not directly speak to the desire and capacity of clients to take on the roles specified by executives, legislatures, and judiciaries. This is where the interest group mobilization framework comes in, pointing our attention to the benefits and costs associated with particular policy areas and choices. By offering a conditional perspective on client activism and influence, this framework recognizes citizens and interest groups as potentially powerful, yet at times unwilling, participants in the hierarchical structures and processes of bureaucratic policymaking.

Importantly, agencies operate not only as agents on the receiving end of delegated authority but also as partners in networks that span agencies and governments as well as the public and private sectors. During his tenure as attorney general, Dick Thornburgh convened a body called the Financial Crimes Task Force. In the words of the attorney general, this organization "brought together on an interagency basis all the people who would be pursuing wrongdoing in that area," including agents from the Federal Bureau of Investigation. The task force, in other words, offered the possibility of coordination across a host of bureaucracies, all of which operated as agents to their own principals. The complexity of this arrangement, which is not at all uncommon, undoubtedly had implications for the mobilization of, and influence exercised by, the intended beneficiaries and targets of executive branch activity in the area of financial crimes. These implications will become clearer after government networks are considered from a theoretical point of view in the following chapter.

Client Participation: Three Lessons and Beyond

At first glance the bureaucracy often appears insular and impervious to outside intervention. Complaints about red tape and out-of-control agencies abound, and at times these complaints have merit. This chapter, however, has demonstrated that the bureaucracy is a surprisingly open and accessible set of institutions and organizations. Three lessons, in particular, seem appropriate to draw regarding the bureaucracy and its clients.

Who Participates Varies

Citizens, women's rights organizations, and the cast and fans of the Broadway musical *Hamilton* all placed enormous pressure on the Department of the Treasury during the debate over the redesign of the nation's currency. This mobilization occurred thanks to the entrepreneurial efforts of organizations such as Women on 20s. Although it might be tempting to conclude that agencies always hear from interested stakeholders, such a conclusion would ignore the variation in client participation that occurs over time and across policy areas. As noted above, in recent decades some iron triangles have been transformed into sloppy hexagons, making participation more fluid and uncertain than in previous eras. Within these hexagons, the activism of particular clients varies across issues as benefits and costs take on unique distributions. Although business organizations will undoubtedly continue to participate extensively in bureaucratic proceedings, given their direct material stake in agency actions, the extent to which this participation will be met by other interests is best assessed on a case-by-case basis.

Venues Vary

Just as the identities of client participants are remarkably diverse, so, too, are the venues through which these participants make their views known. When the Department of the Treasury announced its plan to replace Alexander Hamilton's image on the $10 bill with the portrait of a woman, citizens swamped the agency with comments and Women on 20s pressed forward with a very public online campaign. In general, clients can communicate with agency officials through both direct and indirect channels. Direct channels, such as the advisory committee system, bring clients themselves before agencies. Indirect channels, in contrast, task legislatures and courts with addressing agencies on behalf of specific constituencies or parties. Importantly, venues are distinct in the resources clients must possess to take advantage of opportunities for participation. Clients seeking to comment on agency proposals are best off when exercising significant legal acumen, given the complexity of many contemporary rulemakings. When the goal is to entice legislators to intervene in bureaucratic decisions, clients are most capable when mobilizing large numbers of constituents or filling the campaign coffers of prospective benefactors.

Influence Varies

Most, though not all, interested parties were satisfied with the Department of the Treasury's resolution of the currency redesign controversy. Alexander

Hamilton's place of honor has been preserved and a woman will soon be featured on America's currency, along with a more representative presentation of the nation's democratic history. In other instances, however, influence accrues disproportionately to one interest or set of interests. When revising the way in which the Medicare program pays for physician services, the Health Care Financing Administration proved more responsive to comments submitted by specialists (for example, cardiologists) than to comments submitted by family practitioners and other general providers. These differences in influence were important because the agency had been charged by Congress with redistributing payments away from specialists.[172] The influence patterns, at least as witnessed in the notice and comment process, may have made it difficult for such an outcome to emerge from the rulemaking.

Issues of client influence raise a pair of broader, more normative questions: Does client participation make policymaking in the bureaucracy more democratic? Does this participation enhance the ability of agencies to make high-quality, defensible decisions? Although these questions do not have simple answers, this chapter has provided a framework for thinking about such concerns. Due in part to client participation, policymaking in the bureaucracy is a political process as well as an exercise in administration. Assessments of accountability and performance must be made with both aspects of bureaucracy in mind.

Creating a currency that is both resistant to counterfeiting and reflective of American democracy is not a trivial undertaking. The sustained activism of both Hamiltonians and women's rights advocates—not all of whom were in agreement about the most representative path forward—made the Department of the Treasury's task that much more difficult. Such multifaceted client participation, however, pushed the agency toward an innovative solution that pleased most constituencies. In the words of former Agriculture Secretary Dan Glickman, "equality of engagement" among stakeholders can foster "genuine debate" and ultimately give rise to a policy community that is healthy and anchored by an agency that serves both its clients and the nation with distinction.

Key Terms

Notes

1. U.S. Department of the Treasury, "Secretary Lew Announces Historic Decision to Feature a Woman on the Newly Redesigned Ten Dollar Note," https://www.treasury.gov/press-center/press-releases/Pages/jl0079.aspx (accessed September 12, 2016).

2. http://www.womenon20 s.org/ (accessed September 13, 2016).

3. "Shaheen: It's Time to Put a Woman on the Twenty Dollar Bill," Jeanne Shaheen, U.S. Senator, N.H., April 15, 2015, https://www.shaheen.senate.gov/news/press/release/?id=05739d4a-bb0e-4724-a49a-031aa0797fd3 (accessed September 13, 2016).

4. Harrison Jacobs, "The US Is Changing the Face of the $10 Bill," Business Insider, June 17, 2015, http://www.businessinsider.com/the-us-is-reportedly-going-to-change-the-face-of-the-10-bill-2015-6 (accessed September 13, 2016); "Where Women on 20s Stands Today," http://www.womenon20s.org/ (accessed September 13, 2016).

5. http://www.hamiltonbroadway.com/ (accessed September 13, 2016).

6. Jackie Calmes, "Success of 'Hamilton' May Have Saved Hamilton on the $10 Bill," New York Times, April 16, 2016, http://www.nytimes.com/2016/04/16/us/politics/success-of-hamilton-may-have-saved-hamilton-on-the-10-bill.html (accessed September 13, 2016).

7. Jacobs, "The US Is Changing the Face of the $10 Bill."

8. U.S. Department of the Treasury, "Secretary Lew Announces Historic Decision."

9. "An Open Letter from Secretary Lew," https://medium.com/@USTreasury/an-open-letter-from-secretary-lew-672cfd591d02#.ggn8tlurt (accessed September 13, 2016).

10. Jennifer Schuessler, Binyamin Appelbaum, and Wesley Morris, "Tubman's In. Jackson's Out. What's It Mean?" New York Times, April 21, 2016, http://www.nytimes.com/2016/04/21/arts/design/tubmans-in-jacksons-out-whats-it-mean.html (accessed September 13, 2016).

11. "An Open Letter from Secretary Lew."

12. "An Open Letter to US Treasury Secretary Jack Lew on Why a Woman Needs to Be on the Front of the $10 Bill," Makers Team, April 20, 2016, http://www.makers.com/blog/facts-women-ten-dollar-bill (accessed September 13, 2016).

13. U.S. Department of the Treasury, "Secretary Lew Announces Historic Decision."

14. James Q. Wilson, "The Politics of Regulation," in The Politics of Regulation, ed. James Q. Wilson (New York: Basic Books, 1980); James Q. Wilson, Bureaucracy: What Government Agencies Do and Why They Do It (New York: Basic Books, 1989).

15. Frank R. Baumgartner and Bryan D. Jones, *Agendas and Instability in American Politics* (Chicago: University of Chicago Press, 1993).

16. Lawrence S. Rothenberg, *Regulation, Organizations, and Politics: Motor Freight Policy at the Interstate Commerce Commission* (Ann Arbor: University of Michigan Press, 1994).

17. Wilson, "Politics of Regulation"; Wilson, *Bureaucracy*.

18. Wilson, *Bureaucracy*, 78–79.

19. Daniel Kaufmann, "Corruption and the Global Financial Crisis," *Forbes*, January 27, 2009, http://www.forbes.com/2009/01/27/corruption-financial-crisis-business-corruption09_0127corruption.html (accessed September 14, 2016).

20. "Charlie Rose Interviews Charles Ferguson on His Documentary 'Inside Job,'" https://www.youtube.com/watch? v=vS0hj4kiqsA (accessed September 14, 2016).

21. Susan E. Dudley and Jerry Brito, *Regulation: A Primer*, 2nd ed. (Arlington, VA: Mercatus Center, George Mason University, 2012), http://mercatus.org/sites/default/files/RegulatoryPrimer_DudleyBrito_0.pdf (accessed September 14, 2016).

22. Samuel P. Huntington, "The Marasmus of the ICC: The Commission, the Railroads, and the Public Interest," *Yale Law Journal* 62 (April 1952): 467–509; Grant McConnell, *Private Power and American Democracy* (New York: Knopf, 1966).

23. Kay Lehman Schlozman and John T. Tierney, *Organized Interests and American Democracy* (New York: Harper and Row, 1986).

24. "Lobbying Database," http://www.opensecrets.org/lobby/ (accessed September 14, 2016).

25. "Top Contracts," http://www.opensecrets.org/lobby/top.php? indexType=f&show Year=2016 (accessed September 14, 2016).

26. Baumgartner and Jones, *Agendas and Instability in American Politics*.

27. Steven Mufson, "Why Is the Obama Administration Using Taxpayer Money to Back a Nuclear Plant That's Already Being Built?" *Washington Post*, February 21, 2014, https://www.washingtonpost.com/news/wonk/wp/2014/02/21/why-is-the-obama-administration-using-taxpayer-money-to-back-a-nuclear-plant-thats-already-being-built/ (accessed September 14, 2016).

28. Ibid.

29. Stephen Ansolabehere and David Konisky, *Cheap and Clean: How Americans Think about Energy in the Age of Global Warming* (Cambridge, Mass.: MIT Press, 2014), 50–54.

30. Charles O. Jones, "American Politics and the Organization of Energy Decision Making," in *Annual Review of Energy*, ed. Jack M. Hollander, Melvin K. Simmons, and David O. Wood (Palo Alto, Calif.: Annual Reviews, 1979).

31. Hugh Heclo, "Issue Networks in the Executive Establishment," in *The New American Political System*, ed. Anthony King (Washington, D.C.: American Enterprise Institute, 1978).

32. Elaine B. Sharp, "The Dynamics of Issue Expansion: Cases from Disability Rights and Fetal Research Controversy," *Journal of Politics* 56 (November 1994): 919–939.

33. Michelle Levi, "Republicans Rally against Obama on Stem Cells," CBS News, March 9, 2009, http://www.cbsnews.com/news/republicans-rally-against-obama-on-stem-cells/ (accessed September 14, 2016).

34. Cornelius M. Kerwin, *Rulemaking: How Government Agencies Write Law and Make Policy*, 3rd ed. (Washington, D.C.: CQ Press, 2003).

35. Competitive Enterprise Institute, "Thousands of Pages and Rules in the *Federal Register*," May 3, 2016, https://cei.org/10KC/Chapter-2, (accessed September 14, 2016).

36. American Action Forum, "Regulation Rodeo," https://regrodeo.com/ (accessed September 14, 2016).

37. Each of the fifty states and the District of Columbia have their own administrative procedure acts, which govern rulemaking within their jurisdictions.

38. Steven J. Balla, "Between Commenting and Negotiation: The Contours of Public Participation in Agency Rulemaking," *I/S: A Journal of Law and Policy* 1 (Winter 2005): 59–94; Kerwin, *Rulemaking;* Connor Raso, "Agency Avoidance of Rulemaking Procedures," http://papers.ssrn.com/sol3/papers.cfm? abstract_id=2293455 (accessed September 14, 2016).

39. Schlozman and Tierney, *Organized Interests and American Democracy.*

40. "Quid Pro Quo and Hostile Environment Harassment and Liability for Discriminatory Housing Practices under the Fair Housing Act," *Federal Register,* September 14, 2016, https://www.federalregister.gov/documents/2016/09/14/2016-21868/quid-pro-quo-and-hostile-environment-harassment-and-liability-for-discriminatory-housing-practices (accessed September 14, 2016).

41. Frederick J. Boehmke, Sean Gailmard, and John W. Patty, "Business as Usual: Interest Group Access and Representation across Policy-Making Venues," *Journal of Public Policy* 33 (April 2013): 3–33.

42. Christine Mahoney, *Brussels versus the Beltway: Advocacy in the U.S. and the European Union* (Washington, D.C.: Georgetown University Press, 2008), 131–132.

43. Ibid., 132.

44. These rules were identified by searching the website of the *Federal Register* (https://www.federalregister.gov/, accessed September 14, 2016) for significant rules issued during June, July, and August 2016.

45. The White House, Executive Order 12866, "Regulatory Planning and Review," https://www.whitehouse.gov/sites/default/files/omb/inforeg/eo12866/eo12866_10041993.pdf (accessed September 14, 2016).

46. Animal and Plant Health Inspection Service, "Viruses, Serums, Toxins, and Analogous Products; Packaging and Labeling," https://www.federalregister.gov/documents/2016/08/30/2016-20749/viruses-serums-toxins-and-analogous-products-packaging-and-labeling (accessed September 14, 2016).

47. U.S. General Accounting Office, *Food and Drug Administration: Regulation of Tobacco Products* (Washington, D.C.: GAO, 1997).

48. Grant Gross, "FCC Receives Record 3 Million Net Neutrality Comments: What Now?" http://www.pcworld.com/article/2684395/fcc-gets-record-number-of-net-neutrality-comments-what-now.html (accessed September 14, 2016).

49. Steven J. Balla and Benjamin M. Daniels, "Information Technology and Public Commenting on Agency Regulations," *Regulation and Governance* 1 (March 2007): 46–67.

50. Ibid.; Scott R. Furlong and Cornelius M. Kerwin, "Interest Group Participation in Rule Making: A Decade of Change," *Journal of Public Administration Research and Theory* 15 (July 2005): 353–370; Jason Webb Yackee and Susan Webb Yackee, "A Bias toward Business? Assessing Interest Group Influence on the U.S. Bureaucracy," *Journal of Politics* 68 (February 2006): 128–139.

51. Marissa Martino Golden, "Interest Groups in the Rule-Making Process: Who Participates? Whose Voices Get Heard?" *Journal of Public Administration Research and Theory* 8 (April 1998): 245–270.

52. Ibid.

53. Stuart W. Shulman, "An Experiment in Digital Government at the United States National Organic Program," *Agriculture and Human Values* 20 (Fall 2003): 253–265.

54. Jason Webb Yackee and Susan Webb Yackee, "A Bias toward Business?"; Susan Webb Yackee, "Sweet-Talking the Fourth Branch: The Influence of Interest Group Comments on Federal Agency Rulemaking," *Journal of Public Administration Research and Theory* 16 (January 2006): 103–124.

55. Stuart W. Shulman, "An Experiment in Digital Government at the United States National Organic Program," *Agriculture and Human Values* 20 (Fall 2003): 253–265.

56. Ibid.

57. Marissa Martino Golden, "Interest Groups in the Rule-Making Process"; Kerwin, *Rulemaking;* Wesley A. Magat, Alan J. Krupnick, and Winston Harrington, *Rules*

in the Making: A Statistical Analysis of Regulatory Agency Behavior (Washington, D.C.: Resources for the Future, 1986); David C. Nixon, Robert M. Howard, and Jeff DeWitt, "With Friends Like These: Rule-Making Comment Submissions to the Securities and Exchange Commission," *Journal of Public Administration Research and Theory* 12 (January 2002): 59–76.

58. William F. West, "Formal Procedures, Informal Processes, Accountability, and Responsiveness in Bureaucratic Policy Making: An Institutional Policy Analysis," *Public Administration Review* 64 (January/February 2004): 67.

59. David Nelson and Susan Webb Yackee, "Lobbying Coalitions and Government Policy Change: An Analysis of Federal Agency Rulemaking," *Journal of Politics* 74 (March 2012): 339–353.

60. The White House, Executive Order 12866, "Regulatory Planning and Review," https://www.whitehouse.gov/sites/default/files/omb/inforeg/eo12866/eo12866_10041993.pdf (accessed September 16, 2016).

61. Jeffrey Lubbers, *A Guide to Federal Agency Rulemaking*, 4th ed. (Chicago: American Bar Association, 2006).

62. Steven J. Balla, "Procedural Control, Bureaucratic Discretion, and Public Commenting on Agency Regulations," *Public Administration* 93 (June 2015): 524–538.

63. Ibid.

64. Philip J. Harter, "Negotiated Rulemaking: A Cure for Malaise," *Georgetown Law Journal* 71 (December 1982): 1–113.

65. Kerwin, *Rulemaking;* Cornelius M. Kerwin and Scott R. Furlong, "Time and Rule-making: An Empirical Test of Theory," *Journal of Public Administration Research and Theory* 2 (April 1992): 113–138.

66. Harter, "Negotiated Rulemaking."

67. Administration for Children and Families, "Head Start Performance Standards," https://www.federalregister.gov/documents/2016/09/06/2016-19748/head-start-performance-standards (accessed September 16, 2016).

68. Advisory Committee on Head Start Research and Evaluation, "Final Report," https://www.acf.hhs.gov/sites/default/files/opre/eval_final.pdf (accessed September 16, 2016).

69. Ibid.

70. Administration for Children and Families, "Head Start Performance Standards," https://www.federalregister.gov/documents/2016/09/06/2016-19748/head-start-performance-standards (accessed September 16, 2016).

71. Martha Zaslow et al., "Quality Dosage, Thresholds, and Features in Early Childhood Settings: A Review of the Literature," OPRE 2011-5 (Washington, D.C.: Office of Planning, Research and Evaluation, Administration for Children and Families, U.S. Department of Health and Human Services).

72. The Committee Management Secretariat of the U.S. General Services Administration maintains an online database pertaining to advisory committees, http://www.gsa.gov/portal/content/104514 (accessed March 6, 2007).

73. "Types of Federal Advisory Committees," http://www.facadatabase.gov/rpt/rptq02.asp? hdr=0 (accessed September 16, 2016).

74. Mark P. Petracca, "Federal Advisory Committees, Interest Groups, and the Administrative State," *Congress and the Presidency* 13 (Spring 1986): 83–114.

75. Steven J. Balla and John R. Wright, "Can Advisory Committees Facilitate Congressional Oversight of the Bureaucracy?" in *Congress on Display, Congress at Work,* ed. William T. Bianco (Ann Arbor: University of Michigan Press, 2000), 167–188.

76. Petracca, "Federal Advisory Committees, Interest Groups, and the Administrative State."

77. Jason Ross Arnold, "Has Obama Delivered the 'Most Transparent' Administration in History?" *Washington Post,* March 16, 2015, https://www.washingtonpost.com/blogs/monkey-cage/wp/2015/03/16/has-obama-delivered-the-most-transparent-administration-in-history/ (accessed September 16, 2016).

78. Josh Gerstein, "Judge Tosses Suit against Obama over Health Care Advice," *Politico,* March 15, 2013, http://www.politico.com/blogs/under-the-radar/2013/03/judge-tosses-suit-against-obama-over-health-care-advice-159420 (accessed September 16, 2016).

79. Ibid.

80. The Negotiated Rulemaking Act of 1996, https://www.acus.gov/sites/default/files/documents/Reg%20Neg%20Act%20of%201996_0.pdf (accessed September 16, 2016).

81. Lawrence Susskind and Gerard McMahon, "The Theory and Practice of Negotiated Rulemaking," *Yale Journal on Regulation* 3 (Fall 1985): 133–165.

82. Harter, "Negotiated Rulemaking."

83. Cary Coglianese, "Assessing Consensus: The Promise and Performance of Negotiated Rulemaking," *Duke Law Journal* 46 (April 1997): 1255–1349.

84. Steven J. Balla and John R. Wright, "Consensual Rule Making and the Time It Takes to Develop Rules," in *Politics, Policy, and Organizations: Frontiers in the Scientific Study of the Bureaucracy,* ed. George A. Krause and Kenneth J. Meier (Ann Arbor: University of Michigan Press, 2003), 187–206.

85. Reeve T. Bull, "The Federal Advisory Committee Act: Issues and Proposed Reforms," September 12, 2011, https://www.acus.gov/sites/default/files/documents/COCG-Reeve-Bull-Draft-FACA-Report-9-12-11.pdf (accessed September 16, 2016).

86. Laura I. Langbein and Cornelius M. Kerwin, "Regulatory Negotiation versus Conventional Rule Making: Claims, Counterclaims, and Empirical Evidence," *Journal of Public Administration Research and Theory* 10 (July 2000): 599–632.

87. Coglianese, "Assessing Consensus."

88. U.S. Department of Transportation, Federal Railroad Administration, "Use of Locomotive Horns at Highway-Rail Grade Crossings," *Federal Register,* March 22, 2000, 15298; Mark H. Tessler, Federal Railroad Administration, interview by Balla, March 11, 2002.

89. U.S. Department of Transportation, Federal Railroad Administration, "Use of Locomotive Horns at Highway-Rail Grade Crossings," *Federal Register,* January 13, 2000, 2229.

90. Railton Roy, letter to U.S. Department of Transportation, January 20, 2000, http://dmses.dot.gov/docimages/pdf42/70969_web.pdf.

91. U.S. Department of Transportation, Federal Railroad Administration, "Use of Locomotive Horns at Highway-Rail Grade Crossings," *Federal Register,* December 18, 2003, 70586–70687.

92. Michael Grunwald, "Growing Pains in Southwest Florida," *Washington Post,* June 25, 2002.

93. Ibid. See also "Explore FGCU: Historical Perspective," Florida Gulf Coast University, http://www.fgcu.edu/info/HistoricalPerspective.asp (accessed August 6, 2011).

94. Roger Faith, Donald Leavens, and Robert Tollison, "Antitrust Pork Barrel," *Journal of Law and Economics* 25 (October 1982): 329–342.

95. John Scholz and Feng Heng Wei, "Regulatory Enforcement in a Federalist System," *American Political Science Review* 80 (December 1986): 1249–1270.

96. Eric Katz, "Congress Intervenes to Fix Hiring Regs Written by 'Entrenched Bureaucrats' at OPM," (accessed September 19, 2016).

97. Ibid.

98. Ibid.

99. Ibid.

100. Bill McKibben, "A Pipeline Fight and America's Dark Past," *The New Yorker,* September 6, 2016.

101. James McPherson, "Pipeline Protesters Vow to Stay Camped on Federal Land," *Washington Post,* November 26, 2016; Editorial, "The False Victory at Standing Rock," *Washington Post,* December 7, 2016, p. 18.

102. Julie Turkewitz, "Army Approves Construction of Dakota Access Pipeline," *New York Times,* February 7, 2017.

103. Consumer Financial Protection Bureau, "CFPB Considers Debt Collection Rules," http://www.consumerfinance.gov/about-us/newsroom/cfpb-considers-debt-collection-rules/ (accessed September 19, 2016).

104. Consumer Financial Protection Bureau, "Debt Collection (Regulation F)," http://files.consumerfinance.gov/f/201311_cfpb_anpr_debtcollection.pdf (accessed September 19, 2016).

105. Regulation Room, "Overview," http://regulationroom.org/about/overview (accessed September 19, 2016).

106. Regulation Room, "Consumer Debt Collection Practices," http://regulationroom.org/rules/consumer-debt-collection-practices-anprm (accessed September 19, 2016).

107. Regulation Room, http://regulationroom.org/rules/consumer-debt-collection-practices/discussion/questions-about-email-texting-social-media-debt#nid-197 (accessed September 19, 2016).

108. Consumer Financial Protection Bureau, "Debt Collection (Regulation F)," http://files.consumerfinance.gov/f/201311_cfpb_anpr_debtcollection.pdf (accessed September 19, 2016).

109. Cary Coglianese, "E-Rulemaking: Information Technology and the Regulatory Process," *Administrative Law Review* 56 (2004): 353–402.

110. Stephen M. Johnson, "The Internet Changes Everything: Revolutionizing Public Participation and Access to Government Information through the Internet," *Administrative Law Review* 50 (Spring 1998): 277–337.

111. Kevin A. Hill and John E. Hughes, *Cyberpolitics: Citizen Activism in the Age of the Internet* (Lanham, Md.: Rowman and Littlefield, 1998); Elaine Ciulla Kamarck and Joseph S. Nye, eds., *Democracy.com? Governance in a Networked World* (Hollis, N.H.: Hollis, 1999); Michael Margolis and David Resnick, *Politics as Usual: The Cyberspace "Revolution"* (Thousand Oaks, Calif.: Sage, 2000).

112. Peter M. Shane, *Democracy Online: The Prospects for Political Renewal through the Internet* (New York: Routledge, 2004).

113. Darrell M. West, *Digital Government: Technology and Public Sector Performance* (Princeton, N.J.: Princeton University Press, 2005).

114. USA.gov, "A–Z Index of U.S. Government Departments and Agencies," https://www.usa.gov/federal-agencies/a (accessed September 21, 2016).

115. Paul Ausick, "The 10 Most Popular Government Websites," 24/7 Wall St., April 8, 2015, http://247wallst.com/technology-3/2014/04/08/the-10-most-popular-government-websites/ (accessed September 21, 2016).

116. Rebecca R. Ruiz, "A Real-Time Peek at Traffic to U.S. Government Websites," *New York Times*, March 20, 2015, http://bits.blogs.nytimes.com/2015/03/20/government-website-analytics/?_r=0 (accessed September 21, 2016).

117. Heather Kerrigan, "19 of the Coolest Government Mobile Apps," Govloop, March 18, 2015, https://www.govloop.com/community/blog/cool-gov-mobile-apps/ (accessed September 21, 2016).

118. Tom Fox, "Using Social Media for Your Agency," *Washington Post*, March 18, 2015, https://www.washingtonpost.com/news/on-leadership/wp/2015/03/18/using-social-media-for-your-federal-agency/ (accessed September 21, 2016).

119. Danielle Brigida, "State of Federal Blogging 2016," Digitalgov, January 15, 2016, https://www.digitalgov.gov/2016/01/15/state-of-federal-blogging-2016/ (accessed September 21, 2016).

120. U.S. Department of the Interior, "Social Media Policy," https://www.doi.gov/notices/Social-Media-Policy (accessed September 21, 2016).

121. Lauren Girardin, "5 Website Best Practices from the 2015 Center for Digital Government Award Winners," Govloop, September 9, 2015, https://www.govloop.com/community/blog/5-website-best-practices-2015-center-digital-government-award-winners/ (accessed September 21, 2016).

122. Ibid.

123. Andrew Perrin and Maeve Duggan, "Americans' Internet Access: 2000–2015," Pew Research Center, June 26, 2015, http://www.pewinternet.org/2015/06/26/americans-internet-access-2000-2015/ (accessed September 21, 2016).

124. Lauren Girardin, "5 Website Best Practices from the 2015 Center for Digital Government Award Winners," Govloop, September 9, 2015, https://www.govloop.com/community/blog/5-website-best-practices-2015-center-digital-government-award-winners/ (accessed September 21, 2016).

125. "Federal Rulemaking: Agencies' Use of Information Technology to Facilitate Public Participation," U.S. General Accounting Office, June 30, 2000, www.gao.gov.

126. Balla and Daniels, "Information Technology and Public Commenting on Agency Regulations."

127. Steven J. Balla, "Public Commenting on Federal Agency Regulations: Research on Current Practices and Recommendations to the Administrative Conference of the United States," March 15, 2011, https://www.acus.gov/sites/default/files/documents/Consolidated-Reports-+-Memoranda.pdf (accessed September 21, 2016).

128. Steven J. Balla, "Procedural Control, Bureaucratic Discretion, and Public Commenting on Agency Regulations," *Public Administration* 93 (2015): 524–538.

129. Ibid.

130. Alan Sipress, "Open Call from the Patent Office; Agency Web Site Will Solicit Advice," Washington Post, March 5, 2007.

131. Ibid.

132. Ibid.

133. James Loiselle, Michael Lynch, and Michael Sherrerd, "Evaluation of the Peer to Patent Pilot Program," https://web.wpi.edu/Pubs/E-project/Available/E-project-122109-150816/unrestricted/usptofinalreport.pdf (accessed September 21, 2016).

134. United States Patent and Trademark Office, "USPTO Launches Second Peer to Patent Pilot in Collaboration with New York Law School," http://www.uspto.gov/about-us/news-updates/uspto-launches-second-peer-patent-pilot-collaboration-new-york-law-school (accessed September 21, 2016).

135. http://regulationroom.org/ (accessed on September 21, 2016).

136. Jane E. Fountain, *Building the Virtual State: Information Technology and Institutional Change* (Washington, D.C.: Brookings Institution Press, 2001).

137. Jonathan Rauch, *Demosclerosis: The Silent Killer of American Government* (New York: Times Books, 1994).

138. Jeffrey H. Birnbaum, "Washington's Power 25: Which Pressure Groups Are Best at Manipulating the Laws We Live By? A Groundbreaking Fortune Survey Reveals Who Belongs to Lobbying's Elite and Why They Wield So Much Clout," CNNMoney.com, December 8, 1997, http://money.cnn.com/magazines/fortune/fortune_archive/1997/12/08/234927/index.htm (accessed September 21, 2016); Michelle Leach, "10 Most Powerful Special Interest Groups in America," http://listosaur.com/politics/10-powerful-special-interest-groups-america/ (accessed September 21, 2016); Erik Sherman, "Top 10 Lobbyists Spend $64M on Congress and Agencies in 3 Months," *Forbes*, April 22, 2015, http://www.forbes.com/sites/eriksherman/2015/04/22/top-10-lobbyists-spend-64m-on-congress-and-agencies-in-3-months/#6ccbe30ac7d3 (accessed September 21, 2016).

139. Scott Hovanyetz, "FTC: No Campaign to Promote National DNC List," dmNews.com, www.dmnews.com/cms/dm-news/teleservices/20155.html, March 5, 2007.

140. Wilson, *Bureaucracy.*

141. Joel Aberbach and Bert Rockman, *In the Web of Politics: Three Decades of the U.S. Federal Executive* (Washington, D.C.: Brookings Institution Press, 2000).

142. C. Edward Lindblom, *Politics and Markets* (New York: Basic Books, 1977), 5.

143. Jason Webb Yackee and Susan Webb Yackee, "A Bias toward Business? Assessing Business Group Influence on the U.S. Bureaucracy," *Journal of Politics* 68 (February 2006): 128–139.

144. Ibid.

145. Bloomberg Businessweek, "The 'Anti-Business' President Who's Been Good for Business," http://www.bloomberg.com/features/2016-obama-anti-business-president/ (accessed September 21, 2016).

146. Dan Froomkin, "Cass Sunstein: The Obama Administration's Ambivalent Regulator," *Huffington Post,* June 13, 2011, http://www.huffingtonpost.com/2011/06/13/cass-sunstein-obama-ambivalent-regulator-czar_n_874530.html (accessed September 21, 2016).

147. William T. Gormley Jr., "A Test of the Revolving Door Hypothesis at the FCC," *American Journal of Political Science* 23 (November 1979): 665–683.

148. Judith Layzer, *The Environmental Case: Translating Values into Policy* (Washington, D.C.: CQ Press, 2002).

149. Ibid., 308.

150. Maureen Cropper, "The Determinants of Pesticide Regulation," *Journal of Political Economy* 100 (February 1992): 175–197.

151. William T. Gormley Jr., *The Politics of Public Utility Regulation* (Pittsburgh: University of Pittsburgh Press, 1983).

152. Evan Ringquist, *Environmental Protection at the State Level* (Armonk, N.Y.: M. E. Sharpe, 1993).

153. Finley Peter Dunne, as quoted in Bill Kovach and Tom Rosenstiel, "Are Watchdogs an Endangered Species?" *Columbia Journalism Review* 40 (May/June 2001): 50.

154. Layzer, *Environmental Case,* 107.

155. Paul Sabatier, John Loomis, and Catherine McCarthy, "Hierarchical Controls, Professional Norms, Local Constituencies, and Budget Maximization: An Analysis of U.S. Forest Service Planning Decisions," *American Journal of Political Science* 39 (February 1995): 204–242.

156. David A. Graham, "The Politics of Obama's Greenhouse-Gas Rule," *The Atlantic,* August 3, 2015, http://www.theatlantic.com/politics/archive/2015/08/obama-greenhouse-gas-rule/400382/ (accessed September 21, 2016).

157. Joshua D. Clinton and David E. Lewis, "Expert Opinion, Agency Characteristics and Agency Preferences," *Political Analysis* 16 (2008): 3–20.

158. Sally Cohen, *Championing Child Care* (New York: Columbia University Press, 2001).

159. Ibid.

160. U.S. Department of Health and Human Services, "Obama Administration Announces $500 Million for Race to the Top—Early Learning Challenge," news release, Washington, D.C., May 25, 2011, http://www.hhs.gov/news/press/2011pres/05/20110525a.html.

161. Anne Camissa, *Governments as Interest Groups: Intergovernmental Lobbying and the Federal System* (Westport, Conn.: Praeger, 1995).

162. Helen Boutrous, "Presidential Influence and Regulatory Review" (PhD diss., Georgetown University, 2002), 123.

163. Committee Management Secretariat of the U.S. General Services Administration online database, http://www.gsa.gov/portal/content/104514 (accessed March 6, 2007).

164. William T. Gormley Jr., "Money and Mandates: The Politics of Intergovernmental Conflict," *Publius: The Journal of Federalism* 36 (Fall 2006): 523–540.

165. William Gormley Jr., "An Evolutionary Approach to Federalism in the U.S." (paper presented at the annual meeting of the American Political Science Association, San Francisco, August 31, 2001).

166. Gormley, "Money and Mandates," 523–540.

167. U.S. Department of Education, "ESEA Flexibility," http://www2.ed.gov/policy/elsec/guid/esea-flexibility/index.html (accessed September 21, 2016).

168. Cathleen Willging, Rafael Semansky, and Howard Waitzkin, "New Mexico's Medicaid Managed Care Waiver: Organizing Input from Mental Health Consumers and Advocates," *Psychiatric Services* 54 (March 2003): 289–291.

169. E. E. Schattschneider, *The Semi-Sovereign People* (New York: Holt, Rinehart, and Winston, 1960).

170. Henry Eichel, "Appeals Court Bars Blockade of Plutonium," *Charlotte Observer*, August 7, 2002.

171. David Firestone, "South Carolina Battles U.S. on Plutonium," *New York Times*, April 12, 2002.

172. Steven J. Balla, "Administrative Procedures and Political Control of the Bureaucracy," *American Political Science Review* 92 (September 1998): 663–673.

5 | Bureaucratic Networks

On September 28, 2016, the Centers for Medicare and Medicaid Services (CMS) issued a regulation prohibiting nursing homes that receive federal funding from requiring residents to resolve complaints via arbitration rather than in court.[1] This regulation, which applies to about 1.5 million nursing home residents, is designed to prevent what happened after a woman with Alzheimer's disease was sexually assaulted by residents at a nursing home in Lemon Grove, California. Family members seeking to sue the nursing home in court were denied that opportunity due to an arbitration clause that had been signed when the woman was admitted.[2] Arbitration is less costly than going to court, and the nursing home industry has warned that banning the ban on litigation will drive up costs and potentially drive facilities out of business.

The nursing home in Lemon Grove is not operated by the federal government. In fact, government agencies directly run only about 5 percent of the nation's nursing homes. For-profit firms operate the overwhelming majority of nursing homes, with nonprofit organizations running most of the rest.[3] Although government agencies seldom operate nursing homes themselves, they are intimately involved in funding, licensing, and monitoring nursing homes. In addition to funding nursing homes that care for Medicare and Medicaid clients, CMS oversees the licensing of facilities by state human services agencies. Statutes require regular site visits by state officials, with intermittent visits carried out by federal regulators.

All of these organizations—federal and state agencies, for-profit firms, and nonprofit organizations—belong, in effect, to a **network,** an interorganizational structure in which "one unit is not merely the formal subordinate of the others in some larger hierarchical arrangement."[4] This nursing home network has no official name and is sometimes even hard to detect. Other members of the network include state ombudsman offices representing nursing home patients, trade associations representing nursing homes, and citizen groups representing clients and loved ones.

These arrangements typify what has been called the **hollow state.**[5] Instead of directly delivering policies and services through hierarchical arrangements, government bureaucracies frequently finance and scrutinize the delivery of such outputs by other organizations. This phenomenon, known as contracting out, originated in "hard services" such as road repair, but it has spread over time to other areas, including education, health, and weapons acquisition. Contracting out is one element of a broader trend toward **privatization** of public services.[6]

One way to view contracting out is through the lens of principal-agent theory. Take, for example, the Manor Care nursing home in Bethesda, Maryland. Just as CMS is a bureaucratic agent of Congress and the president, so too is Manor Care an agent of the state and federal governments. Contracts specify Manor Care's obligations to each of these principals. As demonstrated by the prohibition of an arbitration-only rule, government entities have leverage over Manor Care, and other for-profit and nonprofit nursing homes, because of their ability to take actions such as withholding funds and accelerating regulatory enforcement. As predicted by principal-agent theory, monitoring is a constant challenge—and agency loss, evidenced by the fact that in 2007, some 17 percent of nursing homes were cited for violations causing "actual harm or immediate jeopardy" to patients, is an inevitable result.[7]

Yet principal-agent theory may not be the best way to think about the politics of nursing home policy. Consider, for example, the relationship between the federal and state agencies that regulate nursing homes. In the federal system, this relationship is not truly hierarchical. Although the federal government can tell the state of Maryland how to spend federal Medicare dollars, it does not enjoy the same degree of leverage when federal funding is not involved. When it comes to the Medicaid program, the federal government often treats states with kid gloves for fear of stifling innovation or provoking a negative political reaction.

Furthermore, Manor Care is more than just an agent of the state of Maryland and the federal government. As a for-profit firm, Manor Care has obligations to its shareholders and customers that may not coincide with the views of government agencies. Complicating matters even more is the fact that Manor Care in Bethesda is part of a nationwide chain of nursing homes. Although one might treat nursing home politics as a case involving multiple principals, such an approach does not adequately account for relationships that are not easily portrayed in hierarchical terms.

Ultimately, it may be more useful to apply network-based approaches to nursing homes and the agencies that occupy such a prominent place in the delivery of nursing home care. A network approach has several advantages. First, it encompasses both hierarchical and nonhierarchical relationships. Second, it measures information flows, which need to be modeled and documented if complex relationships among organizations are to be understood. Third, it recognizes the extent of interorganizational bargaining that occurs not just over programmatic details but also, more fundamentally, over the goals of programs themselves. Organizations belonging to networks have their own goals, which they can pursue and promote to a greater degree than is typically possible for agents in hierarchies. Fourth, a network approach highlights problems of accountability as policymaking and implementation shift from hierarchical organizational forms to more fluid and complex kinds of relationships.

This chapter focuses on networks that include bureaucracies—how such networks function, how they are changing, and how they might be changed to become more accountable and to improve their performance. The following are the *core questions* explored in the chapter:

- *HOW DO FEDERAL AGENCIES RELATE TO STATE AND LOCAL GOVERNMENT AGENCIES AND WITH WHAT RESULTS?* Many policy areas, such as the environment and health care, historically have been intergovernmental in character. In recent years, other policy areas, such as education, which was not all that long ago regarded as the province of local governments, have become increasingly intergovernmental.

- *WHAT ARE THE ESSENTIAL FEATURES AND KEY CHALLENGES OF PUBLIC-PRIVATE PARTNERSHIPS, SUCH AS CONTRACTING OUT?* For many years, public-private partnerships have marked such fields as trash collection and economic development. Recently, such arrangements have arisen and spread in areas of social and defense policy, at times sparking considerable controversy.

- *HOW DO BUREAUCRACIES COORDINATE WITH OTHER BUREAUCRACIES?* Interagency task forces and cabinet meetings are among the traditional venues through which agencies coordinate with one another. Recent presidents have appointed "czars" to manage such complex issues as energy policy, drug policy, homeland security, and the recovery of the automobile industry. These approaches to network governance have produced notably mixed results.

As detailed below, the chapter addresses these core questions from the perspective of **network theory** and the **tools approach.** Broadly speaking, the concepts described in the chapter are applied to the challenges of accountability and to the question of whether networks alleviate or aggravate these challenges. The concepts are also used to evaluate the tools of government in terms of the potential that networks have in helping, or hindering, the performance of government bureaucracies.

Networks versus Hierarchies

A network is an institution linking persons or organizations. **Interorganizational networks** are of particular interest when considering government bureaucracies. As long as two or more organizations are involved and the relationship between these organizations is not strictly hierarchical, a network of organizations exists. The purposes of such relationships can be multifold— advocacy, information sharing, joint decision making, or some combination of these and other goals.

What is the relative prevalence of networks and hierarchical arrangements? Research suggests that managers in public bureaucracies spend the overwhelming majority of their time working within a hierarchy. Managers spend only 15 to 20 percent of their time collaborating, and even less time specifically collaborating within a network.[8] From this perspective, networks have not displaced hierarchies, although the importance of networks appears to be growing.[9]

From a different vantage point, networks may have already surpassed hierarchies as institutional mechanisms for formulating and implementing public policy. In the 1960s, about one-third of laws enacted by Congress stipulated the involvement of more than one federal agency in the implementation process. By the 1990s, this multiple agency requirement characterized more than half of Congress's actions.[10] In addition, statutes routinely empower not just federal agencies, but state and local governments and nongovernmental actors such as business firms and nonprofit organizations as well.[11] The end result of these legislative decisions are arrangements that require "participation by individuals ensconced in different organizational cultures, influenced by different sets of incentives, often reporting to different oversight committees in Congress, and directed toward somewhat different organizational objectives."[12]

Network Theory

Network theory consists of a set of concepts designed to explicate relationships that cannot be fully described in hierarchical terms. As such, network theory operates as a conceptual alternative to principal-agent theory. In some intergovernmental networks, a state government may be an agent of the federal government on one issue and a "free agent" on another. Within a cabinet-level department, one unit may deliver services directly (a principal-agent relationship), while another unit delivers services through a variety of for-profit and nonprofit contractors (a network).

Whereas principal-agent theory originated in economics, network theory traces its origins to sociology, where it has highlighted the importance of **weak ties** between persons in social networks.[13] Research demonstrates that weak ties (think, for example, of the vast majority of Facebook friends) are primary sources for new ideas and information, much more so than **strong ties** (close friends, generally speaking, are most distinctively important when it comes to offering serious favors and support).[14] Network theory has also provided insight into how organizations share information.[15] For example, networks can serve as vehicles for reducing **substantive uncertainty**, a form of uncertainty caused by insufficient information about the content of vexing economic and social problems.[16] Networks can also help to manage **strategic uncertainty** (not knowing how other actors will respond to problems) and **institutional uncertainty** (a lack of knowledge about the rules of the game in which actors are operating).[17]

Unlike principal-agent theory, which treats the goals of principals as given and relatively fixed, network theory views goals as somewhat fluid. Although each organization affiliated with a network undoubtedly has its own goals, the goals of the network itself can evolve over time through a process of give-and-take.[18] Given that a network's goals can be more tentative and dynamic than those of an organization, and given that a network's stakeholders can be more numerous than those of a single organization, it is often rather difficult to evaluate, and in some instances even to define, the success of a network.[19]

Network theory draws attention to a number of key concepts, including centrality, density, size, complexity, multiplexity, and differentiation. **Centrality** is the degree to which network information flows through a single individual or organization, strategically situated to serve a clearinghouse function. **Density** is the number of actual connections among individuals or organizations divided by the number of potential connections within the network.[20] **Size** is the number of persons or organizations that participate in the work of the network. **Complexity** is the number of different service or product sectors represented by individual and organizational network members.[21] **Multiplexity** is the number of separate relationships between pairs of network actors (for example, two mental health agencies might be linked through referrals, service contracts, and information sharing).[22] **Differentiation** is the degree to which there is functional and service specialization among individual and organizational network members.[23] As depicted in Figure 5.1, these concepts are useful in delineating basic network structures, such as the distinctions between centralized and decentralized networks and between high-density and low-density networks.

Figure 5.1 Networks with Different Characteristics

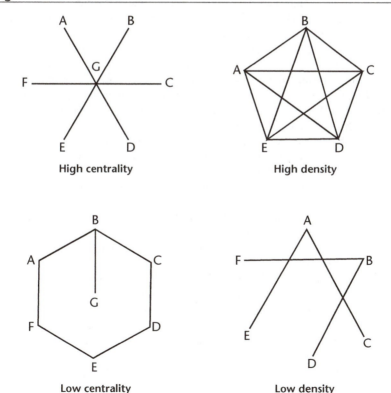

High centrality

High density

Low centrality

Low density

To what extent is there overlap between these different aspects of network structures? Evidence suggests that there is a positive relationship between size and centrality, in that larger networks find it desirable or necessary to route communications through one organization or subunit. It is also the case that larger networks are relatively complex and differentiated. Larger networks, however, are less dense than their smaller counterparts.[24] Interestingly, centrality and density are inversely related. In other words, the presence of a dominant individual or organization discourages connections between other network actors.

A key premise of network theory is that dense networks have advantages over other types of networks, because they facilitate information sharing. In an ingenious test of this hypothesis, researchers devised an experiment in which subjects had to piece together clues or facts, as in the game of Clue, to "connect the dots."[25] The researchers varied the structure of the networks in which individuals participated. The experiment revealed, as expected, that "dense clustering" encouraged individuals to share new information. The experiment also demonstrated, however, that individuals in more densely clustered networks were less likely to propose new theories or ideas. The researchers concluded that dense clustering has positive effects on the search for information but negative effects on the search for solutions. These results suggest that densely clustered networks may be well suited to make routine decisions but not to resolve more difficult problems that require analysts to think outside the box.

Although network theory is general in its orientation, the theory's concepts can be especially useful in particular fields. In law enforcement, for example, the relative centrality of individuals in crime networks can help investigators determine on whom to target their efforts. Another important concept in law enforcement is **equivalence**: "The disruptive effectiveness of removing one individual or a set of individuals from a network depends not only on their centrality, but also upon some notion of their uniqueness. The more unique, or unusual, their role the harder they will be to replace. The most valuable targets will be both central and difficult to replace."[26] The concept of weak ties can also be instructive in alerting investigators to the utility of focusing attention on communication channels that are seldom used but indispensable to the network's operation. A criminal's chance encounter with an old acquaintance may lead to a burglary or some other type of illegal activity. A law enforcement officer's conversation with a casual acquaintance may provide information that is pivotal in leading to a major arrest.

In the years following the September 11, 2001, terrorist attacks, much attention has been paid to understanding the nature of terrorist networks. For example, al-Qaida's internal connections are characterized by extraordinarily low density, with few communications links among conspirators. Generally speaking, "covert networks trade efficiency for secrecy."[27] Given the absence of "moment-to-moment top-down management" within al-Qaida, it appears that leadership (that is, centrality) is essential at the planning stages "but may not be critical for the maintenance of the terrorist activity."[28]

In fighting al-Qaida, U.S. military officials resolved that their best strategy was to mimic the organization's own tactics, especially its trademark preference for the network form. Beginning in 2006, when the United States launched raids against al-Qaida leaders in Iraq, Yemen, and Afghanistan, the military shared intelligence directly with combat troops rather than through the chain of command. This resulted in a sharp increase in the number of raids and in their success rate as well. As Army general Stanley McChrystal put it, "To defeat a networked enemy, we had to become a network ourselves."[29]

But not all terrorist organizations are created equal. The Islamic State, or ISIS, primarily focuses not on attacking the West, but rather on controlling territory in Syria and Iraq.[30] This goal has organizational implications. Despite its localized focus, ISIS has mobilized "lone wolf" attacks in Europe and North America. Such attacks are often perpetrated by individuals who, although inspired by ISIS's ideology and methods, have had little or no contact with ISIS as an organization.[31] Given ISIS's territorial ambitions, the organization operates not merely as a series of loose networks, in the mold of al-Qaida. ISIS has created a "structured institution with a defined power structure" similar to that of a government.[32] This structure includes administrative networks that provide basic services such as education and law enforcement.[33] Under the leadership of Abu Bakr al-Baghdadi, there are cabinet officials as well as provincial governors.[34] ISIS, in other words, combines elements of both hierarchical and networked arrangements.

In sum, network theory provides a means of thinking systematically about the operation of bureaucracy in the context of institutional environments that deviate from purely hierarchical arrangements. Network theory is grounded in concepts, such as size, centrality, and density, that are of great use in differentiating networks from one another. As will become apparent in subsequent sections of the chapter, network theory offers insights into bureaucratic accountability and performance that are distinct from those generated by principal-agent theory and other perspectives on organizational decision making.

The Tools Approach

Another line of inquiry into the operation of networked arrangements is the tools approach. The essence of this approach is an understanding that the choice of a particular policy instrument (for example, regulation, information provision, market competition) typically implies the choice of a particular network or combination of organizations. As a result, network accountability and performance depend not only on the organizational characteristics of the networks themselves but also on the characteristics of the policy tools that undergird networked arrangements.

Policy tools vary in several key respects, including coerciveness, directness, automaticity, and visibility.[35] **Coerciveness** is the degree to which tools compel certain forms of behavior, as opposed to merely encouraging specific actions. **Directness** is the extent to which organizations that authorize, finance, or commence activities actually carry out these activities. **Automaticity** is the extent to which tools rely on existing organizational structures, as opposed to creating new arrangements. **Visibility** is the degree to which resources devoted to tools are featured prominently in budget and review processes.[36]

With these attributes in mind, it is possible to categorize a wide variety of policy tools, such as grants, loans, vouchers, regulation, information provision, and voluntary compliance programs. For example, regulation tends to be high in coerciveness and directness, and low in visibility. In contrast, vouchers tend to be low in directness and high in automaticity and visibility.[37] When public officials favor vouchers over regulation, such decisions about policy tools inevitably advance one set of networked arrangements over alternative organizational forms. In the case of school vouchers, the resulting networks are likely to be decentralized and differentiated, with schools striving to establish distinctive market niches. The success or failure of such networks in no small part depends on the attributes of the vouchers themselves. The high visibility of voucher programs, for example, increases the likelihood that such programs will be controversial. The low directness of vouchers as policy tools fuels demands for systematic evaluations of the accountability and performance of voucher programs.

The tools approach provides a framework for understanding contracting out and the phenomenon of **third-party government,** which occurs when public officials turn to third parties to deliver public services.[38] Third parties include banks, schools, hospitals, day care centers, and other levels of government. In third-party government, the tools utilized to deliver public services are not as direct as in traditional public sector arrangements. Such indirectness emphasizes the importance of looking at the relationships between organizations (that is, the inner workings of networks). Indirectness also draws attention to the extent to which networks help or hinder the process of holding service-delivery organizations accountable for their results.

Third-party government involves at least five different kinds of accountability challenges.[39] First, federal goals are sometimes diverted or compromised because state and local officials do not support these goals. Second, state and local governments often receive fiscal windfalls, with the federal government supporting programs that recipient governments would otherwise have funded themselves. Third, federal support, through insurance and loan guarantee programs, creates moral hazard problems, encouraging third parties to take risks they would not otherwise entertain. Fourth, third parties frequently lack fiscal incentives to avoid waste, fraud, and abuse, as the money is not theirs and they do not benefit from the correction of such problems. Fifth, third-party subsidies can encourage opportunistic behavior by organizations seeking to enhance their profits or, in the case of nonprofit organizations, to increase the size of their customer bases.

To return to the politics of nursing home policy, who is to be blamed if patients at a particular facility are discovered with bedsores and dirty linens? Is it the owner of the facility? If the nursing home is part of a nationwide chain, is it the organization that operates the chain? Is it the state agency that failed to protect the nursing home's residents? Is it the federal agency that did not engage in adequate oversight of the state agency under its jurisdiction? Is it the ombudsman whose intervention was too little, too late? In hierarchical arrangements, it can be at times, though certainly not always, relatively easy to affix blame. In the immortal words of Harry S. Truman, "The buck stops here!" By contrast, accountability can be especially difficult to establish in networks characterized by public and private partners and federal and state officials.

Types of Bureaucratic Networks

Three types of networks are of particular importance when considering public bureaucracy—intergovernmental relationships, public-private partnerships, and interagency coordination. Network theory and the tools approach are directly applicable to all three types of arrangements. In the sections that follow, we examine each of these types of networks, their accountability challenges, and their performance as institutions of policymaking and implementation.

Intergovernmental Relationships

Intergovernmental networks are commonplace in the American system of federalism. Many public policies involve shared decision making on the part of federal, state, and local governments. There are three primary tools that serve as sources of intergovernmental networks. First, Congress assigns responsibility for programs to federal agencies, which in turn delegate authority to state and local governments. This instrument is known as **devolution.** Second, Congress explicitly **mandates** that states and localities implement programs and perform other tasks. Third, Congress appropriates **grants-in-aid**—funds accompanied by requirements that are oriented toward enticing lower levels of government to participate in specific programs.[40] In 2015, grants-in-aid accounted for $648 billion, one-sixth of the federal budget, in such wide-ranging areas as road construction, rural housing, job training, and childhood obesity.[41]

Environmental Protection. Following the passage of a slew of major federal environmental laws in the 1970s, the Environmental Protection Agency (EPA) found it difficult to implement the resulting statutory mandates on its own. At the same time, state governments were pleading with federal officials for greater flexibility in carrying out legal requirements. Specifically, state officials argued that their familiarity with the geographic, topological, economic, and political circumstances of their jurisdictions make them especially well-suited to design and oversee environmental programs. In response to these developments, the EPA devolved considerable authority to state-level decision makers in a number of areas of environmental protection. In the language of network theory, intergovernmental networks decreased in their centrality. As Table 5.1 demonstrates, the end result of this devolution is that, by 2010, two-thirds of states had taken command of the environmental programs that can in principle be delegated to them.

Table 5.1 Number of States Authorized to Run Environmental Programs

Program	Number of States by Delegation Status[1]	
	Fully delegated[2]	Partial delegation[3]
Clean Air Act (CAA)		
New Source Performance Standards (NSPS)	41	9
National Emission Standards for Hazardous Air Pollutants (NESHAP)	38	12
Prevention of Significant Deterioration (PSD)	47	3
Operating Permits (Title V)	39	2
New Source Review (NSR)	44	1
Clean Water Act (CWA)		
Construction Grants	43	0
National Pollution Discharge Elimination System (NPDES)	42	3
Publicly Owned Treatment Works (POTWs)	35	1
Sludge Management	7	4
State Revolving Fund (SRF)	26	0
Wetlands (Section 404)	2	0
Emergency Planning and Community Right to Know Act		
Section 313 Toxic Chemical Release Form	0	0
Section 304 and 312	0	0
Federal Insecticide, Fungicide, and Rodenticide Act (FIFRA)		
Section 23a (State Cooperation, Aid, and Training)	44	1
Section 23b (State Cooperation, Aid, and Training)	45	1
Endangered Species	26	1
Worker Protection	47	2
Groundwater Protection	27	3
Oil Pollution Act		
Prevention and Liability of Oil Spills	0	0

| Program | Number of States by Delegation Status[1] | |
	Fully delegated[2]	Partial delegation[3]
Resource Conservation and Recovery Act (RCRA)		
Hazardous Waste Base Program (subtitle C)	49	0
Hazardous Waste Corrective Action (subtitle C)	37	0
Mixed Waste (subtitle C)	40	1
Regulation of Burning of Hazardous Wastes in Boilers and Industrial Furnaces (BIF)	27	2
Toxicity Characteristics Revisions	41	0
Land Disposal Restrictions: California Wastes	41	0
Land Disposal Restrictions: 1/3 Wastes	39	0
Land Disposal Restrictions: 2/3 Wastes	32	0
Land Disposal Restrictions: 3/3 Wastes	32	2
Solid Waste (subtitle D)	32	3
Underground Storage Tanks (subtitle I)	39	1
Safe Drinking Water Act		
Public Water System Supervision (PWSS)	49	0
Wellhead Protection Program	41	0
Section 1422 Underground Injection Control (UIC)	34	0
Section 1425 UIC	36	1
Toxic Substances Control Act (TSCA)		
Model Accreditation Plan (training for workers)	23	4
The Asbestos Hazard Emergency Response Act (AHERA) Waiver	10	4
Indoor Radon (§306)	6	0

[1] We do not include interim status (pending EPA authorization) in our tallies.
[2] Includes programs that are authorized with an approved state program or a State Implementation Plan (SIP).
[3] Includes programs with partial authorization and approval.

Source: The Environmental Council of the States, "State Delegation of Environmental Acts," February 2016.

The flow of information between the federal government and state policymakers is an important consideration when programmatic authority is devolved to the states. It is incumbent upon the federal government to reduce institutional uncertainty by, for example, distinguishing minimum standards that states must uphold from other domains in which states are more or less free to set their own standards. As for states, they are typically required to furnish to the federal policymakers information about policy outputs and outcomes within their borders. Such information is useful in reducing substantive uncertainty, particularly with respect to evaluating program success in addressing underlying economic and social problems.

In 1995, to improve the quality of information transmitted through environmental networks, the EPA established a new policy tool, the **Performance Partnership Agreement** (PPA). Under this arrangement, states are given the option of negotiating agreements with EPA officials based in their region. These agreements "can range from general statements about how the state and EPA will work together as partners (perhaps identifying joint priorities that will be addressed) to comprehensive, multiprogram documents that detail each party's roles and responsibilities."[42] Frequently, PPAs grant states flexibility in administering federal environmental programs. In return, states agree to improve their environmental performance and to document these improvements in a thorough and transparent manner. Though voluntary, PPAs have been negotiated by twenty-eight states.[43] According to the EPA, "Nearly all of the PPAs cover air quality and water pollution control, and a large majority address enforcement, drinking water, hazardous waste, and underground storage tanks. About half cover wetlands, solid waste, toxic substances, pollution prevention, and environmental justice. Brownfields, pesticides, children's health, and Superfund are included in only about a third of the PPAs."[44]

The use of PPAs as policy instruments has received somewhat mixed reviews from outside observers.[45] On the one hand, state-level environmental performance measures are more widely used and more sophisticated than in years past. On the other hand, states typically continue to rely more on **output measures,** such as the number of inspections conducted, rather than on **outcome measures,** such as changes in air and water quality. Ultimately, outcomes are of greater importance than outputs as indicators of environment protection.

The state of Washington is an example of a jurisdiction that incorporates both output and outcome measures into its agreement.[46] In the area of air pollution, the state's Department of Ecology has committed to measuring compliance with its PPA through various outputs, such as using "listservs, e-mails, and web pages to inform the public about air monitoring results."[47] The agency has also committed to tracking outcomes, such as the number of times $PM_{2.5}$ or ozone exceeds healthy levels, the number of citizens exposed to pollution measurements above federal standards, and the extent to which visibility has improved in scenic parks and wilderness areas.[48] As an earlier version of the PPA acknowledged, the ability of the Department of Ecology to attain its output

Christine Todd Whitman
EPA Administrator
(2001–2003)

"Performance partnerships are really aimed at buy-in, and that of course is a key if you're trying to implement something. The problem you're always faced with with environmental regulations is every time you try to promulgate one you're causing someone to change behavior and spend money for problems they may not have made. When you get into performance partnership agreements you're trying to get buy-in from a wider constituency which will then allow you to move forward.... Overall it's been very helpful."

and outcome goals can be jeopardized by external events beyond its control. For example, the global financial crisis had far-reaching negative consequences for the state's budget: "Washington state, like most other states, is in the midst of unprecedented and severe budget short falls.... As such, it is highly possible that some of the activities and outputs will have to be adjusted."[49]

By definition, PPAs are dyadic relationships between the EPA and state environmental agencies. Other environmental networks and policy tools, by contrast, are regional in orientation. Regional initiatives focus on geographically broad concerns, such as improving the environmental quality of the Chesapeake Bay and the Great Lakes Basin. Evidence suggests that networks in both regions have achieved some successes, thanks to combinations of grants, coordination, technical assistance, and collective efforts to achieve uniform standards.[50] In the Chesapeake Bay, for example, many specific measures aimed at reducing nitrogen and phosphorous discharges have been undertaken. On the other hand, ambitious goals for improving water quality have not yet been reached.[51] Pennsylvania, in particular, has lagged behind both Virginia and Maryland in supporting vigorous clean-up efforts.[52] Perhaps this is because Pennsylvania's economy benefits less from Chesapeake Bay tourism. Such variation is also a reflection of the fact that there has historically not been an emphasis on the use of **coercive policy tools.** Although coercion appeals in principle to federal officials, efforts to compel desired forms of behavior at the state level are often counterproductive, especially when federal and state organizations do not hold basic goals and values in common.[53]

During the Obama administration, coercion came to play a bigger role in the cleanup of the Chesapeake Bay, thanks to an executive order issued by the president several months after taking office. Executive Order 13508 grants the EPA the authority to enforce pollution reduction goals if these goals cannot be achieved by states on their own.[54] The action was praised by some, including Maryland governor Martin O'Malley: "It's not just the enforcement that could be a help. It's a help in terms of their leadership and the dollars they bring to the table."[55] Other network actors objected to the federal government's centralization of authority. The American Farm Bureau Association as well as the attorneys general of twenty-one states filed a lawsuit against the administration. In ruling against the lawsuit, a district court judge acknowledged the federal government's centrality in the Chesapeake Bay policymaking network: "EPA's role is critical to coordinating the Bay Jurisdictions' efforts to ensure pollution reduction."[56] When this decision was appealed to the Supreme Court, the eight justices, conferencing for the first time after Antonin Scalia's death, declined to hear the case that was likely to result in a 4–4 split. A year later, the Trump administration proposed to eliminate funding for the EPA's Chesapeake Bay clean-up effort, in a nod to industrial farms, home builders, and municipalities that have sought to resist federal government mandates.[57]

In recent decades, federal and state agencies have formed hundreds of **watershed partnerships** in an effort to manage natural resources through voluntary cooperation. Such partnerships, which in some instances include third parties, reflect dissatisfaction with **command-and-control regulation** and other similar approaches to environmental protection. Partnerships have arisen most frequently in watersheds characterized by severe pollution from nonpoint sources (for example, agricultural and urban runoff) and relatively weak organized agricultural interests.[58] Partnerships have also commonly been instituted in high-income watersheds. In contrast, partnerships have for the most part not emerged in watersheds with large percentages of black and Hispanic residents.[59] Watershed partnerships therefore have not served as antidotes to concerns over environmental justice, although such arrangements may very well have contributed to environmental protection in general.

The Suwannee River Partnership, which originated in north-central Florida in the late 1990s, illustrates the potential, and limitations, of watershed partnerships as policy tools.[60] The partnership consists of a network of dozens of organizations, including the EPA, Florida Department of Agriculture and Consumer Service, Florida Farm Bureau, and the University of Florida.[61] The partnership was created to reduce nutrient discharges into watersheds when it appeared that command-and-control regulation might follow if a voluntary approach were not to succeed. Farmers participating in the partnership receive cost sharing of up to 75 percent when they pledge to adopt recommended best management practices in areas such as sod farming and manure application.[62] Within a few years of its creation, the partnership had signed up the vast majority of dairies, poultry farms, and crop farms in the Suwannee River basin.[63] Environmental groups, however, have historically been reluctant to join the partnership, fearing that their involvement might compromise lawsuits filed against the state Department of Environmental Protection.[64] This reluctance illustrates the tension that can exist when, as is not uncommon, both hierarchical arrangements (e.g., judicial actions) and networked approaches (e.g., partnerships) are utilized in the same area of public policy.

Health Policy. In addressing the health needs of the poor, the federal government has long relied on intergovernmental networks. The Medicaid program, established in 1965, sets up shared responsibility for funding the health care of Americans with limited income and resources. The federal government provides at least half of the funding, with state governments providing the rest under a formula that favors states with low per capita incomes. State Medicaid agencies determine eligibility standards and benefits, subject to federal rules and regulations. The networks that operate Medicaid typically include federal and state agencies as payers and physicians, hospitals, and nursing homes as payees.

During the administration of George H. W. Bush, the Health Care Financing Administration, the predecessor of CMS, was authorized to grant waivers to state governments in the area of Medicaid policy. Waivers provide states with relief from federal rules, thereby opening up opportunities for states to experiment with policy tools and network arrangements. For example, one of the first Medicaid waivers granted the state of Tennessee the authority to launch TennCare, a program that fundamentally transformed the organizational environment for both payers and payees.[65] The goal of the waiver was to expand health insurance to poor residents who had not previously been covered under Medicaid. This expansion was to be achieved in a budget-neutral manner through managed care practices, such as providing physicians and patients with incentives to select less costly forms of care, selectively contracting with providers, and intensely monitoring high-cost cases.[66] These practices were to be implemented through a competitive bidding process carried out by twelve newly created managed care organizations.[67]

TennCare is an example of kinds of institutional arrangements that can emerge under **1915(b) waivers,** the specific class of waivers that allow states to enroll Medicaid clients in managed care plans. The secretary of health and human services can also authorize **1115 waivers,** which allow states to exercise broad discretion in testing "policy innovations likely to further the objectives of the Medicaid program."[68] Both types of waivers have proven enormously popular with state policymakers. At the beginning of the Clinton administration, only one state (Arizona) had been granted an 1115 waiver.[69] By 2016, there were 509 Medicaid waivers in operation.[70] The vast majority of states, as well as the District of Columbia, now operate 1115 waivers, with a similar expansion having occurred over time in the utilization of 1915(b) waivers.[71]

One consequence of this trend toward waivers is that Medicaid networks have not only become more prevalent but have become more complex and differentiated as well. In 1997, many of these networks expanded further when Congress established the Children's Health Insurance Program (CHIP). The aim of CHIP is to provide health insurance to children in families with incomes that are "modest but too high to qualify for Medicaid."[72] CHIP, like Medicaid, is a shared federal–state program: the U.S. Department of Health and Human Services establishes basic requirements and contributes funds according to a formula, and state governments determine program specifics and provide the remainder of the resources. In implementing CHIP, states have chosen to utilize

"There are enormous partnerships in adoption. Many states, including New York, long ago made a decision to involve private charity agencies in adoption. Our major partnerships at HHS were with HMOs. More generally, we increased contracting out to social service organizations."

a number of different types of policy tools. Fifteen states have created children's health programs that are completely separate from Medicaid. Seven states and the District of Columbia have fully incorporated CHIP into their existing Medicaid programs. Finally, twenty-eight states have adopted hybrid programs that bring together elements of both of these approaches.[73]

Regardless of the policy tools that are utilized, it is not uncommon for coordination issues to arise across Medicaid and CHIP networks. Federal contributions to children enrolled in CHIP are more generous than are those for Medicaid beneficiaries. Seeking to take advantage of this generosity, some states have enrolled in their CHIP programs children who are actually eligible for Medicaid. Such behavior not only exemplifies poor coordination, but it is also illegal. Over time, in part because of pressure from the federal government, states have become better at assigning children to the appropriate program.

Additional assignment problems remain, however. One such problem is "**churning**" between the Medicaid and CHIP programs. Because of changes in parental employment, income, and other related factors, children eligible for CHIP sometimes become eligible for Medicaid. Movement in the reverse direction also happens.[74] This phenomenon makes it imperative that Medicaid and CHIP networks work closely with one another. If such coordination occurs, children and their families are likely to enjoy smooth transitions from one program to the other. In contrast, coordination failures can lead to the interruption of medical services and, ultimately, to harmful consequences for the health of needy children.

The Affordable Care Act generated new tensions between the federal government and the states over health policy. Many states expressed concern over federal mandates, increased caseloads, and rising costs. States took action on these concerns through a number of channels.[75] One prominent channel was a lawsuit—***National Federation of Independent Business v. Sebelius***— filed by twenty-six states against the Obama administration, challenging the constitutionality of Affordable Care Act provisions, such as the mandate that individuals purchase health insurance. By a 5–4 vote, the Supreme Court upheld the individual mandate as a valid exercise of Congress's taxing power. The Court, however, struck down as unconstitutional the ACA's expansion of the Medicaid program on the grounds that it would coerce states to join the expansion or risk losing established Medicaid funding. This ruling departed from prior precedents that treated conditions of aid as legitimate extensions of federal power.[76] In this instance, the Supreme Court decided, in effect, that when federal grants-in-aid become large enough, the threat to withhold them if certain conditions are not met can be construed as coercive.

State resistance also encompassed the "enactment of statutes or constitutional amendments opting out of ACA or challenging mandatory ACA provisions."[77] A total of twenty-one states opposed the ACA through such instruments. For example, six states—Missouri, Montana, New Hampshire, North Carolina, Utah, and Wyoming—enacted laws prohibiting further compliance with the ACA unless such compliance is explicitly approved by the state legislature.[78]

It is much easier for states to resist federal enticements when the financial stakes are relatively small. A good example of that is federal funding available to states for abstinence-only education, which studies have shown to be ineffective.[79] Unlike Medicaid, which involves enormous cash transfers, abstinence-only grants are quite modest. As of 2009, twenty-five states had declined to accept such grants; states with more Democratic public officials and more liberal citizens were more likely to say no.[80] This is a useful reminder that when states have strong views and when the financial consequences are minor, states can avoid becoming reluctant agents in a principal-agent relationship.

Although federal health funding is typically channeled through state governments, local agencies are also participants in health policy networks. Over the past two decades, the visibility of public health networks has increased significantly. For example, in September–October 2001, letters containing anthrax were mailed to media outlets and Senate offices. These attacks, which killed five people and infected seventeen others, drew attention to weaknesses in public health preparedness and responsiveness. At the time, half of all local public health departments did not have access to the Internet. Furthermore, the communications of these departments with the all-important Centers for Disease Control and Prevention (CDC) were often rather limited. As a result of these deficiencies, many departments relied primarily on the mass media for guidance when responding to the fast-moving events.[81] Dr. Julie Gerberding, who was at the time acting deputy director of the CDC's Center for Infectious Diseases, told the *New York Times*, "In retrospect, we were certainly not prepared for layers and levels of collaboration among a vast array of government agencies and professional organizations that would be required to be efficient and successful in the anthrax outbreak."[82]

Immediately following the terrorist attacks of 2001, federal funding for state and local public health initiatives increased dramatically, from $67 million to $1 billion annually.[83] Within three years, the number of epidemiologists working in state health departments had increased by 27 percent.[84] Despite these promising developments, the capacity of public health networks to respond to catastrophes has remained uncertain. Although the number of epidemiologists in state health departments increased substantially, nearly one-third of these employees lacked any formal training or academic coursework in epidemiology.[85] Furthermore, regardless of the capacity of health departments at the state level, many local public health agencies have not demonstrated adequate preparedness for emergencies such as infectious disease outbreaks. Researchers at the RAND Corporation tested the readiness of nineteen local health agencies in eighteen states by reporting "urgent" cases in telephone calls to these organizations. In a subset of calls, the researchers described symptoms of botulism, anthrax, smallpox, and bubonic plague. Although some officials responded appropriately by asking relevant questions and probing for details, other officials did not take such important steps. After listening to a description of the classic symptoms of bubonic plague, one official told the caller not to worry and to "go back to bed" because no similar cases had been reported. Upon hearing about a case with symptoms of botulism, another official said, "You're right, it does sound like botulism. I wouldn't worry too much if I were you."[86]

Despite such examples, local agencies have proven in other contexts to be capable members of health networks, crafting policy tools designed to address issues in public health. In recent years, localities across the country have instituted smoking bans of a variety of types. Such bans restrict smoking in places ranging from restaurants to government buildings.[87] Local governments have been especially inclined to adopt smoking bans in states where statewide prohibitions have not been instituted. For example, there is no statewide smoking ban in Kentucky, despite recent efforts to change the situation.[88] A total of twenty-eight cities and eleven counties in Kentucky, however, have restricted smoking in public places in some way.[89] In general, local antismoking networks are characterized by high degrees of centrality, in that larger cities are typically the first jurisdictions to adopt smoking bans. Such bans are then imitated, whether appropriately or not, by smaller cities and counties that have observed the decisions of their early-adopting neighbors.[90]

Race to the Top in Education. Within months of taking office, President Barack Obama made good on a campaign promise by announcing the creation of a federal education program dubbed the Race to the Top. Under this initiative, the Department of Education has allocated $4.35 billion for grants to states and localities that pursue certain types of reforms in their education systems.[91] Requests for grants are judged on a number of specific criteria, such as conducting performance-based assessments of teachers and principals, adopting common standards for student assessments, providing favorable environments for charter schools, and turning around the lowest-achieving schools.[92]

Although forty-one states initially applied for Race to the Top grants, the program has been criticized on a number of grounds. For example, Texas governor Rick Perry explained his administration's decision not to apply for funding by stating that "we would be foolish and irresponsible to place our children's future in the hands of unelected bureaucrats and special interest groups thousands of miles away in Washington."[93] In addition, a number of civil rights organizations, including the Urban League and the NAACP Legal Defense Fund, protested that the Race to the Top "reinstates the antiquated and highly politicized frame for distributing federal support to states that civil rights organizations fought to remove in 1965."[94]

The importance of networks in Race to the Top is evidenced by Florida's quest to participate in the program. In the first round of Race to the Top competition, Florida was handicapped by a lack of support from state teachers' unions.[95] As one union representative said, "When it came down to the collaboration, the state said, 'No.' They believe they have a strong enough proposal without union backing. We'll see."[96] In the end, Florida did not receive funding in the first round of the competition, although it did secure $700 million in the second round five months later.[97]

Welfare Reform. One of the most significant policy outcomes in recent decades was the drop in the 1990s in the number of Americans receiving welfare benefits. Between 1993 and 1996, nearly three million Americans left the welfare rolls, the largest such decline in more than half a century.[98] One reason for this decline was the economic growth that occurred in the aftermath of the recession of the early 1990s. In addition, intergovernmental networks, by devolving authority from the federal government to the states, contributed to the nationwide drop in welfare receipt. As was the case with Medicaid policy, welfare waivers increased dramatically in their prevalence as a policy tool during the Clinton administration.[99] Many states instituted limits on the length of time recipients are permitted to receive welfare benefits. Another common waiver required recipients to participate in job training programs. Family caps, under which household benefits are not increased when additional children are born, also proved popular among state policymakers. Overall, the White House Council of Economic Advisers estimated that approximately one-third of the reduction in welfare receipts was attributable to waivers granted to the states by the Department of Health and Human Services.[100] Welfare waivers, like policy tools in the areas of the environment, health, and education, have resulted in networks that are not only intergovernmental in nature but are also characterized by partnerships between public and private organizations. It is to such partnerships that we now turn.

Public-Private Partnerships

Many networks involving government bureaucracies also include private sector actors as members. Such public-private partnerships may or may not include interagency or intergovernmental relationships. In some instances, public-private partnerships involve direct contracts between government agencies and for-profit firms or nonprofit organizations. In other instances, public-private partnerships involve relationships where cooperative behavior emerges without explicit contractual obligations.

Contracting Out. **Contracting out** is a public-private partnership in which a government agency establishes a contractual arrangement with a for-profit firm or nonprofit organization to perform some task. Contracting out offers the promise, and sometimes the reality, of improving bureaucratic performance in areas such as reducing the expenditures required to produce given services. The privatization of garbage collection, for example, has generally resulted in cost savings, with no diminution in the quality of services provided.[101] Contracting out, however, presents government officials with significant organizational challenges. Monitoring and influencing the delivery of services is difficult enough when implementing agents are subordinate government officials. When service providers are employees of private organizations that are members of networks, the pursuit of accountability can become that much more difficult. A key problem with recent trends is that while contracting out has increased sharply there has been no commensurate increase in government officials capable of monitoring contracts. The aging of the federal workforce and the expectation of numerous retirements over the next few years could exacerbate the problem by depriving the federal government of some of its most experienced officials.[102]

Soon after taking office, President Obama issued a memorandum on government contracting to the heads of executive branch departments and agencies.[103] The memorandum stressed that, with the rapid expansion in contracting out in recent decades, activities that are inherently governmental are now being performed by nongovernmental actors. In addition, the White House emphasized the importance of awarding contracts through an open and competitive process, in contrast to the single-source arrangements that have increasingly come to define contracting out. Toward the end of the Obama administration, the Labor Department issued a regulation ordering federal contractors to pay sick leave to their workers.[104]

Actions such as these prompted associations representing federal contractors to write a letter to the White House. Signed by organizations such as the National Defense Industrial Association and Aerospace Industries Association, the letter requested that "no further presidential directives primarily focused on government contractors be issued for the foreseeable future."[105] According to estimates, as much as thirty cents of every contracting dollar is spent complying with government regulations. Although understandable from an accountability perspective, government regulations can negatively affect performance to the extent that innovative private sector organizations are deterred from seeking contracts.

Energy policy
In carrying out its duties, the Department of Energy (DOE) relies extensively on contracts with private firms. In fact, for every DOE employee, there are thirty-five contractor employees.[106] The DOE, in other words, is "little more than an administrative shell over a vast empire of contractors."[107] With so many contracts and with extraordinarily technical tasks being performed by contractors, DOE employees at times find it difficult to pursue network accountability.

In 1989, for example, government investigators uncovered serious problems at a nuclear weapons production facility in Rocky Flats, Colorado. This facility was being run by Rockwell International, a private sector contractor. Officials discovered a wide array of health and safety problems inside the plant, as well as illegal dumping of hazardous wastes outside the plant. The severity of these problems led to an FBI raid, a temporary shutdown of operations, and the hiring of a new contractor. These findings and actions contrasted sharply with the DOE's prior ratings of the plant, which had been positive across the board.[108] Ultimately, such discrepancies suggest that DOE officials had not been receiving accurate information about what was actually happening on the ground.

The events at Rocky Flats are indicative of the incongruity in goals that are at times manifested in public-private networks. From the perspective of the DOE, the primary goal was the production of nuclear weapons. Although environmental considerations were certainly salient to DOE officials, such considerations took a back seat to production priorities. From the perspective of Rockwell International, the overarching goal was profit maximization, with environmental concerns mattering even less to the firm than to the government. Given this combination of circumstances, it is no wonder that the DOE found it difficult to convey to its network partner the need to dispose of nuclear waste in a safe and legal manner.

Transportation

Toll roads, which charge motorists a fee for the use of certain roads, are not new, but they have experienced a resurgence in recent years. As of 2014, twenty-nine states have toll roads.[109] For example, Florida drivers pay tolls on 719 miles of roads. States that have privatized public roads have done so primarily to raise cash in the short run, to avoid tax increases. In 2005, Indiana privatized 157 miles of northern Indiana roads, receiving $3.85 billion from an Australian–Spanish consortium in return.[110] The toll road arrangement enabled Governor Mitch Daniels to keep his campaign pledge not to raise new taxes. On the other hand, it generated some controversy when estimates indicated that the state could be foregoing $121 billion in revenue over the seventy-five-year duration of the contract with the consortium.[111] In recent years, Texas has also privatized some of its roads. Citizen opposition has slowed the pace of privatization, but Texas remains one of the nation's leaders in the scope of its toll road system.[112]

There is a distinction between privatizing roads that have already been built and contracting out to private firms the construction of new highways. A study by the University of Melbourne discovered that private sector infrastructure projects in Australia were less likely to have cost overruns and more likely to be finished on time than government projects.[113] Similarly, the state of Virginia was stymied by the $3 billion price tag to widen a section of the Capital Beltway, only to find that private companies were able to take on the project for $1.34 billion. Despite such outcomes, contracting out the construction of toll roads can raise accountability problems, as "many states lack the technical capacity and expertise to consider such deals and fully protect the public interest."[114]

Welfare privatization

During the 1990s, a number of state governments opted for public-private partnerships as part of their broader welfare reform initiatives. Under the Wisconsin Works program, for example, county governments in Wisconsin were stripped of the exclusive right to run welfare programs within their borders. In the aftermath of this reform, for-profit firms and nonprofit organizations came to manage approximately 70 percent of the state's welfare caseload.[115] In Milwaukee County, the local government completely ceded the administration of Wisconsin Works to such organizations as the YMCA, Goodwill Industries, and Maximus, Inc. At times, these organizations have used innovative mechanisms to help clients succeed in the changing welfare environment. Maximus developed a "doorbell" service, in which clients are called on the telephone to ensure that they wake up early enough to get their children off to school and themselves off to work.[116]

The privatization of welfare service delivery has been described as a shift from "the welfare state" to "Opportunity, Inc."[117] The CEO of Fedcap Rehabilitation Services, a nonprofit with government welfare contracts, described the organization's mission as assisting individuals to make a "long-term pivot out of poverty."[118] Examples of this "opportunity" phenomenon can be found in policy areas such as child welfare, employment and training, and child support enforcement. In at least three states—Kansas, Michigan, and Texas—the child welfare systems are substantially privatized.[119] Many states use private firms or nonprofit organizations to assist in some aspect of child support collection, such as identifying parents and maintaining payment systems. In all of these instances, public and private organizations belong to networks responsible for delivering social services to clients.

Unfortunately, the privatization of welfare services has sometimes been disastrous. In 2007, Texas canceled an $899 million contract with Accenture, following numerous complaints about jammed call centers, incorrect routing instructions, and wrongful terminations.[120] In 2010, Indiana canceled a $1.34 billion contract with IBM, which was handling approximately one-third of the state's 1.2 million person caseload. Accusations against IBM included lost documents, slow approvals, and high error rates.[121] Interestingly, both states switched contractors and tightened oversight procedures (i.e., increased government centrality) but did not abandon privatization. In Indiana, for example, the new system is a hybrid system, with some public provision and some contracting out.

Correctional facilities

In recent decades, state governments around the country have turned over the administration of some of their prisons to for-profit firms. These firms operate hundreds of correctional facilities that collectively house in the vicinity of 100,000 inmates.[122] The contracting out of prison operations has been most prevalent in the South. In 1984, Tennessee, the home state of Corrections Corporation of America (CCA), became the first jurisdiction to privatize a prison facility. By 2000, Texas, another early adopter of privatization, had nineteen private prisons operating within its borders.[123]

There is considerable debate about whether private prisons perform better than their public counterparts. On the one hand, evidence suggests that states have been able to save up to $15 million annually by privatizing some of their prison operations.[124] On the other hand, the lower wages paid by companies have led to higher personnel turnover in private prisons than in government facilities. Studies indicate that there have been more assaults by inmates on both staff and other inmates in private prisons than in public facilities. In addition, private prisons utilize less reliable methods of classifying prisoners for security purposes than do facilities operated by government agencies.[125]

Regardless of the performance implications of private prisons, such facilities certainly present accountability challenges. For example, after securing approval to operate a prison in Youngstown, Ohio, CCA did not fully inform state and local officials about the security risks present at the facility. When five convicted murderers escaped from the prison in July 1998, company officials tried to cover up the event. In response, officials in Ohio took steps to terminate the government's contract with CCA. Although this effort failed, CCA eventually agreed to move out of the Youngstown facility inmates who were deemed to be unsuitable for a medium-security prison.[126]

In 2016, the Department of Justice (DOJ) announced that it will stop using private prisons for federal inmates.[127] The DOJ's action, however, does not apply to state facilities or detention centers run by Immigration and Customs Enforcement. In making this announcement, the DOJ stated that, when compared to government facilities, private prisons "do not provide the same level of correctional services, programs and resources; they do not save substantially on costs; and . . . they do not maintain the same level of safety and security."[128] In addition, private prisons raise social justice issues that have been emphasized in the Black Lives Matter movement, which has argued that the profit motive can encourage mass incarceration.

Several months later, in early 2017, Attorney General Jeff Sessions reversed this policy. This change reflected what Donald Trump had said on the campaign trail: "I do think we can do a lot of privatizations and private prisons. It seems to work a lot better."[129] In anticipation of this move, the stock price of CCA (now renamed CoreCivic) jumped 43 percent the day after the election. By February 2017, stocks in CCA and the GEO Group (its leading competitor in operating private prisons) had gone up by 100 percent.[130]

Partnerships without Contracts. Despite their fundamental importance, contracts are not the only policy tools for achieving collaboration between public and private organizations. In many contexts, informal conversations and **memorandums of understanding** are sufficient to create relatively durable relationships between public agencies and private organizations. Many watershed partnerships, for example, rely on memorandums of understanding rather than formal contracts.[131] The choice of policy tools in part depends on the levels of trust that exist between network actors and the nature of the incentives to sustain informal agreements. If levels of trust are high and incentives are compelling, contracts may not be necessary.

Environmental Protection. In southern California, public officials, developers, and environmental groups created a cooperative governance arrangement with the aim of avoiding the gridlock that is sometimes associated with enforcement of the Endangered Species Act. State and county parks and wildlife officials meet regularly with developers and environmentalists in an effort to anticipate problems with sensitive species and prevent the triggering of lengthy legal disputes. Under this informal arrangement, developers receive permits to build on parts of land parcels they own. In return, other parts of these parcels are set aside for wildlife habitats. In addition, developers agree to fund environmental restoration work on their properties. For their part, environmental organizations provide volunteers to assist in restoration activities.[132] Hundreds of habitat conservation plans like this cooperative governance arrangement are in operation around the United States.[133]

The nonhierarchical configuration of networks is readily observable in habitat conservation plans. Such plans can be constructive in bringing together organizations with divergent goals that are not connected via supervisor–subordinate relationships. A potential danger, however, is that environmental groups may find themselves co-opted by developers: "Democratic accountability may be compromised as environmental groups receive funding for collaboration in restoration activities they are supposed to monitor."[134] Such dangers may be mitigated by the organizational diversity of the environmental community, in that any movement in the direction of **co-optation** on the part of specific groups likely triggers outcries by other, more adversarial advocates.

Regardless of their advantages and disadvantages, voluntary programs in the area of environmental protection are growing in prevalence and importance as policy instruments.[135] Sponsors of voluntary programs are oftentimes government agencies, but business firms and nonprofit organizations have also taken the lead in promoting partnerships without contracts. One prominent example is **ISO 14001,** a voluntary program sponsored by the International Organization for Standardization (ISO), a powerful standard-setting body composed of representatives from more than 100 nations. The ISO promulgates standards of conduct in particular areas of organizational behavior. Although these standards are costly and difficult for organizations to attain, the "brand name" of ISO certification offers a strong incentive for companies to make such investments.

Under ISO 14001, business firms agree to adopt stringent environmental management systems. Such adoptions entail conducting comprehensive reviews of their existing environmental practices and developing action plans to correct identified problems.[136] The primary benefit of ISO 14001 adoption is to acquire ISO certification. As Honda boasted on its website, "All major Honda plants worldwide already meet the toughest international environmental management standards (ISO 14001)."[137] In the United States alone, there are thousands of ISO 14001 registered facilities.[138]

Although it is not the lead organization, the EPA is part of the ISO 14001 network. The agency's general stance is that voluntary programs have the potential to address problems that have not been amenable to resolution through command-and-control approaches.[139] Specifically, the EPA is optimistic that ISO 14001 increases businesses' compliance with environmental regulations and ultimately leads to better outcomes in terms of pollution reduction. This optimism is borne out by various firms' experiences. Evidence indicates that, even after accounting for variation in firms' propensities to join ISO 14001, facilities that are ISO 14001 members spend on average 7 percent less time (twenty-five fewer days per year) out of compliance with EPA regulations than do facilities that are not ISO members. These improvements are reflective of reductions in both willful noncompliance and ignorance on the part of firms.[140] **Willful noncompliance** is addressed through the stringent standards that ISO 14001 members must demonstrably meet, while **ignorance** is mitigated against by directing members' attention to the root causes of noncompliant behavior.

Education. Public schools collaborate with various nongovernmental partners in efforts to promote organizational goals. In Chicago, for example, dozens of businesses and nonprofit organizations have established informal partnerships with public schools in areas such as curriculum, school management, and auxiliary services. The Executive Service Corps, a consulting group, has operated a work observation program enabling high school students to learn how financial institutions really work. The Suzuki-Orff School of Music, through an outreach program with public and private schools, has enabled thousands of children to develop a repertoire of songs and rhymes using rhythm instruments and xylophones. The Second Federal Savings Bank has established a student loan program. Other businesses that have partnered with Chicago public schools include McDonald's, JCPenney, the Wrigley Company, and McKinsey & Company. In Tulsa, Oklahoma, Growing Together, a local nonprofit organization, partners with six public schools to promote safe and supportive neighborhoods and schools.[141] For example, Growing Together deploys and supervises near-peer mentors in Clinton Middle School and Webster High School to help at-risk students overcome educational and social problems. In McDonald, Pennsylvania, the South Fayette Township High School has a long-standing informal partnership with All-Clad Metalcrafters, a local firm that produces kitchenware, where students help to improve and design commercial products in return for valuable mentoring and assistance.[142]

There is growing evidence that public-private partnerships in education can work. Take, for example, the Strive Together partnership, aimed at helping young people in Cincinnati and two nearby Kentucky cities achieve success from "cradle to career." Since 2006, early childhood educators, school superintendents, college presidents, business leaders, and nonprofit leaders have shared ideas on how to improve educational outcomes. By issuing annual "report cards," they have monitored and publicized progress toward shared goals. Thanks in part to these efforts, school readiness levels, fourth-grade reading and math scores, high school graduation rates, and college graduation rates have increased in Cincinnati.[143] Explanations for success include the involvement of top leaders from multiple sectors of society, shared goals, and high levels of interaction and data sharing. Strive Together has attracted such favorable notice that it has exported its ideas to other jurisdictions. As of 2015, Strive Together's "Cradle to Career Network" encompassed sixty-three community partnerships from thirty-two states and Washington, D.C.[144]

Regional Economic Development. Metropolitan areas—where people live, work, and play—often spill across local and state jurisdictional boundaries. As a result, it is difficult to use formal policy tools to pursue regional economic development objectives such as improving infrastructure and attracting and retaining workers. Such tools—laws, regulations, taxation—are the domain of local, state, and national governments that do not neatly overlap with metropolitan geography. Under these circumstances, stakeholders naturally turn to indirect policy tools that are grounded in partnerships without contracts.[145]

The keys to regional economic development partnerships are networks that span government, nonprofits, and the private sector. Oftentimes these networks are interpersonal in nature: "The cohesion of cities is generated by the cohesion of their social networks, which are created through face-to-face meetings and supported by extant means of transport and communication."[146] In cities such as Atlanta and Houston, it is documented that nonprofit and private sector actors have cultivated relationships with mayors and other government decision makers through events such as breakfasts and basketball games.[147]

Evidence also suggests that crucial differences in network structures have enabled Allentown, Pennsylvania, to respond more effectively than Youngstown, Ohio, to the difficulties that have plagued Rust Belt cities in recent decades.[148] Networks in Allentown have been characterized by high levels of multiplexity. For example, otherwise unconnected private sector actors found themselves linked by overlapping memberships on the boards of civic organizations.[149] Such linkages fostered cooperation among community leaders, who then devised innovative policies to hold off some of the most devastating consequences of post-industrialism. In Youngstown, by contrast, overlocking boards were not prevalent, thereby depriving policymakers of forums for working collectively on behalf of the region, which slipped into a cycle of steep decline.[150]

Interagency Networks

Perhaps the most fundamental of all networks in which bureaucracies participate is the **interagency network.** Within any given level of government (federal, state, or local), executive branch organizations coordinate their programs, activities, and public testimonies. At the very least, coordination implies the sharing of information across agencies. In some contexts, coordination also entails efforts to reach a consensus and to speak with one voice. What are the characteristics of such interagency networks? What types of policy tools are typically utilized in the quest for coordination?

The Cabinet. Since the presidency of George Washington, the heads of cabinet departments have met on a regular basis to offer advice to the president, learn from one another, and hear about the president's priorities and decisions. Despite the longevity of this interagency network, it is widely understood that the cabinet has failed to live up to its potential, both as a policymaking institution and as a coordinating body. During the administration of Lyndon B. Johnson, in the late 1960s, cabinet officials at times concealed their true views of the Vietnam War in order to avoid antagonizing a president who demanded fierce loyalty from his top officials.[151] A few years later, at least one of Richard Nixon's cabinet members (the attorney general, no less) sanctioned illegal acts, including the infamous Watergate burglary.[152] More generally, the cabinet's natural lack of coherence and limited ability to coordinate policy contribute to its weakness as an interagency network.[153]

Another root cause of the limitations of the cabinet is the process by which members are selected.[154] The president typically seeks to placate important electoral constituencies and make symbolic appointments that satisfy objectives such as ideological congruence (President Reagan) and ethnic diversity (President Clinton). President Obama took a somewhat different tack, selecting as cabinet members some of his primary election opponents (Joe Biden as vice president, Hillary Clinton as secretary of state, and, initially, Bill Richardson as secretary of commerce), to form a **team of rivals,** as Abraham Lincoln had done in 1860.[155] Obama's stated goal was to form a cabinet that would not hesitate to challenge his preconceptions. By some accounts, President Obama did a good job of seeking out multiple viewpoints as president and learned enough about policy details to ask probing questions at cabinet meetings and White House staff meetings.[156] Like his predecessors, however, Obama often sided with the White House staff when they disagreed with key cabinet officials. Initially, Obama gave Attorney General Eric Holder considerable discretion. However, after Holder received criticism from Congress and White House staff members, Obama later reined him in.

Donald Trump's cabinet selections, in contrast, did not feature appointees who were likely to challenge the notoriously thin-skinned president-elect. Instead, Trump selected individuals who were long on business experience and short on government experience, especially federal government experience. In fact, several of Trump's appointees were openly hostile to the federal agencies they were being asked to lead. Scott Pruitt, chosen to lead the EPA, had joined in two lawsuits seeking to overturn the EPA's antipollution and carbon-reduction plans, in addition to expressing doubts about climate change.[157] Rick Perry, chosen to lead the Department of Energy, had proposed abolishing that department when he ran for president in 2012.[158] Ben Carson, asked to head the Department of Housing and Urban Development (HUD), had expressed opposition to HUD's pressure on local governments to desegregate, which he denounced as "social engineering" reminiscent of "communist countries."[159]

Critics of the new president, like Sen. Chuck Schumer, D-N.Y., argued that, in many instances, he had appointed a fox to guard the chicken coop.[160] In some ways, Trump's appointees were reminiscent of Ronald Reagan's appointees, who shared Reagan's skepticism toward the federal bureaucracy. However, Trump's appointees were expected to be even more disruptive than Reagan's, in keeping with Trump's admonition that we need to "drain the swamp."[161] Trump's appointees were also expected to enjoy considerable discretion in managing their departments. During the transition, one observer likened Trump's management style to that of a Fortune 500 CEO: "He's finding the best people he can and he's going to turn the reins over to them to see what they can do."[162] On the other hand, this could end abruptly, given Trump's penchant for sudden policy shifts and sweeping pronouncements. As one Trump transition official put it, referring to the cabinet secretaries: "They'll have as much room as they need—until they don't."[163]

Given competing political pressures, it is perhaps not surprising that presidents often ignore the advice emanating from both individual members and the cabinet as a collective body. Despite inherent shortcomings, cabinet meetings do at times facilitate exchanges between department secretaries and their organizations. The very knowledge that cabinet officials meet with one another on a regular basis can be enough to encourage cooperative behavior.[164] Ongoing interactions between small numbers of department secretaries may be particularly useful to the president, especially when such networks focus on relatively discrete issue areas such as national security.

Office of Management and Budget. In recent decades, the Office of Management and Budget (OMB) has come to rival, and perhaps even supersede, the importance of the cabinet as an interagency presidential network. The mission of OMB is to "serve the President of the United States in implementing his vision across the Executive Branch."[165] The work of OMB is divided into five main functions: (1) budget development and execution; (2) management of tasks, such as procurement, paperwork reduction, information, and technology; (3) review of executive branch regulatory actions, as discussed in Chapter 3; (4) coordination of agency communications with Congress; and (5) issuance of presidential memorandums and executive orders.[166]

OMB is organizationally located inside the Executive Office of the President. Dating back to 1939, the Executive Office of the President is overseen by the White House chief of staff and is staffed by many of the president's most trusted advisers.[167] In addition to OMB, the Executive Office of the President includes organizations such as the National Security Council and the Council of Economic Advisers. Given their network centrality, these organizations are well positioned to serve the coordination and policymaking functions that historically have proven to be beyond the motivations and capabilities of cabinet secretaries as a group.

<table>
<tr><td>Inside
Bureaucracy
with</td><td>Donna Shalala
Secretary of Health and Human Services
(1993–2001)</td></tr>
</table>

"The best way to coordinate across federal agencies is to build relationships over time, to make sure that the general counsels and inspectors general know each other. We convened groups from the Department of Justice and HHS and the Census Bureau on data issues, to make sure we knew what we were doing. For disease outbreaks, Agriculture and the EPA and HHS had to be coordinated.

"Coordination depends a lot on goodwill at the top and at the middle levels of the bureaucracy. On the Patients' Bill of Rights, Alexis Herman from DOL and I convened everybody and said, 'Look, we've been friends for years. Don't try to play us against each other! Work together!'

"Federal agencies are very turf conscious. Our biggest problem was always the FBI and the Department of Justice. They protected information and didn't share. The FBI simply would not share. The CIA and the security agencies were much more cooperative. The FBI was awful! And they didn't know anything! It's no different today."

There are a variety of regular ways in which OMB coordinates policymaking in executive branch agencies. OMB issues **circulars** containing information that has continuing effects of at least two years.[168] For example, OMB Circular A-11 instructs agencies how to prepare, submit, and execute the federal budget.[169] OMB officials also write memoranda to agencies, documents seeking to foster consistency across the executive branch on specific issues. On October 7, 2015, OMB ordered agencies to "develop and institutionalize policies to promote consideration of ecosystem services, where appropriate and practicable, in planning, investments, and regulatory contexts."[170]

Interagency Coordination. Despite specialization and differentiation in the executive branch, many agencies have overlapping jurisdictions. For example, the foreign affairs bureaucracy is characterized by "bureaucratic interconnectedness."[171] The State Department has strong incentive to pay attention to the design and operation of the Defense Department, and vice versa. The Central Intelligence Agency has good reason to stay informed about the norms and decisions of the National Security Council, and vice versa.

Although agencies in the area of domestic policy are generally not so tightly connected, occasions arise when **interagency coordination** is paramount in the production of bureaucratic outputs. All new cars and light-duty trucks sold in the United States are required to have labels that display information about the vehicle's fuel economy.[172] In 2010, the EPA and the Department of

Transportation (DOT) jointly initiated an effort to update label requirements. This effort sought both to make fuel economy labels easier for consumers to understand and to incorporate into the labels new information about greenhouse gas emissions.[173] Given the environmental and transportation implications of fuel economy labels, coordination between the EPA and DOT was essential in ensuring that the decision-making process resulted in an output that was satisfactory on both dimensions.

According to some observers, the Obama administration tried hard to "break down stovepipes." Information sharing between the Department of Education and the Department of Health and Human Services is noticeable, especially on early childhood education issues, as is information sharing between the Department of Education and the Department of Labor, especially on job training issues. President Obama alluded to the challenges of interagency coordination in his 2011 State of the Union speech: "The Interior Department is in charge of salmon while they're in fresh water, but the Commerce Department handles them when they're in saltwater. I hear it gets even more complicated once they're smoked."[174] Most salmon would probably agree with that! Implicit in Obama's comment is the assumption that we might want to streamline jurisdiction over salmon under the aegis of one federal agency.

For agencies with overlapping jurisdictions, **interagency task forces** are frequently used as coordinating techniques. For example, in 1999–2000, the Task Force on Export Control Reform brought together representatives from the Commerce Department, Defense Department, and State Department in an effort to modernize and liberalize U.S. export control practices. Specifically, the task force focused on how long it takes to process licenses, what types of technologies should be easier to export, and how the United States should treat different countries. In 2007, President George W. Bush established an interagency task force, headed by the secretary of veterans affairs, to address problems in meeting the needs of veterans of the wars in Iraq and Afghanistan.[175] The President's Interagency Task Force to Monitor and Combat Trafficking in Persons, which has operated during the past four administrations, brings together officials from seventeen executive branch organizations.[176] The breadth of organizations represented on the task force reflects the multifaceted nature of the effort to eliminate human trafficking, which requires data gathering, law enforcement, education and public awareness, and foreign diplomacy.

As discussed in Chapter 4, the Bush administration launched in 2002 an initiative to increase access to agency records and to stimulate public participation in the regulatory process. This eRulemaking Program is governed by an interagency task force comprising dozens of federal organizations.[177] The EPA serves as the managing partner of the eRulemaking Program. In addition, as illustrated in Figure 5.2, the eRulemaking Program has an executive committee composed of "Chief Information Officers (CIO), Regulatory Policy Officers, and/or Deputy Secretaries from 40 Federal Departments and Agency partners."[178] The eRulemaking Program's governance structure is rounded out by an advisory board of senior officials from partner agencies and workgroups that

Figure 5.2 Interagency Coordination under the eRulemaking Program

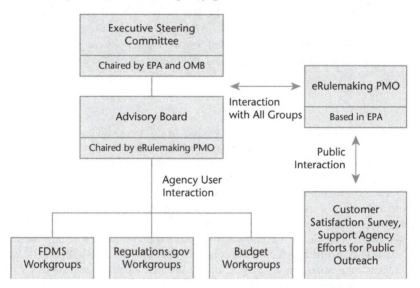

eRulemaking Program Governance Structure

Multiple levels of cross-agency governance and collaboration

Source: U.S. Environmental Protection Agency, Program Management Office, regulations.gov, "About Us," https://www.regulations.gov/aboutUs (accessed October 6, 2016).

provide expertise on specific budget, legal, and other issues that arise during the task force's deliberations.[179]

Although interagency task forces serve clear coordination purposes, such networks have at times aroused skepticism. Some of this skepticism comes from within the bureaucracy itself: "Interagency committees are the crab grass in the garden of government. Nobody wants them, but everyone has them. Committees seem to thrive on scorn and ridicule, and multiply so rapidly that attempts to weed them out appear futile."[180] As a case in point, the eRulemaking Program is funded through contributions from member agencies. Because these contributions divert resources from other valued activities, agencies face incentives to minimize their support of the task force's mission.[181]

Czars. Another form of interagency networking is the creation of **czars** to coordinate government actions. Presidents have found czars especially appealing as policy tools during times of crisis. For example, President Nixon empowered a czar to coordinate the administration's handling of the 1973 energy crisis. The job of energy czar proved so challenging and frustrating that five

Donna Shalala
Secretary of Health and Human Services
(1993–2001)

"Bureaucrats solve problems by talking to each other a lot, particularly as a way of minimizing risk. They ask whether the problem to be solved will result in reward or punishment. The reward could be either financial or someone saying that was a good thing you did."

individuals held the position within a twelve-month period. The experience of former Colorado governor John Love was typical in that, despite an important title and job description, he lacked by his own admission both the staff and the authority to effectively carry out his duties.[182]

Since 1988 each president has had a drug czar on his staff. The drug czar is officially known as the director of national drug control policy. Although the position is located within the Executive Office of the President, the Office of National Drug Control Policy has been criticized as ineffectual and has at times suffered from a lack of resources. As is always the case with efforts at interagency coordination, a key part of the problem is that responsibility for policymaking and enforcement is scattered across the federal bureaucracy. When it comes to drug policy, this responsibility is shared by no fewer than sixty agencies, many of which have missions and cultures that are at odds with other network actors.[183]

Prior to the creation in 2002 of the Department of Homeland Security, the White House tapped Tom Ridge, a former governor of Pennsylvania, to serve as the director of the Office of Homeland Security. When President Bush first announced Ridge's appointment as homeland security czar on September 21, 2001, the announcement provoked two strong reactions—praise for Ridge's leadership ability and skepticism that Ridge, or anyone else for that matter, would be able to function effectively without adequate authority.[184] Although some observers asserted that Ridge was indeed the right man for the job, many experts believed that he was being asked to carry out an impossible mission.

The mission of the Office of Homeland Security was to "lead, oversee and coordinate a comprehensive national strategy to secure the United States from terrorist threats or attacks."[185] The executive order that created the office granted Ridge, as director, cabinet membership. Ridge enjoyed an office in the West Wing of the White House, in close proximity to the president. In the weeks after his appointment, Ridge emerged as the administration's leading spokesman on terrorism, holding press conferences several times a week.[186]

Despite these symbolic steps, the Office of Homeland Security and its director were severely handicapped. The ultimate goal was to coordinate the forty or fifty federal agencies that shared responsibility for the security of the nation's homeland. Unfortunately, however, the office had no direct line authority over any agency with significant staff or program responsibility. By late 2001, Ridge was directing a skeleton staff of thirty members.[187] The fact that the office's limited mandate was rooted in an executive order, and not a statute, further weakened Ridge's legitimacy as a central network actor.[188] In a scathing editorial, the *New York Times* put it bluntly: "Washington seems to have swallowed up Tom Ridge since he arrived in time last fall to take charge of domestic security. Instead of forcefully coordinating the work of a host of federal agencies, Mr. Ridge has bumped from one humiliation to another as various cabinet departments have openly flouted his advice and failed to address security problems identified by their own inspector general."[189]

Inside Bureaucracy with	Tom Ridge *Secretary of Homeland Security* *(2003–2005)*

"There was some resistance and understandable and predictable resistance because you had been under one agency for a long time, you were comfortable with the leadership, comfortable with your role. I was not surprised—in spite of the horrific events of 9/11 and this being a response to it—that there was some resistance to moving into a new department. There was certainly a lot of misinformation on the street, particularly with real conservative political figures who said, 'Well, you're creating 180,000 new people.' No, we inherited about 179,900 people. So we weren't creating, maybe a new agency, but it was a very appropriate agency. We should have built a border sensitive agency a long time ago given the globalization of the economy, the globalization of the threat. . . . The TSA for management reasons was probably the most difficult challenge coming in simply because it was new. The department writ large is a piñata for the politicians on the Hill. But the TSA was a particular target because we had never had that kind of security before. So, fortunately, there were good people. It wasn't difficult to manage because of the people. It's just difficult to manage because it was constantly under the critical scrutiny of the Hill and I think it took a lot of unfair shots (although it wasn't as efficient and as effective as I wanted it to be). On the flip side of that, the Secret Service has always had a good relationship with the White House, and while they technically reported to me on occasions and I tried to get them to adjust things I thought needed to be done, they weren't necessarily willing to do it. But it was at the margins and so I didn't really worry about it too much."

Frustrated by these problems, Congress and President Bush agreed to the creation of a cabinet-level Department of Homeland Security. The new department began operating in March 2003, with Ridge as its first secretary. Among other agencies, the department comprises the Coast Guard, Customs and Border Protection, Citizenship and Immigration Services, Secret Service, Federal Emergency Management Agency, and Transportation Security Administration.[190] Because the department included former employees from twenty-two other federal agencies (see Table 5.2), it faced considerable integrative challenges.

Table 5.2 Agencies Shifted to Create the Department of Homeland Security

Animal and Plant Health Inspection Service	Department of Agriculture
Plum Island Animal Disease Center	Department of Agriculture
National BW Defense Analysis Center	Department of Defense
National Communications System	Department of Defense
CBRN Countermeasures Programs	Department of Energy
Energy Security and Assurance Program	Department of Energy
Environmental Measurements Laboratory	Department of Energy
Nuclear Incident Response Team	Department of Energy
Strategic National Stockpile and the National Disaster Medical System	Department of Health and Human Services
Domestic Emergency Support Teams	Department of Justice
Immigration and Naturalization Service	Department of Justice
Office for Domestic Preparedness	Department of Justice
Transportation Security Administration	Department of Transportation
U.S. Coast Guard	Department of Transportation
Federal Law Enforcement Training Center	Department of the Treasury
U.S. Customs Service	Department of the Treasury
U.S. Secret Service	Department of the Treasury
National Domestic Preparedness Office	Federal Bureau of Investigation

National Infrastructure Protection Center	Federal Bureau of Investigation
Federal Computer Incident Response Center	General Services Administration
Federal Protective Service	General Services Administration
Federal Emergency Management Agency	*Previously an independent agency*

Source: U.S. Department of Homeland Security, "Who Joined DHS," https://www.dhs.gov/who-joined-dhs (accessed March 2, 2017).

During eight years in office, President Obama approved more than thirty czar positions. As Table 5.3 indicates, the responsibilities of these czars cover many of the most pressing policy concerns faced by the nation in recent times, including border security, climate change, health care reform, and the subprime mortgage crisis. Observers have pointed out that President Obama's aggressive use of czars reflected a personal predilection, dating back to his campaign for the White House, for delegating to top personnel responsibility for large areas of decision making. This approach served Senator Obama well on the campaign trail. A key question for all chief executives who rely on czars is "whether the president is adept at managing the kind of pathologies that can flow out of setting up these rival power centers."[191]

If czars arouse some jealousies and suspicions within the executive branch, they also rankle members of Congress, who believe that it is easier for Congress to oversee cabinet departments than it is to oversee White House staff members, who do not need Senate confirmation and whose communications can be protected through executive privilege. In 2011, House Republicans insisted on eliminating funding for four policy czars—those who assisted President Obama on health care, climate change, automobiles and manufacturing, and urban affairs.[192] Perhaps in anticipation of such retribution, three of the four czars had already resigned or accepted a new job within the administration. When signing the budget bill, President Obama issued a statement disputing Congress's authority to prevent him from hiring czars, should he wish to do so.[193]

In 2014, when President Obama made good on this statement and named Ron Klain, a former aide to Vice President Biden, as the coordinator of the government's response to an outbreak of the Ebola virus, this action was met by vociferous opposition: "Mr. Klain is not a doctor. He's not a health care professional. He doesn't have background in these issues. But what he is, is a political operative."[194] The administration's response to this criticism reflects the inherently nonhierarchical nature of the interagency networks in which czars are enmeshed: "You don't need to be a healthcare person, you need to be somebody who is a good organizer. And his experience is extraordinary. He has been chief of staff to a couple of vice presidents. He has a lot of experience."[195]

Table 5.3 Czars under President Obama

1. Afghanistan–Pakistan Czar
2. AIDS Czar
3. Asian Carp Czar
4. Auto Recovery Czar
5. Border Czar
6. California Water Czar
7. Car Czar
8. Climate Czar
9. Counterterrorism Czar/Homeland Security Czar
10. Cyber Czar
11. Diversity Czar
12. Domestic Violence Czar
13. Drug Czar
14. Ebola Czar
15. Economics Czar
16. Energy Czar
17. Government Performance Czar
18. Great Lakes Czar
19. Green Jobs Czar
20. Guantánamo Closure Czar
21. Health Czar
22. Healthcare.gov Czar
23. Information Czar
24. Intelligence Czar
25. Iran Czar
26. Manufacturing Czar
27. Mideast Czar
28. Pay Czar
29. Performance Czar
30. Regulatory Czar
31. Safe Schools Czar
32. Science Czar
33. Stimulus Accountability Czar
34. TARP Czar
35. Technology Czar/Infotech Czar
36. Technology Czar
37. Urban Affairs Czar
38. Weapons Czar
39. Weapons of Mass Destruction Czar

Sources: Arit John, "The Encyclopedia of All 34 of Obama's Czars, From A to Zients," http://www.bloomberg.com/politics/articles/2014-10-25/the-encyclopedia-of-all-34-of-obamas-czars-from-a-to-zients (accessed October 6, 2016); University of Pennsylvania, Annenberg Public Policy Center, http://www.factcheck.org/UploadedFiles/Czars.pdf (accessed November 5, 2010).

President Trump continued his predecessors' predilections for employing czars, especially in areas at the top of the administration's agenda. Investor Carl Icahn was named a special adviser on regulatory reform. Economist Peter Navarro was tapped as the president's trade policy czar.[196]

Network Effectiveness

As this chapter's examples of intergovernmental relations, public-private partnerships, and interagency coordination have demonstrated, networked arrangements vary in their effectiveness. What are the conditions under which networks are, broadly speaking, effective forms of bureaucratic policymaking? Put differently, are there conditions under which networks are not well suited to advance accountability and performance in the executive branch?

Evaluating the effectiveness of networks is a rather difficult task. Network participants are diverse, encompassing government organizations, nonprofits, and the private sector. What constitutes an effective network—and the importance of accountability and performance in making such judgments—can vary significantly across the perspectives of "those organizations that make up the network, those who are served by the network, and those whose policy and funding actions affect the network."[197]

An analysis of fifteen social service networks in upstate New York identified a number of factors that predict a "performance gap" between the status quo and an idealized standard, based on the perceptions of caseworkers and administrators.[198] On the one hand, vertical dependency was negatively related to performance measures. On the other hand, network autonomy served to enhance the performance of the network actors. These findings suggest support for **resource dependency theory,** which posits that a lack of control over resources weakens an organization or cluster of organizations such as a network. Finally, although complexity undermined network performance, larger numbers of communication channels were associated with performance enhancements.

A study of mental health networks in four cities reached rather different conclusions.[199] Defining effectiveness as case managers' perceptions of the overall well-being of severely mentally ill clients, this research concluded that direct external control exerted a positive influence on network effectiveness. The performance of these networks was also enhanced by integration, system stability, and the presence of substantial resources.

In an analysis that brought together information about nineteen interagency collaboratives encompassing diverse geographic sites and policy sectors, four factors emerged as those most likely to produce effective networks: a technically clear mission, external demands to perform better, vigorous leadership, and a culture of pragmatism.[200] Generally speaking, it is imperative that network managers work hard to create and sustain atmospheres of mutual trust. In addition, research on state and local government efforts to coordinate employment and training programs suggests that leadership and mutual respect are particularly important as predictors of network success.[201]

Taken together, the evidence highlights the potential importance of leadership, mutual respect, and external control in determining the effectiveness of bureaucratic networks. Given that different analyses have reached somewhat different conclusions, it is reasonable to infer that the kinds of networks that are appropriate for advancing accountability and performance in certain settings may not be effective in other contexts.

The Effectiveness of Policy Tools

The examples in this chapter have made it clear that the policy tools available to public officials vary significantly in their characteristics. What are the conditions that govern the effectiveness of different types of tools? To address this question, the following sections evaluate the effectiveness of three of the most widely used policy tools—grants-in-aid, regulation, and information.

Grants-in-Aid

In intergovernmental relations, the federal government utilizes grants-in-aid to encourage state and local governments to allocate resources toward particular policy problems. Such grants-in-aid take different forms. **Categorical grants** must be used for relatively narrow, specific program categories. The Head Start program, which disburses money to local communities for the purpose of improving the school readiness of disadvantaged preschoolers, is an example of a categorical grant. In contrast, **block grants** can be used for a variety of purposes within broad program areas. The Child Care and Development Block Grant is a case in point, in that funds may be used to pay for child care for low-income families, to increase the availability of child care facilities, or to improve the quality of child care for all families.

Although grants-in-aid have a variety of specific purposes, a key motivating factor has been the promotion of redistributive spending by state and local governments.[202] As a general matter, state and local governments are not all that willing to allocate substantial resources to disadvantaged residents, out of a fear that poor citizens living in other jurisdictions might migrate across boundaries and take advantage of generous social benefits. In the context of welfare policy, this phenomenon is known as the **welfare magnet effect** because states with generous welfare payments may exert a magnetic pull on disadvantaged citizens.[203] Although welfare payment levels affect interstate migration less than do other factors, such as family ties, the effects of program generosity can be considerable. For example, evidence suggests that if California were to increase its welfare benefits by 10 percent, the number of households in the state headed by single mothers would likely increase by more than 2,500 after five years.[204]

Some grants-in-aid programs have produced relatively clear positive results. The interstate highway program, inaugurated in the 1950s during the Eisenhower administration, produced within two decades a remarkable latticework of roads that facilitates commerce and tourism all across the nation. The Medicaid program has enabled millions of low-income individuals, especially children and senior citizens, to receive timely medical attention. The Head Start program has generated generally favorable reviews, although doubts remain as to the persistence of the program's impact on children's cognitive development.[205]

Grants-in-aid programs not only affect policy outcomes but also the attention that recipients pay to particular types of solutions to public problems. President Obama's Race to the Top program, for example, brought to the fore of state-level policy agendas a series of education reforms that were controversial and stood no chance of being enacted by Congress and many state legislatures.[206] Research indicates that such reforms—the development of common assessments, evaluations of teacher and principal performance, funding for charter schools—were adopted at higher rates after Race to the Top took effect.[207] This increase occurred not only in states that received Race to the Top grants but in others states as well. Alaska, which did not apply for a grant, nevertheless increased the weight placed upon standardized test results in making teacher assessments, an approach closely associated with Race to the Top reforms.[208]

In some areas, by contrast, grants-in-aid programs essentially substitute federal dollars for expenditures that state and local governments would have undertaken even without encouragement from policymakers in Washington, D.C. This substitution is known as the **crowd-out phenomenon**.[209] Evidence suggests that the extent of crowd-out depends on various aspects of tool design, such as the generosity of matching federal funds and whether there is a ceiling on this matching.[210] Through careful calibration of such elements of **grant-in-aid** programs, public officials may be able to mitigate the extent to which state and local governments substitute federal dollars for already planned state and local spending.

Other issues with grants-in-aid have been even more vexing. Political factors often play a major role in determining how grants-in-aid are distributed. As a result, the federal government allocates funds not just to the neediest of states and communities but to less needy governments as well. A congressional report made the following argument: "Millions of dollars that are supposed to fight terror are actually going to the very worst kind of pork barrel programs. Meanwhile, many real homeland security needs—like those in New York City—remain unmet."[211] As evidence, the report criticizes allocations such as $55,000 to the fire department in Crawfordsville, Indiana, to "buy gym equipment, provide nutritional counseling and instruct firefighters on how to become fitness trainers" and $36,200 to Kentucky's Office of Charitable Gambling to "prevent terrorists from trying to raise money for their plots at the state's bingo halls."[212]

Another concern is that grants undermine accountability by creating a disjunction between the level of government that raises the money and the level of government that spends the money. If an intergovernmental program becomes embroiled in controversy, as Medicaid sometimes does, then who should be blamed? Should blame be placed on the federal government that failed to prevent waste, fraud, and abuse? Or should blame fall to the state government that perpetrated the problems?

In recent years, many grants-in-aid have taken the form of block grants, which permit state and local governments to exercise considerable flexibility in how they spend federal dollars. The Social Services Block Grant and the Community Development Block Grant are two prominent examples. When the White House Office of Management and Budget rated different types of policy tools, it awarded the block grant its second lowest rating among seven program types.[213] Such criticisms reflect the fact that block grants are spent for wide varieties of purposes and that funding levels are typically determined by formulas and population counts rather than by merit or need. From time to time, congressional Republicans have proposed to convert the Medicaid program from a categorical grant into a block grant, which they believe would be more efficient and more cost-effective. Congressional Democrats have opposed this because experience shows that the creation of a block grant is often accompanied by a reduction in federal funding. Such a reduction, Democrats believe, would harm Medicaid clients, who are primarily poor, and make it more difficult for them to obtain basic health care services.

A nongovernmental assessment of grants-in-aid concluded that "grants merit an overall moderate rating in terms of effectiveness."[214] When properly administered, grants-in-aid enable federal officials to promote redistributive goals and to compensate for externalities that cross state boundaries (for example, air and water pollution). More broadly, grants-in-aid are hortatory controls that can be extremely useful as alternatives to more coercive mechanisms that often produce dysfunctional results.[215]

Regulation

If grants are carrots, then regulations are sticks. By definition, regulation is a coercive policy instrument, though the degree of coercion varies considerably across specific manifestations. A regulation mandating a coal-burning utility to use low-sulfur coal is far more coercive than a regulation requiring the same utility to open its doors to periodic inspections. A regulation compelling a day care center to maintain child–staff ratios of seven to one for preschool children is far more restrictive than a regulation dictating the center to arrange for periodic in-service training experiences for its professional staff.

Regulations can make a difference in policy outcomes. Research on state air pollution standards has found that states with strong regulatory standards experience sharp reductions in sulfur dioxide and nitrogen dioxide.[216] A study of day care centers in four states found the poorest quality in the state with the weakest standards.[217]

Regulatory enforcement can also affect policy outcomes. Evidence suggests that the imposition of monetary penalties by Occupational Safety and Health Administration inspectors improves the safety records of penalized firms.[218] Reduced surveillance of day care centers with reasonably good track records can lead to higher numbers of code violations at the neglected centers.[219]

One difficulty in evaluating the efficacy of regulation is the dearth of **retrospective reviews** of rules that are on the books. In 2011, President Obama instructed agencies to "consider how best to promote retrospective analysis of rules that may be outmoded, ineffective, insufficient, or excessively burdensome, and to modify, streamline, expand, or repeal them in accordance with what has been learned."[220] By 2016, twenty-six agencies—from the Department of Agriculture to the Environmental Protection Agency to the Social Security Administration—had conducted reviews of their stocks of regulation.[221]

President Obama touted the results of retrospective review in his State of the Union address in 2012: "We got rid of one rule from 40 years ago that could have forced some dairy farmers to spend $10,000 a year proving that they could contain a spill—because milk was somehow classified as an oil. With a rule like that, I guess it was worth crying over spilled milk."[222] Some assessments of retrospective review, however, have not been so optimistic (or vivid!): "retrospective reviews mostly reflect business-as-usual management, with little discernible new work on the retrospective analysis and measurement called for in the executive order."[223] Retrospective review is at this point far less robust than established practices for the initial development of regulations.[224] As one researcher has argued, "retrospective review is today where prospective analysis was in the 1970s: ad hoc and largely unmanaged."[225] President Trump has sought to advance the cause of retrospective review by placing, in every federal agency, task forces charged with identifying regulations for modification or elimination. Sen. James Lankford, R-Okla., chair of the Senate Subcommittee on Regulatory Affairs and Federal Management, was optimistic about this development: "I applaud this action by the president. This new action adds some teeth to retrospective review by putting processes in place and holding agencies accountable."[226]

Is regulation as a policy tool less efficient than reliance on markets or market-like incentives? It has been demonstrated that, under favorable circumstances, market-like approaches produce positive results. For example, the Clean Air Act authorizes emissions trading as a means for encouraging industrial plants to agree to larger than average emissions reductions in return for cash payments if they can achieve such reductions at lower costs than other plants. Cap and trade, as emissions trading is also known, has proven successful in specific contexts.[227] It has also proven politically contentious. In the aftermath of the 2010 midterm elections, in which the Democratic Party lost control of the U.S. House of Representatives, President Obama acknowledged that his administration's cap and trade proposals had no chance of moving forward in the face of Republican opposition: "Cap and trade was just one way of skinning the cat; it was not the only way. It was a means, not an end. And I'm going to be looking for other means to address this problem."[228]

The cases for and against regulation depend in part on the types of regulation in question. Consider, for example, **economic regulation,** which seeks to improve the functioning of markets through mechanisms such as entry and exit restrictions and price controls. Such regulation can be useful in the context of industries characterized by natural monopolies, in which the presence of competitive firms might bring about inefficiencies. For years, analysts considered telephone companies and electric utilities to be natural monopolies. With technological advances, however, it has become possible to achieve even greater efficiency through the introduction of competition, at least on a limited basis. Under such circumstances, **deregulation** can be useful. Deregulation, however, can also backfire, as when the state of California deregulated its electric utilities without providing for adequate safeguards.[229] As a result of this hasty deregulation, California's electric utilities experienced dramatic increases in wholesale electricity prices. When utilities could not pay their bills, some suppliers balked at selling electricity to them, an action that precipitated the occurrence of intermittent blackouts throughout the state.

In contrast, **social regulation** seeks to curb or restrict behavior by individuals or firms that interfere with public health or safety. The case for social regulation is particularly strong when liability and tort systems prove cumbersome as mechanisms for correcting market failures.[230] Much of the success of social regulation, however, depends on the willingness of individuals and firms to comply with government requirements. When the federal government first mandated the use of seatbelts, many citizens balked at what seemed like a ridiculous requirement. Over time, seatbelt use has become common enough to save thousands of lives, which in turn has encouraged even higher levels of seatbelt buckling.[231]

Information

A central aim of interagency coordination is the sharing of information. Information sharing can foster agency specialization, the diffusion of best practices, and joint movement toward mutually held goals. Information sharing is also an important policy tool when it comes to intergovernmental relations and in public-private.

Law enforcement officials are among the leading users of interagency and intergovernmental databases. For example, prior to a gun purchase, individuals are checked against the FBI's **National Instant Criminal Background Check System** to see whether they have committed a felony, have a serious mental illness, or are otherwise ineligible to purchase a gun. After an individual attempts to buy a gun, the FBI has three days to investigate and either prohibit the sale or allow it to proceed.

This system failed tragically just weeks before Dylann Roof shot nine African Americans to death at a historic black church in Charleston, South Carolina, on June 17, 2015. Because he had recently been arrested for drug possession, Roof should have been ruled ineligible to purchase a gun. However, when the FBI's agent checked the database, she read that Roof had been arrested by Lexington County, South Carolina, officials. In fact, Roof had been arrested by Columbia, South Carolina, police, though he was detained in a Lexington County jail, which might explain the original error. When contacted by the agent, Lexington County officials indicated that they knew nothing about the arrest and recommended that she contact Columbia police. Unfortunately, the FBI's list of law enforcement agencies for South Carolina, amazingly, did not include Columbia, though it did include West Columbia. The FBI agent, based in West Virginia, was not familiar with the nuances of South Carolina's local jurisdictions. When the FBI agent contacted West Columbia police, they too knew nothing about the incident. Then, the agent, inexplicably, dropped the matter instead of looking independently for the Columbia police department's phone number, which could easily have resolved the matter. When the three-day waiting period expired, Roof was free to purchase the gun; he did so, and he killed the nine victims approximately two months later.[232]

This tragic set of circumstances illustrates one of the central themes of this chapter—namely, the vital importance of communications and coordination to bureaucratic performance, with profound consequences for public safety, public health, and public well-being. It also illustrates how easily things can unravel when a network involving federal and local agencies is involved. The information was there; it just wasn't accessed because of several human errors along the way—an incorrect arrest report, an incomplete contact sheet, and a federal official who tried to get to the bottom of things but did not try hard enough. Clearly, Roof, whose racism was the apparent motivation for the murders, was the culprit here. Just as clearly, a more effective criminal background check system could have made it difficult, if not impossible, for Roof to obtain the gun he used to commit mass murder.

In recent decades, bureaucracies have devoted substantial resources to sharing information with the general public. The Federal Trade Commission requires cigarette manufacturers to place warning labels on their products, and the Food and Drug Administration mandates companies to prepare nutrition labels clarifying the contents of foods, beverages, and other products. The evidence suggests that labeling can have an impact on target behaviors. For example, eight months after the implementation of alcohol warning labels in 1990, researchers documented a decline in drinking during pregnancy.[233] By contrast, although nutrition labels contributed to a decline in fat consumption during the early 1990s, total calorie consumption did not decline, and fat consumption quickly rose again.[234]

In 2010, the Health Department in Erie County, New York, turned to nutrition labels as a policy tool in a new context, becoming the first such agency in the nation to offer restaurant chefs the opportunity to place nutrition labels on their menus.[235] By the end of the Obama administration, chain-restaurant menus and vending-machine products were required to display nutritional information, and the "much-maligned" food pyramid had been replaced by MyPlate (see Figure 5.3), a simple and informative image divided into fruits, grains, vegetables, and protein.[236]

As first lady, Michelle Obama made child nutrition her highest priority, helping to secure passage of the Healthy, Hunger-Free Kids Act in December 2010. That act expanded the number of children receiving school lunches by

Figure 5.3 MyPlate Graphic

Source: U.S. Department of Agriculture, choosemyplate.gov.

115,000; increased the reimbursement rate to school districts for meals by six cents per meal; and replaced junk food in school vending machines with healthier food options.[237] In signing the bill, President Obama acknowledged his wife's strong commitment to child nutrition legislation: "Had I not been able to get this bill passed, I would be sleeping on the couch."[238] Once the Obamas moved out of the White House, however, efforts began to repeal certain aspects of the act, notably its healthy school lunch program. These efforts were led by the House Freedom Caucus, which, citing researchers at the University of Vermont, argued that: "The regulations have proven to be burdensome and unworkable for schools to implement. Schools are throwing food away that students are not eating."[239]

Public bureaucracies have promoted the use of **organizational report cards,** which compare the performance of two or more organizations. Studies show that such report cards can affect both organizational and public behavior. Following the introduction of a hospital report card in New York State, deaths resulting from botched heart surgery declined more rapidly in New York than in other states.[240] Following the introduction of a public school report card in North Carolina, schools whose students had performed poorly on standardized tests did better in the next iteration.[241]

In 1986, Congress mandated a report card of a different kind. The **Toxics Release Inventory** (TRI) is a database that makes available information about business firm releases into the atmosphere of hundreds of toxic chemicals. The first round of disclosures negatively affected the stock market prices of some of the heaviest polluters.[242] In response, Monsanto and other top polluters announced ambitious air toxics reduction goals.[243] The TRI data also provided environmental groups and journalists with valuable information they were able to use in press releases, briefing reports, and news stories. Although circulation of the TRI data clearly affected the behavior of private firms and supplied information to interested third parties, the general public's response was much weaker. Only 11 percent of all citizens indicated that they were familiar with the law. Furthermore, approximately half of these same citizens claimed to be familiar with a program that didn't even exist![244] Finally, evidence of the TRI's effect on housing prices is mixed. Some evidence suggests that housing prices decline as proximity to publicly identified polluting plants increases, while other evidence does not uncover such a link.[245]

At the beginning of his second term, President Obama signaled his intent to create a "scorecard" for colleges and universities, with ratings based on affordability, timely graduation rates, and other factors. As it solicited feedback on this project, the Obama administration encountered both technical and political obstacles. It is hard to measure longer-term outcomes, such as adult earnings, and it is equally hard to construct a credible value-added model that controls for student ability when assessing college performance. The Obama administration drew fire from for-profit colleges, whose timely graduation rates are extremely low, and from historically black colleges, who objected to a "one-size-fits-all" rating system that ignored the special challenges facing disadvantaged minority youth.[246] Powerful members of Congress also expressed opposition to the proposal. Confronted by both sets of obstacles, the Obama administration reconsidered its approach and announced a much less ambitious scheme in 2015.[247] In a nutshell, the U.S. Department of Education will make relevant data available to consumers but will resist the urge to rate individual colleges and universities using clear metrics.

Under what conditions, then, is information effective as a policy tool? It has been argued that information is most useful under the following circumstances:

- when the problem is caused by information asymmetry or information that is difficult to obtain;
- when the targets of public policy are very broadly dispersed but not organized;
- when the interests of policymakers and those of targeted individuals or groups are closely aligned so that voluntary compliance is likely to occur;
- when there is broad agreement about desired outcomes; and
- when no legal or politically acceptable alternative tools are available or when policy outcomes occur in partnerships or coalitions in which command-and-control approaches are impermissible.[248]

In the end, it is likely that information is an especially potent policy tool when it is combined with other instruments, such as financial incentives and the threat of government regulation.

Networks and Public Bureaucracy

Although public bureaucracies might prefer to act in isolation, much of what they do occurs in concert with other agencies, other levels of government, nonprofit organizations, and for-profit firms. In short, bureaucracies routinely exercise their authority through interorganizational networks. A key characteristic of such networks is that each organization has its own distinctive goals. Furthermore, organizations that belong to networks often differ in political and economic resources. Finally, the relationships between networked organizations are not purely hierarchical in operation.

For some types of networks to be effective, much is required. In many intergovernmental networks and public-private partnerships, some modus vivendi must be achieved between organizations with differing missions and goals. Absent such agreement, organizations are bound to be pulled in different directions, and performance will ultimately suffer. In addition, some consensus must be reached in terms of which organizations are responsible for the success or failure of particular tasks. Without such assignment, citizens and politicians will be unable to hold networks accountable.

For other types of networks to be effective, less is required. Interagency coordination, for example, oftentimes entails nothing more than information sharing. When one organization is not being asked to implement another organization's policies, it can be sufficient for organizations to share timely and salient information about activities and initiatives so that agencies with overlapping jurisdictions can avoid conflict and duplication. To be sure, one can easily underestimate the difficulty of information sharing across public bureaucracies. Nevertheless, it is, in principle, more feasible to share information than to change another agency's point of view.

As a means of organizing its presentation and evaluation of bureaucratic networks, this chapter has drawn from two conceptual traditions. The first tradition is network theory. Network theory emphasizes such concepts as centrality and density and seeks to map network structures. As highlighted above, some progress has been made in identifying key network characteristics and in linking such characteristics to network performance. On balance, however, systematic empirical assessments of the insights of network theory are relatively sparse, especially when it comes to bureaucratic outcomes. The second tradition is the tools approach. On the one hand, the theoretical propositions of the tools approach are not all that cohesive and empirical applications are often restricted to a single type of network, such as public-private partnerships or intergovernmental relations. On the other hand, the tools approach clearly draws both theoretical and empirical attention toward explaining variations in the performance of bureaucratic networks.

From network theory, it can be concluded that networks function more effectively if they possess ample resources and strong leadership. The role of external control in facilitating performance is less clear. Although some evidence points to the advantages of network autonomy, other evidence suggests that external control enhances performance, perhaps because control naturally strengthens accountability.

From the tools approach, it can be concluded that the effectiveness of particular policy instruments is highly contextual. Grants-in-aid can be useful tools for federal policymaking if they are designed to promote goals that state and local governments would not otherwise pursue (for example, redistribution) and to inhibit state and local governments from substituting federal dollars for their own resources. Contracts can be useful tools for officials at all levels of government if contractors are selected not just to reduce costs but also with the quality of services in mind. Regulations can be useful tools, provided that the economics of a given industry (child care, air transportation, occupational health and safety) is well understood by government decision makers.

As for information, it is the one indispensable tool that makes networks and policy tools function effectively. Without timely and accurate information, federal policymakers have no way of knowing how state and local officials are using federal tax dollars. Without information about the private sector, bureaucracies cannot be sure that contractors are accomplishing designated goals. Without regularly updated information, government regulators cannot correct for unexpected consequences that have the potential to undermine government policies. In these respects, network theory is right on target—communication between organizations that share responsibility for service delivery is essential. However, as the tools approach reminds us, what matters is not just who communicates with whom, but also what actors say to one another and how much leverage various parties have over one another.

Key Terms

Notes

1. Jessica Silver-Greenberg and Michael Corkery, "U.S. Just Made It a Lot Less Difficult to Sue Nursing Homes," *New York Times*, June 29, 2016, www.nytimes.com/2016/09/29/business/dealbook/arbitration-nursing-homes-elder-abuse-harassment-claims.html?_r=0 (accessed September 30, 2016).

2. Ibid.

3. Lester Salamon, *America's Nonprofit Sector* (New York: Foundation Center, 1992), 65.

4. Laurence J. O'Toole Jr., "Treating Networks Seriously: Practical and Research-Based Agendas in Public Administration," *Public Administration Review* 57 (January/February 1997): 45.

5. H. Brinton Milward, "Symposium on the Hollow State," *Journal of Public Administration Research and Theory* 6 (April 1996): 193–195.

6. E. S. Savas, *Privatization: The Key to Better Government* (Chatham, N.J.: Chatham House, 1987); William Gormley Jr., "The Privatization Controversy," in *Privatization and Its Alternatives*, ed. William Gormley Jr. (Madison: University of Wisconsin Press, 1991), 3–16; and Harvey Feigenbaum, Jeffrey Henig, and Chris Hamnett, *Shrinking the State: The Political Underpinnings of Privatization* (Cambridge, UK: Cambridge University Press, 1998).

7. Daniel R. Levinson, "Trends in Nursing Home Deficiencies and Complaints," U.S. Department of Health and Human Services, September 18, 2008, https://oig.hhs.gov/oei/reports/oei-02-08-00140.pdf (accessed March 31, 2017).

8. Robert Agranoff, "Inside Collaborative Networks: Ten Lessons for Public Managers," *Public Administration Review* 66 (December 2006, special issue): 57.

9. Ibid.

10. Kenneth J. Meier and Laurence J. O'Toole Jr., *Bureaucracy in a Democratic State: A Governance Perspective* (Baltimore: Johns Hopkins University Press, 2006), 45–66.

11. Ibid.

12. Ibid., 56.

13. Mark Granovetter, "The Strength of Weak Ties," *American Journal of Sociology* 78 (May 1973): 1360–1380.

14. Nancy Darling, "Facebook and the Strength of Weak Ties," *Psychology Today,* May 14, 2010, http://www.psychologytoday.com/blog/thinking-about-kids/201005/facebook-and-the-strength-weak-ties; and Malcolm Gladwell, "Small Change: Why the Revolution Will Not Be Tweeted," *New Yorker*, October 4, 2010, http://www.newyorker.com/reporting/2010/10/04/101004fa_fact_gladwell (accessed March 31, 2017).

15. Edward O. Laumann and David Knoke, *The Organizational State: Social Choice in National Policy Domains* (Madison: University of Wisconsin Press, 1987), 206–225.

16. Joop Koppenjan and Erik-Hans Klijn, *Managing Uncertainties in Networks: A Network Approach to Problem Solving and Decision Making* (New York: Routledge, 2004), 19–38.

17. Ibid., 7.

18. Walter J. M. Kickert, Erik-Hans Klijn, and Joop F. M. Koppenjan, "Introduction: A Management Perspective on Policy Networks," in *Managing Complex Networks: Strategies for the Public Sector,* ed. Walter J. M. Kickert, Erik-Hans Klijn, and Joop F. M. Koppenjan (London, UK: Sage, 1997), 7–11; Paul Posner, "Accountability Challenges of Third-Party Government," in *The Tools of Government: A Guide to the New Governance,* ed. Lester Salamon (New York: Oxford University Press, 2002), 546.

19. Keith Provan and H. Brinton Milward, "Do Networks Really Work? A Framework for Evaluating Public-Sector Organizational Networks," *Public Administration Review* 61 (July/August 2001): 416.

20. John Scott, *Social Network Analysis: A Handbook,* 2nd ed. (Beverly Hills, Calif.: Sage, 2001), 82, 71.

21. Catherine Alter and Jerald Hage, *Organizations Working Together* (Newbury Park, Calif.: Sage, 1993), 155, 157.

22. We are indebted to Brint Milward for bringing this concept to our attention.

23. Alter and Hage, *Organizations Working Together,* 158.

24. Ibid., 163.

25. Jesse Shore, Ethan Bernstein, and David Lazer, "Facts and Figuring: An Experimental Investigation of Network Structure and Performance in Information and Solution Spaces," *Organization Science,* 2015.

26. Malcolm Sparrow, "The Application of Network Analysis to Criminal Intelligence: An Assessment of the Prospects," *Social Networks* 13 (September 1991): 266.

27. Valdis Krebs, "Mapping Networks of Terrorist Cells," *Connections* 24 (Winter 2001): 43–52, 46.

28. Richard Rothenberg, "From Whole Cloth: Making Up the Terrorist Network," *Connections* 24 (Winter 2001): 37.

29. Peter Finn, Ian Shapira, and Marc Fisher, "A Victory Built on Lessons Learned from the Enemy," *Washington Post,* May 6, 2011.

30. Daniel L. Bynam, "Comparing Al Qaeda and ISIS: Different Goals, Different Targets," prepared testimony before the Subcommittee on Counterterrorism and Intelligence of the House Committee on Homeland Security, April 29, 2015, https://www.brookings .edu/testimonies/comparing-al-qaeda-and-isis-different-goals-different-targets/ (accessed September 30, 2016).

31. Robert Brown, "Al Qaeda vs. ISIS: Similarities, Differences, and Everything In-Between," LinkedIn, November 9, 2015, https://www.linkedin.com/pulse/al-qaeda-vs-isis-similarities-differences-everything-in-between (accessed September 30, 2016).

32. Ibid.

33. "ISIS: Portrait of a Jihadi Terrorist Organization," Meir Amit Intelligence and Terrorism Information Center, Israeli Intelligence and Heritage Commemoration Center, November 2014, http://www.terrorism-info.org.il/Data/articles/Art_20733/E_101_14_163836165.pdf (accessed September 30, 2016).

34. Ruth Sherlock, "Inside the Leadership of Islamic State: How the New 'Caliphate' Is Run," *The Telegraph,* March 29, 2017, http://www.telegraph.co.uk/news/worldnews/middleeast/iraq/10956280/Inside-the-leadership-of-Islamic-State-how-the-new-caliphate-is-run.html (accessed September 30, 2016).

35. Lester Salamon, "The New Governance and the Tools of Public Action: An Introduction," in Salamon, *Tools of Government,* 1–47.

36. Ibid.

37. Ibid., 24–37.

38. Ibid., 2.

39. Posner, "Accountability Challenges of Third-Party Government," 528–532.

40. Denise Scheberle, *Federalism and Environmental Policy* (Washington, D.C.: Georgetown University Press, 1997), 13–14.

41. James L. Buckley, "How Congress Bribes States to Give Up Power," *Wall Street Journal,* December 25, 2014, http://www.wsj.com/articles/james-l-buckley-how-congress-bribes-states-to-give-up-power-1419541292 (accessed September 30, 2016).

42. U.S. Environmental Protection Agency, "Performance Partnership Agreements," http://www.epa.gov/ocirpage/nepps/pp_agreements.htm (accessed July 31, 2011).

43. Environmental Protection Agency, Office of Congressional and Intergovernmental Relations, "National Environmental Performance Partnership System (NEPPS)," https://www.epa.gov/sites/production/files/2015-12/documents/2014_nepps_program_implementation_summary_final.pdf (accessed September 30, 2016).

44. U.S. Environmental Protection Agency, "Performance Partnership Agreements."

45. National Academy of Public Administration, *Environment.gov* (Washington, D.C.: NAPA, 2000), 135–153.

46. Department of Ecology, State of Washington, and U.S. Environmental Protection Agency, "Environmental Performance Partnership Agreement for July 1, 2015–June 30, 2017," July 2015, https://fortress.wa.gov/ecy/publications/documents/1501005.pdf (accessed September 30, 2016).

47. Ibid., 31.

48. Ibid., 24.

49. Department of Ecology, State of Washington, and U.S. Environmental Protection Agency, "Environmental Performance Partnership Agreement for July 1, 2009–June 30, 2011," July 2009, http://www.ecy.wa.gov/pubs/0901009.pdf (accessed September 30, 2016).

50. Barry Rabe, "Power to the States: The Promise and Pitfalls of Devolution," in *Environmental Policy: New Directions for the Twenty-First Century,* ed. Norman Vig and Michael Kraft (Washington, D.C.: CQ Press, 2000), 43.

51. Paul Posner, "Networking and the Chesapeake Bay Program," in *Unlocking the Power of Networks: Keys to High-Performance Government,* ed. Stephen Goldsmith and Donald Kettl (Washington, D.C.: Brookings Institution Press, 2009), 81–82.

52. "A Failing Bay Cleanup," editorial, *Washington Post,* July 27, 2015, p. 14.

53. William Gormley Jr., *Taming the Bureaucracy: Muscles, Prayers, and Other Strategies* (Princeton, N.J.: Princeton University Press, 1989), 3–31, 173–193.

54. Ashley Halsey III, "Obama Orders EPA to Take the Lead in Chesapeake Bay Cleanup Efforts," Department of Ecology, State of Washington, http://www.ecy.wa.gov/pubs/0901009.pdf (accessed September 30, 2016).

55. Ibid.

56. Annie Snider, "The War over Chesapeake Bay," *Politico,* May 25, 2016, http://www.politico.com/agenda/story/2016/05/obama-chesapeake-bay-restoration-000127 (accessed September 30, 2016).

57. "The Trump Administration's Attack on the Chesapeake Bay," editorial, March 21, 2017, https://www.washingtonpost.com/opinions/the-trump-administrations-attack-on-the-chesapeake-bay/2017/03/21/d7b5f6ec-0db6-11e7-ab07-07d9f521f6b5_story.html?utm_term=.0e129b3f1cf1 (accessed March 31, 2017).

58. Mark Lubell et al., "Watershed Partnerships and the Emergence of Collective Action Institutions," *American Journal of Political Science* 46 (January 2002): 148–163.

59. Ibid., 158.

60. Aysin Dedekorkut, "Suwannee River Partnership: Representation Instead of Regulation," in *Adaptive Governance and Water Conflict: New Institutions for Collaborative Planning,* ed. John T. Scholz and Bruce Stiftel (Washington, D.C.: Resources for the Future Press, 2005), 25–39.

61. Cooperative Conservation America, "Suwannee River Partnership," http://cooperativeconservation.org/viewproject.asp?pid=783 (accessed September 30, 2016).

62. Aysin Dedekorkut, "Suwannee River Partnership: Representation Instead of Regulation," in *Adaptive Governance and Water Conflict: New Institutions for Collaborative Planning,* ed. John T. Scholz and Bruce Stiftel (Washington, D.C.: Resources for the Future Press, 2005), 25–39.

63. Ibid.

64. Ibid.

65. "TennCare," http://www.tn.gov/tenncare (accessed July 31, 2011).

66. "Managed Care," http://en.wikipedia.org/wiki/Managed_care#cite_note-0 (accessed October 26, 2010).

67. "TennCare."

68. U.S. Department of Health and Human Services, Centers for Medicare and Medicaid Services, "Medicaid State Waiver Program Demonstration Projects—General Information," http://www.cms.gov/MedicaidStWaivProgDemoPGI (accessed July 31, 2011).

69. William Gormley Jr., "An Evolutionary Approach to Federalism in the U.S." (paper presented at the annual meeting of the American Political Science Association, San Francisco, August 31, 2001).

70. Medicaid.gov, "Demonstrations and Waivers," https://www.medicaid.gov/medicaid-chip-program-information/by-topics/waivers/waivers_faceted.html (accessed October 1, 2016).

71. Ibid.

72. "State Children's Health Insurance Program," http://en.wikipedia.org/wiki/State_Children%27s_Health_Insurance_Program (accessed August 16, 2011).

73. Henry Kaiser Family Foundation, "CHIP Program Name and Type," http://kff.org/other/state-indicator/chip-program-name-and-type, January 14, 2013 (accessed July 13, 2015).

74. Centers for Medicare and Medicaid Services, *The State Children's Health Insurance Program: Annual Enrollment Reports* (Baltimore: CMS, February 6, 2002).

75. Steven J. Balla and Christopher J. Deering, "Salience, Complexity, and State Resistance to Federal Mandates," *Journal of Public Policy* 35 (December 2015): 459–476.

76. *South Dakota v. Dole,* 483 U.S. 203 (1987).

77. Ibid., 467.

78. National Conference of State Legislatures, "State Legislation and Actions Opting-out or Opposing Certain Health Reforms," http://www.ncsl.org/documents/

summit/summit2013/online-resources/State-Legislation-Opt-out.pdf (accessed October 1, 2016).

79. Laura Stepp, "Study Casts Doubt on Abstinence-Only Programs," *Washington Post,* April 14, 2007.

80. Alesha Doan and Deborah McFarlane, "Saying No to Abstinence-Only Education: An Analysis of Decision Making," *Publius* 42, no. 4 (Fall 2012): 613–635.

81. Tara O'Toole, "Institutional Issues in Biodefense," in *Governance and Public Security,* ed. Alasdair Roberts (Syracuse, N.Y.: Campbell Public Affairs Institute, 2002), 98–110.

82. Lawrence K. Altman and Gina Kolata, "A Nation Challenged: Anthrax Missteps Offer Guide to Fight Next Bioterror Battle," *New York Times,* January 6, 2002.

83. "Brief Report: Terrorism and Emergency Preparedness in State and Territorial Public Health Departments—United States, 2004," *Journal of the American Medical Association* 294 (August 3, 2005): 549–550.

84. "Assessment of Epidemiologic Capacity in State and Territorial Health Departments—United States, 2004," *Journal of the American Medical Association* 293 (June 22/29, 2005): 2993–2994.

85. Ibid., 2993.

86. Mike Mitka, "Readiness of Local Public Health Agencies to Respond to Bioterrorism Questioned," *Journal of the American Medical Association* 294 (October 19, 2005): 1885.

87. Charles R. Shipan and Craig Volden, "The Mechanisms of Policy Diffusion," *American Journal of Political Science* 52 (October 2008): 840–857.

88. Tom Loftus, "Smoking Ban Dead for This Year," Louisville *Courier-Journal,* March 2, 2015.

89. John Gregory, "A History of Smoking Restrictions in Kentucky," Kentucky Educational Television, February 10, 2014, http://www.ket.org/legislature/posts/1003 (accessed July 10, 2015).

90. Charles R. Shipan and Craig Volden, "The Mechanisms of Policy Diffusion," *American Journal of Political Science* 52 (October 2008): 840–857.

91. "Obama Offers 'Race to the Top' Contest for Schools," *Guardian,* January 23, 2008.

92. U.S. Department of Education, "Race to the Top Program: Executive Summary," http://www2.ed.gov/programs/racetothetop/executive-summary.pdf (accessed July 31, 2011).

93. Office of Governor Rick Perry, "Gov. Perry—Texas Knows Best How to Educate Our Students: Texas Will Not Apply for Federal Race to the Top Funding," press release, Austin, Texas, January 13, 2010, http://www.texasinsider.org/gov-perry-texas-knows-best-how-to-educate-our-students/ (accessed March 31, 2017).

94. Seyward Darby, "The New Republic: Defending Obama's Education Plan," NPR, July 29, 2010, http://www.npr.org/templates/story/story.php?storyId=128843021 (accessed March 31, 2017).

95. Brandon Larrabee, "Union Opposition Dogs Florida Application for Education Race to the Top Funds," *Florida Times-Union,* February 8, 2010, http://jacksonville.com/2016-03-07/stub-796# (accessed October 1, 2016).

96. Ibid.

97. U.S. Department of Education, "Awards," http://www2.ed.gov/programs/racetothetop/awards.html (accessed October 1, 2016).

98. Council of Economic Advisers, "Explaining the Decline in Welfare Receipt, 1993–1996," May 9, 1997, http://clinton4.nara.gov/WH/EOP/CEA/Welfare/Report.html (accessed March 31, 2017).

99. Jeffrey Grogger and Lynn Karoly, *Welfare Reform: Effects of a Decade of Change* (Cambridge, Mass.: Harvard University Press, 2005), 20.

100. Council of Economic Advisers, "Explaining the Decline in Welfare Receipt."

101. Savas, *Privatization,* 124–131.

102. Phillip Cooper, "The Duty to Take Care: President Obama, Public Administration, and the Capacity to Govern," *Public Administration Review* 71 (January/February 2011): 7–18.

103. The White House, "Memorandum for the Heads of Executive Departments and Agencies—Subject: Government Contracting" (accessed October 1, 2016).

104. Noam Scheiber, "U.S. Will Require Its Contractors to Provide Paid Sick Leave," *New York Times*, September 30, 2016, http://www.nytimes.com/2016/09/30/business/economy/paid-sick-leave-government-contractors.html?_r=0 (accessed October 1, 2016).

105. Emily Kopp, "Contractors Say They've Had It with White House Executive Orders," Federal News Radio, August 11, 2015, http://federalnewsradio.com/acquisition-policy/2015/08/contractors-say-theyve-white-house-executive-orders/ (accessed October 1, 2016).

106. Paul Light, cited in Donald F. Kettl, "Managing Indirect Government," in Salamon, *Tools of Government*, 490.

107. Donald Kettl, *Sharing Power: Public Governance and Private Markets* (Washington, D.C.: Brookings Institution Press, 1993), 131.

108. Ibid., 134–138.

109. Laris Karklis and Reid Wilson, "The United States of Toll Roads," *Washington Post*, May 1, 2014.

110. Pat Choate, "Toll Roads—the Wrong of Way," *Texas Observer*, October 31, 2008.

111. Ibid.

112. Karklis and Wilson, "The United States of Toll Roads"; Choate, "Toll Roads."

113. "Performance of PPPs and Traditional Procurement in Australia," Allen Consulting Group, November 30, 2007, http://www.irfnet.ch/files-upload/knowledges/IPA_Performance%20of%20PPPs_2007.pdf (accessed on October 1, 2016).

114. Brad Plumer, "More States Privatizing Their Infrastructure. Are They Making a Mistake?" *Washington Post*, March 31, 2012, https://www.washingtonpost.com/blogs/ezra-klein/post/more-states-privatizing-their-infrastructure-are-they-making-a-mistake/2012/03/31/gIQARtAhnS_blog.html (accessed October 1, 2016).

115. Mark Rom, "From Welfare State to Opportunity, Inc.: Public-Private Partnerships in Welfare Reform," in *Public-Private Policy Partnerships*, ed. Pauline Rosenau (Cambridge, Mass.: MIT Press, 2000), 161–182.

116. Lawrence Mead, *Government Matters: Welfare Reform in Wisconsin* (Princeton, N.J.: Princeton University Press, 2004), 172.

117. Rom, "From Welfare State to Opportunity., Inc.," 161–182.

118. Marina Villeneuve, "Paul LePage Says He Doesn't Get 'Hoopla' over Welfare Contract," *Boston Globe*, September 13, 2016, https://www.boston.com/news/politics/2016/09/13/paul-lepage-says-he-doesnt-get-hoopla-over-welfare-contract (accessed October 1, 2016).

119. Mead, *Government Matters*, 161, 170.

120. Robert Garrett, "Exclusive: State Privatization Champion Gets Contract to Help Clear Up Welfare Mess," *Dallas Morning News*, March 13, 2010, http://www.dallasnews.com/news/local-politics/2010/03/13/Exclusive-State-privatization-champion-gets-1424 (accessed March 31, 2017).

121. Associated Press, "Daniels' Highly Touted Privatization Plan Runs into Trouble," *Indianapolis Times*, July 8, 2009, http://indianapolistimesblog.blogspot.com/2009/07/daniels-highly-touted-privatization.html; Associated Press, "Indiana, IBM Sue Each Other over Welfare Contract," *Indianapolis Business Journal*, May 13, 2010, http://www.ibj.com/articles/19928-indiana-ibm-sue-each-other-over-welfare-contract (accessed March 31, 2017).

122. Frank Schmalleger and John Smykla, *Corrections in the 21st Century*, 4th ed. (New York: McGraw-Hill, 2009).

123. Anne Schneider, "Public-Private Partnerships in the U.S. Prison System," in Rosenau, *Public-Private Policy Partnerships*, 203.

124. James F. Blumstein, Mark A. Cohen, and Suman Seth, "Do Government Agencies Respond to Market Pressures? Evidence from Private Prisons," Social Science Research Network, December 2007, https://papers.ssrn.com/sol3/papers.cfm?abstract_id=441007 (accessed March 31, 2017).

125. Judith Greene, "Bailing Out Private Jails," *American Prospect*, September 10, 2001, 23–27.

126. Pauline V. Rosenau, "The Strengths and Weaknesses of Public-Private Policy Partnerships," in Rosenau, *Public-Private Policy Partnerships*, 227; Greg Jaffe and Rick Brooks, "Violence at Prison Run by Corrections Corp. Irks Youngstown, Ohio," *Wall Street Journal*, August 5, 1998.

127. Ben Norton, "Incarceration Nation: U.S. Has Miles to Go in Ending Private Prisons, Legal Advocates Warn," *Salon*, September 7, 2016, http://www.salon.com/2016/09/07/incarceration-nation-the-u-s-has-miles-to-go-in-fixing-private-prisons-legal-advocates-warn/ (accessed October 1, 2016).

128. Ibid.

129. "Under Mr. Trump, Private Prisons Thrive Again," editorial, *New York Times*, February 24, 2017, https://www.nytimes.com/2017/02/24/opinion/under-mr-trump-private-prisons-thrive-again.html (accessed March 31, 2017).

130. Ibid.

131. John T. Scholz, personal communication, January 26, 2007.

132. Steven R. Smith and Helen Ingram, "Policy Tools and Democracy," in Salamon, *Tools of Government*, 565.

133. Charles Sabel, Archon Fung, and Bradley Karkkainen, *Beyond Backyard Environmentalism* (Boston: Beacon Press, 2000), 5.

134. Smith and Ingram, "Policy Tools and Democracy," 565.

135. Virginia Haufler, *A Public Role for the Private Sector: Industry Self-Regulation in a Global Economy* (Washington, D.C.: Carnegie Endowment for International Peace, 2001).

136. Matthew Potoski and Aseem Prakash, "Green Clubs and Voluntary Governance: ISO 14001 and Firms' Regulatory Compliance," *American Journal of Political Science* (April 2005): 235–248.

137. Ibid., 238.

138. Ibid.

139. Global Environment and Technology Foundation, "Final Report: The US EPA Environmental Management System Pilot Program for Local Government Entities," http://www.epa.gov/owm/is014001/emsrepor.pdf (accessed November 3, 2010).

140. Potoski and Prakash, "Green Clubs and Voluntary Governance," 236.

141. Mike Averill, "Growing Together, National Partners Support Tulsa Neighborhoods," *Tulsa World*, August 21, 2013; Nour Habib, "Growing Together Says New Data System Will Help Track Student Achievement," *Tulsa World*, October 16, 2015.

142. William Gormley Jr., *The Critical Advantage: Developing Critical Thinking Skills in School* (Cambridge, Mass.: Harvard Education Press, 2017).

143. David Bornstein, "Coming Together to Give Schools a Boost," *New York Times*, March 7, 2011, https://opinionator.blogs.nytimes.com/2011/03/07/coming-together-to-give-schools-a-boost/ (accessed March 31, 2017).

144. Strive Together, "Strive Together Welcomes Two New Network Members," Cincinnati, Ohio, press release, http://www.strivetogether.org/news/strive-releases/strivetogether-welcomes-eight-new-network-members, June 18, 2015 (accessed March 31, 2017).

145. Donald F. Norris, *Metropolitan Governance in America* (Farnham, UK: Ashgate Publishing Limited, 2015).

146. Géraldine Pflieger and Céline Rozenblat, "Introduction. Urban Networks and Network Theory: The City as the Connector of Multiple Networks," *Urban Studies* 47, no. 13 (2010): 2723–2735, 2728.

147. Robert E. Parker and Joe R. Feagin, "A 'Better Business Climate' in Houston," in Dennis Judd and Michael Parkinson, eds., *Leadership and Urban Regeneration: Cities in North America and Europe* (Newbury Park, Calif.: Sage, 1990), 216–238; Clarence N. Stone, *Regime Politics: Governing Atlanta, 1946–1988* (Lawrence: University of Kansas Press, 1989).

148. Sean Safford, *Why the Garden Club Couldn't Save Youngtown: The Transformation of the Rust Belt* (Cambridge, Mass.: Harvard University Press, 2009).

149. Ibid.

150. Ibid.

151. David Halberstam, *The Best and the Brightest* (New York: Random House, 1972).

152. Carl Bernstein and Bob Woodward, *All the President's Men* (New York: Simon and Schuster, 1974).

153. Jeffrey Cohen, *The Politics of the U.S. Cabinet* (Pittsburgh: University of Pittsburgh Press, 1988), 33–42.

154. James Pfiffner, *The Modern Presidency* (New York: St. Martin's Press, 1994), 117–128.

155. Christi Parsons, "Obama Hopes to Appoint a 'Team of Rivals,'" *Chicago Tribune,* November 15, 2008. The concept of a "team of rivals" comes from Doris Kearns Goodwin, *A Team of Rivals: The Political Genius of Abraham Lincoln* (New York: Simon and Schuster, 2005).

156. James Pfiffner, "Decision Making in the White House," *Presidential Studies Quarterly* 41 (June 2011): 244–262.

157. Chris Mooney, Brady Dennis, and Steven Mufson, "Trump Names Scott Pruitt, Oklahoma Attorney General Suing EPA on Climate Change, to Head the EPA," *Washington Post,* December 8, 2016.

158. Coral Davenport, "Rick Perry, Ex-Governor of Texas, Is Trump's Pick as Energy Secretary," *New York Times,* December 13, 2016.

159. Lorraine Woellert and Louis Nelson, "Trump Picks Ben Carson to Be HUD Secretary," *Politico,* December 5, 2016.

160. Kira Bindrim, "Donald Trump Is Picking People to Run Agencies They Hate," Quartz, December 13, 2016, http://qz.com/861897/fox-in-the-henhouse-trumps-cabinet-nominees-are-being-chosen-to-run-agencies-they-hate/; Michael Shear, "Outsiders Selected by Trump Aim to Unnerve Washington," *New York Times,* December 18, 2016, p. 1.

161. Philip Wallach, "What Trump Can Learn from Jimmy Carter's Failure to 'Drain the Swamp,'" *Fortune,* November 15, 2016, http://fortune.com/2016/11/15/trump-drain-swamp-establishment/ (accessed March 31, 2017).

162. Josh Dawsey and Andrew Restuccia, "Trump Planning to Give Cabinet Unusually Wide Latitude," *Politico,* January 9, 2017.

163. Ibid.

164. For numerous examples of this general phenomenon, see Robert Axelrod, *The Evolution of Cooperation* (New York: Basic Books, 1984).

165. Office of Management and Budget, "The Mission and Structure of the Office of Management and Budget," http://www.whitehouse.gov/omb/organization_mission (accessed October 6, 2016).

166. Ibid.

167. Executive Office of the President, https://www.whitehouse.gov/administration/eop (accessed October 6, 2016).

168. Office of Management and Budget, "Circulars," https://www.whitehouse.gov/omb/circulars_default (accessed October 6, 2016).

169. Office of Management and Budget, "OMB Circular A-11," https://www.whitehouse.gov/omb/circulars_a11_current_year_a11_toc (accessed October 6, 2016).

170. Office of Management and Budget, "Memoranda 2016," https://www.whitehouse.gov/omb/memoranda_default (accessed October 6, 2016).

171. Amy Zegart, *Flawed by Design: The Evolution of the CIA, JCS, and NSC* (Stanford, Calif.: Stanford University Press, 1999), 52.

172. U.S. Environmental Protection Agency, "Fuel Economy Labels," http://epa.gov/fueleconomy (accessed November 4, 2010).

173. Ibid.

174. "Obama's Second State of the Union" (text), *New York Times,* January 25, 2011, www.nytimes.com/2011/01/26/us/politics/26obama-text.html?scp=1&sq=obama   second state of the union&st=cse (accessed March 31, 2017).

175. Josh White, "Dole, Shalala to Lead Troop-Care Panel," *Washington Post,* March 7, 2007.

176. U.S. Department of State, "President's Interagency Task Force to Monitor and Combat Trafficking in Persons," http://www.state.gov/j/tip/response/usg/ (accessed October 6, 2016).

177. U.S. Environmental Protection Agency, Program Management Office, regulations.gov, "About Us," https://www.regulations.gov/aboutUs (accessed October 6, 2016).

178. Ibid.

179. Ibid.

180. Harold Seidman, *Politics, Position and Power* (New York: Oxford University Press, 1970), 171.

181. Committee on the Status and Future of Federal e-Rulemaking, "Achieving the Potential: The Future of Federal e-Rulemaking," http://resource.org/change.gov/ceri-report-web-version.fixed.pdf (accessed October 6, 2016).

182. David Howard Davis, *Energy Politics,* 2nd ed. (New York: St. Martin's Press, 1978), 93.

183. Luis Payan, "Cops, Soldiers, and Diplomats" (PhD diss., Georgetown University, 2001), chap. 3, 41.

184. Edward Walsh, "Challenges Familiar to Bush Pick," *Washington Post,* September 22, 2001.

185. Michael Wermuth, "Mission Impossible? The White House Office of Homeland Security," in Roberts, *Governance and Public Security,* 31.

186. Mike Allen, "White House to Increase Ridge's Exposure," *Washington Post,* October 28, 2001.

187. Eric Pianin and David Broder, "Ridge Defends His Role as 'Coordinator,'" *Washington Post,* November 18, 2001.

188. For example, the executive order used the words *coordinate* and *coordinating* thirty-seven times but never used the words *direct* or *directing*. See Wermuth, "Mission Impossible?" 32.

189. "Faltering on the Home Front," editorial, *New York Times,* May 12, 2002.

190. Helen Dewar, "Senate Passes Homeland Security Bill," *Washington Post,* November 20, 2002; "Department Subcomponents and Agencies," U.S. Department of Homeland Security, www.dhs.gov/xabout/structure/#1 (accessed August 16, 2011).

191. Steve Holland, "Obama Fashions a Government of Many Czars," Reuters, May 29, 2009, http://www.webcitation.org/5jquvIhG1 (accessed March 31, 2017).

192. Robin Bravender, "Budget Deal Axes 'Czars' Already Gone," *Politico,* April 12, 2011.

193. James Risen, "Obama Takes on Congress over Policy Czar Positions," *New York Times,* April 16, 2011.

194. Jake Miller, "GOP: Ebola 'Czar' Ron Klain Steeped in Politics, Not Medicine," CBS News, October 19, 2014, http://www.cbsnews.com/news/gop-ebola-czar-ron-klain-steeped-in-politics-not-medicine/ (accessed October 6, 2016).

195. Ibid.

196. David Dayen, "Trump Kicks Off the Return of the Czars," *The Nation,* https://www.thenation.com/article/trump-kicks-off-the-return-of-the-czars/ (accessed March 31, 2017).

197. Keith G. Provan and H. Brinton Milward, "Do Networks Really Work? A Framework for Evaluating Public-Sector Organizational Networks," *Public Administration Review* 61 (July–August 2001): 414–423.

198. Alter and Hage, *Organizations Working Together,* 210.

199. Keith G. Provan and H. Brinton Milward, "A Preliminary Theory of Interorganizational Network Effectiveness: A Comparative Study of Four Community Mental Health Systems," *Administrative Science Quarterly* 40 (1995): 1–33.

200. Eugene Bardach, *Getting Agencies to Work Together* (Washington, D.C.: Brookings Institution Press, 1998).

201. Edward Jennings, "Building Bridges in the Intergovernmental Arena: Coordinating Employment and Training Programs in the American States," *Public Administration Review* 54 (January/February 1994): 52–60.

202. Paul Peterson, Barry Rabe, and Kenneth Wong, *When Federalism Works* (Washington, D.C.: Brookings Institution Press, 1986).

203. For studies that have found evidence in support of the welfare magnet theory, see Paul Peterson and Mark Rom, *Welfare Magnets: A New Case for a National Standard* (Washington, D.C.: Brookings Institution Press, 1990); and Michael Bailey, "Welfare and the Multifaceted Decision to Move," *American Political Science Review* 99 (February

2005): 124–135. For evidence to the contrary, see Sanford Schram, Lawrence Nitz, and Gary Krueger, "Without Cause or Effect: Reconsidering Welfare Migration as a Policy Problem," *American Journal of Political Science* 42 (January 1998): 210–230.

204. Bailey, "Welfare and the Multifaceted Decision to Move," 133.

205. William Gormley Jr., "Early Childhood Care and Education: Lessons and Puzzles," *Journal of Policy Analysis and Management* 26 (Summer 2007): 633–671; Michael Puma, Stephen Bell, Ronna Cook, and Camilla Heid, "Head Start Impact Study: Final Report," U.S. Department of Health and Human Services, Administration for Children and Families, Washington, D.C., January, 2010.

206. William G. Howell, "Results of President Obama's Race to the Top," *EducationNext* 15, no. 4 (Fall 2015), http://educationnext.org/results-president-obama-race-to-the-top-reform/ (accessed October 7, 2016).

207. Ibid.

208. Ibid.

209. David Bradford and Wallace Oates, "Towards a Predictive Theory of Intergovernmental Grants," *American Economic Review* 61 (May 1971): 440–448; Brian Knight, "Endogenous Federal Grants and Crowd-Out of State Government Spending: Theory and Evidence from the Federal Highway Aid Program," *American Economic Review* 92 (March 2002): 71–92.

210. Knight, "Endogenous Federal Grants and Crowd-Out of State Government Spending," 88.

211. Anthony D. Weiner and Jeff Flake, "Security or Pork? A Review of National Homeland Security Funding Boondoggles," March 1, 2007, https://www.hsdl .org/?view&did=477656 (accessed March 31, 2017).

212. Ibid.

213. Office of Management and Budget, *Analytical Perspectives: Budget of the United States Government, Fiscal Year 2007* (Washington, D.C.: U.S. Government Printing Office, 2006), 12.

214. David Beam and Timothy Conlan, "Grants," in Salamon, *Tools of Government,* 371.

215. Gormley, *Taming the Bureaucracy,* 173–193.

216. Evan Ringquist, *Environmental Protection at the State Level* (Armonk, N.Y.: M. E. Sharpe, 1993), 126–154.

217. Suzanne Helburn, ed., *Cost, Quality, and Child Outcomes in Child Care Centers, Technical Report* (Denver: Economics Department, University of Colorado–Denver, January 1995).

218. Wayne Gray and John Scholz, "Does Regulatory Enforcement Work? A Panel Analysis of OSHA Enforcement," *Law and Society Review* 27 (1993): 177–213.

219. William Gormley Jr., *Everybody's Children: Child Care as a Public Problem* (Washington, D.C.: Brookings Institution Press, 1995), 113–117.

220. Executive Order 13563, "Improving Regulation and Regulatory Review," https:// www.gpo.gov/fdsys/pkg/FR-2011-01-21/pdf/2011-1385.pdf (accessed October 7, 2016).

221. Office of Management and Budget, "Retrospective Review of Regulations," https:// www.whitehouse.gov/omb/oira/regulation-reform (accessed October 7, 2016).

222. The White House, "Remarks by the President in State of the Union Address," https://www.whitehouse.gov/the-press-office/2012/01/24/remarks-president-state-union-address (accessed October 7, 2016).

223. Randall Lutter, "The Role of Retrospective Analysis and Review in Regulatory Policy," Mercatus Center at George Mason University, April 2012, http://mercatus.org/sites/ default/files/publication/Role-Retrospective-Analysis-Review-Regulatory-Policy-Lutter.pdf (accessed October 7, 2016).

224. Susan Dudley, "A Retrospective Review of Retrospective Review," George Washington University Regulatory Studies Center, May 7, 2013, http://regulatorystudies .columbian.gwu.edu/sites/regulatorystudies.columbian.gwu.edu/files/downloads/20130507-a-retrospective-review-of-retrospective-review.pdf (accessed October 7, 2016).

225. Cary Coglianese, "Moving Forward with Regulatory Lookback," *Yale Journal on Regulation* 30 (2013): 59.

226. Eric Katz, "New Trump Order Will Create Agency Task Forces to Eliminate Regulations," http://www.govexec.com/management/2017/02/new-trump-order-will-create-agency-task-forces-eliminate-regulations/135700/ (accessed March 31, 2017).

227. J. Clarence Davies and Jan Mazurek, *Pollution Control in the United States* (Washington, D.C.: Resources for the Future, 1998), 140–142.

228. Chip Nappenberger, "Post-Election, Post-Cap-and-Trade: Obama Clings to an Anti-CO_2 Agenda," November 9, 2010, https://www.masterresource.org/obama-energy-policy/post-cap-and-trade-obama/ (accessed March 31, 2017).

229. Peter Schrag, "Blackout," *American Prospect,* February 26, 2001, 29–33.

230. Peter May, "Social Regulation," in Salamon, *Tools of Government,* 171.

231. According to the National Highway Traffic Safety Administration, seatbelts have saved approximately 135,000 lives since 1975. See Rick Popely and Jim Mateja, "Life Savers," *Chicago Tribune,* April 21, 2002.

232. See Kevin Johnson, "FBI Chief Says Accused Shooter Shouldn't Have Been Able to Buy Gun," *USA Today,* July 10, 2015; Michael Schmidt, "Background Check Flaw Let Dylann Roof Buy Gun, F.B.I. Says," *New York Times,* July 10, 2015; Carrie Johnson, "FBI Says Background Check Error Let Charleston Shooting Suspect Buy Gun," NPR, July 10, 2015; FBI, "Statement by FBI Director James Comey Regarding Dylann Roof Gun Purchase," Washington, D.C., July 10, 2015.

233. James Hankin et al., cited in Janet Weiss, "Public Information," in Salamon, *Tools of Government,* 242.

234. David Weil et al., "The Effectiveness of Regulatory Disclosure Policies," *Journal of Policy Analysis and Management* 25 (Winter 2006): 170–171.

235. Chris Caya, "Restaurants to Offer Food Labels," WNED, Buffalo, N.Y., November 8, 2010, http://www.publicbroadcasting.net/wned/news.newsmain/article/1/0/1722995/WNED-AM.970.NEWS/Restaurants.to.Offer.Food.Labels (accessed March 1, 2012).

236. Rebecca Flint Marx, "What Obama Has Meant for Food," *New Yorker,* September 28, 2016, http://www.newyorker.com/culture/culture-desk/what-obama-has-meant-for-food (accessed October 7, 2016).

237. Nia-Malika Henderson, "President Obama Signs Child Nutrition Bill, a Priority for First Lady," *Washington Post,* December 13, 2010.

238. Ibid.

239. "Republicans Look to Scrap Michelle Obama School Lunch Plan," Fox News, January 25, 2017, http://www.foxnews.com/politics/2017/01/25/republicans-look-to-scrap-michelle-obama-school-lunch-plan.html (accessed March 31, 2017).

240. William Gormley Jr. and David Weimer, *Organizational Report Cards* (Cambridge, Mass.: Harvard University Press, 1999), 141–142.

241. Charles Clotfelter and Helen Ladd, cited in Gormley and Weimer, *Organizational Report Cards,* 156.

242. James Hamilton. "Pollution as News: Media and Stock Market Reactions to the Toxics Release Inventory Data," *Journal of Environmental Economics and Management* 28 (1995): 98–113.

243. James T. Hamilton, *Regulation through Revelation: The Origin, Politics, and Impacts of the Toxics Release Inventory Program* (New York: Cambridge University Press, 2005), 224–226.

244. Mark Atlas, Michael Vasu, and Michael Dimock, cited in Hamilton, *Regulation through Revelation,* 218.

245. Hamilton, *Regulation through Revelation,* 218–219; Weil et al., "Effectiveness of Regulatory Disclosure Policies," 171–172.

246. Michael Shear, "With Website to Research Colleges, Obama Abandons Ranking System," *New York Times,* September 12, 2015.

247. Goldie Blumenstyk, "White House Unveils College Scorecard That Replaces Its Scuttled Ratings Plan," *Chronicle of Higher Education,* September 12, 2015.

248. Weiss, "Public Information," 233–234.

6 | The Politics of Disaster Management

MANY BUREAUCRATIC DECISIONS involve the application of standard operating procedures to routine situations. For example, when inspectors at the Environmental Protection Agency (EPA) conduct reviews of pesticide labels, these reviews are guided by a three-page inspection checklist.[1] Among other things, the checklist reminds inspectors to scrutinize labels for the name of the manufacturer, the company's EPA registration number, and the statement of product ingredients. In general, pesticide inspections entail clear chains of command and established patterns of interaction among agency officials, manufacturers, and other relevant parties.

Contrast all of this regularity with EPA decision making in the area of climate change. No EPA office has sole jurisdiction over the agency's policy response to this threat to the planet. In fact, the U.S. Global Change Research Program, which is run out of the Executive Office of the President, brings together thirteen federal agencies, including the Department of Defense and National Aeronautics and Space Administration (NASA).[2] When it comes to climate change itself, although many key facts are established (temperatures are rising, human activities are negatively affecting the atmosphere), other fundamental aspects of the issue are not yet fully understood. There is uncertainty, for example, regarding how much warming will occur, how fast this warming will take place, and how increasing temperatures will affect precipitation and ocean acidity.[3]

Clearly, climate change represents in many respects a greater challenge to EPA decision makers than does the review of pesticide labels. Generally speaking, catastrophic events and potentially disastrous threats provide public bureaucracies with some of their stiffest tests. That said, not all crises are alike in the nature of the specific difficulties they present to government agencies. Some crises are preceded by similar occurrences, such as the tropical storms and hurricanes that are spawned each summer and fall in the Atlantic Ocean. Other crises lack such immediate precedent, as when terrorists used hijacked airplanes as bombs in their attacks on the World Trade Center and the Pentagon. On top of this, agencies are charged not only with reacting to crises, but also with taking steps to prospectively ameliorate or even avert disasters altogether.

Disasters also pose tough tests for the theories we have described and applied in the preceding chapters. All four of these approaches are designed to be general ways of understanding bureaucracies and their governmental and nongovernmental environments. How well do these general theories hold up in the specific context of disaster management? Do these theories provide a solid analytical basis for evaluating the successes and failures that bureaucracies experience in times of crisis?

In this chapter, we examine bureaucratic preparations for and responses to four major crises: Hurricane Katrina and the *Deepwater Horizon* oil spill, two disasters in the Gulf of Mexico with ample precedent; the terrorist attacks of September 11, 2001, an unprecedented tragedy; and an avian influenza pandemic, a potential threat that has not yet materialized. Our analyses of these cases focus on two *core questions:*

- *WHAT ACCOUNTS FOR THE BUREAUCRATIC SUCCESSES AND FAILURES THAT WERE AND ARE BEING REALIZED IN THE MANAGEMENT OF THESE DISASTERS?* In judging the relevant bureaucracies, we focus on both key structural and procedural elements in agency decision making and the outcomes that result from these decisions.

- *CAN THE THEORIES AND CONCEPTS THAT HAVE BEEN INTRODUCED IN THE PRECEDING CHAPTERS INFORM OUR UNDERSTANDING OF HOW BUREAUCRACIES HAVE COPED WITH RECENT DISASTERS AND ARE PREPARING FOR FUTURE CATASTROPHIC THREATS?* All four of these crises have been examined by journalists, pundits, and public officials. Our aim is to take an analytical approach to understanding the politics of disaster management.

At the outset, we want to emphasize the importance of being frank in our assessments without setting the bar unreasonably high for bureaucracies operating in the midst of crises. Agencies experience accountability and performance failures in all of their activities, even routine tasks such as pesticide label inspections. To use a sports analogy, we are asking whether a team can win the Super Bowl or the World Cup, whether it can succeed under the most trying of circumstances. Disaster management is, to be sure, a very demanding assignment for government bureaucracies.

The Gulf of Mexico: Two Crises with Precedent

The Gulf of Mexico is one of the United States' most treasured natural resources. The white sands of Gulf Coast beaches attract millions of visitors every year.[4] The waters of the Gulf, teeming with shrimp, oysters, and fish, sustain a sprawling industry that supplies seafood to the entire nation and provides jobs crucial to the region's fragile economy.[5]

In recent years, the Gulf of Mexico has also been the site of two of the largest and most tragic disasters in American history. In August 2005,

Hurricane Katrina claimed nearly 2,000 lives and caused in excess of $80 billion in property damage in Louisiana and other Gulf states.[6] Five years later, the biggest oil spill in history occurred when a well being drilled thousands of feet below the Gulf's surface blew out and destroyed the ***Deepwater Horizon,*** the mammoth rig that was conducting the exploration. Eleven rig workers lost their lives and approximately 4.9 million barrels of oil gushed into the Gulf before the well was capped nearly two months later.[7]

Although these disasters were historically unrivaled in their respective magnitudes, both crises were preceded by events with which they share fundamental characteristics. The Gulf Coast is routinely buffeted by hurricanes and tropical storms. Oil exploration in deep waters and other remote locations, such as the Arctic, has resulted in deaths and catastrophic spills around the world. In this section, these two crises with precedent are recounted and evaluated through the lenses of the four theoretical frameworks that have been developed in the preceding chapters.

Hurricane Katrina

The United States has thousands of miles of coastline, and, according to the National Oceanic and Atmospheric Administration, 123.3 million people (39 percent of the nation's population) live in a county directly on the East, West, or Gulf Coast shorelines.[8] Inland, many of the nation's oldest and largest cities are situated on the banks of major rivers or other significant bodies of water, such as the Great Lakes. As the U.S. population has moved westward over the years, more and more residents make their homes in locations that are particularly at risk of experiencing earthquakes and wildfires. In general, recurring natural disasters are a fact of life for millions of Americans who live in highly desirable, and highly vulnerable, parts of the country.

This certainty aside, specific weather events often strike in ways that defy pinpoint prediction. Tornadoes offer little warning to people caught in their fast-moving tracks. We know that weather disasters will occur, but we do not have the capacity to forecast beyond a reasonable doubt just when, where, and with what severity nature will unleash its fury. Also, earthquakes, much like extreme weather, vary tremendously in their magnitudes as measured on the Richter scale.

This combination of certainty and doubt aptly describes the situation when Hurricane Katrina struck. On the one hand, it was not a surprise that a hurricane would strike the Gulf Coast in late August 2005. On the other hand, the sheer size and strength of the storm, combined with the proximity of its landfall to New Orleans, made Hurricane Katrina anything but a routine tropical weather event.

Many government officials and organizations at the federal, state, and local levels came under heavy criticism in the aftermath of the storm. No bureaucracy endured more scorn than the **Federal Emergency Management Agency** (FEMA), the nation's primary disaster mitigation and relief organization. The FEMA director at the time of Hurricane Katrina, Michael Brown, lost his job,

Table 6.1 Jokes about the Government's Bungled Response to Hurricane Katrina

"No word yet on Mr. Brown's future plans, though sources say he does want to spend more time doing nothing for his family." —Jon Stewart

"Many Americans are calling on President Bush to fire the head of FEMA Michael Brown because of the slow response to the crisis. Unfortunately, due to the red tape, firing Brown will take 6 to 8 months." —Conan O'Brien

"So no one's going to be held accountable for this at all?" —Jon Stewart "No. In fact, if history is any indication, they'll be hard-pressed finding enough medals to pin on these guys. My sources tell me the head of FEMA will be dipped in bronze and turned into an award to be given to other officials." —Ed Helms

"Yesterday President Bush made his fifth visit to the area that received the most damage from Hurricane Katrina. In other words, the White House." —Conan O'Brien

Source: Daniel Kurtzman, "Hurricane Katrina Jokes," http://politicalhumor.about.com/od/hurricanekatrina/a/katrinajokes.htm (accessed October 19, 2016).

and the entire agency suffered great damage to its reputation (see Table 6.1 for some of the jokes that were told at the time by late-night comedians). What went so wrong in FEMA's preparation and response? Did anything go right in the bureaucracy's handling of Hurricane Katrina? A good place to start in addressing these questions is to take a historical look at the development of FEMA, both its high points and low points.

FEMA's Evolution. For many years after its creation in 1979, FEMA was roundly criticized for being long on promises and short on results. In the wake of the agency's poor handling of relief efforts following Hurricane Hugo in 1989, Sen. Ernest "Fritz" Hollings, D-S.C., referred to FEMA as the "sorriest bunch of bureaucratic jackasses I've ever known."[9] When FEMA responded ineptly to Hurricane Andrew in 1992, a local official appeared on national television and began to cry. "Enough is enough," she said. "Quit playing like a bunch of kids. Where the hell is the cavalry on this one? For God's sake, where are they?"[10]

Much of this changed in 1993, when President Bill Clinton appointed James Lee Witt as FEMA administrator. Witt was a longtime friend of the president and, unlike previous administrators, had extensive experience in disaster management, having served for four years as the director of the Arkansas Department of Emergency Services. Upon arriving at FEMA, Witt announced an "open door" policy so that employees would have easy access to him. On Witt's recommendation, the president filled political posts in FEMA with individuals who had backgrounds in disaster relief and intergovernmental relations. With this change in staffing orientation, FEMA was positioned to transform itself from the "political dumping ground" it had been for so many years.[11] To the surprise of many and consternation of some, Witt insisted that senior managers rotate jobs. The idea was that senior managers should not get too complacent or parochial, that they would perform better if they developed a keen sense of the agency's multiple responsibilities. As Witt put it, the goal was to "disassemble the **stovepipe structure** and reassemble it as a mass of connecting pipes."[12]

Under Witt's leadership, FEMA turned out to be one of the most impressive bureaucratic success stories in recent decades. An agency that had been vilified won many new friends, including disaster victims, state and local officials, members of Congress, and an admiring press corps. Whereas the old FEMA waited for a disaster to strike before sending food, water, and equipment, Witt's FEMA sent supplies to the scene as soon as a disaster loomed. Whereas the old FEMA procrastinated in providing relief to victims, Witt's FEMA got checks to victims in record time.[13] Whereas the old FEMA often seemed more interested in credit claiming and blame avoidance than problem solving, Witt did his best not to upstage state and local officials. As Sen. Bob Graham, D-Fla., put it, FEMA effected a "180-degree turnaround" from its response to Hurricane Andrew.[14]

One of Witt's more important changes was to articulate a clear mission for FEMA: "reduce the loss of life and property and protect our institutions from all hazards by leading and supporting the Nation in a comprehensive, risk-based emergency management program of mitigation, preparedness, response, and recovery."[15] This **all hazards approach** represented a marked departure from FEMA's historical preoccupation with preparation for a possible nuclear war. With FEMA's new stature as an effective, anticipatory, and responsive agency came a huge surge in agency morale. As one employee noted, "We don't have to wear bags over our heads when we go to meetings with other departments."[16] Another employee put it this way: "Everyone likes to wear their FEMA jackets now."[17]

And then things got worse. Upon assuming the presidency, George W. Bush appointed Joe Allbaugh as FEMA's director. Allbaugh, who had served as Bush's chief of staff in Texas and as his national campaign director in 2000, had good access to the president (like Witt) but no disaster management experience (unlike Witt). When the Mississippi River flooded Davenport, Iowa, in April 2003 for the third time in eight years, Allbaugh publicly upbraided local officials for not having built levees. He asked, "How many times will the American taxpayer have to step in and take care of this flooding, which could be easily prevented by building levees and dikes?"[18] Regardless of the merits of his argument, Allbaugh came off as blaming the victim. He subsequently apologized, but his credibility—and FEMA's—was damaged.

If public relations were a problem, internal changes were even more troublesome. Agency officials close to Witt were viewed with suspicion, and morale deteriorated. By the end of 2002, twenty-two senior staff members had quit or were fired.[19] At the same time, FEMA was struggling to rethink its mission in the wake of the September 11, 2001, terrorist attacks. In March 2003,

FEMA was absorbed into the newly created Department of Homeland Security (DHS), despite protests from Allbaugh and **Michael Brown,** who was the agency's recently appointed deputy director. When Tom Ridge was named to head the department, Allbaugh announced his resignation. Brown, whose résumé famously included a stint as director of the International Arabian Horse Association, took over as acting director and then became director.

FEMA fared poorly under the Department of Homeland Security. Instead of turning to FEMA to take the lead in drafting the **National Response Plan** for domestic incidents, Secretary Ridge asked the RAND Corporation to handle the assignment.[20] As a result, FEMA's role in crafting this important document was marginal at best. Authorized to reshape FEMA's budget virtually at will, Secretary Ridge reallocated substantial amounts of money from flood mitigation to the war on terrorism. He also transferred responsibility over preparedness grants from FEMA to state and local officials.[21] When a new secretary, Michael Chertoff, took over Homeland Security in early 2005, he reduced FEMA's authority even further. Although Brown argued against these changes, he lacked friends in high places. As one FEMA staffer put it, "Mike was often his own worst enemy. . . . He never cultivated any friends in the department or anywhere in Washington for that matter that I could see who were willing to go to bat for him. And the sad truth is FEMA suffered for it. FEMA suffered because people were making stupid decisions and Brown could not stop them."[22]

Despite the friction between FEMA and almost everyone else, the agency managed to respond reasonably well to a rapid series of four hurricanes that hit Florida in 2004. Politically and administratively, conditions were favorable. Florida, perhaps more than any other state, was battle tested and prepared for the hurricane season. Gov. Jeb Bush, the president's brother, was well situated to ask for and receive federal assistance. The fact that Florida was a key electoral battleground and that 2004 was a presidential election year may also have been important. Whatever the reasons, the federal government opened up its coffers to Florida, which made FEMA's job much easier. As the *Wall Street Journal* put it, "Washington pulled out all the stops to ensure that the state—and its voters—got everything they needed."[23]

Katrina Strikes. Hurricane Katrina struck the Gulf Coast with pitiless ferocity on August 29, 2005. In addition to the nearly 2,000 people who died, more than 200,000 homes were destroyed and another 45,000 residences were assessed as unlivable.[24] The storm also destroyed close to 19,000 businesses.[25] Combined with Hurricane Rita, which made landfall near the Texas–Louisiana border less than a month later, damage was inflicted on more than 90,000 square miles of territory.[26] The toll was particularly heavy in New Orleans. In addition to the many hundreds who died, about half of the city's nearly 500,000 residents did not return after the storm.[27]

All of this occurred, unfortunately, at a time when FEMA was particularly weakened. Approximately 500 of the agency's 2,500 positions were vacant, and eight of ten regional directors were working in an acting capacity when Hurricane Katrina struck.[28] Furthermore, lines of authority in the

Department of Homeland Security were uncertain and untested in the face of such a massive natural disaster. Perhaps it is not surprising, then, that Terry Ebbert, head of emergency operations in New Orleans, had this to say: "This is a national disgrace. FEMA has been here three days, yet there is no command and control."[29]

FEMA's blunders before, during, and after Hurricane Katrina were committed by officials all the way up and down the organization's **chain of command,** including those working for the scores of private firms with whom the agency had service contracts. Basic supplies—power generators, medical equipment, emergency communications systems—were not effectively transported to areas where they were needed the most. "Where's my god-dam ice?" was the question one state official heatedly posed during a telephone argument with Michael Brown.[30] FEMA even had great difficulty getting Jim Strickland, its designated Hurricane Katrina team leader, into New Orleans.[31] With road signs down, Strickland's convoy accidentally separated on the way to the city. Without a scout or global positioning system, Strickland received faulty information about conditions in and around the Morial Convention Center, causing him to bypass the center city altogether and establish a base camp in the parking lot of a suburban Sam's Club.

FEMA, of course, was not the only bureaucracy overwhelmed by Hurricane Katrina's destruction. The mayor of New Orleans, C. Ray Nagin, made a colossal mistake by not issuing a mandatory evacuation order well in advance of the storm.[32] With education, economic development, and other pressing issues on the agenda, Nagin's administration had not placed much of an emphasis on improving the city's hurricane preparedness.[33] In fact, Nagin was one of the few public officials in the so-called hurricane belt who had not established a working relationship with Max Mayfield, the director of the National Hurricane Center (NHC).[34] Lacking a direct channel into NHC, Nagin missed out on valuable information and insights that may have changed his decision making and reduced Hurricane Katrina's toll on New Orleans.

Applying the Theories. Without denying the role that lackluster leadership played in the bureaucracy's handling of Hurricane Katrina, the four theoretical perspectives direct our attention to additional considerations. When it comes to bureaucratic reasoning, decision makers put into practice a variety of elements of bounded rationality, both before and after Hurricane Katrina made landfall. The results were decidedly mixed.

In 2004, FEMA funded a week-long test designed to simulate what it would be like if a major hurricane hit New Orleans. The scenario, dubbed **Hurricane Pam,** was eerily evocative of what happened just a year later, with levee failures, ten-foot-high floodwaters, and a city teeming with hazardous debris.[35] Although simulations can enhance decision making based on bounded rationality, this particular test was limited in several key respects. Because of funding shortfalls, many FEMA officials were unable to attend the Hurricane Pam event and other exercises similar to it.[36] Furthermore, follow-up workshops were not convened until July 2005, too late to be of much use when Hurricane Katrina struck the following month.[37]

As documented in Chapter 2, bounded rationality often entails the application of standard operating procedures to recurring circumstances. In the aftermath of Hurricane Katrina, FEMA arranged, with great difficulty, for commercial airlines to evacuate remaining residents out of New Orleans. Then, consistent with its usual practices, the Transportation Security Administration insisted that all passengers and luggage be screened before any planes left Louis Armstrong International Airport.[38] This normally laudable practice was hindered by the fact that the electricity required to operate screening machines was not readily available in a city still without power! In addition, the Department of Homeland Security mandated that undercover air marshals, a standard and undoubtedly useful element of contemporary aviation security, be present on all departing flights.[39] In the end, the evacuation took two long days to arrange, demonstrating how the invocation of standard operating procedures can under certain circumstances produce dysfunctional outcomes. These particular procedures certainly made it more difficult for FEMA to do its job.

One of the main lessons of Chapter 3 is that the delegation of policymaking authority to the bureaucracy varies systematically across types of issues. Disaster management is high in both salience and complexity, a combination that often results in significant levels of discretion for agencies. This discretion, however, is often accompanied by procedural constraints on the exercise of delegated authority. For example, FEMA had the authority to purchase 145,000 trailers and mobile homes as a way of housing some of those displaced by Hurricane Katrina. Yet when more than 8,000 of these units went unused, procedures imposed on FEMA by Congress greatly restricted the agency's ability to sell the units or allot them to house victims of subsequent disasters.[40] To be sure, FEMA made its share of mistakes in the acquisition process, such as purchasing modular homes that could not be used in flood zones.[41] That said, many of the problems associated with the units were ultimately attributable to delegation decisions made by political principals.

Some of FEMA's leadership shortcomings can also be traced back to elected officials. As discussed earlier, President Bush appointed a pair of FEMA administrators who lacked prior experience in disaster management. One of these agents, Michael Brown, did not serve his principal well during Hurricane Katrina, despite the president's infamous assertion, "Brownie, you're doing a heck of a job." In retrospect, the appointment of Brown was an instance where adverse selection came back to haunt the administration.

But Brown was only part of the problem. Lines of authority changed abruptly when FEMA became part of the Department of Homeland Security. At a time when the administration, and the nation, was directing its attention more toward terrorist threats than natural disasters, even a highly competent, highly experienced FEMA director would have struggled to get his agency's mission noticed and funded. Furthermore, it was the secretary of homeland security, not the FEMA administrator, who was ultimately in charge of the federal government's actions. The day after Hurricane Katrina made landfall, Secretary Chertoff declared the disaster an "incident of national significance" and activated the National Response Plan.[42] Chertoff also named Brown as his "principal federal official," a designation that in some respects curtailed the FEMA administrator's ability to act independently.[43] At one point, Chertoff gave this order to Brown: "I don't want you running around, flying around all over the place, I want you to go to Baton Rouge and not leave Baton Rouge."[44] Brown was thus in the difficult administrative position of being closely monitored by one of his principals while at the same time attempting to direct the behavior of his own agents.

In general, these types of **vertical communications** were a major problem during Hurricane Katrina. In severe natural disasters, commercial landline and cellular phone systems are often compromised or destroyed, which means that emergency systems must be in place.[45] Unfortunately, adequate **emergency communications systems** were not in place in New Orleans. During a radio interview, Chertoff demonstrated a lack of awareness of just how dire things were getting for evacuees at the Convention Center: "Actually I have not heard a report of thousands of people in the Convention Center who don't have food and water."[46] As this lack of accurate information suggests, the ability of leaders at the top of the bureaucracy to communicate with agents in the field was drastically compromised during key moments in the rescue and recovery operations.

The seeds of New Orleans's destruction had been sown many years and decades before Hurricane Katrina unleashed its disruptive fury. Local officials consistently made decisions to favor economic development over the protection of wetlands. Members of Congress made careers out of sanctioning public works projects that were of debatable merit. Historically, Louisiana has received more funding from the Army Corps of Engineers than any other state, with the lion's share of resources going to oil, fishing, and navigation projects.[47] Levees constructed along the Mississippi River had the effect of reducing the amount of silt carried out to the Gulf of Mexico, which in turn stunted the creation and preservation of coastal marshes and swamps. These wetlands, which serve as "hurricane speed bumps," have been vanishing at a rate of twenty-four square miles per year.[48] In addition, the **Mississippi River Gulf Outlet,** an artificial navigation channel connecting downtown New Orleans with the Gulf of Mexico, cuts right through a series of pristine marshes and natural levees. Its path, some experts say, has created a hurricane superhighway that amplifies the height and ferocity of storm surges, perhaps by as much as two feet during Hurricane Katrina.[49]

This combination of long-term conditions is strikingly reminiscent of what Chapter 4 described as "client politics." Water projects along the Mississippi River and the Gulf Coast are usually characterized by concentrated benefits and diffuse costs. In other words, local interests reap gains that are paid for by the nation as a whole. There is little wonder, then, that the Louisiana congressional delegation and the Army Corps of Engineers have been able to secure a steady stream of funding for their preferred projects without needing to justify these efforts in the context of national water priorities. Although these projects no doubt fueled economic growth beneficial to those living in and around New Orleans, they also played no small role in the chain of events that exacerbated the death and destruction left behind by Hurricane Katrina.

Client politics persisted after the storm as well. Well-connected firms received **no-bid contracts,** which meant they did not have to compete with other companies to prove they could do the work better, faster, and cheaper. The Shaw Group, represented by former FEMA administrator Joe Allbaugh, won a $100 million no-bid contract to provide housing to displaced residents and another $100 million contract to pump water out of flooded New Orleans. Another Allbaugh client, KBR (an engineering, procurement, and construction company), secured $88 million in contracts in just over a month.[50] Some of these no-bid awards were so objectionable that the Department of Homeland Security was forced to reopen negotiations and allow other firms to enter the competitions. The bipartisan outrage that was directed at these awards points to the constraints client-based iron triangles face when diffuse constituencies become interested in issues they had formerly ignored.

In an ideal world, a network of public, nonprofit, and for-profit organizations would have responded promptly and vigorously to Hurricane Katrina. In reality, organizations both inside and outside government did too little too late. According to one estimate, as many as 533 organizations engaged in response operations after the hurricane struck. Few of these organizations intervened in advance of the storm, however, and many waited days or even weeks before taking action.[51] What eventually emerged was a loosely connected network, with an extremely low level of centralization.[52] This lack of centralization may have hindered the network's overall effectiveness, as there was no core agency or set of agencies through which organizational participants were connected to one another.[53]

One of the more notable network failures was the poor coordination between FEMA and the Red Cross.[54] The Red Cross did not get significantly involved in relief efforts until September 15, more than two weeks after Hurricane Katrina had made landfall.[55] In fact, the Red Cross never opened up a shelter in New Orleans, owing to its long-standing policy of not operating facilities in locations near or below sea level.[56] Even in areas where the Red Cross maintained an active presence, such as Houston and Baton Rouge, organization officials complained about FEMA's inability to process and respond in a timely manner to requests for cooperation.[57] For their part, FEMA officials found it difficult to work with the Red Cross's constantly rotating workforce of staff and volunteers.[58] In light of these failures, the National Response Plan was modified after Hurricane Katrina to place FEMA in charge of shelters, food, and first aid. In taking these steps, the plan in effect relegated the Red Cross to a subsidiary role.[59] The relationship between these longtime network partners, in other words, was transformed into more of a hierarchical arrangement.

The Coast Guard and Other Success Stories. Although FEMA was widely scorned for its performance during Hurricane Katrina, another federal agency, the Coast Guard, won nearly universal acclaim. The Coast Guard's leaders took decisive action two days before the storm. In anticipation of a major disaster, the agency moved its regional headquarters from New Orleans to

Inside Bureaucracy with	Tom Ridge *Secretary of Homeland Security* *(2003–2005)*

"The Coast Guard is the most heavily tasked, multitasked, underfunded, underappreciated, lean-forward organization in the federal government and they've got nothing but a can-do attitude. Everybody is trained to do multiple things. They do multiple missions, and they do multiple missions with the same personnel and the same equipment. So the coastee who is pulling a civilian off of a flooded street or neighborhood is the same coastee a couple years later who could be running down drug dealers in the Gulf of Mexico, is the same coastee who could be working on port security. So there's this mindset within the U.S. Coast Guard. . . . They have so many missions. So there's great leadership from the top to the bottom. It's an attitude. They're just damn good at what they do and they're called on to do a lot of things. There's an esprit there that I think is exceptional. They really always rise to the occasion. And they are grossly underfunded, grossly underfunded."

St. Louis and established another command center in Alexandria, Virginia.[60] When Hurricane Katrina struck, the agency deployed 3,000 personnel to the region, along with a fleet of cutters and helicopters. Coast Guard employees, many of whom had lost their own homes in the flooding, demonstrated considerable valor and resourcefulness throughout the ordeal. What's more, these responders were indefatigable. As one official recalled, "The pace we kept up was amazing. When I say we were working around the clock, I mean it. Both boat and air. We were all go, go, go. Every minute of delay meant a possible loss of life."[61] Thanks to the Coast Guard's interventions, more than 33,000 people were rescued.[62]

What enabled the Coast Guard to respond so effectively while other agencies were dropping the ball? First, the Coast Guard performs a wide variety of missions, such as intercepting drugs, patrolling war zones, offering humanitarian relief, rescuing refugees on dilapidated boats, cleaning up oil spills, and identifying terrorist threats.[63] While employees tend to specialize in specific types of operational tasks, all personnel are trained to meet **across-the-board standards.** As a result, teams can quickly form up in emergencies, with each member knowing what every job entails and how it fits into the overall mission.[64] Second, the Coast Guard possesses an excellent emergency communications system. When the power went out throughout the Gulf region, the Coast Guard's system continued to function, enabling agency officials in disparate locations to communicate and coordinate with one another. Third, the Coast Guard had strong, experienced leadership. Admiral Thad Allen, the Coast Guard's chief of staff during Hurricane Katrina, had headed up the agency's maritime response to the September 11, 2001, terrorist attacks. At that time, Allen earned praise for acting decisively, by blocking the Potomac River and securing ports in New York and Boston. Within days of Hurricane Katrina, Allen was tapped to replace Michael Brown as the official in charge of federal recovery efforts in New Orleans.[65]

Other federal agencies also performed well during Hurricane Katrina. The National Weather Service provided accurate forecasts of the storm's intensity and location, which gave public officials enough time to mobilize an evacuation effort. Although many citizens remained behind, this was certainly not the fault of the National Weather Service, which warned that the storm would be fierce and devastating. One of its bulletins presciently stated: "Hurricane Katrina . . . A most powerful hurricane with unprecedented strength . . . Most of the area will be uninhabitable for weeks . . . perhaps longer."[66] Likewise, the Forest Service behaved admirably during the ordeal, supplying more than 600,000 people with 2.7 million meals, 4 million gallons of water, and 40 million pounds of ice.[67] And when the delivery of Social Security checks was disrupted, the Social Security Administration responded resourcefully by making emergency payments to destitute senior citizens.[68]

Success stories such as these do not erase, of course, the failures in accountability and performance that plagued much of the bureaucracy before, during, and after Hurricane Katrina. These successes do serve as reminders, however, that failure was not inevitable. How, then, have the theories helped us understand the difference between bureaucratic victory and defeat?

All of the agencies and nongovernmental organizations we have considered applied standard operating procedures to the decisions they confronted during Hurricane Katrina. In many instances, these procedures broke down in the face of the sheer size and strength of the storm and the exceptional vulnerability of its Gulf Coast targets. The primary exceptions were those procedures explicitly designed to meet the specific challenges that emerged. For example, the Coast Guard's prior experience with dangerous air missions allowed the agency's operatives to carry out exceedingly difficult, and lifesaving, rooftop rescues.

The theories point out that standard operating procedures are designed to fulfill tasks handed to agencies by their bosses and requested by their clients. In many respects, these outside actors redesigned the bureaucracy for the worse prior to Hurricane Katrina. Many agencies, including FEMA, had shifted their emphasis toward terrorism and away from natural disasters. Agencies throughout the government had long pursued questionable policies that fostered development beneficial to Gulf Coast legislators, economic interests, and residents themselves. Ultimately, failures inside the bureaucracy were in no small part a reflection of failures in the larger political system within which the agencies were embedded.

The Deepwater Horizon *Oil Spill*

In recent decades, the search for oil has taken the government and the petroleum industry to remote areas that are home to some of the world's most pristine ecosystems. From Alaska to Washington, D.C., for example, a debate has raged regarding the economic benefits and environmental costs of drilling for oil in the Arctic National Wildlife Refuge, the largest wildlife refuge in the entire United States.[69] In the Gulf of Mexico, it is not uncommon for oil reserves to be located thousands of feet beneath the surface of the water and the salt, sandstone, and other geological features that characterize the deep ocean floor. Although such drilling is inherently risky in a number of respects, the occurrence of disasters of the magnitude of the *Deepwater Horizon* blowout is by no means preordained. What, then, went so tragically wrong on the day of the explosion, as well as in the days, months, and years leading up to the oil spill?

April 20, 2010, was an important day on board the *Deepwater Horizon,* a state-of-the-art, semisubmersible rig that specialized in deepwater oil and gas exploration.[70] The crew of the *Deepwater Horizon,* more than 100 managers, engineers, and auxiliary workers, was completing the lengthy and exceedingly difficult process of drilling an undersea well that was two-and-a-half miles deep. All that remained was for specialists to verify the structural integrity of the well, after which the *Deepwater Horizon* was scheduled to move on to another exploratory project elsewhere in the Gulf of Mexico.

A key element in remotely assessing the construction of undersea wells is the performance of pressure tests.[71] For example, in a **negative-pressure test,** rig workers decrease the pressure inside a well and then close the well off. If the pressure inside the well remains steady, the evidence suggests that the well's steel casings and concrete sealants are holding steady in the seabed's high-pressure environment. If, however, the well's internal pressure builds back up, there is an indication that the structural integrity of the well may be compromised.

This latter result is exactly what was discovered when the crew on the *Deepwater Horizon* conducted its negative-pressure test. Faced with this unwelcome evidence of rising pressure levels, crew members came to two very different conclusions. One interpretation, derived from prior experiences with negative-pressure tests, was that the readings were anomalous and not indicative of actual levels inside the well.[72] Another expressed opinion was that "something wasn't right."[73]

The primary danger associated with a well that is structurally compromised is that oil and gas can gush in an uncontrolled manner up though the drilled column. Sure enough, shortly after the negative-pressure tests were concluded, mud and seawater suddenly began spewing out of the Gulf of Mexico onto the *Deepwater Horizon,* a surefire indication that the well was blowing out.[74] Before frantic crew members were able to close the well off, gas that had shot all the way up from under the ocean floor ignited on the rig's platform, triggering deadly explosions and engulfing the *Deepwater Horizon* in flames. Thirty-six hours later, the rig that had cost hundreds of millions of dollars to construct capsized and sank to the bottom of the Gulf.[75]

Bounded Rationality on the Deepwater Horizon. How might the decisions that were made on board the *Deepwater Horizon* regarding the negative-pressure test and its interpretation be understood from a theoretical point of view? As discussed in Chapter 2, bounded rationality is an approach to decision making that is frequently employed in the context of difficult problems. Making inferences about natural and man-made conditions 5,000 feet below the water and an additional 13,000 feet below the surface of the seafloor certainly classifies as a difficult decision-making environment.

Under conditions of bounded rationality, decision makers routinely rely on standard operating procedures as a means of decomposing complex environments into manageable, discrete judgments. Unfortunately, such procedures had not been adequately developed in the context of negative-pressure tests, even though such tests constitute ordinary practice in deep-sea exploratory drilling. Sam Sankar, deputy chief counsel of the presidentially appointed **National Commission on the BP *Deepwater Horizon* Oil Spill and Offshore Drilling,** described the situation in this way: "Why would these men not have realized that this was a bad negative pressure test? Nobody in industry or in government had set forth any procedures governing what the negative pressure test is, how to conduct it, or how to interpret it."[76]

Given this lack of well-developed guidance, crew members on the *Deepwater Horizon* were faced with making a real-time, high-stakes choice between two very different courses of action. The negative-pressure test could have been deemed a failure, a decision that would have prompted the initiation of remedial efforts aimed at shoring up the structural integrity of the well. This remediation would have required at least one week of additional work, at an estimated cost to BP of as much as $10 million.[77]

The alternative course of action was to declare the negative-pressure test a success, despite the realization of readings indicating that pressure levels inside the well were increasing without abatement. Why did crew members settle on this interpretation of the negative-pressure test and conclude that rising pressure levels were anomalous and not indicative of underlying problems in structural integrity? The evidence does not suggest a "conscious decision to sacrifice safety to save money."[78] Rather, crew members relied on prior experiences with the results of negative-pressure tests to come to their judgments. For example, Jason Anderson, a veteran driller who had worked on the *Deepwater Horizon* since it had first been commissioned years earlier, stated that he had observed this particular configuration of pressure readings in the context of other explorations.[79] In the view of Anderson and others, the collection of additional information and the imposition of remedial efforts were unnecessary given the presence of a plausible, benign explanation for the pressure readings. In the end, this decision, which was made without the benefit of clearly articulated standard operating procedures, was an immediate contributing factor to the blowout that occurred shortly thereafter.

Networks and Oil Exploration. Although a focus on decision making in the moments leading up to the *Deepwater Horizon* explosion is undoubtedly insightful, such a perspective naturally begs a broader question: Why, in the first place, were there problems of structural integrity with the well that had been drilled? From the perspective of this book's theoretical frameworks, the prevalence of networks of organizations spanning the oil industry is a salient factor deserving detailed consideration.

From a private sector perspective, no single organization in existence possesses the wherewithal to conduct deepwater oil exploration on its own. At the **Macondo well,** the name for the site where the *Deepwater Horizon* was stationed in the spring of 2010, three main companies were responsible for the operations that were being carried out. In 2008, **BP,** one of the largest energy companies in the world, had purchased from the federal government a lease that conferred exclusive drilling rights in an area of the Gulf of Mexico known as the Mississippi Canyon. It was under the terms of this lease that BP was conducting a search for an oil and gas reservoir thousands of feet below the surface of the water and seafloor.[80]

In carrying out this exploration, BP was fundamentally reliant on two other major corporations. One of these corporations was **Halliburton,** an oilfield services company that was responsible for cementing in the Macondo well.[81] The other corporation was **Transocean,** a company that owns nearly half of the world's deepwater drilling platforms.[82] The *Deepwater Horizon* was the pride of Transocean's fleet, as it commanded daily leasing fees of hundreds of thousands of dollars for its work on the frontiers of deepwater exploration.[83]

As discussed in Chapter 5, a key attribute of networks is differentiation, the extent to which network participants engage in functional and service specialization. The network of private sector organizations operating at the Macondo well site certainly was characterized by extensive differentiation. For example, although BP engineers were engaged in designing the formula for the cement sealant and the process by which the sealant would be pumped down into the well, it was Halliburton engineers who were primarily responsible for creating the cement blend and analyzing its properties.[84] As Halliburton's work on the project progressed, a number of laboratory tests indicated that the cement blend would likely be unstable in the conditions under which it was to be deployed. The evidence suggests that in some instances the results of these tests were never reported to officials at BP.[85] In one instance in which Halliburton did transmit results, it is far from certain that BP decision makers ever examined the report's information about the potential instability of the cement blend.[86] Given the eventual failure of the cement sealant to hold back oil and gas from the reservoir, the differentiated nature of the corporate network involved in the Macondo well project appears to have been a major contributing factor to the blowout and subsequent oil spill.

As an instance of vital, highly technical safety information not adequately making its way through communications channels in a differentiated network, the *Deepwater Horizon* oil spill shares much in common with the Space Shuttle *Challenger* disaster. On January 28, 1986, the *Challenger* broke apart seventy-three seconds after it was launched from Kennedy Space Center. The proximate cause of the breakup was the failure of an O-ring seal in one of the vehicle's solid rocket boosters; the function of the seal was to keep pressurized hot gases from reaching an external fuel tank being used to propel the ascent.[87] According-ing to the Presidential Commission on the Space Shuttle *Challenger* Accident, information about design flaws inherent in the O-rings was not sufficiently circulated among government and private sector organizations involved in the Space Shuttle network.[88] For example, managers at the George C. Marshall Space Flight Center, a research organization operated by NASA, had known about such O-ring problems for nearly a decade, but they had never discussed the matter outside their reporting channels with Morton Thiokol, the private contractor that had designed the solid rocket boosters.[89] This egregious violation of NASA regulations meant that crucial information about "internal flight safety problems" had not been communicated to "key Shuttle managers." In general, both the *Deepwater Horizon* and the Space Shuttle *Challenger* disasters demonstrate that differentiated networks can impede the flow of technical information, thereby increasing the difficulty of preserving the safety of complex, potentially dangerous systems.

The Minerals Management Service: A Problematic Principal. From its creation in 1982 until the *Deepwater Horizon* oil spill, the **Minerals Management Service** (MMS) operated as the federal agency with jurisdiction over the offshore oil and gas industry.[90] Located within the Department of the Interior, the MMS was explicitly designed to bring together into a single organization a pair of functions that proved over time to be inherently conflictual. The first function was to regulate the industry and its activities, as a means of enhancing the safety of exploration and extraction processes and, more broadly, safeguarding for future generations treasured aquatic resources. The second function was to ensure a continued flow into government coffers of royalties and revenues from oil and gas resources under federal control.

Over time, this income-generation function came to dominate the mission of the MMS. MMS directors who served under Presidents Barack Obama and George W. Bush have stated that royalty issues consumed the bulk of their time on the job.[91] The reasons for this domination are not difficult to comprehend. By the 1980s, royalties and revenues from oil and gas resources constituted one of the largest and most dependable streams of income for the federal government. In 2008 alone, federal **offshore royalty revenues** totaled more than $18 billion, a record haul bolstered by a lease sale in Alaska's Chukchi Sea that brought in $2.6 billion.[92]

With the organizational focus of the MMS fixed predominantly on revenue generation, industry safety and environmental protection suffered accordingly. During 1995, for example, nearly 100 fires, explosions, and other incidents associated with the oil and gas industry in the Gulf of Mexico were reported to the MMS.[93] These accidents injured and, in some instances, claimed the lives of workers on drilling rigs and offshore supply vessels. One commander with the Coast Guard explained in colorful terms the industry attitude that flourished in the absence of sustained, effective regulatory oversight: "There's a cowboy mentality out there: 'Don't think about it, do it.'"[94]

Over time, episodes of cozy relations between the MMS and industry officials were documented. For example, Randall Luthi, who served as MMS director from 2007 until 2009, subsequently became president of the National Oceans Industries Association, an organization seeking to secure a "favorable regulatory and economic environment for the companies that develop the nation's valuable offshore energy resources."[95] In general, the revolving door between government service and employment in regulated industry that was discussed in Chapter 4 is not uncommon in the area of offshore oil and gas exploration and extraction.

Despite such connections between the MMS and the industry it regulated, the organization's fundamental difficulties did not stem from a lack of commitment and ethical behavior on the part of agency executives, managers, and operators.[96] Rather, the agency lacked the resources necessary to design and enforce regulations in an environment characterized by rapidly changing technology and industrial practices. During the latter half of the 1990s, when deepwater oil production for the first time outstripped production from shallow water wells, the budget of the MMS fell to an all-time low.[97] In assessing this combination of realities, the National Commission on the BP *Deepwater Horizon* Oil Spill and Offshore Drilling concluded that "MMS was unable to maintain up-to-date technical drilling-safety requirements to keep up with industry's rapidly evolving deepwater technology."[98]

To employ the language of principal-agent theory, the MMS inherently faced substantial moral hazard difficulties in pursuing the daunting task of regulating the offshore oil and gas industry. Unfortunately, the institutional design of the agency fundamentally handicapped the ability of regulators to establish and carry out effective oversight of industry equipment and practices. At the Macondo well site, a number of federal statutes, including the Clean Water Act and the Endangered Species Act, could potentially have been utilized to review aspects of the *Deepwater Horizon*'s drilling operations.[99] In the end, however, none of these instruments of reducing moral hazard and mitigating agency loss was invoked by officials at the MMS.

In the weeks following the *Deepwater Horizon* explosion and oil spill, Secretary of the Interior Ken Salazar bestowed upon the tarnished MMS a new name—the **Bureau of Ocean Energy Management, Regulation, and Enforcement.**[100] Secretary Salazar further divided the organization into a number of separate entities, each with its own distinct mission.[101] For example, the **Office of Natural Resources Revenue** is now charged with collecting payments derived from offshore oil and gas exploration and extraction. Workplace safety and environmental protection is now the province of the **Bureau of Safety and Environmental Enforcement.**

As mentioned in Chapter 2, bureaucratic restructuring (as a manifestation of the availability heuristic) frequently follows the occurrence of disasters. In the long run, will the breaking apart of the MMS result in sufficient attention being paid to both the preservation of natural resources and the procurement of financial and energy resources upon which the United States is economically, socially, and politically dependent? In 2016, the Obama administration made millions of acres in the Gulf of Mexico available for oil and gas drilling.[102] This profitable lease sale, which was held in New Orleans, was praised by the National Ocean Industries Association. It was also vehemently protested by community and climate change activists: "Our rallying cry is to take on fossil fuel extraction and, in particular, challenge the Obama administration to stop the sale of fossil fuels on our public lands."[103] Given that much of the pressure placed on MMS to aggressively pursue revenue generation historically came from elected officials, the reorganization of MMS, while useful in certain respects, leaves in place principal-agent dynamics that have long defined the politics of oil and gas exploration.[104]

Of Booms, Berms, and Client Politics. **Booms** are artificial barriers used to contain oil spills and prevent harmful substances from contaminating beaches, marshes, and other environmentally sensitive areas. As a means of responding to the oil gushing out of the Macondo well, booms were distinctive from other widely utilized approaches, such as skimming, burning, and spraying chemical dispersants.[105] In contrast to such approaches, booms are physical objects that stop encroaching oil slicks in ways that are highly visible from the air, water, and coast. According to one cynical Louisiana resident, booms were "eye candy," offering a sense of satisfaction that something was being done to protect cherished ways of life and natural resources.[106]

Although booms offer a number of advantages, the efficacy of physical barriers in containing oil spills is in part a function of tidal and meteorological conditions. Ocean currents can carry oil underneath booms that are not appropriately placed. Storms can blow oil over the top of booms and push the barriers themselves into environmentally fragile areas that they are designed to protect.[107]

Booms and other types of physical barriers are also distinctive in the mobilization of societal interests by which they are typically characterized. The benefits of the deployment of booms most immediately accrue to concentrated interests, namely, residents of coastal areas who are affected by oil spills and comforted by the sight of protective barriers. The costs of booms, in contrast, are typically borne by diffuse interests, such as multinational corporations and government organizations. As discussed earlier in the context of Hurricane Katrina, such combinations of concentrated benefits and diffuse costs are associated with client politics in which mobilization on the part of specific interests outstrips the activism of broad constituencies.

One by-product of client politics is bureaucratic decision making in which agencies are especially responsive to the interests of concentrated beneficiaries. Responsiveness to local interests is precisely what occurred in the context of boom deployment. Scientifically, the placement of booms is a function of forecasts regarding the trajectory of oil spills, within an overall framework of prioritizing the protection of environmentally sensitive areas. In the aftermath of the *Deepwater Horizon* oil spill, however, the Coast Guard adopted a strategy of distributing booms according to the dictates of client politics. Hundreds of miles of boom were deployed along the Gulf Coast, in an explicit effort to "keep the parishes happy."[108]

Client politics also characterized decision making regarding the construction of **berms,** sand barriers designed to prevent oil spills from reaching areas of shallow water. During a visit to the Gulf Coast, President Obama pressured Admiral Thad Allen, who had again been tapped to coordinate the federal government's response to a disaster in the region, to prioritize an investigation into the efficacy of berms as instruments of containment.[109] This pressure was politically astute in that the administration's efforts to prevent oil from reaching the Gulf's shores were being roundly criticized by local officials and residents.[110]

Although motivated in part by the dictates of client politics, the Obama administration's embrace of berm construction was not without scientific justification. As pointed out by a researcher at the Pontchartrain Institute for Environmental Studies at the University of New Orleans: "One of the reasons it's so easy for the oil to get into the wetlands in Louisiana is that the barrier shoreline is so degraded."[111] From a logistical point of view, however, information collected by the Army Corps of Engineers suggested that it was not possible to construct berms in time to stop the flow of significant amounts of oil. Furthermore, there were concerns that hastily assembled berms might result in significant, unanticipated harm to environmentally sensitive areas.[112]

In the end, such scientific debates were no match for the imperatives of client politics. Within days of President Obama's visit to the Gulf region, hundreds of millions of dollars of berm construction had been commissioned.[113] Months later, Louisiana Governor Bobby Jindal aptly summarized the concentrated benefits that continued to flow from this decision: "We are thrilled that this has become the state's largest barrier island restoration project in history."[114]

It is important to recognize that the combination of concentrated benefits and diffuse costs does not as a matter of course ensure the flow of desired benefits into local areas affected by disasters. On June 16, 2010, at the urging of President Obama, BP established the **Gulf Coast Claims Facility** (GCCF) as a means of compensating individuals and businesses for costs and damages incurred as a result of the *Deepwater Horizon* oil spill.[115] BP allocated $20 billion to the GCCF, which was administered by Kenneth R. Feinberg, an attorney who had previously overseen the operation of the September 11th Victim Compensation Fund. In the months following the GCCF's creation, both BP and the federal government found themselves on the receiving end of criticisms from local residents who were unhappy with the pace of claims processing and the amounts of the awards that were being dispersed. Referring to Feinberg, Sheila Newman, the owner of a beach wedding business, had this to say: "I think he's just trying to wear everybody down; they'll take such a small amount and just give up."[116] One year after the Macondo well blowout, the GCCF had allocated a grand total of only $4 billion and had begun the process of winding down its operations, despite opposition on the part of local residents and public officials.[117]

BP and Beyond. The BP oil spill, like Hurricane Katrina, triggered a barrage of withering jokes from late-night comedians. Common themes were greed, incompetence, and insensitivity (see Table 6.2). Unlike Hurricane Katrina, where most ridicule was directed at a government agency (FEMA), the primary target of comedians after the oil spill was a private company (BP). Although the Obama administration came in for some criticism over the oil spill, it was nothing like the criticism that the Bush administration received for the government's response to Katrina.

Like the late-night comedians, we have focused much of our attention on BP. We have also hinted at an organizational culture that placed greater emphasis on profits than on safety. However, the problems we have identified are more complex and more prosaic than simple greed. In the case of the BP oil spill, clear standard operating procedures for dealing with worrisome results from negative-pressure tests were not in place. Strong communication links between BP officials and other critical members of the oil drilling network (most notably, Halliburton engineers) did not exist. A consensus among technical experts on how to proceed when an oil spill occurred was not evident.

Parallels between the BP oil spill and other disasters—most notably, Hurricane Katrina and the Space Shuttle *Challenger* debacle—are almost eerie. Poor communication within and between organizations, standard operating procedures poorly designed for emergency situations, and a reluctance to invest

Table 6.2 Jokes about the BP Oil Spill

"The BP president said yesterday that the company would survive. That's like someone running over your dog and saying, 'Don't worry, my car is fine.'" —Jimmy Fallon

"I love this. On the news today, the CEO of British Petroleum says he believes the overall environmental impact of this oil spill will be very, very modest. Yeah, if you live in England!" —Jay Leno

"The president met with BP CEO Tony Hayward, and Obama was demanding that BP clean up the Gulf. And I'm thinking, good luck. They can't even clean up their gas station restrooms." —David Letterman

"Today, President Obama finally met with BP's CEO, Tony Hayward, but the meeting was only scheduled [for] 20 minutes. Call me crazy, but I think it should take more time to discuss an oil spill than it does to get your oil checked." —Jimmy Fallon

"A new poll found that 43 percent of Americans think President Obama is doing a good job at handling the BP oil spill. Of course, the same poll found that 43 percent of Americans hate pelicans." —Jimmy Fallon

Source: About.com, http://political humor.about.com/od/currentevents/a/oil-spill-jokes.htm (accessed December 7, 2010).

scarce resources in safety are common denominators. At times, it seems that both government agencies and private companies have forgotten the fundamentals of good organizational behavior. When that occurs, the possibility of a catastrophe is much more likely.

September 11, 2001: A Crisis without Precedent

Throughout its history, the United States has largely been free from foreign attacks on its own soil. Part of this security is due to the vast oceans that separate the United States from potentially hostile European and Asian regimes, while part of it is due to the worldwide economic and military power the country has projected since the early twentieth century. There have been occasions, of course, when this security has been disrupted. The British burned much of official Washington, including the White House, during the War of 1812. The Japanese attacked Pearl Harbor on December 7, 1941, a date President Franklin D. Roosevelt declared will "live in infamy." For the better part of two centuries, though, the U.S. mainland was essentially free from direct foreign intervention.

It is this freedom that made the terrorist attacks of September 11, 2001, such an unprecedented crisis. The attacks were also unprecedented in their origin (an international terrorist network), their scope (the use of airplanes at multiple sites to take approximately 3,000 lives), and their targets (civilians and buildings of economic and political significance). For many Americans, the attacks were likely the most shocking world event of their entire lives.

That said, however, the idea that terrorists might target domestic sites was not completely incomprehensible. On February 26, 1993, a car bomb was detonated in a parking garage underneath the World Trade Center. Sheik Omar Abdel Rahman was convicted of masterminding the bombing, and several other conspirators were imprisoned for their roles in planning and carrying out the attack, which claimed six lives and caused more than a thousand injuries.

In addition, in the months before the September 11 attacks, intelligence agents had warned Central Intelligence Agency officials, who in turn warned the White House that "spectacular" terrorist attacks were being planned.[118] On two separate occasions in June 2001, Richard Clarke, the chair of the administration's **Counterterrorism Security Group**, informed National Security Adviser Condoleezza Rice that **al-Qaida** personnel had predicted a pending attack and that the terrorist network's activity had reached a "crescendo."[119] A July 2001 memo from an FBI agent in Phoenix to bureau headquarters noted that an "inordinate number of individuals of investigative interest" were attending flight schools.[120] A month later, a memo from an FBI agent in Minneapolis to the CIA warned that an Islamic extremist, Zacarias Moussaoui, was learning how to fly.[121] A daily briefing prepared for President George W. Bush by CIA analysts on August 6, 2001, carried the title "Bin Laden Determined to Strike US."[122]

In fairness, the federal government had been receiving warnings about possible terrorist attacks on U.S. soil for at least a decade. Furthermore, none of these reports was specific enough to allow decision makers to pinpoint a specific date or particular targets. As historian Roberta Wohlstetter has noted, it is "much easier *after* the event to sort the relevant from the irrelevant signals. After the event, of course, a signal is always crystal clear; we can now see what disaster it was signaling since the disaster has occurred. But before the event it is obscure and pregnant with conflicting meanings."[123]

Not surprisingly, the events of September 11, 2001, have been the subject of great debate and scrutiny. Arguably, the most comprehensive investigation was carried out by the **National Commission on Terrorist Attacks upon the United States,** an independent, bipartisan group chartered by Congress and President Bush. On June 22, 2004, the so-called 9/11 Commission issued a 567-page report covering everything from advance preparations to immediate response to the prevention of terrorist attacks in the future. Given all of this general attention, our aim in this section is rather specific: What insights can the four theoretical perspectives provide when it comes to the bureaucracy's behavior before, during, and after the unprecedented crisis that occurred on September 11, 2001?

The First Response

In New York City, the immediate response to the attacks on the World Trade Center entailed both individual heroism and systemic breakdown. Police officers and firefighters placed themselves in mortal peril, knowing full well they stood a good chance of dying in their efforts to rescue workers inside the burning towers. Thanks to their efforts, countless lives were saved that morning.

Hundreds of firefighters, however, entered the buildings with their hands figuratively tied behind their backs. Communications between firefighters and their superiors were poor. For example, although firefighters possessed new radios, they had not been trained to use these radios properly. Furthermore, coordination between the fire department and other key units—the police department, the Port Authority, the Office of Emergency Management—was severely limited by ineffective communications.[124] Some of these problems arose from the fact that the Office of Emergency Management was located inside 7 World Trade Center, a forty-seven-story building that was damaged and ultimately collapsed as a result of the attacks.[125] All told, 343 firefighters as well as 60 police officers perished in New York City on September 11, 2001.[126]

By contrast, the bureaucratic response to the attack on the Pentagon was relatively timely, safe, and effective. In large part, these differences are attributable to the fact that the logistics were much less daunting at the site in Arlington, Virginia, where a single airplane had crashed into a low-lying building. In addition, local officials were especially well prepared and organized. **Incident command** was established quickly, thanks to a formalized management structure for emergency response that had been put into place throughout the Washington, D.C., area prior to the attack.[127] Different agencies played distinct, well-defined roles. For example, the Arlington County fire department was the incident commander, with the Department of Justice serving as the lead federal agency.

These arrangements were familiar to many of the officials who were first on the scene, as federal, state, and local agencies regularly took part in regional events and training exercises. In fact, many of these agencies had been working together that very day on plans related to the World Bank–International Monetary Fund meetings that were to be held later that month in the nation's capital.[128]

This history of communication and cooperation paid immediate dividends. Within five minutes of the attack, FBI officials had arrived and fire department commanders had established their headquarters at the scene.[129] Evacuation of the area impacted by the crash was ordered minutes before the building partly collapsed. As a result of this quick action, no **first responder** was injured by falling debris.[130]

A common thread that emerges from the Pentagon and World Trade Center experiences is that when disaster strikes, dedicated public servants will immediately arrive upon the scene ready to do whatever they can to make things better. Can the theoretical perspectives offer any insight into how successful these responders are likely to be in their initial efforts?

At both locations, bureaucratic networks were crucial forms of organization. No one agency possessed all the tools necessary to cope with the multitude of problems that were occurring at the same time—fires, injuries, airplane crashes, building collapses. Nor was there a single agency, or even a small set of agencies, with the authority to command the large numbers of organizations that were responding from all levels of government. These attributes would appear to be descriptions of the immediate aftermath of major disasters in general, suggesting that networked arrangements are likely to be inevitable in this area of policymaking and implementation.

Network failures too would seem to be unavoidable in times of great crisis, especially failures related to communications of one sort or another. It is hard enough for principals to keep in touch with their own agents, let alone for officials to coordinate with one another across agency lines. Even at the Pentagon, cell phones proved to be of little value, and radio channels quickly became overwhelmed. Although pagers turned out to be the most reliable means of communication, many first responders were not equipped with these particular devices.[131] In the end, well-established, well-functioning networks are organizational tools for mitigating, though not eliminating, communication problems that threaten the lives of both disaster victims and their would-be rescuers.

Bureaucracy after 9/11

Once the dust had settled, the events of September 11, 2001, precipitated one of the most significant transformations of public bureaucracy in recent times. Six weeks after the attacks, Congress passed and President Bush signed into law the **USA PATRIOT Act.**[132] The Patriot Act strengthened the power of bureaucrats all across the government, especially at the federal level. Officials were given greater authority to track electronic communications, investigate and disrupt money laundering, detain and deport individuals suspected of having terrorist ties, and obtain so-called sneak-and-peek (covert entry) search warrants.[133]

A year later, many of these disparate bureaucratic functions were consolidated into a single organization, when Congress and President Bush agreed to create the **Department of Homeland Security.** As mentioned in Chapter 3, this new cabinet department brought together twenty-two agencies and 170,000 employees. Figure 6.1 illustrates why this action has been called the "most complicated restructuring of the federal government ever."[134] Agencies ranging from the Department of Transportation to the Federal Bureau of Investigation to the General Services Administration were altered, sometimes in fundamental ways, by the changes instituted in the Homeland Security Act.

These changes in bureaucratic power and organization were inspired by the fact that members of al-Qaida had been living and training in the United States for months, even years, prior to carrying out the attacks. Although the suspicions of individual bureaucrats had been raised in certain instances, the failure to connect the dots and uncover the hijacking plot pointed to the need for an expansion and reconfiguration of government authority in the area of homeland security.

From the beginning, these changes were met with skepticism from various quarters. Civil libertarians were concerned that individual rights would be seriously and unnecessarily eroded. Conservatives were opposed to the creation of a new federal department and the increase in the size of the government workforce that was bound to go with it.

What impacts have these changes had on the accountability and performance of the homeland security bureaucracy? As Chapter 3 suggests, there is

Figure 6.1 Organizational Highlights of the Creation of the Department of Homeland Security

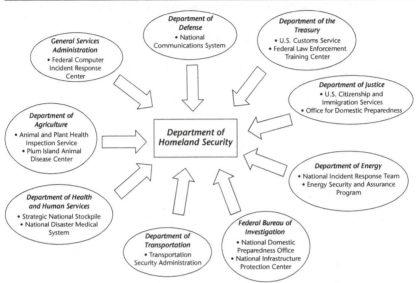

Source: "History: Who Became Part of the Department?" U.S. Department of Homeland Security, https://www.dhs.gov/creation-department-homeland-security (accessed March 31, 2017). Figure prepared by authors.

normally a strenuous, multifaceted competition between the executive and legislative branches for influence over bureaucratic agencies. Such competition certainly occurred in the years after creation of the Department of Homeland Security. Certain features of this competition clearly favored the White House. The appointment of Tom Ridge as the department's first administrator, on the heels of his stint as President Bush's homeland security czar, gave the White House a strong ally in the single most important antiterrorism position in the U.S. government. In addition, many of the initial applications of the bureaucracy's new powers and organization came in the context of military interventions in Afghanistan and Iraq. Historically, presidents are much more formidable in the conduct of foreign affairs than in the making of domestic policy.[135] For example, after Democrats gained control of the Senate and the House of Representatives in 2007, they found it difficult to influence policy regarding the withdrawal of U.S. troops from Iraq, even though the conflict was by that time widely unpopular among the American people.

This is not to say that Congress did not exert sway over the homeland security bureaucracy. Secretary Ridge, by his own count, found himself and the department being overseen by "over 100 committees and subcommittees in the House and the Senate."[136] This sprawling oversight resembles the politics of iron triangles that were discussed in Chapter 4, in that specific agencies within the Department of Homeland Security operated in close alignment with congressional overseers on particular committees and subcommittees.[137] The aim of such alignments was to protect concentrated benefits that accrued to certain actors in the homeland security industry. From the perspective of Secretary Ridge, as an official operating outside of established iron triangles, such oversight required an enormous investment of time and resources that did not necessarily assist in the integration of homeland security that the White House and Congress in general were hoping for.[138]

When it comes to performance, there have been both security success stories and **civil liberties** failures. Hundreds of millions of dollars in assets tied to international terrorist organizations and state sponsors of terrorism have been frozen by the U.S. government in the years since the September 11, 2001, terrorist attacks.[139] Most Americans have experienced nothing more than inconveniences, such as long lines and uncomfortable body searches at airport security checkpoints, as a result of tightened homeland security policies. Over the years, however, a number of citizens have had their lives profoundly affected. In the fall of 2006, for example, six Muslim imams were ordered off a flight from Minneapolis–St. Paul to Phoenix after passengers complained about their praying, conversation, and behavior.[140] At about the same time, the U.S. government agreed to pay $2 million to settle a lawsuit filed by Brandon Mayfield, an Oregon attorney who was mistakenly linked to train bombings in Madrid, Spain, that had killed 191 people two years earlier.[141] Mayfield and civil liberties advocates argued that his arrest and two-week detainment serve as reminders of just how easy it is for bureaucrats to abuse powers, such as relaxed standards of probable cause, conferred by the Patriot Act.

The Iraq War and the Intelligence Community

It was in this uncertain post–September 11, 2001, environment that the Bush administration, with Congress's consent, embarked on a war in Iraq. The White House contended that Iraq was harboring terrorists and possessed **weapons of mass destruction** that could be used to inflict great damage upon American interests. In August 2002, for example, Vice President Dick Cheney asserted, "There is no doubt that Saddam Hussein now has weapons of mass destruction [and] there is no doubt that he is amassing them to use against our friends, against our allies, and against us."[142]

Assertions such as this ultimately proved false. The United States and its allies succeeded in toppling Saddam Hussein from power but never located the weapons of mass destruction that had served as such a crucial justification for the war effort. This startling failure has been the subject of much controversy and investigation. An independent, bipartisan commission came to this general conclusion: "the Intelligence Community was dead wrong in almost all of its pre-war judgments about Iraq's weapons of mass destruction."[143] From the perspective of the book's theoretical frameworks, this general finding raises specific questions regarding bureaucratic accountability and performance: Why did intelligence agencies and other bureaucracies get it so wrong when it came to Saddam Hussein's weapons program? How might the theoretical perspectives provide insight into the mistakes that were made up and down the chain of command?

For starters, it is important to recognize that **United Nations weapons inspectors** had been absent from Iraq since 1998, making the intelligence community's job inherently difficult.[144] In this information vacuum, and based on the Hussein regime's past behavior, a prevailing assumption emerged that Iraq had resumed its weapons program.[145] This assumption affected the way in which the often sketchy information coming out of Iraq was interpreted and used. In bounded rationality terms, intelligence analysts had grounded much of their work in the idea that Iraq was making significant progress in developing biological, chemical, and nuclear weapons. These premises rendered unattractive other schools of thought and courses of action regarding the Hussein regime.

These limitations in decision making were magnified as information was passed through the bureaucracy from analysts up to policymakers. From the perspective of high-level officials, intelligence reports took on the appearance of making relatively certain claims when, in fact, there was much to be contested in their content.[146] For example, the **President's Daily Brief** often touched on Iraq's weapons program. These reports sometimes carried titles that were far more alarmist than the accompanying texts would seem to have called for. In addition, information about the credibility of the sources used to generate the intelligence was sometimes exaggerated or not discussed at all.[147] In this environment, the president and other principals faced a significant information deficit when it came to evaluating the orientation and work of their agents on the ground. These principals, in other words, confronted serious adverse selection and moral hazard problems, both of which appear to have contributed greatly to the poor policy choices that were eventually made.

These hierarchical problems were compounded by shortcomings in intelligence networks. There are many bureaucracies that collect intelligence information—the Central Intelligence Agency, the Defense Intelligence Agency, and the National Geospatial-Intelligence Agency, to name just three. Given this organizational diversity, it might have been useful if there had been a regularized way for intelligence agencies to coordinate their collection and analytical efforts. Unfortunately, no such central clearinghouse existed.[148] In fact, there was a bias in the intelligence community against sharing information across jurisdictional lines. The National Security Agency, for example, was hesitant to share its raw data with anyone from outside the organization.[149]

In an effort to address this lack of centrality in the intelligence network, Congress and President Bush created, in late 2004, the position of **director of national intelligence** (DNI). Early on, some commentators decried the DNI position as a "toothless figurehead."[150] Over time, however, the intelligence community has drawn praise for its enhanced predisposition to coordinate across agencies the sharing and analysis of information. At a hearing conducted by the Senate Homeland Security and Governmental Affairs Committee in the aftermath of the May 2, 2011, killing of Osama bin Laden, Sen. Susan Collins, R-Maine, had this to say: "Last week's welcome news that Osama bin Laden was killed demonstrates the kind of successful collaboration of intelligence and operations that we envisioned in reforming our capabilities and intelligence community in the wake of the attacks of 9-11-01."[151] And there have been other, lower-profile successes as well. In 2009, Najibullah Zazi, an al-Qaida operative who was planning a suicide bombing in the New York City subway system, was identified and arrested several days before he was ready to carry out his mission.[152]

Despite these laudable successes, there have been intelligence failures that continue to highlight the difficulties faced by the intelligence network in assembling and analyzing information across organizational boundaries. On Christmas Day of 2009, Umar Farouk Abdulmutallab nearly detonated plastic explosives hidden in his underwear on an airplane that was approaching Detroit. In the aftermath of this potentially deadly incident, Secretary of Homeland Security Janet Napolitano stated that the "system worked."[153] This assertion drew widespread criticism because Abdulmutallab had been "allowed to fly to the United States on a valid visa without extra screening even though he was listed in a terrorism database, his ticket was bought with cash, and he checked no luggage."[154] Napolitano later backtracked from her initial assessment, acknowledging that "Our system did not work in this instance. No one is happy or satisfied with that."[155]

Making the intelligence community's job all the more difficult is the fact that the terrorist threat continually evolves in its specific ways and means. At a September 27, 2016, congressional hearing, Secretary of Homeland Security

Jeh Johnson described a movement away from attacks specifically directed by terrorist organizations to a "world that also includes the threat of terrorist-inspired attacks."[156] The latter types of attacks, often perpetrated by U.S. citizens who have "self-radicalized," are difficult to detect and prevent, especially by a homeland security bureaucracy designed to fight organizations such as al-Qaida.[157]

Beyond the Department of Homeland Security

One crucial challenge that federal agencies face in preventing future terrorist attacks is communicating to state and local officials, and the American people, information about potential terrorist threats inside their jurisdictions. In 2002, the Department of Homeland Security established a **color-coded threat level system** for the nation as a whole, as well as for specific industries and geographic regions. Whatever its utility as a means of transmitting information, the color-coded system served as an easy target for late-night comedians such as Jay Leno, who joked, "Yesterday the alert went from blue to pink; now half the country thinks we're pregnant."[158]

In 2011, the color-coded system was scrapped in favor of a new system, the **National Threat Advisory System** (NTAS).[159] The Department of Homeland Security describes NTAS as follows:

> When there is specific, credible information about a terrorist threat against the United States, DHS will share an NTAS Alert with the American public when circumstances warrant doing so. The Alert may include specific information, if available, about the nature of the threat, including the geographic region, mode of transportation, or critical infrastructure potentially affected by the threat, as well as steps that individuals and communities can take to protect themselves and help prevent, mitigate or respond to the threat. The Alert may take one of two forms: **Elevated**, if we have credible threat information, but only general information about timing and target such that it is reasonable to recommend implementation of protective measures to thwart or mitigate against an attack, or **Imminent**, if we believe the threat is credible, specific, and impending in the very near term.[160]

Four years after its inception, the NTAS had still not issued a single alert, even though a number of terrorist attacks had occurred, both on U.S. soil and abroad. By 2015, the NTAS Twitter feed had attracted 23,500 followers but had never issued a single tweet. The NTAS's Facebook page had been liked by 33,864 people, yet its timeline was completely devoid of posts.[161] To fill in this information vacuum, Secretary of Homeland Security Jeh Johnson announced a modification of the system. In place of alerts, the DHS lowered the threshold for sharing information and began issuing bulletins that are available to the public.[162]

Given the ever-changing nature of homeland security communications, how do local officials rate information sharing on the part of federal and state agencies? Survey data indicate that most local officials agree, either somewhat or strongly, that homeland security information provided by federal principals is easy to understand.[163] The same officials, however, report that information from state-level principals is even more easily understood. When it comes to timeliness, most local officials agree that homeland security information from the federal government reaches them expeditiously. Once again, though, these officials report that information emanating from state governments is even timelier.

The efficacy of homeland security efforts depends not only on the nature of the information being shared by higher-level governmental units but also on the capabilities of lower-level units. For example, in cities with populations of more than 500,000, some 78.1 percent of public health officials report that they have collaborated with the Department of Health and Human Services, the lead federal agency on matters such as bioterrorism. Unfortunately, the level of collaboration is much lower in smaller jurisdictions, with only 29 percent of local officials reporting these kinds of interactions with their federal counterparts.[164]

A survey of county and city officials in Florida suggests that intergovernmental networks have become stronger as a result of homeland security initiatives and expenditures. Increased levels of cooperation on homeland security after September 11, 2001, were reported by 64 percent of county officials and 60 percent of city officials. Very few of these officials reported a surge in conflict across jurisdictions.[165] Furthermore, 96 percent of counties and 92 percent of cities in Florida reported having established a homeland security network with officials in Tallahassee, the home of Florida's state government. Smaller yet still sizable percentages—76 percent of counties and 84 percent of cities—reported having established a homeland security network with officials in the federal government.[166] It would thus appear that, if developments in Florida are any indication, substantial progress has been made in fostering network arrangements in the area of homeland security. Within these networks, bonds between local officials and state government are at this point stronger than bonds between local officials and government at the federal level.

Although governments at all levels are better prepared for terrorist threats than they were in 2001, the general public's level of awareness and information leaves much to be desired. Only 20 percent of Americans are familiar with their state or local government's plan for a terrorist attack, and only 37 percent have worked out arrangements with family members and friends for responding to an emergency.[167] When asked how they would respond to a terrorist attack, Americans offer a wide variety of answers. This variety suggests that the public's response to actual terrorist attacks is unpredictable and difficult to manage from a governmental point of view.

A key problem is that, politically, it is difficult for politicians to talk about **mitigation and recovery,** as opposed to prevention. Although it is impossible for politicians to reduce to zero the threat of another terrorist attack, many citizens naively expect them to do exactly that. To even talk about how to respond to a massive terrorist attack strikes many citizens as defeatist. Until such attitudes change, politicians are likely to do most of their planning for mitigation and recovery behind the scenes, rather than engaging the general public.[168]

In fact, bureaucracies have done little to educate citizens about proper preparations for and responses to an emergency. Bureaucracies have improved the government's standard operating procedures, but they have not adequately assisted ordinary citizens in developing their own, equally important standard operating procedures. Without stronger, sustained public education efforts across the nation, the next massive terrorist attack on U.S. soil may find well-prepared public officials but poorly prepared citizens.

The mobilization of interest groups has implications, often not for the better, for decisions that are made in some areas of homeland security. Consider the allocation of **homeland security grants.** These grants are federal funds awarded to states and localities to shore up port security, protect critical infrastructure, equip and train first responders, and so forth. At times, these funds are allocated with an eye more toward constituency considerations than objective need. For example, Congress has in some contexts decreed that no state shall receive less than 75 percent of the average per capita grant allotment.[169] As a result of this decree, there are documented instances of smaller states receiving far more funding per capita than larger states with a preponderance of terrorist targets. In one such case, New York and New Jersey, which together handle 12 percent of the nation's cargo, received only 1 percent of the federal funds available for port protection.[170] This pattern is consistent with Congress's usual preference for distributing funds across many states and localities as a way of maximizing political support for federal programs.[171]

Even DHS officials concede that homeland security grants have not always been well spent. Chip Fulghum, chief financial officer for DHS, puts it this way: "Right after 9/11, the spigot got turned on and a fire hose of money poured out. Much of it was badly monitored and much of it was for stuff that just didn't work."[172]

Competition for homeland security grants has become a rather fierce business. In the years following the September 11, 2001, attacks, government **outsourcing** on homeland security increased by $130 billion.[173] A particularly controversial example of this type of network arrangement occurred in 2006, when it was revealed that Dubai Ports World, a firm controlled by the government of the United Arab Emirates, had come into position to run ports in Baltimore, Miami, New Jersey, New Orleans, New York, and Philadelphia.[174] Opponents argued that it would not be appropriate for this kind of authority to be given to a country that has "historically been used as a base of terrorist operations and financing."[175] Proponents countered that the decision had been approved by the Federal Bureau of Investigation and the Departments of Commerce, Defense, Homeland Security, and the Treasury. In the end, the transfer of authority never took place, as Dubai Ports World bowed to political pressure and transferred all of its U.S. operations to an American company.[176]

This episode illustrates two important points about homeland security and the war on terrorism as they are likely to be carried out in the years ahead. The first point is that public bureaucracies will surely retain primary, day-to-day responsibility for making decisions on everything from advance planning to first response to tactical operations. The second point is that the bureaucracy's bosses and clients will continue to use their influence and authority to shape bureaucratic decision making, but only in those instances where the political stakes are visibly elevated. Together these insights mean that it will not always be easy to assign credit and blame for homeland security successes and failures. All such efforts should naturally start with the bureaucracies of the executive branch, yet it must also be recognized that these agencies function as part of a larger political system that itself is subject to various, often contradictory, outside impulses.

The broader challenge for public officials who seek to assess the performance of DHS and, more broadly, the war on terrorism, is that it's extremely difficult to specify with any precision the number of terrorist threats averted and the number of lives saved. For example, we can say that the Transportation Security Administration seized 2,500 guns in carry-on luggage in 2015, and that 83 percent of these guns were loaded. [177] But we can't say whether any of those guns, if not confiscated, would have led to a hijacking attack. An additional problem, as noted earlier, is that the nature of the terrorist threat has undoubtedly changed since September 11, 2001, with a growing emphasis on "lone wolf attacks" and with the frightening specter of a "dirty bomb" or a chemical attack looming ominously over the horizon. One thoughtful observer sums up the current state of events in this way: "Are we safer? Yes, we're safer from the kind of orchestrated attack that shocked us. . . . It's harder for terrorists to get into the country, and harder for them to pull off something spectacular if they do. But we have not plugged some of the most threatening security gaps. . . . Our defenses are far stronger, but what we have to defend against has outpaced our progress."[178]

Avian Influenza: A Crisis in the Making?

On June 4–6, 2004, an international agricultural conference held in California drew speakers and participants from all over the world. Unknowingly, some presenters were ill from a strain of avian influenza (also called "bird flu") and, during the course of the proceedings, transmitted the virus to other attendees. Within days, the news media were issuing reports of a sudden flu outbreak that had infected large numbers of people and had even resulted in some deaths. Health departments across the state were ordered to open mass clinics as a means of delivering a newly developed avian flu vaccine to all residents.

We can all be thankful that this scary-sounding series of events never actually occurred. Rather, the Health Department of Yolo County, California, created this mock scenario for a flu vaccination drill that it carried out on June 10, 2004, in collaboration with other government agencies, the local Red Cross chapter, community health care institutions, and individual volunteers.[179] Drills such as this are one element, along with monitoring, scientific research, and economic and policy forecasting, of an overall preparation strategy for a public health catastrophe that has yet to come, but one day might very well affect the lives and livelihoods of millions of Americans.

The possibility of an avian flu pandemic, an outbreak of global proportions, is salient today in large part because of the ongoing spread of the **H5N1 virus.** H5N1 is a particularly virulent strain of avian flu that, since 2003, has infected 856 people around the world, killing 452 of them.[180] As Table 6.3 indicates, none of the reported cases have occurred in the United States. Nor has the virus thus far been detected in domestic poultry stocks. These conditions, however, are potentially at risk of deteriorating rapidly, given the ease of international travel and the fact that H5N1 is continually being carried to far-off locations by migratory birds.[181]

For H5N1 to spawn a pandemic, the virus would have to evolve from its current form, in which it can readily spread from an infected bird to a person but not from one person directly to another. If the virus were to acquire this latter ability, the results could be catastrophic, as humans possess little natural immunity to such mutated strains of influenza. Extrapolating from past pandemics, the Department of Health and Human Services estimates that somewhere between 200,000 and 2 million Americans would lose their lives, with tens of millions more suffering nonfatal illnesses.[182] In addition to these staggering losses, H5N1 has the potential to cause severe economic dislocations, impacting activities and industries as diverse as "travel, trade, tourism, food, consumption and eventually, investment and financial markets."[183]

Clearly, an **avian influenza pandemic** would provide public bureaucracies with a host of disaster management challenges. What is less certain is just when such an outbreak might occur, as well as whether H5N1 is in fact the strain most likely to mutate into a human virus. Indeed, in 2015–2016, **Zika,** a mosquito-borne virus that can be transmitted from person to person through sexual activity, traveled quickly from South America to the United States, infecting thousands and causing several deaths.[184] As one scientist summed up the uncertainty of the spread of H5N1, "There's no sense of 'imminence' here. . . . The virus could move closer to human-to-human transmission, and it could move farther away."[185]

When it comes to this disaster that has not yet happened, government officials thus find themselves in a difficult spot. On the one hand, if officials overestimate the likelihood of an H5N1 pandemic, they run the risk of misallocating valuable emergency preparedness resources, resources that could be utilized more effectively in getting ready for other prospective crises. In addition, by drawing extensive public attention to a crisis that does not in short order manifest itself, officials could unwittingly cast themselves in the role of Chicken Little, desensitizing citizens to dangers in public health and other important areas of collective concern. On the other hand, if the threat of an H5N1 outbreak is too steeply discounted, officials might find themselves woefully unprepared when poultry and people suddenly begin to exhibit symptoms in large numbers.

Table 6.3 Confirmed Bird Flu Cases and Deaths

Country	Number of Cases	Number of Deaths
Egypt	356	119
Indonesia	199	167
Vietnam	127	64
Cambodia	56	37
China	53	31
Thailand	25	17
Turkey	12	4
Azerbaijan	8	5
Bangladesh	8	1
Iraq	3	2
Pakistan	3	1
Laos	2	2
Canada	1	1
Djibouti	1	0
Myanmar	1	0
Nigeria	1	1
Total	856	452

Source: "Cumulative Number of Confirmed Human Cases of Avian Influenza A/(H5N1) Reported to WHO," World Health Organization, http://www.who.int/influenza/human_animal_interface/2016_10_03_tableH5N1.pdf?ua=1 (accessed October 26, 2016).

National Strategy for Pandemic Influenza

More than a decade in the making, a national strategy for anticipating and responding to an influenza pandemic was announced by the Bush administration on November 1, 2005, and was followed, six months later, by the release of an accompanying **implementation plan.**[186] The strategy lays out three guiding principles—preparedness and communication, surveillance and detection, and response and containment. When it comes to implementing these laudable principles, the plan tasks the Department of Homeland Security with coordinating the overall federal effort, while placing the Department of Health and Human Services in charge of medical readiness and management. The primary responsibilities of the federal government are limited to working with international authorities; procuring and distributing vaccines and antiviral medications; modifying laws and regulations as needed; and offering guidance to states, localities, and other organizations. For their part, state and local governments are charged with managing both the medical and nonmedical impacts of the avian flu within their jurisdictions over the many months an outbreak is projected to last. This arrangement means that the "center of gravity" before and during a pandemic will be located not in Washington, D.C., but in communities all around the country.[187]

After its release, a number of the plan's features came under criticism. By fragmenting authority across agencies and failing to empower a single, national leader on matters of avian flu preparation and response, the plan runs the risk of producing, as former House Speaker Newt Gingrich has put it, little more than "confusion, finger-pointing and neglect."[188] In addition, most state and local health departments are poorly equipped to carry out their designated responsibilities, such as instituting quarantines, delivering vaccines, and providing medical care to those who become sick.[189]

The private sector may also be an unreliable partner for the federal government. In the area of vaccines, domestic manufacturing capacities are rather limited, which would make it difficult for drug companies to bring a newly developed pandemic treatment to the market in short order.[190] To make matters worse, a dispute between the Bush administration and congressional Democrats resulted in the United States falling well behind other nations in stockpiling Tamiflu, an antiviral drug that is known to be efficacious when taken shortly after the onset of flu-like symptoms.[191] Despite these initial difficulties, by 2009 the federal government had procured 50 million courses of Tamiflu.[192] The accumulation of this stockpile, although certainly a welcome development, brought with it a new challenge for government decision makers, namely, the crafting of a strategy for safely disposing of millions of courses of Tamiflu that have gone unused and have reached their expiration dates.[193] In 2016, the Food and Drug Administration approved the first generic version of Tamiflu, with the expectation that other generics would soon compete for market share in the lucrative flu-fighting industry.[194]

The **National Strategy for Pandemic Influenza** was put to an unanticipated test when, in April 2009, the **H1N1 virus** was detected in the United States. H1N1 is a strain of swine flu that had never previously been identified in either animal stocks or human beings.[195] First observed in a ten-year-old living in California, H1N1 quickly spread across the country, eventually infecting an estimated 43 million to 89 million Americans.[196] According to the Centers for Disease Control and Prevention (CDC), as many as 20,000 deaths were ultimately attributable to the virus.[197]

Within two weeks of the initial case, the federal government declared a **public health emergency.**[198] Consistent with this statement and the national strategy's implementation plan, the CDC began releasing stockpiled supplies of antiviral drugs and protective equipment such as masks, gloves, and gowns.[199] By the fall of 2009, President Obama ratcheted up the government's response by declaring that the swine flu outbreak constituted a **national emergency.**[200] This additional declaration enabled state and local officials to establish special facilities, such as clinics located in school gymnasiums, for treating swine flu victims.[201] The national emergency declaration also facilitated the disbursement of swine flu vaccinations that had been approved after successful clinical trials. Initially, demand far outstripped supplies, resulting in criticisms that the

Obama administration was slow in delivering essential protections to vulnerable groups such as children and pregnant women. By December, however, tens of millions of doses had been administered and swine flu vaccinations were made available to the entire population.[202]

In calibrating its response to the swine flu outbreak, the Obama administration relied heavily on the national strategy that had been developed during the presidency of George W. Bush. As President Obama stated, "I think the Bush administration did a good job of creating the infrastructure so that we can respond."[203] The president's sentiment was echoed by House minority leader John Boehner, R-Ohio: "I have no complaints about how they're proceeding."[204]

Although such bipartisan praise and cooperation is reassuring, the national strategy has not yet been put to its most demanding test. An outbreak of H5N1 avian influenza would differ from the swine flu experience by orders of magnitude in its public health, economic, and social consequences. In what follows, the book's four theoretical perspectives are utilized to assess the areas of preparation and response where bureaucratic success stories, as well as government failures, are most likely to be manifested in the event of an H5N1 outbreak.

Using the Theories to Forecast

An avian flu pandemic would appear to be a case ripe for an application of the logic and lessons of bounded rationality. On the one hand, bureaucratic decision makers might very well know their preferences—to minimize the likelihood of an H5N1 pandemic and to contain illness, death, and harmful economic consequences were such a pandemic to occur. On the other hand, decision makers will likely find it extremely difficult to consider all or even most applicable prevention and response strategies, and will likely have an even harder time anticipating the outcomes that will follow from various policy choices. Satisficing, in other words, is more likely to be an apt descriptor of bureaucratic reasoning than is optimization.

As discussed in Chapter 2, satisficing has a lot to offer as a mode of decision making, in that it allows for quick actions that are often either close to right or right on target in their intended effects. Nevertheless, satisficing does at times lead to off-the-mark decisions and therefore has the potential to produce disastrous results when the stakes are extraordinarily high, as in the context of the H5N1 virus. With these possibilities in mind, what are some of the ways in which boundedly rational processes are being used in preparing for an avian flu pandemic?

One key element of bounded rationality is problem disaggregation, the breaking down of complex challenges into their component parts. Such disaggregation is evident throughout the national strategy. Not only does the plan, as highlighted earlier, call for three distinct conceptual focal points, it also disaggregates in terms of specific activities and functions. The plan lays out more than 300 actions that are to be taken or have already been implemented by the federal government. Examples of these actions include establishing surveillance capacity in at-risk countries, developing standards for the isolation and quarantine of travelers, assembling vaccine stockpiles adequate to immunize millions of Americans, and providing guidance to law enforcement officials at the state and local levels.[205]

One advantage of problem disaggregation is that it opens the door for bureaucracies to conduct simulations and tests in areas of specific responsibility. The Yolo County Health Department focused its avian flu exercise on a handful of discrete tasks, including the delivery of mock vaccinations to several hundred volunteers within a short period of time.[206] The department did not concern itself at all with larger issues surrounding the development, manufacturing, and distribution of these vaccinations, duties that clearly fall outside its immediate domain. With such a narrow focus, the department was readily able to evaluate the lessons, both positive and negative, that were learned from the drill. On the positive side, participants gained confidence with respect to the roles they would be called upon to play in the event of an actual avian flu outbreak. Conversely, the department discovered that its incident command center did not operate very effectively and that its control measures were inadequate for containing the spread of the virus.[207]

No matter how laudable, the department's simulation may ultimately be irrelevant if avian flu vaccinations never make it to Yolo County. This failure is a distinct possibility because of the current state of the domestic vaccine industry. Pharmaceutical companies, which collectively constitute one of the most powerful organized interests in contemporary American politics, have shied away from increasing their vaccine manufacturing capacities, primarily because of their concerns about liability and profitability.[208] During the 2003–2004 flu season, one of these companies, Wyeth, exited the market rather than incurring the required costs of upgrading its facilities.[209] And manufacturing pandemic vaccines is even more economically challenging than bringing seasonal vaccines to market. Because of the population's lack of prior exposure to viruses such as H5N1, pandemic vaccines typically require multiple doses that are higher in content than seasonal vaccines.[210] It is no wonder, then, that only a handful of companies have contracts with the Department of Health and Human Services to produce pandemic vaccines.[211] In 2013, to address this deficiency, the Department of Health and Human Services awarded four pharmaceutical companies contracts totaling $40 million to establish a manufacturing network capable of increasing influenza vaccine production by 20 percent.[212] In general, reluctance on the part of the pharmaceutical industry has led some public health experts to call for an abandonment of the existing private sector system in favor of a government-led initiative, modeled perhaps after the World War II–era Manhattan Project that produced the atomic bomb.[213] As highlighted in Chapter 4, it would take entrepreneurial behavior on the part of such experts, along with similarly inclined officeholders, to impose concentrated costs on the drug industry in order to deliver potential benefits to a diffuse set of millions of Americans.

Questions surrounding the division of responsibility between the federal government and other public and private entities can be considered through the lens of principal-agent theory. This approach is particularly relevant in the context of the delegation of policymaking and implementation authority to state and local governments. In addition to Yolo County's successful avian flu simulation, governments in cities such as Seattle and New York have made significant progress in pandemic planning, and effective action that saved dozens of lives was taken during the H1N1 pandemic by state and local health departments in Ohio.[214] Despite these success stories, it is nevertheless the case that the vast majority of local health departments remain ill-prepared to exercise their delegated authority in a reasonable manner.[215] These collective shortcomings might well be viewed as manifestations of adverse selection, with a principal (the federal government) selecting agents (local health departments) that are generally not well suited for the tasks at hand.

As discussed in Chapter 3, a common solution to the problem of adverse selection is for principals to screen agents carefully before delegating responsibilities. Unfortunately, the federal government has little choice in the matter because local health departments face little, if any, competition in their areas of jurisdiction. What this lack of competition suggests is that agency loss, here visible through poor planning and response on the part of local health departments, will be inherently difficult for the federal government to mitigate in a serious way.

When it comes to networks, many interagency, intergovernmental, and public-private arrangements are reasonable candidates for theoretical scrutiny. Arguably, the most important network arises out of the allocation of pandemic flu authority across multiple agencies of the federal government. In addition to the aforementioned duties of the Department of Homeland Security and the Department of Health and Human Services, at least six other agencies—the Departments of Agriculture, Defense, Labor, State, Transportation, and the Treasury—have jurisdictional responsibilities enumerated in the implementation plan of the National Strategy for Pandemic Influenza.[216]

Although such a division of authority is natural in the face of a multidimensional threat like the H5N1 virus, it immediately raises difficulties regarding cross-agency coordination and the manner in which policy disagreements are aired and resolved. Cognizant of these difficulties, officials who drew up the plan placed the secretary of homeland security in charge of the federal government's overall response to an avian flu pandemic. These policymakers also established a process for dealing with issues that cannot be successfully addressed at the departmental level. This process involves two organizations located inside the Executive Office of the President—the Homeland Security Council and the National Security Council.[217]

On the surface, cabinet-level and White House attention to the most pressing and stubborn problems in the area of avian flu preparation and response would appear to be exactly what is needed. A closer look, however, reveals that the key officials and organizations involved have portfolios extending well beyond the H5N1 virus. The day-to-day war on terrorism consumes much of the time and energy of these policymakers, a fact that might well have the impact of diluting coordination and decisiveness when it comes to an avian flu pandemic. As noted in Chapter 5, without vigorous and sustained leadership, interagency networks are not likely to be especially effective in achieving their core tasks. One promising sign in this regard occurred a few years ago at an H1N1 Influenza Preparedness Summit that was held by the federal government. One of the opening speakers at the summit was John Brennan, President Obama's homeland security adviser and the head of the Homeland Security Council.[218] Brennan's presence suggests that leadership resources may indeed be forthcoming during an avian influenza outbreak, resources that are vital in mobilizing the federal government's sprawling pandemic policymaking and implementation network. Similarly, in 2016, President Obama requested a congressional appropriation of $1.9 billion to combat the Zika virus.[219] The fact that this request occurred shortly after the World Health Organization declared Zika to be a Public Health Emergency of International Concern was a sign of fast and decisive leadership at the top of the nation's public health network.

In sum, the possibility that the H5N1 virus might mutate into a strain of pandemic influenza presents public bureaucracies in the United States with a host of accountability and performance challenges. This public health crisis in the making would seem to call for an aggressive federal planning effort, much like previous bureaucratic initiatives that resulted in the detonation of the atomic bomb and other successful responses to prospective dangers. At the same time, an avian flu pandemic would be the ultimate localized disaster, with its effects being felt in neighborhoods, schools, and workplaces throughout the country.

As our theoretical consideration of the avian flu case has demonstrated, there have been bureaucratic success stories in terms of both coordinated action and independent preparations. Boundedly rational actors at the federal and local levels have utilized techniques of problem disaggregation and simulations as ways of beginning to understand the scope and complexity of the problem they may one day confront. Nevertheless, if an avian flu pandemic were to strike the United States sooner rather than later, it is almost certain that bureaucracies at all levels of government would quickly be overwhelmed. At first glance, this verdict may read like an indictment of the bureaucracy. It bears emphasizing, though, that institutions throughout government, civil society, and the economy would find themselves in much the same situation, responding to a crisis that naturally stretches organizational capacities like few other disasters the world has experienced.

Evaluating Bureaucracy in Light of the Theories

At the outset, we noted that emergency situations pose greater challenges for public bureaucracies than do ordinary decisions made under routine circumstances. We also observed that the theoretical perspectives provide us with four vantage points from which to think systematically about the management of major disasters. Along the way, we have encountered examples of strong bureaucratic performance, as well as instances in which agencies have taken courses of action that leave much to be desired. We have also argued that some agency successes and failures emanate from pressures external to the bureaucracy, such as directives from political principals and claims raised by societal clients. Our final task, then, is to look for general patterns that come out of the experiences of Hurricane Katrina; the *Deepwater Horizon* oil spill; the September 11, 2001, terrorist attacks; and the H5N1 avian influenza. What, in the broadest sense, have we learned about bureaucracy and the politics of disaster management?

Five particular lessons stand out. The first is that simulations and tests are likely to be crucial elements in planning for and responding to disasters of all varieties, given the unusual nature of especially large crises, both natural and those caused by human error or intent. Hurricane Pam and the Yolo County vaccination drill provided valuable information to first responders as well as to organizational supervisors. In the end, though, what matters are the concrete ways in which new information is used once the enthusiasm generated by a test fades away. In the case of New Orleans and the Gulf Coast, unfortunately, even a well-conceived simulation did not lead to needed changes in preparation and response protocols.

Second, communications, both horizontal and vertical, are crucial in preventing and reacting to disasters. Communication failures of both kinds are revealed when we consider the September 11, 2001, terrorist attacks. Well in advance of the attacks, intelligence officers in multiple agencies uncovered evidence that al-Qaida operatives were learning to fly various types of airplanes. These disparate pieces of information, however, were hard to assemble across a bureaucracy characterized by long-standing organizational boundaries and even rivalries. Once the hijacked airliners had struck their targets, police, fire, and rescue supervisors found it difficult, if not impossible, to keep in touch with their subordinates inside the World Trade Center, although, for a variety of reasons, communications were better at the Pentagon.

Third, centralized networks appear to be a plus when it comes to managing disasters. As discussed earlier, no one agency or small group of agencies is likely to possess the personnel or the mandate to truly lead when it comes to making emergency preparations and responding to crises as they occur. Even if networks are not already in place prior to a disaster, such organizational arrangements are likely to emerge naturally in the immediate aftermath of the event. In this kind of environment, centralization is a commonly called for, if not always realized, component of disaster networks. It was conspicuously lacking in the years, months, and days preceding and immediately following the blowout of the Macondo well. Similarly, the lack of centralization in planning for an H5N1 pandemic has led observers to worry about the sustainability of the bureaucracy's attention to what could turn out to be a disaster of historic proportions.

Fourth, political principals and societal clients sometimes help but often hinder the bureaucracy's ability to plan for and respond to emergency situations. The threat that Osama bin Laden and his terrorist network posed to the United States was well known among elected officials all the way up to the president many years before the September 11 attacks. These officials, however, failed to take a number of steps that experts agree would have been useful in reorienting the bureaucracy away from conventional, Cold War–era modes of operation to approaches more appropriate in the face of a new, very different type of threat. In the Gulf of Mexico region, economic interests pressured for continued expansion in shipping, tourism, and energy exploration, even when such growth came at the expense of valuable natural buffers that would have protected New Orleans and other low-lying areas from storms and oil slicks that everyone reasonably anticipated and feared.

Finally, as these last statements indicate, the level of death and destruction associated with major disasters is a function of not only the immediate event itself but also the forces that operate over the long run. If the H5N1 virus ever mutates into a global health crisis, its personal and economic toll will be determined in no small part by preparations that are under way now and have been for many years. These preparations include steps being taken by innumerable individuals and organizations here in the United States and around the world. With such a diverse cast of characters, it is naturally rather difficult to sort out cause-and-effect relationships, to associate particular outcomes with actions that were, or were not, taken by specific actors. This inherent interconnectedness signals just how hard it is to evaluate bureaucracies that are operating inside larger political systems.

The four theoretical perspectives have been extremely useful in unpacking these types of complex problems. The theories have pointed to processes and institutions that are especially crucial to consider when we try to understand certain decisions and outcomes. The theories have also provided useful criteria by which to judge decision makers, criteria that are linked to well-established social scientific benchmarks. In the end, the theories have painted what we think is a realistic portrait of bureaucratic accountability and performance under some of the most difficult circumstances in which public servants find themselves.

Key Terms

across-the-board standards, 240
all hazards approach, 234
al-Qaida, 251
avian influenza pandemic, 262
berms, 248
booms, 247
BP, 244
Michael Brown, 235
Bureau of Ocean Energy Management, Regulation, and Enforcement, 247
Bureau of Safety and Environmental Enforcement, 247
chain of command, 236
civil liberties, 255
color-coded threat level system, 258
Counterterrorism Security Group, 251
Deepwater Horizon, 232
Department of Homeland Security, 253
director of national intelligence, 257

elevated (threat), 258
emergency communications systems, 238
Federal Emergency Management Agency, 232
first responder, 252
Gulf Coast Claims Facility, 249
H1N1 virus, 264
H5N1 virus, 262
Halliburton, 244
homeland security grants, 260
Hurricane Katrina, 232
Hurricane Pam, 236
imminent (threat), 258
implementation plan, 263
incident command, 252
Macondo well, 244
Minerals Management Service, 245
Mississippi River Gulf Outlet, 238
mitigation and recovery, 259

Notes

1. United States Environmental Protection Agency, "Federal Insecticide, Fungicide, and Rodenticide Act (FIFRA) Inspection Manual," 137–139, https://www.epa.gov/sites/production/files/2014-01/documents/fiframanual.pdf (accessed October 19, 2016).

2. U.S. Global Change Research Program, http://www.globalchange.gov (accessed October 19, 2016).

3. U.S. Environmental Protection Agency, "Overview of Climate Change Science," https://www.epa.gov/climate-change-science/overview-climate-change-science#Emissions (accessed October 19, 2016).

4. Florida beaches alone host 80 million visitors on an annual basis. See Richard Luscombe, "Gulf of Mexico Oil Spill: The Threat to Tourism," *Telegraph,* May 6, 2010, http://www.telegraph.co.uk/travel/travelnews/7686150/Gulf-of-Mexico-oil-spill-the-threat-to-tourism.html (accessed October 19, 2016).

5. Patrik Jonsson, "Oil Spill: What Is the Threat to Gulf of Mexico Seafood?" *Christian Science Monitor,* April 29, 2010, http://www.csmonitor.com/USA/2010/0429/Oil-spill-What-is-the-threat-to-Gulf-of-Mexico-seafood (accessed October 19, 2016).

6. Richard D. Knabb, Jamie R. Rhome, and Daniel P. Brown, "Tropical Cyclone Report: Hurricane Katrina," National Hurricane Center, December 20, 2005, http://www.nhc.noaa.gov/data/tcr/AL122005_Katrina.pdf (accessed October 19, 2016).

7. National Commission on the BP *Deepwater Horizon* Oil Spill and Offshore Drilling, *Deep Water: The Gulf Oil Disaster and the Future of Offshore Drilling,* Report to the President, January 11, 2011, https://www.gpo.gov/fdsys/pkg/GPO-OILCOMMISSION/pdf/GPO-OILCOMMISSION.pdf (accessed October 19, 2016).

8. National Oceanic and Atmospheric Administration, "What Percentage of the American Population Lives Near the Coast?" http://oceanservice.noaa.gov/facts/population.html (accessed October 19, 2016).

9. Douglas Brinkley, *The Great Deluge: Hurricane Katrina, New Orleans, and the Mississippi Gulf Coast* (New York: Morrow, 2006), 247.

10. Christopher Cooper and Robert Block, *Disaster: Hurricane Katrina and the Failure of Homeland Security* (New York: Times Books, 2006), 57.

11. Stephen Barr, "Transforming FEMA," in *Triumphs and Tragedies of the Modern Presidency: Seventy-six Case Studies in Presidential Leadership,* ed. David Abshire (Westport, Conn.: Praeger, 2001), 268–270.

12. James Lee Witt and James Morgan, *Stronger in the Broken Places: Nine Lessons for Turning Crisis into Triumph* (New York: Times Books, 2002), 172.

13. In fiscal 1998, FEMA took an average of eight days to get relief checks to disaster victims, down from a high of twenty days in 1992; see Jerry Ellig, "Learning from the Leaders: Results-Based Management at the Federal Emergency Management Administration" (Arlington, Va.: George Mason University, Mercatus Center, March 29, 2000), 2, https://www.mercatus.org/system/files/MC_GAP_RBMatFEMA_000329.pdf (accessed October 19, 2016).

14. Ibid., 7.

15. Ibid., 8.

16. Ibid., 22.

17. Ibid.

18. Cooper and Block, *Disaster,* 72.

19. Ibid., 73.

20. Ibid., 82.

21. Ibid., 85–86.

22. Bill Carwile, quoted in ibid., 90.

23. Cooper and Block, *Disaster,* 86.

24. Brinkley, *The Great Deluge,* 620.

25. "Katrina, One Year Later," editorial, *Washington Post,* August 29, 2006, http://www.washingtonpost.com/wp-dyn/content/article/2006/08/28/AR2006082801244.html (accessed October 19, 2016).

26. "Catastrophic Disasters: Enhanced Leadership, Capabilities, and Accountability Controls Will Improve the Effectiveness of the Nation's Preparedness, Response, and Recovery System," Report no. GAO-06-618 (Washington, D.C.: U.S. Government Accountability Office, September 2006), 10, http://www.gao.gov/assets/260/251287.pdf (accessed October 19, 2016).

27. Kevin F. McCarthy, D. J. Peterson, Narayan Sastry, and Michael Pollard, *The Re-population of New Orleans after Hurricane Katrina* (Santa Monica, Calif.: RAND Corporation, 2006), www.rand.org/pubs/technical_reports/2006/RAND_TR369.pdf (accessed October 19, 2016).

28. Donald Menzel, "The Katrina Aftermath: A Failure of Federalism or Leadership?" *Public Administration Review* 66 (November/December 2006): 808–812.

29. Josh White and Peter Whoriskey, "Planning, Response Are Faulted," *Washington Post,* September 2, 2005, http://www.washingtonpost.com/wp-dyn/content/article/2005/09/01/AR2005090102428.html (accessed October 19, 2016).

30. Cooper and Block, *Disaster,* 102.

31. Brinkley, *The Great Deluge,* 230–234.

32. Ibid., 34.

33. Ibid., 21.

34. Ibid., 57–58.

35. Ibid., 18–19.

36. Eric Klinenberg and Thomas Frank, "Looting Homeland Security," *Rolling Stone,* December 29, 2005, 44–54.

37. See Menzel, "Katrina Aftermath," 809.

38. Cooper and Block, *Disaster,* 202–203.

39. Ibid.

40. Spencer S. Hsu, "FEMA Taking Hit on Sale of Surplus Trailers," *Washington Post,* March 8, 2007, http://www.washingtonpost.com/wp-dyn/content/article/2007/03/07/AR2007030702628.html (accessed October 19, 2016).

41. Ibid.

42. Brinkley, *The Great Deluge,* 173.

43. Ibid.

44. Ibid., 170.

45. "Catastrophic Disasters," 40.

46. Brinkley, *The Great Deluge*, 205.

47. Michael Grunwald and Susan Glasser, "The Slow Drowning of New Orleans," *Washington Post*, October 9, 2005, http://www.washingtonpost.com/wp-dyn/content/article/2005/10/08/AR2005100801458.html (accessed October 19, 2016).

48. Michael Grunwald, "Par for the Corps; A Flood of Bad Projects," *Washington Post*, May 14, 2006, http://www.washingtonpost.com/wp-dyn/content/article/2006/05/13/AR2006051300037.html (accessed October 19, 2016).

49. Cooper and Block, *Disaster*, 26–27; Grunwald, ibid.

50. Klinenberg and Frank, "Looting Homeland Security."

51. Louise Comfort, "The Dynamics of Policy Learning: Catastrophic Events in Real Time" (paper presented at the annual meeting of the American Political Science Association, Philadelphia, September 1, 2006).

52. Ibid., 9.

53. Keith Provan and H. Brinton Milward, "A Preliminary Theory of Interorganizational Network Effectiveness: A Comparative Study of Four Community Mental Health Systems," *Administrative Science Quarterly* 40 (March 1995): 1–33.

54. "Catastrophic Disasters," 30.

55. Comfort, "Dynamics of Policy Learning."

56. Brinkley, *The Great Deluge*, 17–18.

57. Ibid., 588–589; Spenser S. Hsu, "FEMA to Take Lead Role in Coordinating Disaster Aid," *Washington Post*, April 18, 2007, http://www.washingtonpost.com/wp-dyn/content/article/2007/04/17/AR2007041701985.html (accessed October 19, 2016).

58. Hsu, ibid.

59. Ibid.

60. Paul Purpura, "Coast Guard Stands Up Well to Its Biggest Task," *New Orleans Times-Picayune*, October 2, 2005.

61. Brinkley, *The Great Deluge*, 213.

62. Stephen Barr, "The Coast Guard and Its Chief, Models of Excellence," *Washington Post*, April 20, 2006, http://www.washingtonpost.com/wp-dyn/content/article/2006/04/19/AR2006041902438.html (accessed October 19, 2016).

63. Ibid.

64. Stephen Barr, "Coast Guard's Response to Katrina a Silver Lining in the Storm," *Washington Post*, September 6, 2005, http://www.washingtonpost.com/wp-dyn/content/article/2005/09/05/AR2005090501418.html (accessed October 19, 2016).

65. Josh White, "Coast Guard's Chief of Staff to Assist FEMA Head Brown," *Washington Post*, September 7, 2005, http://www.washingtonpost.com/wp-dyn/content/article/2005/09/06/AR2005090601677.html (accessed October 19, 2016).

66. Brinkley, *The Great Deluge*, 79.

67. "Catastrophic Disasters," 48.

68. Ibid., 50.

69. Elizabeth Shogren, "For 30 Years, a Political Battle over Oil and ANWR," *All Things Considered*, National Public Radio, November 10, 2005, http://www.npr.org/templates/story/story.php?storyId=5007819 (accessed October 19, 2016).

70. The National Commission on the BP *Deepwater Horizon* Oil Spill and Offshore Drilling, which was appointed by President Obama and chaired by former senator Bob Graham, D-Fla., and former administrator of the Environmental Protection Agency William K. Reilly, reconstructed the events of April 20, 2010, in painstaking detail. See National Commission, *Deep Water*.

71. Ibid.

72. Ibid.

73. Ibid., 6.

74. Ibid.

75. Patrik Jonsson, "Ecological Risk Grows as *Deepwater Horizon* Oil Rig Sinks in Gulf," *Christian Science Monitor*, April 22, 2010, http://www.csmonitor.com/USA/2010/0422/

Ecological-risk-grows-as-Deepwater-Horizon-oil-rig-sinks-in-Gulf (accessed October 19, 2016).

76. Mark Clayton, "Gulf Oil Spill: Greed Didn't Trump Safety, Says *Deepwater Horizon* Panel," *Christian Science Monitor,* November 8, 2010, http://www.csmonitor.com/USA/2010/1108/Gulf-oil-spill-Greed-didn-t-trump-safety-says-Deepwater-Horizon-panel (accessed October 19, 2016).

77. Russell Gold and Neil King Jr., "Red Flags Were Ignored aboard Doomed Rig," *Wall Street Journal,* May 13, 2010, http://www.wsj.com/articles/SB10001424052748703339304575240210545113710 (accessed October 19, 2016).

78. Clayton, "Gulf Oil Spill."

79. National Commission, *Deep Water.*

80. Ibid.

81. Ibid.

82. Clifford Krauss and Tom Zeller Jr., "A Behind-the-Scenes Firm Is Caught in the Spotlight," *New York Times,* May 24, 2010, http://query.nytimes.com/gst/fullpage.html?res=9E07E0D61038F936A15756C0A9669D8B63&pagewanted=all (accessed October 19, 2016).

83. National Commission, *Deep Water.*

84. Ibid.

85. Ibid.

86. Ibid.

87. In the aftermath of the *Challenger* disaster, President Reagan chartered the Presidential Commission on the Space Shuttle *Challenger* Accident to conduct an investigation and make recommendations regarding the future of the Space Shuttle program. The commission's report, issued June 6, 1986, focuses in detail on the O-ring failure; it is available at http://history.nasa.gov/rogersrep/genindex.htm (accessed October 19, 2016).

88. Ibid.

89. Ibid.

90. Ibid., 82.

91. U.S. Department of the Interior, Minerals Management Service, "About the Minerals Management Service," https://web.archive.org/web/20100701031314/http://www.mms.gov/aboutmms/ (accessed October 19, 2016).

92. National Commission, *Deep Water.*

93. U.S. Department of the Interior, Office of Natural Resources Revenue, "Total Federal Offshore Reported Royalty Revenues, Fiscal Year 2008," http://www.onrr.gov/ONRRWebStats/FedOffReportedRoyaltyRevenues.aspx?yeartype=FY&year=2008&datetype=AY (accessed May 17, 2011); National Commission, *Deep Water.*

94. Ibid.

95. Danielle Brian and Mandy Smithberger, "Our Government, Serving the Energy Industry," *New York Times,* May 5, 2010.

96. U.S. Department of the Interior, Office of Inspector General, "MMS Oil Marketing Group—Lakewood," http://www.doioig.gov/images/stories/reports/pdf/RIKinvestigation.pdf (accessed May 17, 2011).

97. Bureau of Ocean Energy Management, Regulation and Enforcement, Office of Administration and Budget, Budget Division, "Congressional Budget Justifications," http://www.boemre.gov/adm/budget.html (accessed May 17, 2011); U.S. Department of the Interior, Minerals Management Service, "U.S. Offshore Milestones," http://www.boemre.gov/stats/PDFs/milestonesAUG2006.pdf (accessed May 17, 2011).

98. National Commission, *Deep Water,* 73.

99. Ibid.

100. U.S. Department of the Interior, "Change of the Name of the Minerals Management Service to the Bureau of Ocean Energy Management, Regulation, and Enforcement," http://www.doi.gov/deepwaterhorizon/loader.cfm?csModule=security/getfile&PageID=35872 (accessed May 17, 2011).

101. U.S. Department of the Interior, "Salazar Divides MMS's Three Conflicting Missions," http://www.doi.gov/news/pressreleases/Salazar-Divides-MMSs-Three-Conflicting-Missions.cfm (accessed May 17, 2011).

102. Maria Gallucci, "Obama Administration's Plan to Expand Oil and Gas Drilling in the Gulf of Mexico Draws Protests in New Orleans," http://www.ibtimes.com/obama-administrations-plan-expand-oil-gas-drilling-gulf-mexico-draws-protests-new-2341921 (accessed October 19, 2016).

103. Ibid.

104. Christopher Carrigan, *Structured to Fail? Explaining Regulatory Performance under Competing Mandates* (New York: Cambridge University Press, forthcoming); Christopher Carrigan, "Captured by Disaster? Reinterpreting Regulatory Behavior in the Shadow of the Gulf Oil Spill," in *Preventing Capture: Special Interest Influence, and How to Limit It,* ed. Daniel Carpenter and David A. Moss (New York: Cambridge University Press, 2014), 239–291.

105. National Commission, *Deep Water.*

106. Ibid., 151.

107. Carrie Kahn, "The Boom in Boom: Will Oil Spill Defenses Hold?" National Public Radio, *All Things Considered,* June 15, 2010, http://www.npr.org/2010/06/15/127834220/the-boom-in-boom-will-oil-spill-defenses-hold (accessed October 19, 2016).

108. National Commission, *Deep Water,* 153

109. Ibid.

110. Anne E. Kornblut, "Amid Criticism over Oil Spill, Obama Will Visit Gulf Coast Again," *Washington Post,* May 26, 2010, http://www.washingtonpost.com/wp-dyn/content/article/2010/05/25/AR2010052504996.html (accessed October 19, 2016).

111. David Quinn, "Gulf Oil Spill: Louisiana's Berm Plan Bold but Full of Uncertainty," *Christian Science Monitor,* June 7, 2010, http://www.csmonitor.com/USA/2010/0607/Gulf-oil-spill-Louisiana-s-berm-plan-bold-but-full-of-uncertainty (accessed October 19, 2016).

112. U.S. Army Corps of Engineers, "Corps Decision on State's Emergency Permit Request," http://www.mvn.usace.army.mil/Portals/56/docs/PAO/EmergPermitDoc.pdf (accessed October 19, 2016).

113. National Commission, *Deep Water.*

114. State of Louisiana, Office of the Governor, "Governor Jindal Issues Statement on National Oil Spill Commission Report," http://www.gov.louisiana.gov/index.cfm?md=news room&tmp=detail&catID=2&articleID=2611&navID=3 (accessed May 17, 2011).

115. The website for the Gulf Coast Claims Facility is http://www.gulfcoastclaimsfacility .com/index (accessed October 19, 2016).

116. Debbie Elliott, "On Gulf Coast, Frustration at BP Claims Process," National Public Radio, *Morning Edition,* February 24, 2011, http://www.npr.org/2011/02/24/134009002/on-gulf-coast-frustration-at-bp-claims-process (accessed October 19, 2016).

117. Reuters, "BP Spill Fund Winding Down after $4 Billion Paid Out: Report," May 29, 2011, http://www.reuters.com/article/us-bp-fund-idUSTRE74S18I20110529 (accessed October 19, 2016); Paul Rioux, "Poor Shrimp Season Means BP Oil Spill Claims Offices Should Stay Open, Jefferson Parish Officials Say," *New Orleans Times-Picayune,* May 25, 2011, http://www.nola.com/news/gulf-oil-spill/index.ssf/2011/05/poor_shrimp_season_means_bp_oi.html (accessed October 19, 2016).

118. National Commission on Terrorist Attacks upon the United States, *The 9/11 Commission Report: Final Report of the National Commission on Terrorist Attacks upon the United States* (New York: Norton, 2004), 257, https://www.9-11commission.gov/ (accessed October 26, 2016).

119. Ibid., 257.

120. Ibid., 272.

121. Ibid., 273–275.

122. Ibid., 260.

123. Roberta Wohlstetter, quoted in ibid., 339.

124. Ibid., 301.

125. See Jonathan Mahler, "Aftershock," *New York Times Book Review,* November 12, 2006, 57, http://www.nytimes.com/2006/11/12/books/review/aftershock.html (accessed October 26, 2016).

126. Donald Kettl, *System under Stress: Homeland Security and American Politics* (Washington, D.C.: CQ Press, 2004), 1.

127. National Commission, *The 9/11 Commission Report,* 314.

128. Ibid.

129. Kettl, *System under Stress,* 29.

130. National Commission, *The 9/11 Commission Report,* 315.

131. Ibid., 315.

132. The name of this act is an acronym for Uniting and Strengthening America by Providing Appropriate Tools Required to Intercept and Obstruct Terrorism Act of 2001.

133. Kettl, *System under Stress,* 96–97.

134. Ibid., 49.

135. Bryan W. Marshall and Richard L. Pacelle Jr., "Revisiting the Two Presidencies: The Strategic Use of Executive Orders," *American Politics Research* 33 (January 2005): 81–105.

136. Author interview with Tom Ridge, September 27, 2016.

137. Ibid.

138. Ibid.

139. U.S. Department of the Treasury, Office of Foreign Assets Control, "Terrorist Assets Report," https://www.treasury.gov/resource-center/sanctions/Programs/Documents/tar2015.pdf (accessed October 26, 2016).

140. Bob von Sternberg and Pamela Miller, "Uproar Follows Imams' Detention; The Removal of Six Muslim Clerics from a Twin Cities Flight Ignited Outrage," *Star Tribune* (Minneapolis, Minn.), November 22, 2006.

141. Dan Eggen, "U.S. Settles Suit Filed by Ore. Lawyer; $2 Million Will Be Paid for Wrongful Arrest after Madrid Attack," *Washington Post,* November 30, 2006.

142. Bob Woodward, *Plan of Attack* (New York: Simon and Schuster, 2004), 164.

143. Commission on the Intelligence Capabilities of the United States Regarding Weapons of Mass Destruction, *Report to the President of the United States,* March 31, 2005, https://fas.org/irp/offdocs/wmd_report.pdf (accessed October 26, 2016).

144. Ibid., 157.

145. Ibid., 162.

146. Ibid., 172.

147. Ibid., 181.

148. Ibid., 166.

149. Ibid., 177.

150. Fred Kaplan, "You Call That a Reform Bill?" *Slate,* May 17, 2011, http://www.slate.com/id/2110767 (accessed October 26, 2016).

151. Jim Kouri, "Intelligence Agency Cooperation Still Uncertain, Say Lawmakers," *Canada Free Press,* May 16, 2011, http://canadafreepress.com/article/intelligence-agency-cooperation-still-uncertain-say-lawmakers (accessed October 26, 2016).

152. Ibid.

153. Peter Baker and Scott Shane, "Obama Seeks to Reassure U.S. after Bombing Attempt," *New York Times,* December 28, 2009.

154. Ibid.

155. Ibid.

156. Associated Press, "Bombings in N.J., N.Y. Not Linked to Larger Terror Cell, FBI Director Says," http://www.nj.com/union/index.ssf/2016/09/bombings_in_nj_ny_not_linked_to_larger_terror_cell.html (accessed October 26, 2016).

157. Ibid.

158. "Homeland Security Jokes," ThoughtCo.com, http://politicalhumor.about.com/library/blhomelandsecurity.htm (accessed May 18, 2011).

159. Judith Miller, "Be 'Alert,' Not Afraid—Janet Napolitano and America's New Terror Alert System," Fox News, April 21, 2011, http://www.foxnews.com/opinion/2011/04/21/alert-afraid-janet-napolitano-dhs-offer-new-terror-alert (accessed March 31, 2017).

160. Department of Homeland Security, "NTAS Frequently Asked Questions," https://www.dhs.gov/ntas-frequently-asked-questions (accessed October 26, 2016).

161. Emily Kopp, "DHS Rethinks the Terror Alert System It Never Used," Federal News Radio, October 15, 2015, http://federalnewsradio.com/management/2015/10/dhs-rethinks-terror-alert-system-never-used/ (accessed October 26, 2016).

162. Rebecca Shabad, "DHS to Roll Out Changes to Terror Alert System on Wednesday," CBS News, December 14, 2015, http://www.cbsnews.com/news/dhs-to-roll-out-changes-to-terror-alert-system-on-wednesday/ (accessed October 26, 2016).

163. Carmine Scavo, Richard Kearney, and Richard Kilroy Jr., "Challenges to Federalism: Homeland Security, Disaster Response, and the Local Impact of Federal Funding Formulas and Mandates" (paper presented at the annual meeting of the American Political Science Association, Philadelphia, September 1, 2006), 23.

164. Ibid., 19.

165. Kiki Caruson and Susan A. MacManus, "Mandates and Management Challenges in the Trenches: An Intergovernmental Perspective on Homeland Security," Public Administration Review 66 (July/August 2006): 527.

166. Ibid., 529.

167. Paul Light, "What Citizens Don't Know," Governing, October 2005, A1, https://wagner.nyu.edu/files/performance/What%20Citizens%20Don't%20Know.pdf (accessed October 26, 2016).

168. Steven Brill, "Are We Any Safer?" Atlantic Monthly, September 2016, 86–87.

169. Peter Eisinger, "Imperfect Federalism: The Intergovernmental Partnership for Homeland Security," Public Administration Review 66 (July/August 2006): 537–545.

170. Klinenberg and Frank, "Looting Homeland Security," 44–54.

171. Donald F. Kettl, Managing Community Development in the New Federalism (New York: Praeger, 1980).

172. Brill, "Are We Any Safer?" 66.

173. Klinenberg and Frank, "Looting Homeland Security."

174. "Bush, Congress Clash over Ports Sale," CNN, February 22, 2006, http://archive.li/AesLg (accessed March 31, 2017).

175. Ibid.

176. "Dubai Company Gives Up on Ports Deal," CBS News, March 9, 2006, http://www.cbsnews.com/news/dubai-company-gives-up-on-ports-deal/ (accessed October 26, 2016).

177. Brill, "Are We Any Safer?" 74.

178. Ibid., 62.

179. For information about the drill, see Yolo County, Health Council, "Avian Flu Drill," http://www.yolocounty.org/health-human-services/community-health/prepare-for-an-emergency/exercises-drills/avian-flu-drill-2004 (accessed October 26, 2016).

180. World Health Organization, "Cumulative Number of Confirmed Human Cases of Avian Influenza A/(H5N1) Reported to WHO," http://www.who.int/influenza/human_animal_interface/2016_10_03_tableH5N1.pdf?ua=1 (accessed October 26, 2016).

181. Information about the avian flu and pandemic flu in general can be found at http://www.flu.gov/about_the_flu/h5n1/index.html, a website managed by the U.S. Department of Health and Human Services (accessed October 26, 2016).

182. U.S. Department of Health and Human Services, "Pandemic Planning Assumptions," http://www.flu.gov/professional/pandplan.html (accessed May 18, 2011).

183. U.S. Department of Labor, Occupational Safety and Health Administration, "Pandemic Influenza," http://www.osha.gov/dsg/topics/pandemicflu/index.html (accessed May 18, 2011).

184. Centers for Disease Control and Prevention, "Case Counts in the US," http://www.cdc.gov/zika/geo/united-states.html (accessed October 26, 2016); Debra Goldschmidt, "Utah

Resident Is First Zika-Related Death in Continental U.S.," http://www.cnn.com/2016/07/08/health/utah-zika-death/ (accessed October 26, 2016).

185. E. J. Mundell, "Outbreaks Show Bird Flu Virus Is Changing," *Washington Post,* November 22, 2006, https://consumer.healthday.com/infectious-disease-information-21/flu-news-314/outbreaks-show-bird-flu-virus-is-changing-536220.html (accessed October 26, 2016).

186. Homeland Security Council, "National Strategy for Pandemic Influenza: Implementation Plan," http://www.flu.gov/planning-preparedness/federal/pandemic-influenza-implementation.pdf (accessed October 26, 2016).

187. Ibid., 2.

188. Newt Gingrich and Robert Egge, "To Fight the Flu, Change How Government Works," *New York Times,* November 6, 2005, http://www.nytimes.com/2005/11/06/opinion/to-fight-the-flu-change-how-government-works.html?_r=0 (accessed October 26, 2016).

189. Donald G. McNeil Jr., "States and Cities Lag in Readiness to Fight Bird Flu," *New York Times,* February 6, 2006, http://www.nytimes.com/2006/02/06/politics/states-and-cities-lag-in-bird-flu-readiness.html (accessed October 26, 2016).

190. Rick Weiss, "Bush, Executives Consider Strategies to Ramp Up Vaccine Production; Spurred by Concern about Avian Flu, Officials Focus on Capacity to Fight Possible Pandemic," *Washington Post,* October 8, 2005.

191. Sebastian Mallaby, "A Double Dose of Failure," *Washington Post,* November 7, 2005, http://www.washingtonpost.com/wp-dyn/content/article/2005/11/06/AR2005110601013.html (accessed October 26, 2016).

192. "H1N1 (Swine Flu) Pandemic and the Imminent Expiration of Millions of Courses of Tamiflu," Scribd, April 30, 2009, http://www.scribd.com/doc/14812224/Tamiflu-Stockpile-Millions-Expiring-20092010 (accessed October 26, 2016).

193. Ibid.

194. Tracy Staton, "With FDA Generic Nod, Roche's Once-Blockbuster Tamiflu Faces Its First Copycat Assault," FiercePharma, August 4, 2016, http://www.fiercepharma.com/pharma/fda-generic-nod-roche-s-once-blockbuster-tamiflu-faces-its-first-copycat-assault (accessed October 26, 2016).

195. Centers for Disease Control and Prevention, "The 2009 H1N1 Pandemic: Summary Highlights, April 2009–April 2010," http://www.cdc.gov/h1n1flu/cdcresponse.htm (accessed October 26, 2016).

196. Centers for Disease Control and Prevention, "Updated CDC Estimates of 2009 H1N1 Influenza Cases, Hospitalizations and Deaths in the United States, April 2009–April 2010," http://www.cdc.gov/h1n1flu/estimates_2009_h1n1.htm (accessed October 26, 2016).

197. Ibid.

198. Centers for Disease Control and Prevention, "2009 H1N1 Pandemic."

199. Ibid.

200. Betsy McKay, Cam Simpson, and Jeanne Whalen, "Obama Targets Swine Flu Response," *Wall Street Journal,* October 26, 2009, http://www.wsj.com/articles/SB125640028120405945 (accessed October 26, 2016).

201. Ibid.

202. Centers for Disease Control and Prevention, "2009 H1N1 Pandemic."

203. Brian Naylor, "Obama Flu Response Relied on Bush Plan," NPR, WBUR, Boston, May 7, 2009, http://www.wbur.org/npr/103908247/obama-flu-response-relied-on-bush-plan (accessed October 26, 2016).

204. Scott Wilson and Spencer S. Hsu, "Bush Team Strategy Now Obama's Swine Flu Playbook," *Washington Post,* May 1, 2009, http://www.washingtonpost.com/wp-dyn/content/article/2009/04/30/AR2009043003910.html (accessed October 26, 2016).

205. The White House, Office of the Press Secretary, "Fact Sheet: Advancing the Nation's Preparedness for Pandemic Influenza," May 3, 2006, https://2001-2009.state.gov/r/pa/ei/wh/65790.htm (accessed October 26, 2016).

206. Yolo County, "Avian Flu Drill."

207. Yolo County Health Department Emergency Preparedness and Response, "Lessons Learned from the Avian Flu Outbreak and Vaccination Drill, June 10, 2004," http://www.yolocounty.org/home/showdocument?id=290 (accessed October 26, 2016).

208. Rick Weiss, "Bush, Executives Consider Strategies to Ramp Up Vaccine Production; Spurred by Concern about Avian Flu, Officials Focus on Capacity to Fight Possible Pandemic," *Washington Post,* October 8, 2005; M. Asif Ismail, "Prescription for Power: Drug Makers' Lobbying Army Ensures Their Legislative Dominance," Center for Public Integrity, April 28, 2005, https://www.publicintegrity.org/2005/04/28/6564/prescription-power (accessed October 26, 2016).

209. Congressional Budget Office, "U.S. Policy Regarding Pandemic-Influenza Vaccines," September 2008, https://www.cbo.gov/sites/default/files/110th-congress-2007-2008/reports/09-15-pandemicflu.pdf (accessed October 26, 2016).

210. Ibid.

211. David Brown and Rob Stein, "U.S. Asks Firms to Make Swine Flu Vaccine," *Washington Post,* May 23, 2009.

212. Department of Health and Human Services, "HHS Boosts National Capacity to Produce Pandemic Flu Vaccine," http://www.hhs.gov/about/news/2013/09/30/hhs-boosts-national-capacity-to-produce-pandemic-flu-vaccine.html (accessed October 26, 2016).

213. Rick Weiss, "Unknowns Pose a Challenge for Preparedness Plan; Report Highlights U.S. Weaknesses in Infrastructure, Vaccine Dispersal," *Washington Post,* November 3, 2005.

214. Ellen Kleinerman, "Study Lauds Ohio Teamwork in 2009 Flu Pandemic," *Cleveland Plain Dealer,* May 3, 2011, http://www.cleveland.com/healthfit/index.ssf/2011/05/study_lauds_ohio_teamwork_in_2.html (accessed October 27, 2016).

215. McNeil, "States and Cities Lag in Readiness to Fight Bird Flu."

216. Homeland Security Council, "National Strategy for Pandemic Influenza: Implementation Plan."

217. Ibid.

218. The White House, "Media Advisory: The White House Announces H1N1 Flu Preparedness Summit," https://obamawhitehouse.archives.gov/the-press-office/media-advisory-white-house-announces-h1n1-flu-preparedness-summit (accessed March 31, 2017).

219. The White House, "Letter from the President—Zika Virus," https://www.whitehouse.gov/the-press-office/2016/02/22/letter-president-zika-virus (accessed October 27, 2016).

7 | Why Are Some Bureaucracies Better Than Others?

As THE THEORETICAL FRAMEWORKS and case studies throughout this book have demonstrated, executive branch bureaucracies are policymaking organizations that operate as institutions of American democracy. As one observer has put it, agencies "shape decisions that influence the quality of the air you breathe, how safe your car is, which immigrants will enter and stay in this country, how airports will be protected from terrorism, what you can expect from your employer in terms of working conditions and pension, and how safe that hamburger is that you just put in your mouth."[1] In terms of affecting our lives on a day-to-day basis, the bureaucracy has no peer among government institutions.

Although this influence is exercised by organizations not directly connected to the elections that form the backbone of U.S. democracy, it is inaccurate to portray the bureaucracy as being aloof from citizens and their elected representatives. From oversight by powerful congressional committees to testimony by the most common of folk, agencies stay in constant contact with their political supervisors and those in society upon whom their actions bestow benefits and impose costs. In the context of these interactions, two standards have become paramount in judging agencies as public policymakers: accountability and performance. Accountability has been a concern since the bureaucracy emerged as a policymaking force early in the twentieth century. More recently, strength in performance has come to rival clear accountability as a desirable, even necessary, trait in public bureaucracies.

Success in measuring up to accountability and performance standards varies from one agency to another. Such variation can also be seen within agencies, as organizations move from issue to issue and from one policy area to another. Many of the reasons for these differences have been highlighted in the preceding chapters. We now bring these insights together and amplify them in important ways by taking on two *final questions:*

- *WHICH AGENCIES ARE THE HIGHEST, AND LOWEST, PERFORMING ORGANIZATIONS IN THE EXECUTIVE BRANCH?*

- *WHAT FACTORS, INCLUDING ACCOUNTABILITY, HELP TO EXPLAIN DIFFERENCES IN BUREAUCRATIC BEHAVIOR AND OUTCOMES?*

Rating the Performance of Agencies

As the twenty-first century began, a team of researchers set out to document differences in the performance of federal agencies. This was no easy task! To account for the fact that performance is a multifaceted concept, the researchers developed a rating scheme that evaluated agencies on thirty-four criteria in five crosscutting areas—financial management, capital management, human resources, information technology, and managing for results. After conducting hundreds of interviews with individuals from the legislative and executive branches, think tanks, the press, interest groups, academic institutions, and many other organizations, the researchers deliberated and reached conclusions about the performance of fifteen agencies.[2]

The results of the **Federal Performance Project** demonstrated great variation in agency performance, with grades ranging from A (the Social Security Administration) to C– (the Immigration and Naturalization Service, since renamed Citizenship and Immigration Services). Over the next three years, twelve more agencies were evaluated, including the Postal Service (USPS) and the Army Corps of Engineers. The researchers also rated six agencies a second time in an effort to track changes in performance over time. In the last year of the Federal Performance Project, the Internal Revenue Service received a B–, a modest improvement over the C it had received three years earlier.

The Federal Performance Project confirms that some agencies perform better than others. On occasion, as in the case of the Social Security Administration and Immigration and Naturalization Service, these differences are dramatic. More often than not, however, the distinctions are much subtler. For example, the Federal Emergency Management Agency (with a grade of B) was by a small margin a higher performing agency than the Environmental Protection Agency (which received a B–). Figure 7.1 presents grades for a selection of agencies that were evaluated in the Federal Performance Project.

Although rating the performance of government organizations presents a stiff challenge, the Federal Performance Project is not the only effort at ranking federal agencies. Other approaches, which will be discussed later in the chapter, rely on the input of government workers and the general public. In addition, presidential administrations have sought to measure performance as a means of informing budgetary and programmatic decisions. From among these approaches, the Federal Performance Project stands out as a thorough, objective, and reasoned assessment of bureaucracy. As such, its report cards provide a solid basis for helping to explain variation in performance across organizations.

Figure 7.1 Report Cards for Selected Federal Agencies

1999	Immigration and Naturali-zation Service	Customs Service	Health Care Financing Administration	Environmental Protection Agency	Social Security Administration
	C–	C	C	B–	A

2000	National Park Service	Occupational Safety and Health Administration	Veteran Benefits Administration	Army Corps of Engineers	Coast Guard
	C	C	B–	B	A

2001	Bureau of Indian Affairs	Bureau of Consular Affairs	National Aeronautics and Space Administration	Postal Service	National Weather Service
	D	C	B	A–	A

2002	Immigration and Naturali-zation Service	Centers for Medicare and Medicaid Services	Internal Revenue Service	Federal Aviation Administration	Social Security Administration
	D	C–	B–	B	B

Source: Government Executive, February 1999, March 2000, April 2001, May 2002. Consolidated table prepared by the authors.

Note: In 2001, the Health Care Financing Administration was renamed the Centers for Medicare and Medicaid Services. In 2003, when the Department of Homeland Security was created, the functions of the Immigration and Naturalization Service were transferred to three new agencies—Citizenship and Immigration Services, Immigration and Customs Enforcement, and Customs and Border Protection. At the same time, the duties of the Customs Service were placed in Customs and Border Protection and Immigration and Customs Enforcement.

Explaining Variations in Performance

To what extent are variations in performance systematic, as opposed to reflections of idiosyncrasies in agencies and their evaluators? To answer this question, we return to the insights generated by the theoretical frameworks and case studies. On the basis of these insights, we believe four factors are particularly relevant in distinguishing agencies in their performance: **tasks, relationships, political support,** and **leadership.** Some agencies deal with relatively clear, easy, and manageable tasks; other agencies have more imposing responsibilities. Some agencies communicate and coordinate well with other organizations; other agencies experience great difficulties in building effective network ties.

Some agencies benefit from sustained accountability to diverse sovereigns and clients; other agencies lack solid political support. Some agencies enjoy competent, sensitive, and creative leadership; other agencies suffer from leadership that fails in fundamental respects. From these key premises flow twelve specific propositions about the performance of public bureaucracies.

Tasks

At times agencies engage in policymaking, while at other times they implement decisions made elsewhere in the political system. Although **implementation** can pose significant problems, policymaking is, generally speaking, a more difficult responsibility. For this reason agencies that primarily engage in routine implementation tasks are likely to perform better than those whose central mission is resolving complex and contentious policy issues. This holds especially for implementation tasks viewed favorably by the agency's clients.

- **PROPOSITION 1: AGENCIES WHOSE PRIMARY TASK IS TO DISTRIBUTE MONEY TO INDIVIDUALS TEND TO PERFORM WELL.**

The Social Security Administration, which received an A in the first year of the Federal Performance Project and a B three years later, exemplifies this proposition. Much of what the agency does is write checks to retirees and disabled individuals. Once eligibility has been determined, the rest is really quite straightforward. The criteria for retirement payments are crystal clear, and agency officials have extensive documentation of individual work histories at their fingertips. Determining eligibility for disability payments is somewhat trickier, but even here statutory criteria exist and are supplemented by more specific administrative rules and judicial decisions.

By way of contrast, consider the Centers for Medicare and Medicaid Services (CMS), the lead agency in delivering health care services to the elderly, poor, and other segments of the population. In carrying out the Medicaid portion of this task, CMS relies on state governments to decide who is eligible for the program and who is authorized to provide the program's services. Since the passage of the Affordable Care Act, states have varied in their willingness to expand eligibility to adults who earn up to 138 percent of the federal poverty level, further complicating CMS management and oversight of the program. For their part, state governments rely on hospitals, managed care plans, cooperatives, and other health care organizations to hire, deploy, and compensate personnel. Finally, health care organizations rely on physicians, nurses, and other medical professionals to deliver services in accordance with program rules. With such a long chain of responsible parties, performance difficulties are bound to arise.[3] Not surprisingly, then, CMS received a C– from the Federal Performance Project.[4]

Not all implementation tasks, however, are created equal or viewed with favor. At times agencies engage in routine behaviors that stakeholders do not find at all endearing, such as collecting money. Whereas agencies distributing money are likely to be blessed, agencies **extracting money** are likely to be cursed.

- **PROPOSITION 2: AGENCIES WHOSE PRIMARY TASK IS TO COLLECT MONEY TEND TO PERFORM POORLY.**

The Internal Revenue Service (IRS), which has never received a grade higher than a B–, epitomizes this proposition. It goes without saying that hardly anyone likes the IRS, and many people fear it. Despite this fear, a number of taxpayers cheat, banking on the fact that the agency audits only a relatively small portion of tax returns. In fact, the IRS estimates that the annual tax gap, the difference between what taxpayers owe and what they voluntarily pay, is approximately $450 billion.[5] Two decades ago, revelations that some IRS officials were overzealous in their efforts to combat tax evasion made it more difficult for the agency to perform auditing duties. In a series of highly publicized hearings and the subsequent Internal Revenue Service Restructuring and Reform Act of 1998, Congress made it clear that it wanted the IRS to be relatively benign in its enforcement efforts. Congress also undoubtedly wants the IRS to offer better services, such as timely and accurate advice to taxpayers, but legislators have not provided the funding necessary to bring about such performance enhancements. In fact, from 2015 to 2016, the IRS's budget was reduced by 18 percent.[6] Yet even if Congress increases funding levels for popular improvements, the IRS, by the very nature of its core task, would likely continue to suffer from a negative image.

The Office of Student Financial Assistance (OSFA; today known as the Office of Federal Student Aid) is an interesting agency to consider because it both distributes money and collects it. Like the Social Security Administration, it writes checks, in its case mainly to students of relatively modest means who wish to attend college. These payments, however, are primarily loans that must eventually be repaid. Like the IRS, then, the OSFA is also a revenue collection operation. Its task is particularly difficult because recent college graduates, if saddled with substantial debt, may lack the resources necessary to make rent payments, car payments, and student loan payments at the same time. Sixty-eight percent of college students graduate with loan debt.[7] This debt is, on average, $30,100 per student,[8] and the national student loan default rate is 11.3 percent.[9] Given these gloomy statistics, it is not surprising that the OSFA earned no better than a C from the Federal Performance Project.

Throughout the preceding chapters we have highlighted the variety of **missions** bestowed upon agencies by political principals. Many of these missions reflect the fact that public problems are often hard to solve, especially without running afoul of powerful constituencies. The Forest Service's delicate balancing act between the conservation of natural resources and the fostering of rural economic development offers just one example of such a mission. In general, **ambiguity** and **conflict** in missions make it difficult for agencies to satisfy the desires and needs of their stakeholders and political supervisors.

- **PROPOSITION 3: AGENCIES WITH AMBIGUOUS OR CONFLICTING MISSIONS TEND TO PERFORM POORLY.**

U.S. Citizenship and Immigration Services (CIS) is an example of a bureaucracy bedeviled by competing goals. The agency is expected to protect the homeland by "strengthening the security and integrity of the immigration system" while at the same time advancing "America's promise as a nation of immigrants."[10] It is extremely difficult, and perhaps impossible, to fully reconcile these goals. A looser touch allows necessary agricultural workers and welcome foreign tourists into the country, but unintentionally whisks in individuals seeking to harm the United States. The stakes of getting this trade-off right were never so apparent as on September 11, 2001. Several months after the terrorist attacks, the agency received a D, lower than the C– it had received three years earlier. Even today, many years after the attacks, it remains difficult to strike a balance between the often competing economic and security rationales for the nation's immigration system.[11] Absent a consensus, CIS is likely to remain caught in the middle, unable to perform well on either dimension.

By contrast, the National Weather Service (NWS), which suffers no existential angst as it contemplates its raison d'être, received an A from the Federal Performance Project. Everyone inside and outside the agency knows that the NWS is responsible for predicting the weather as accurately as possible. Nothing cloudy about that mission! Fully aware of its mission, and equipped with the personnel and technology to carry it out, the NWS tracks hurricanes and other disturbances in the atmosphere with considerable finesse and precision. An agency with such a clear mission is likely to perform well, especially when that mission enjoys wide support. No one doubts the need for good weather forecasts to anticipate emergencies and to enhance the quality of our lives. By acquitting itself admirably during the Hurricane Katrina disaster, the NWS demonstrated that it is capable of providing these valuable services in an accurate and dependable (and lifesaving) manner.

The distinction between outputs (the activities of agencies) and outcomes (the results of these activities) is salient when thinking about performance. For example, the observability of these facets of bureaucratic behavior varies across policy areas and agencies.[12] As a result, the difficulty of the moral hazard problem facing political principals and their constituents is best not treated as constant.

In dealing with the SSA, one question the agency's supervisors and clients ask is, *How quick and accurate are Social Security payments?* Fortunately, for all concerned parties, the information necessary to gauge these outputs and outcomes is readily available. Similarly, it is relatively easy for those inside and outside the USPS to keep tabs on the agency's activities and results. No great mystery exists about how long it takes a letter carrier to deliver the mail or a first-class letter to reach its destination.

Agencies such as the SSA and the USPS are known as **production organizations.** In such organizations, clarity in outputs and outcomes makes it relatively easy for agency leaders to see what is being done and what is being accomplished. This clarity also helps interested parties outside the organization; agency mistakes, for example, are relatively transparent to bosses and clients. For these reasons production organizations, in most cases, perform with considerable strength and precision.

- **PROPOSITION 4: AGENCIES WHOSE OUTPUTS AND OUTCOMES BOTH ARE OBSERVABLE TEND TO PERFORM WELL.**

The National Aeronautics and Space Administration (NASA), which received a B, would seem to qualify at least in some respects as a production agency. Granted, the long-term implications of space exploration are difficult to assess. For example, it is hard to say whether President Barack Obama's 2010 charge to NASA to send human beings to Mars by the 2030s was executed effectively during his administration.[13] However, there are immediate consequences of NASA's outputs that are easy to spot. In 2003, a piece of foam insulation broke off the main propellant tank of the Space Shuttle *Columbia* and struck the leading edge of the craft's left wing. This accident damaged the shuttle's thermal protection system, and the vehicle disintegrated when hot gases penetrated its structure upon reentry into the Earth's atmosphere, causing the deaths of all seven crew members.[14] Two-and-a-half years later, safety modifications to the shuttle fleet's external fuel tank system were put to the test when *Discovery* lifted off from Florida's Kennedy Space Center. During the course of their two-week mission, *Discovery*'s crew members engaged in a first-of-its-kind spacewalk to perform repairs on the International Space Station.[15] Both the repairs and the flight itself were resounding successes. In general, NASA has performed reasonably well in executing a very difficult, and decidedly observable, mission.

What about agencies whose outputs and outcomes are difficult to observe? Such agencies, known as **coping organizations,** often find it difficult to perform well.[16] Leading examples of coping organizations include public schools and police departments. Diplomacy—the State Department's stock in trade—is also emblematic of this state of affairs. Perhaps not surprisingly, the State Department's Bureau of Consular Affairs (BCA) received a C from the Federal Performance Project. The BCA takes care of American citizens overseas—reissuing lost passports, for example—and gives visas to foreigners who wish to visit the United States. Because the BCA's consulates are scattered throughout the world, and because its information technology has lagged behind that of other agencies, it has been challenging for agency leaders to manage the organization's tasks and for members of Congress to keep tabs on what the organization is doing.[17] The BCA's weaknesses became painfully apparent to many would-be travelers in the spring of 2007, when the agency's backlog of passport applications escalated sharply as a result of new regulations governing international travel. Even destinations such as the Caribbean islands were affected by the new rules.[18] Many Americans did not know if their passport application had been approved until just prior to their scheduled departure. Since that time, BCA's performance seems to have improved somewhat, thanks to increased staffing and improved technology.

The Interior Department's Bureau of Indian Affairs (BIA), which received a D, also possesses some coping organization characteristics. The agency's activities, such as supporting education on tribal reservations, are difficult to measure and monitor. Although test scores offer some indication of how much students have learned, it is exceedingly tough to disentangle the effects of teacher intervention from those of student initiative and home environment. In short, the BIA's management lapses arise in part from the complexity of the tasks it is charged with carrying out.[19]

The much-maligned Citizenship and Immigration Services and related agencies, such as Customs and Border Protection (whose predecessor, the Customs Service, received a C), suffer from multiple problems, including the difficulty of discerning outputs and outcomes. To cite the clearest problem, illegal immigration is extremely hard to document because those who enter the country without documentation have compelling incentives to remain hidden from government authorities. It is, of course, possible to gather statistics on the number of individuals apprehended at U.S. borders. During 2016, more than 300,000 illegal border crossers were apprehended in Texas, New Mexico, Arizona, and California.[20] The ratio of successful to unsuccessful illegal border crossings is for all intents and purposes unknowable. However, a common estimate is that 12 million undocumented immigrants currently reside in the United States.[21]

Relationships

Despite the importance of agency tasks, many bureaucracies with identical missions perform very differently. For example, some state environmental agencies have effectively controlled air pollution, while others have not. Some local police departments have successfully reduced violent crime, while others have not. Many factors help to explain these differences, among them relationships between bureaucrats (for example, **communications**) and relationships between bureaucracies (for example, **coordination**). These relationships are so integral to the daily lives of bureaucrats that we often take them for granted. Yet just as winning in basketball depends on certain relationships (crisp passing, solid team defense), so too does good bureaucratic work.

The transmission of information, though lacking in glamour, is of critical importance if bureaucrats, their bosses, and their clients are to know what is happening and what is expected of them. This is true in both emergencies and in more routine situations. Communications are an especially pressing concern for the National Park Service (NPS), which received a C from the Federal Performance Project. The NPS has tens of thousands of employees who serve more than 275 million visitors each year.[22] In recent decades, the NPS has relied on focus groups to assess what the public knows about the agency, what visitors expect from parks, and how the agency can best communicate with its constituents. According to agency personnel, these communication efforts "help the agency better understand its future needs, as well as educate the public about the importance of natural resource stewardship."[23]

- **PROPOSITION 5: AGENCIES THAT ESTABLISH GOOD COMMUNICATION SYSTEMS TEND TO PERFORM WELL.**

According to former surgeon general Jocelyn Elders (and many others), coordination is an "unnatural act between non-consenting adults."[24] Unnatural though it may be, coordination between agencies is of vital importance. The challenges of coordination are especially acute in an intergovernmental setting, where bureaucrats work for different bosses and for organizations with different cultures and norms. These challenges help to explain why intergovernmental programs are often rated so poorly. Consider the Chesapeake Bay Commission (CBC), a tristate body charged with restoring one of the nation's most treasured natural resources. Although three states (Pennsylvania, Maryland, and Virginia) comprise the membership of the CBC, other jurisdictions (New York, Delaware, West Virginia, and the District of Columbia) also help to determine water quality in the region.[25] Furthermore, as discussed in Chapter 5, Pennsylvania has not been as supportive as Virginia and Maryland of aggressive clean-up efforts.[26] Reconciling conflicts between states, and between states and federal agencies (especially during the Obama administration, which gave EPA the authority to enforce pollution reduction goals in the watershed), is a constant challenge.[27] Even if a consensus is reached at the policy formulation stage, that consensus may erode at the policy implementation stage, where different actors are involved. As Paul Posner notes, "The network for policy development is actually quite different from the network for policy implementation."[28] Unfortunately, such delays can have devastating consequences for the environment. As one EPA official said in a critical assessment of the CBC, "If we go at the current rate that we're doing, we're talking about restoring the Chesapeake decades from now, a generation or two."[29]

- **PROPOSITION 6: AGENCIES THAT COORDINATE ACTIVITIES INTERNALLY, AS WELL AS WITH OTHER AGENCIES, TEND TO PERFORM WELL.**

Sometimes embattled agencies learn to coordinate better than they have done in the past. Over the years, the Bureau of Land Management (BLM) has been on the receiving end of numerous lawsuits filed by environmental groups. To decrease the frequency of these lawsuits, some BLM officials have opted to improve interagency planning and coordination. For example, BLM officials in California's San Joaquin Valley led an effort to create an interagency council that developed a regional plan to protect biodiversity.[30] In the long run, such constructive efforts are likely to reduce levels of environmental litigation.

Political Support

As has been emphasized throughout, accountability and performance are the two main standards by which public bureaucracies are judged. Though distinct in some respects, these standards are inextricably linked in others. For decades, one of the central ways in which chief executives, legislatures, and judiciaries have sought to foster bureaucratic accountability has been by influencing the processes through which agencies go about producing outputs. The Administrative Procedure Act of 1946, with its dictates regarding proposed rules and public comments, is a classic example of this fundamental connection.

But what about the linkage in the reverse direction? In what ways does accountability facilitate performance? Are there forms of accountability, and political support more generally, that hinder the ability of agencies to perform their most crucial tasks?

In iron triangles, political support comes from narrow constituencies that stand to benefit greatly from bureaucratic decision making. Opposing, broader interests do not typically mobilize against these narrow constituencies. Such a pattern can lead to difficulties in both processes and results. For decades the Interstate Commerce Commission had the authority to regulate the rates charged by railroads and motor carriers. Working closely with these interests, the agency developed what has been called "congenital schizophrenia."[31] In other words, taking care of the needs of the rail and trucking industries case by case took precedence over consistent application of particular standards or rationalizations, to the detriment of other interested parties, including consumers and members of Congress.

· PROPOSITION 7: AGENCIES THAT ARE PRESSURED BY DIVERSE SETS OF CONSTITUENCIES TEND TO PERFORM WELL.

In general, **support from diffuse constituencies** is a way to avoid the kinds of problems that eventually contributed to the demise, in 1995, of the Interstate Commerce Commission. The EPA is perhaps the leading example of an agency that, from its inception, has been exposed to diverse points of view, including business interests, environmental advocates, and state and local regulators charged with carrying out federal policies. At times this exposure has proved frustrating for agency officials, who must negotiate political minefields when making decisions. Such negotiations have to be undertaken with great care and deliberation, and as a result the agency seldom sets records for the speed of its policymaking. Nevertheless, the EPA's diverse constituency helps guarantee that it will pay at least some attention to both economic efficiency and ecological concerns whenever it makes a decision. As a case in point, reductions in air and water pollution over the past three decades owe a great deal to the persistent efforts of environmentalists, while technological advances and the enhanced importance of economic incentives reflect the input of regulated industries. Although the agency's grades have not been perfect (a B– in the first year of the Federal Performance Project and a B three years later), they almost certainly would have been worse had the agency been consistently dominated by either business firms or environmental activists.

In contrast, the Customs Service suffered from **lopsided external pressure** prior to the terrorist attacks of September 11, 2001. Shipping interests, eager to speed the flow of goods and therefore to increase their profits, lobbied the agency to expedite checks at the nation's borders. Security interests were poorly represented in this lobbying process. In the aftermath of the attacks, investigations revealed that every year the agency had been allowing millions of containers to enter the country with minimal scrutiny for bombs or biological weapons. In retrospect, the C received by the agency accurately captured an organization poorly prepared to prevent terrorists from gaining a toehold inside the United States.

· PROPOSITION 8: AGENCIES WHOSE PROGRAMS AND POLICIES ENJOY DIFFUSE SUPPORT TEND TO PERFORM WELL.

A closely related covariate of performance is the level of support enjoyed by the programs and policies under an agency's jurisdiction. Consider, at one end of the spectrum, the Social Security Administration (SSA), U.S. Postal Service

(USPS), and National Weather Service (NWS), three agencies that have received very good or excellent ratings. Social Security is probably the most popular income support program in the United States. Senior citizens anxiously wait to receive their monthly check or bank deposit, and most working Americans hope that when they retire, they too will receive a minimum pension from the federal government. Mail delivery, which dates back to the nation's earliest days, also enjoys widespread public support, despite periodic increases in the price of stamps. Even with a growing number of alternatives to traditional mail delivery, such as faxes, e-mails, instant messaging, and Federal Express and similar private services, Americans continue to rely heavily upon the USPS for personal and professional communications. Though not as old as the USPS, the NWS is just as familiar and highly regarded. Weather reports are particularly useful for farmers and travelers. The work of the agency's forecasters is also of critical importance for those who find themselves in the path of blizzards, hurricanes, tornadoes, and other natural disasters. As each one of us can undoubtedly attest, this work helps to enhance the quality of our daily lives, as when we choose to picnic on Saturday rather than Sunday because the weather looks more promising.

At the other end of the spectrum, the BIA is an agency whose programs and policies enjoy specific support from some Native Americans but not diffuse support from the general American public. One reason is that in an effort to build consensus, the agency has deliberately disaggregated issues, thus conveying the impression that its actions will probably promote nothing more than local benefits.[32] Another reason is the succession of highly conflictive issues the agency has had to deal with in recent decades, including various disputes over Native American treaty rights. Because such controversies tend to pit Native Americans against other Americans, these issues are unlikely to generate diffuse support for an agency badly in need of performance enhancements.[33]

Support, or a lack thereof, for agencies and their jurisdictions comes not only from societal clients but from political supervisors as well. These supervisors seek to foster accountability through several different techniques of control. A **catalytic control** places on an agency's agenda an issue requiring some kind of response but allows the agency considerable discretion in crafting its approach. A **hortatory control** offers incentives, such as financial rewards, to encourage an agency to take specific actions. Finally, a **coercive control** compels an agency to behave in a certain way, regardless of the preferences of the agency's leaders, managers, and operations staff. As a general rule, coercive controls inhibit creative problem solving and produce unintended, negative side effects. Although coercion is sometimes necessary, as when civil rights or civil liberties are threatened, it is usually a suboptimal technique for controlling the bureaucracy.[34]

- *PROPOSITION 9: AGENCIES SUBJECT TO CATALYTIC CONTROLS OR HORTATORY CONTROLS TEND TO PERFORM BETTER THAN THOSE SUBJECT TO COERCIVE CONTROLS.*

Congress's intervention in the area of ergonomics policy offers a good example of a coercive control. Rather than relying on legislative appropriations and oversight hearings to encourage an ergonomics rule that reflected its priorities,

Congress waited for the Occupational Safety and Health Administration (OSHA) to adopt a rule and then, with the help of the newly inaugurated George W. Bush administration, promptly overturned it. Repudiated by Congress, and consistent with the aims of its new leadership, the agency declined to revise and reissue the regulation. Rather, OSHA, in 2002, established a four-pronged approach designed to change the behavior of employers and workers through voluntary measures.[35] This approach included guidelines, inspections, outreach, and the ongoing work of the National Advisory Committee on Ergonomics. On the one hand, the plan was hailed by the U.S. Chamber of Commerce and other business interests as putting "science ahead of politics."[36] On the other hand, labor unions such as the AFL-CIO argued that the plan provided "no real protections" against repetitive stress injuries.[37] Labor unions' dissatisfaction with ergonomics policy continued into the Obama administration. In January 2011, citing small-business opposition, OSHA withdrew a proposed regulation requiring firms to count repetitive stress injuries.[38] This withdrawal occurred just hours before President Obama delivered a State of the Union address that heavily emphasized job creation.[39]

By way of contrast, Congress has historically given the USPS considerable discretion and autonomy. Under an arrangement dating back to 1970, an independent Postal Rate Commission makes recommendations on rate increases to an independent board of governors, which then makes the final decisions. The requirements that members be appointed to nine-year terms and can be removed only under the rarest of circumstances insulate the board from political pressure. Such noncoercive controls free the USPS to take actions that raise little political ire, even when they entail rate hikes that are inevitably unpopular with consumers.

As these examples illustrate, political support is not an all-or-nothing proposition. Agencies that most clearly recognize the opportunities and constraints presented by different types of accountability put themselves in a position to generate the political capital necessary to perform their tasks effectively. This awareness often comes from the top, with skillful, visionary leaders.

Leadership

Although it is commonly acknowledged that leadership matters in public bureaucracies, much less agreement exists regarding the specific ingredients that make for an effective leader. This lack of agreement should not be viewed as surprising, as the qualities that make for strong leadership at some agencies may not be the qualities that facilitate appropriate leadership at others. For example, a moribund agency with programs escalating in economic, social, and political importance may benefit from a bold leader willing to rock the boat, even if this rocking causes some inside and outside the agency to feel queasy. In contrast, an embattled agency with programs constantly being challenged may benefit from a coalition builder who can effectively reach out to influential constituencies prior to making crucial decisions. Still, despite these complexities and subtleties, several general propositions about bureaucratic leadership can be advanced.

Agency heads are appointed for a variety of reasons—their qualifications, their demographic characteristics, their long-standing friendship with the president, their support from influential backers or constituencies, and so forth. Of these factors, effective leadership derives primarily from **professional expertise** and **prior work experience.** Without these qualities, agency heads will probably flounder, no matter how much support key bosses and clients provide. With these qualities, success is much more likely, even for agency heads who are not the president's personal friends or closely aligned with powerful societal interests.

- **PROPOSITION 10: AGENCIES WITH LEADERS WHO POSSESS THE REQUISITE EXPERTISE AND EXPERIENCE TEND TO PERFORM WELL.**

Carol Browner, who led the EPA during the Clinton administration, had headed Florida's Department of Environmental Protection prior to serving in the federal government. Browner had also worked on Capitol Hill, assisting Sen. Al Gore, D-Tenn., on environmental issues. Importantly, Browner made good use of the substantive knowledge and political connections she had accumulated prior to her EPA stint. During her tenure, the agency launched a number of major initiatives, including Project XL, which allowed businesses and state and local governments to experiment with innovative, cost-effective approaches for achieving environmental goals.[40]

Consider as well the background of John D. Graham, who headed the Office of Information and Regulatory Affairs (OIRA) until October 2005 in the administration of George W. Bush. Prior to taking the reins at OIRA, Graham founded the Harvard Center for Risk Analysis and wrote several books and dozens of articles on topics such as automotive safety and environmental policy.[41] This body of work established Graham as one of the nation's leading experts on the application of analytical techniques to the setting of regulatory priorities, the weighing of risks, and the design of cost-effective public policies. It was this expertise that in part enabled Graham to survive the contentious Senate confirmation process that inevitably follows the president's nomination of a new regulatory czar (as the OIRA administrator is commonly known in policymaking circles). During his productive tenure, Graham not only blocked proposed regulations that did not pass analytical muster, but he also prompted agencies to issue rules in a number of important areas that otherwise might have been neglected. The trans-fat labels that have become standard elements of food packaging are one example of how Graham's prior expertise in risk analysis served as the impetus for a policy change that is likely to benefit the health and well-being of millions of Americans.

Regardless of their experience, leaders can also enhance bureaucratic performance by taking actions that advance their agencies' long-term interests, even if such actions undermine their personal interests in the short run. By making such **credible commitments,** leaders foster a sense of cooperation and esprit de corps among agency managers and operators, which in turn boost the prospects that the organization will take major strides toward achieving its most fundamental goals.[42]

- **PROPOSITION 11: AGENCIES WITH LEADERS WHO MAKE CREDIBLE COMMITMENTS TEND TO PERFORM WELL.**

Credible commitments can be made and demonstrated in a variety of ways. One way is to state clear goals upfront and stick to them, despite intense political pressure. Michelle Rhee, who became chancellor of D.C. public schools in June 2007, exemplifies this point. An unconventional choice to head the District's school system, Rhee was an outspoken critic of politicians, unions, school administrators, and teachers who stood in the way of students' progress. As chancellor, she committed herself to improving the education of D.C. schoolchildren, even if it meant firing inept principals and incompetent teachers, closing under-enrolled schools, upsetting parents, antagonizing union officials, and infuriating politicians. She promised to put students first. Her stern visage on the cover of *Time* magazine, wielding a broom, conveyed the image that she was a "take-no-prisoners" reformer.[43]

During a tumultuous three-and-a-half years as chancellor, Rhee closed 27 schools, fired nearly 50 principals, hired approximately 900 new teachers, laid off 266 teachers for budgetary reasons, fired 165 teachers for incompetence, and placed approximately 700 teachers on probation because of poor performance.[44] She reduced the size of central office staff by nearly 50 percent. She established a new system for evaluating teachers, known as IMPACT, which based teachers' performance evaluations on a combination of assessments by principals (the norm), assessments by master educators (a new procedure), and a value-added model that linked teachers to students' test score changes over time (a new and very controversial initiative). She won a union contract that officially acknowledged the new performance assessment system and gave principals new freedom to hire the best available teachers. In numerous meetings, speeches, and press conferences, Rhee made it clear that she would do whatever it took to turn student test scores around. And she did. In 2009, high school graduation rates improved. Between 2007 and 2009, National Assessment of Educational Progress scores for reading and math, for both fourth graders and eighth graders, improved—a remarkable achievement for such a troubled school district. In 2010, it was announced that more children were enrolling in the D.C. public schools than in the previous year for the first time in four decades.[45]

Another local administrator who made a credible commitment to her city was Janette Sadik-Khan.[46] Appointed as New York City's transportation commissioner by Mayor Michael Bloomberg in April 2007, Sadik-Khan vowed to promote the twin goals of safety and sustainability, by encouraging biking. Despite political opposition, she added more than 250 miles of bicycle lanes and converted Times Square into a car-free zone.[47] During her tenure as commissioner, traffic accidents and fatalities on New York City streets declined. In a nutshell, Sadik-Khan's resolve and determination paid off, in the form of safer streets, healthier lifestyles, and a cleaner environment.

At one time or another, most agencies need leaders who are adept at **attracting external support.** Leaders who are savvy in this respect find it relatively easy to capture the attention and enthusiasm of not only the democratic public but also agency bosses and clients. Generating favorable coverage in the mass media has become an essential component of this leadership skill. Positive reputations can enhance performance by making it easier, for example, for the organization to attract valuable resources and political capital.

- ## PROPOSITION 12: AGENCIES WITH LEADERS WHO HAVE A FLAIR FOR POSITIVE PUBLICITY TEND TO PERFORM WELL.

Jane Garvey, who led the Federal Aviation Administration from 1997 to 2002, attracted nationwide attention by vowing to be airborne when midnight struck on January 1, 2000. Her promise, which she kept with great fanfare, was broadcast on nightly news programs and reported in morning papers all across the country. Garvey's publicity stunt was substantively important because it helped reassure the public that the safety of air travel would be not be compromised by the year 2000 (Y2K) computer bug.[48] Overall, the agency's performance improved markedly during Garvey's tenure, as indicated by its jump from a C to a B three years later.

More recently, another transportation agency leader made headlines. Ray LaHood, a Republican chosen by President Obama to head the federal Department of Transportation, generated considerable mass media interest (including a guest appearance on the *Oprah Winfrey Show* and a joint event with pop music star Jordin Sparks) for his opposition to texting while driving.[49] At a time of scarce resources, when a new federal program was unlikely, LaHood used his "bully pulpit" to urge state legislatures to ban texting while driving. His efforts seem to have paid off. Within two years after the launch of the campaign, thirty-three states and the District of Columbia had banned texting while driving—a significant increase since LaHood began his tenure as secretary of transportation.[50]

William Bratton, the only person ever to be the chief of police in both New York City and Los Angeles, was also a master of publicity. In both cities, he used the media to cultivate a brash and bold style that attracted both admirers and detractors. In New York, he famously spearheaded a crackdown, with the encouragement of Mayor Rudy Giuliani, on the city's infamous "squeegee men" (who intimidated motorists into accepting unwanted windshield-washing services at busy intersections) and other forms of petty criminal behavior. Upon arriving in Los Angeles, he colorfully informed the department's commanders that he would not tolerate opposition to his strategies: "If you don't want to work in the department, get the hell out."[51] Bratton's signature achievement—crime rates in New York City that plunged to their lowest levels in decades—was in no small part a reflection of his ability to capture external attention and support.

Bratton's successful track record demonstrates that leaders hold in their hands one of the keys to effective performance in executive branch bureaucracies. They cannot, however, unlock the door to praiseworthy outputs and outcomes on their own. Leadership does not operate in a vacuum but in a context colored by the tasks assigned to agencies and the level of political support provided by agency bosses and clients.

While some leaders have a flair for positive publicity, others have a knack for undermining their own cause by **generating unfavorable publicity.** Both Michelle Rhee and Janette Sadik-Khan fit this description. Rhee's bluntness and aversion to compromise made her many enemies, some of whom lashed out at Rhee in newspaper articles and columns, in the *Washington Post* and elsewhere. It didn't help that Rhee seemed to have a tin ear when it came to politics and public perceptions. Ultimately, Rhee's boss, Mayor Adrian Fenty, was defeated at the polls, in part because of Rhee, who had become a polarizing figure.[52] Rhee resigned in October 2010. While Rhee's relentless commitment to education reform produced short-term improvements for students, she also made it more difficult for her successors and her supporters to build on these results. As Rhee herself acknowledged, "We made a ton of mistakes. I thought, very naively, that if we just put our heads down and we worked hard and produced the results, people would be so happy that they would want to continue the work. We were absolutely incorrect about that."[53]

Sadik-Khan also generated lots of negative publicity. Critics complained that she failed to consult local residents and that she generated unnecessary conflict. *New York Post* columnist Cindy Adams derided her as "the wacko nutso bike commissioner."[54] As her support from Mayor Bloomberg and other key officials eroded, Sadik-Khan attempted to be less confrontational and more conciliatory. One local politician put it this way: "The old way the mayor and the D.O.T. approached these street design issues was 'my way or the highway.' . . . The test of Janette is whether she can take all of these great ideas and bold proposals and actually sit down with the community and get them accomplished in a way that can be long-lasting."[55]

Alternative Ways of Gauging Agency Performance

Although the Federal Performance Project (FPP) has been useful as a means of separating highly performing agencies from organizations that generate less-than-stellar outputs and outcomes, this rating system is limited in a number of important respects. For starters, the FPP's agency report cards, approaching two decades old, are somewhat dated. As the FPP itself demonstrates, agency performance can change, sometimes dramatically, in response to evolutions and sharp alterations in organizational tasks, relationships, political support, and leadership. Furthermore, the FPP, with its evaluations grounded in dozens of specific management criteria, all of which are assessed by expert researchers, represents just one basic approach to measuring the performance of public bureaucracies. So how does the FPP stack up next to more recent rating systems that are constructed through alternative methodologies?

On an annual basis, the Partnership for Public Service (PPS) releases ratings of the "**Best Places to Work in the Federal Government**."[56] Using information collected about hundreds of thousands of executive branch employees, PPS ranks 391 federal organizations in terms of worker satisfaction and commitment.[57] Although PPS scores are more current and cover more agencies than the Federal Performance Project, worker satisfaction and commitment represent a manifestation of performance that is quite distinct from the outputs and outcomes we have focused on throughout the book.

Despite such differences, there are reasons to suspect that employee assessments match up well with evaluations of organization management. For example, workers are more likely to be satisfied with and committed to their agency if the organization is well managed. As Table 7.1 illustrates, such matching does indeed occur at many agencies. The Coast Guard, the highest graded FPP agency in the table, is one of the top scoring organizations as measured by employee sentiments as well. The most notable outlier is OSHA, which scores quite poorly on management, but nevertheless maintains above average worker satisfaction and commitment.

A third source of information about agency performance is **public opinion polls.** Once again, it is reasonable to expect that the public's experience with agencies, although a rather different means of gauging performance, is not unrelated to organization management. In 2015, the Pew Research Center asked Americans what they think about a number of agencies of the federal government.[58] Although the survey covered a limited set of agencies, the responses provide an opportunity to juxtapose public opinion with expert assessments of some organizations. Agencies such as the Internal Revenue Service and Veterans Benefits Administration not only receive mediocre grades on management, but are also viewed favorably by less than half of the American public. Compared to these two agencies, NASA is both better managed and more popular with citizens.

A final source of performance assessment comes directly from the government itself. Presidential administrations normally have a keen interest in a well-managed bureaucracy, as executive branch organizations collectively offer an institutional venue for making the president's priorities a reality. Presidents operate outside of iron triangles and therefore must assess from a distance the agencies that offer the greatest prospects for effective policymaking and implementation.[59] Presidents of both parties have long aspired to link assessments of bureaucracy with budgetary allocations, rewarding well-performing agencies with funding increases and punishing organizations that have not proven worthy of the investment.

In recent administrations, the most noteworthy effort in this regard was George W. Bush's **Program Assessment Rating Tool** (PART). For hundreds of programs across the executive branch, the Bush administration collected from agencies information about program purpose and design, strategic planning, program management, and program results.[60] From this information, each program was scored as either effective, moderately effective, adequate, or ineffective.[61]

Given that PART scores were generated by the White House, concerns naturally arise that the ratings favor the administration's allies and are biased against more hostile agencies. From our point of view, a more fundamental difficulty is that PART scores were constructed for individual programs, rather than for agencies as a whole. For example, fifty programs within the EPA were given grades, with none of the programs rated as effective, sixteen rated as moderately effective, thirty-two rated as adequate, and two rated as ineffective.[62]

For comparison purposes, we enter for each agency in Table 7.1 its most common PART score. For the EPA, this means the adequate rating that was given to thirty-two of its fifty programs. Note that no agency received effective as its most common program rating. For all organizations other than the EPA and OSHA (both of which are entered as adequate), the most common

Table 7.1 Comparing Ratings of Agency Performance

Agency	Federal Performance Project	Best Places to Work	Public Favorability	PART Scores
Coast Guard	A	upper quartile	—	moderately effective
Social Security Administration	A/B	above median	55%	moderately effective
Federal Aviation Administration	B	above median	—	moderately effective
National Aeronautics and Space Administration	B	upper quartile	70%	moderately effective
Environmental Protection Agency	B–	below median	52%	adequate
Internal Revenue Service	B–	below median	42%	moderately effective
Veterans Benefits Administration	B–	lower quartile	39%	moderately effective
Occupational Safety and Health Administration	C	above median	—	adequate

Sources: Federal Performance Project: http://www.govexec.com/magazine/2001/04/federal-performance-project/30225/ (accessed November 2, 2016). Best Places to Work: http://bestplacestowork.org/BPTW/ (accessed November 3, 2016). Public Favorability: http://www.people-press.org/2015/11/23/4-ratings-of-federal-agencies-congress-and-the-supreme-court/ (accessed November 3, 2016). PART Scores: https://www.whitehouse.gov/sites/default/files/omb/assets/OMB/expectmore/part.html (accessed November 4, 2016).

Notes: These eight agencies are a sample of the seventeen organizations rated by the Federal Performance Project. A selection of highly graded and more poorly performing agencies was selected. The Social Security Administration has two letter grades because it was rated in multiple years. The Partnership for Public Service's ratings of the "Best Places to Work in the Federal Government" are divided into quartiles—organizations scoring in the top 25 percent (upper quartile), in the 50–75th percentile (above median), in the 25–50th percentile (below median), and the bottom 25 percent (lower quartile). The Pew Research Center's public favorability ratings are available for only five of the sampled agencies. For public favorability and PART scores, the information entered for the Veterans Benefits Administration (VBA) is the respective percentage and rating given to the Department of Veterans Affairs as a whole (information specific to the VBA is not available).

program assessment was moderately effective. In this regard, PART scores are not particularly useful in separating out strong and weak performing bureaucracies. The scores do suggest, however, that whether rated by outside experts (the FPP) or White House officials, the EPA and OSHA are not the strongest performing organizations in the federal government.

In sum, this juxtaposition of various approaches to measuring agency performance indicates that reliance on the FPP does not produce insights that are markedly different than what we would have found had we focused primarily on some other methodology. Given the objective, expert-based focus of the FPP, it provides a reasonable foundation for presenting the performance propositions that have been developed in this chapter. Nevertheless, three final points about other means of assessing agency performance should be noted. First, an agency that enjoys the confidence of its own employees has advantages over other agencies when it comes to recruiting, retaining, and motivating personnel. Agencies should care about employee job satisfaction, they should invest in management practices that provide valuable feedback on which programs are performing better or worse, and they should nurture leadership at all ranks of the bureaucracy. Second, an agency that enjoys the confidence of the public has advantages over other agencies when it comes to securing appropriations and avoiding micromanagement by congressional overseers. Agencies that cultivate a positive reputation are better able to acquire the resources and the flexibility that facilitate high-level performance. Finally, an agency that enjoys the confidence of the president has advantages over other agencies when it comes to securing political appointments and White House clearance for its high-priority initiatives. Agencies with capable leaders who are close to the president and agencies that operate in areas of seminal importance for the president's agenda are naturally advantaged when it comes to building the relationships and generating the political support necessary to perform their tasks with skill and great effect.

Bureaucracy in the Twenty-first Century

As we have seen from the outset, public bureaucracies are institutions of democratic policymaking that are constantly evolving and being transformed. Consider the prominent, and by now familiar, example of education reform.

Many education reforms have been tried in recent decades, ranging from smaller classrooms to stronger testing requirements to school voucher programs enabling disadvantaged children to use public dollars to attend private schools. One innovation that has attracted considerable interest is Success for All, a comprehensive reform model for early childhood education through middle school. Success for All was initiated in Baltimore in 1987 and is now utilized in approximately 1,000 U.S. schools in forty-eight states.[63] Thousands of teachers are working with hundreds of thousands of students, and two million Success for All alumni are currently attending college.[64]

Success for All, which focuses primarily on reading, seeks to ensure that virtually every student will reach the third grade on schedule with adequate basic skills and will build on those skills throughout elementary school. Its elements include a schoolwide curriculum, specially trained tutors, preschool and kindergarten programs, eight-week assessments of elementary school students, a family support team to work with parents, and a facilitator to help teachers implement the program.

A systematic comparison of Success for All schools with a group of control schools suggests that the program works. For each grade, from grade 1 through grade 5, Success for All students performed better on standardized reading tests than did other students with similar socioeconomic backgrounds (see Figure 7.2). Although Success for All is not without its critics,[65] numerous evaluations of the program have reached positive conclusions.[66] The program is especially noteworthy for its ability to improve the educational performance of African American and Latino students.[67] In recognition of such accomplishments, the Obama administration awarded Success for All a $50 million Investing in Innovation (i3) grant designed to double the number of schools implementing the program.[68]

Early childhood education has also generated a great deal of interest in recent years. Most of the momentum for early childhood education programs has been at the state level, where states literally doubled the percentage of four-year-olds enrolled in state-funded pre-kindergarten (pre-K) programs in less

Figure 7.2 Mean Reading Scores: Success for All Schools versus Control Schools

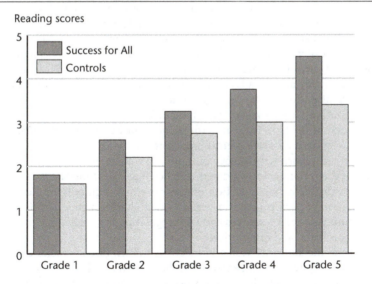

Source: Robert Slavin and Nancy Madden, "'Success for All' and African American and Latino Student Achievement," in *Bridging the Achievement Gap,* ed. John Chubb and Tom Loveless (Washington, D.C.: Brookings Institution Press, 2002), 80.

than a decade.[69] Most pre-K programs were targeted at disadvantaged children, but some (Florida, Georgia, Oklahoma, West Virginia) were universally available. Local governments also expressed growing interest, with Washington, D.C., Boston, Denver, Los Angeles, New York City, San Antonio, and Seattle establishing universal pre-K (UPK) programs that offered or pledged to offer free pre-K to all four-year-olds.

Recent empirical studies have shown, conclusively, that high-quality, large-scale, state-funded pre-K programs can produce substantial improvements in school readiness.[70] In Tulsa, Oklahoma, for example, researchers found that the school-based pre-K program generated big gains in pre-reading, pre-writing, and pre-math skills.[71] In Boston, Massachusetts, researchers found that the school-based pre-K program generated big improvements in cognition, and some more modest gains in executive functioning as well.[72]

One interesting feature of the movement to expand early childhood education, in the United States and in Canada, is that research evidence on positive effects has played a significant role in convincing policymakers to establish and expand these programs.[73] Without strong evidence on performance, it is doubtful that state and local governments would have invested heavily in early childhood education programs. There are limits, however, to the impact of program evaluations. When President Obama proposed a national universal pre-K program in 2013, citing evidence from multiple studies, Congress turned a deaf ear.

In all of these efforts, bureaucrats played a leading role. School superintendents and top staff members helped to design and implement successful UPK programs in Boston and Tulsa. Top officials in the U.S. Department of Health and Human Services and the U.S. Department of Education helped to craft President Obama's UPK proposal. And the success of many state-funded pre-K programs is largely due to the efforts of school administrators and teachers, who have translated powerful ideas into powerful practices.

In bureaucratic policymaking, several broad trends encapsulate the changes that have been occurring recently and that will likely continue to occur in the years and decades ahead. First, the emergence of **performance as a standard of evaluation** has brought concepts from the private sector to bear on organizations at all levels of government. These concepts are articulated in actions such as the Government Performance and Results Act of 1993, which broke new ground by placing great emphasis on strategic plans and the measurement and reporting of agency outputs and outcomes. There are, however, aspects of the movement toward performance that reflect the fact that bureaucracies are distinctly public institutions. For example, equity is an inescapable manifestation of performance for organizations charged with distributing and redistributing societal resources and with regulating the behavior of individuals, business firms, and other private actors.

Second, the authority vested in executive branch bureaucracies continues to increase, despite some appearances to the contrary. In his 1996 State of the Union address President Bill Clinton declared, to much bipartisan applause, that "the era of big government is over." By only one measure is this claim sustainable. From 1968 to 2014, the number of full-time permanent civilian federal workers dropped from 2.3 million to 1.8 million.[74] Once the activities of institutions such as the **shadow government**—the nongovernmental positions created by public sector grants and contracts—are factored in, however, the size of the federal workforce had reached approximately 14.6 million in 2005, with no abatement in sight.[75] Policymaking in the United States simply cannot be understood without paying close attention to executive branch organizations and their partners.

Third, as the bureaucracy continues to expand in scope and responsibility, the resulting organizational apparatus increasingly reflects a **combination of hierarchical and network arrangements.** Such a combination is certainly present in the newest cabinet agency, the Department of Homeland Security. The agency's leadership possesses stronger than normal authority to hire, fire, and reassign subordinate personnel. This authority provides principals inside and outside the department with an unusually robust way of dealing with adverse selection and moral hazard difficulties. At the same time, defending the nation's homeland inevitably entails public-private partnerships, such as those embodied in contracting-out relationships. Firms such as General Electric and L-3 Communications play a fundamental role in the area of transportation security by manufacturing the explosives detection devices that have been installed in airports in the decade and a half since the September 11, 2001, terrorist attacks.

Fourth, **public involvement in bureaucratic proceedings** continues to evolve. During the past five decades, the portfolio of organized interests playing an active role in policymaking has diversified greatly. On the heels of this diversification has come a veritable revolution in the venues of public participation. The application of principles of bargaining and negotiation to the rulemaking process has been a significant addition in an area long governed by the notice and comment requirements of the Administrative Procedure Act. The Internet is changing, at least in some ways, how agencies interact with the beneficiaries and targets of their activities.

In the face of all these changes, a set of analytical tools that transcends the particulars of agencies, policy areas, and time periods is necessary to foster an ongoing understanding of the bureaucracy and its place in American democracy. The four **social scientific frameworks** presented here—bounded rationality, principal-agent theory, interest group mobilization, and network theory—offer just such an array of overarching perspectives. As the problems that agencies address evolve (as does the constellation of agencies themselves), these theoretical orientations toward the bureaucracy's people, bosses, clients, and networks will remain fruitful sources of guidance for students puzzling over policymaking inside the executive branch.

Key Terms

Notes

1. Cindy Skrzycki, *The Regulators: Anonymous Power Brokers in American Politics* (Lanham, Md.: Rowman and Littlefield, 2003), 4.

2. The website of the Federal Performance Project is http://www.govexec.com/magazine/2001/04/federal-performance-project/30225/ (accessed November 2, 2016). Researchers have also rated the performance of state and local governments. See, for example, the website of the Government Performance Project, http://www.pewtrusts.org/en/archived-projects/government-performance-project (accessed November 2, 2016).

3. Jeffrey Pressman and Aaron Wildavsky, *Implementation* (Berkeley: University of California Press, 1973).

4. Its predecessor agency, known as the Health Care Financing Administration (HCFA), received a C in 1999.

5. Internal Revenue Service, "The Tax Gap," https://www.irs.gov/uac/the-tax-gap (accessed November 2, 2016); "IRS Updates Tax Gap Estimates," IR-2006-28, Internal Revenue Service, February 14, 2006, https://www.irs.gov/uac/irs-updates-tax-gap-estimates (accessed April 3, 2017).

6. Daniel Bendtsen, "As IRS Budget Shrinks, So Does the Number of Audits," *Deseret News*, December 5, 2015, http://www.deseretnews.com/article/865643069/As-IRS-budget-shrinks-so-does-the-number-of-audits.html (accessed November 2, 2016).

7. Project on Student Debt, "State by State Data," http://ticas.org/posd/map-state-data (accessed November 2, 2016).

8. Ibid.

9. Danielle Douglas-Gabriel, "Student Loan Default Rate Dips, but 'Considerable Work Remains,' Education Secretary Says," *Washington Post*, September 28, 2016, https://www.washingtonpost.com/news/grade-point/wp/2016/09/28/student-loan-default-rate-dips-but-considerable-work-remains-education-secretary-says/ (accessed November 2, 2016).

10. U.S. Citizenship and Immigration Services, "About Us," https://www.uscis.gov/aboutus (accessed April 3, 2017).

11. Jonathan Weisman, "Backers of Immigration Bill Optimistic; Lawmakers Cite Sense of Urgency," *Washington Post*, June 4, 2007.

12. James Q. Wilson, *Bureaucracy: What Government Agencies Do and Why They Do It* (New York: Basic Books, 1989), 158–171.

13. Mark Schrope, "Obama Outlines Vision for Space," *Nature*, April 16, 2010, http://www.nature.com/news/2010/100416/full/news.2010.189.html (accessed November 2, 2016).

14. National Aeronautics and Space Administration, Columbia Accident Investigation Board, http://govinfo.library.unt.edu/caib/ (accessed November 2, 2016).

15. National Aeronautics and Space Administration, "STS-114 Return to Flight," http://www.nasa.gov/returntoflight/main (accessed November 2, 2016).

16. Wilson, *Bureaucracy,* 168–171.

17. Susannah Figura, "Travel Advisory," *Government Executive*, April 1, 2001, 79.

18. See Gary Lee, "Island Hoppers, Pack Your Passports," *Washington Post,* March 4, 2007, http://www.washingtonpost.com/wp-dyn/content/article/2007/03/02/AR2007030200421.html (accessed November 2, 2016).

19. Katherine Peters, "Trail of Trouble," *Government Executive*, April 1, 2001, 91.

20. Stephen Dinan, "Illegal Immigration Surges Past 2015 Total with Two Months Still to Go in Fiscal Year," *Washington Times,* August 14, 2016, http://www.washingtontimes.com/news/2016/aug/14/illegal-immigration-surges-past-2015-total-with-tw/ (accessed November 2, 2016).

21. "Getting to No," editorial, *Washington Post,* June 10, 2007.

22. National Park Service, "About Us," http://www.washingtontimes.com/news/2016/aug/14/illegal-immigration-surges-past-2015-total-with-tw/ (accessed November 3, 2016); Susannah Zak Figura, "Progress in the Parks," *Government Executive,* March 1, 2000, www.govexec.com/gpp/0300nps.htm (accessed April 3, 2017).

23. Figura, "Progress in the Parks."

24. Thomas E. Backer, ed., *Evaluating Community Collaborations* (New York: Springer Publishing Company, 2003), 10.

25. Paul Posner, "Networking and the Chesapeake Bay Program," in *Unlocking the Power of Networks: Keys to High-Performance Government,* ed. Stephen Goldsmith and Donald Kettl (Washington, D.C.: Brookings Institution Press, 2009), 72–78.

26. "A Failing Bay Cleanup," editorial, *Washington Post,* July 27, 2015, p. 14.

27. Ashley Halsey III, "Obama Orders EPA to Take the Lead in Chesapeake Bay Cleanup Efforts," Department of Ecology, State of Washington, http://www.ecy.wa.gov/pubs/0901009.pdf (accessed September 30, 2016).

28. Ibid., 82.

29. David A. Fahrenthold, "A Revitalized Chesapeake May Be Decades Away; EPA Official Warns of Slow Progress toward 2010 Goals," *Washington Post,* January 5, 2007.

30. Craig W. Thomas, *Bureaucratic Landscapes: Interagency Cooperation and the Preservation of Biodiversity* (Cambridge, Mass.: MIT Press, 2003), 267–268.

31. Theodore J. Lowi, *The End of Liberalism: The Second Republic of the United States,* 2nd ed. (New York: W. W. Norton, 1979), 109.

32. Cathy Johnson, *The Dynamics of Conflict between Bureaucrats and Legislators* (Armonk, N.Y.: M. E. Sharpe, 1992), 71–73.

33. Ibid., 78–80.

34. William Gormley Jr., *Taming the Bureaucracy: Muscles, Prayers, and Other Strategies* (Princeton, N.J.: Princeton University Press, 1989).

35. U.S. Department of Labor, Occupational Safety and Health Administration, https://www.osha.gov/pls/oshaweb/owadisp.show_document?p_table=TESTIMONIES&p_id=307 (accessed November 3, 2016).

36. R. Michael, "Reaction to OSHA's Ergonomics Strategy," Ergoweb, April 8, 2002, https://ergoweb.com/reaction-to-oshas-ergonomics-strategy/ (accessed November 3, 2016).

37. Ibid.

38. Mark Gruenberg, "OSHA Backtracks on Documenting Ergonomic Injuries," *People's World,* February 1, 2011, http://www.peoplesworld.org/article/osha-backtracks-on-documenting-ergonomic-injuries/ (accessed November 3, 2016).

39. Fred Hosier, "OSHA Withdraws Ergonomics Proposal; 2nd Such Action in a Week," *Safety/NewsAlert,* January 26, 2011, http://www.safetynewsalert.com/osha-withdraws-ergonomics-proposal-2nd-such-action-in-a-week (accessed April 3, 2017).

40. W. Anthony Rosenbaum, "Escaping the 'Battered Agency Syndrome': EPA's Gamble with Regulatory Reinvention," in *Environmental Policy,* 4th ed., ed. Norman Vig and Michael Kraft (Washington, D.C.: CQ Press, 2000), 176–181.

41. "John D. Graham Appointed Dean of Pardee RAND Graduate School," RAND Corporation, October 17, 2005, www.rand.org/news/press.05/10.17.html (accessed November 3, 2016).

42. Gary J. Miller, *Managerial Dilemmas: The Political Economy of Hierarchy* (New York: Cambridge University Press, 1992).

43. Dakarai Aarons, "Rhee Reflects on Her Stormy Tenure in D.C.," *Education Week,* September 22, 2010, http://www.edweek.org/ew/articles/2010/09/17/04rhee_ep.h30.html (accessed November 3, 2016).

44. Richard Whitmire, *The Bee Eater: Michelle Rhee Takes on the Nation's Worst School District* (San Francisco: Jossey-Bass, 2011); Bill Turque, "Rhee Assertive Right to the End," *Washington Post,* October 29, 2010, http://www.washingtonpost.com/wp-dyn/content/article/2010/10/28/AR2010102807383.html (accessed November 3, 2016).

45. Whitmire, *The Bee Eater,* 203.

46. Michael Grynbaum, "For City's Transportation Chief, Kudos and Criticism," *New York Times,* March 4, 2011; Michael Grynbaum, "New York Transportation Chief Defends Bike Lanes," *New York Times,* March 9, 2011.

47. Grynbaum, "New York Transportation Chief Defends Bike Lanes."

48. Matthew Brelis, "Earning Her Wings: When Jane Garvey Took the Controls, the Federal Aviation Administration Was Having a Bumpy Flight. Can She Smooth It Out?" *Boston Globe Magazine,* September 6, 1998; Michael Skapinker and Charles Batchelor, "Aviation Chief Puts Faith in Flight: FAA Head Jane Garvey Will Be Airborne When the Millennium Midnight Hour Strikes. But Not in a Third World Airliner," *Financial Times,* November 27, 1998.

49. U.S. Department of Transportation, "Transportation Secretary Ray LaHood Joins Oprah for 'No Phone Zone Day' to End Distracted Driving," press release, April 30, 2010.

50. U.S. Department of Transportation, "U.S. Transportation Secretary Ray LaHood Commends Maine for Enacting Tough Ban on Texting While Driving," press release, June 3, 2011.

51. Rene Sanchez, "L.A.'s New Top Cop Undertakes Tough Task; Style Lauded, but Reform Is Daunting," *Washington Post,* November 3, 2002.

52. Tim Craig and Bill Turque, "Rhee to Resign as Schools Chancellor," *Washington Post,* October 13, 2010.

53. Turque, "Rhee Assertive Right to the End."

54. Grynbaum, "For City's Transportation Chief, Kudos and Criticism."

55. Ibid.

56. "Best Places to Work in the Federal Government," http://bestplacestowork.org/BPTW/ (accessed November 3, 2016).

57. "Best Place to Work in the Federal Government, About" http://bestplacestowork.org/BPTW/about/methodology.php (accessed November 3, 2016).

58. Pew Research Center, "Ratings of Federal Agencies, Congress, and the Supreme Court," http://www.people-press.org/2015/11/23/4-ratings-of-federal-agencies-congress-and-the-supreme-court/ (accessed November 3, 2016).

59. Morris P. Fiorina, "Congressional Control of the Bureaucracy: A Mismatch of Incentives and Capabilities," in Lawrence Dodd and Bruce Oppenheimer, eds., *Congress Reconsidered,* 2nd ed. (Washington, D.C.: CQ Press, 1981).

60. The White House, "Assessing Program Performance," https://www.whitehouse.gov/sites/default/files/omb/assets/OMB/expectmore/part.html (accessed November 4, 2016).

61. Ibid.

62. Ibid.

63. Success For All Foundation, http://www.successforall.org/ (accessed April 3, 2017).

64. Ibid.

65. Nicholas Lemann, "Ready, Read!" http://www.theatlantic.com/past/docs/issues/98nov/read2.htm, *The Atlantic*, November 1998 (accessed November 4, 2016). Three critiques of Success for All are that it is too regimented; its effects do not persist beyond the first year of the program; and, more fundamentally, it prepares students to do well on selected standardized tests—preparation that control group students do not receive.

66. Geoffrey Borman et al., "Comprehensive School Reform and Student Achievement: A Meta-Analysis," *Review of Educational Research* 73 (2003): 125–230; Geoffrey Borman et al., "The National Randomized Field Trial of Success for All: Second-Year Outcomes," *American Educational Research Journal* 42 (2005): 673–696.

67. Robert Slavin and Nancy Madden, "'Success for All' and African American and Latino Student Achievement," in *Bridging the Achievement Gap*, ed. John Chubb and Tom Loveless (Washington, D.C.: Brookings Institution Press, 2002), 74–90; Margarita Calderon, Robert Slavin, and Marta Sanchez, "Effective Instruction for English Learners," *Future of Children* 21 (Spring 2011): 108–109.

68. Nick Anderson, "A Once-Stalled Reading Program Drops Old Rules and Helps Teachers Who Want More Structure," *Washington Post*, January 1, 2011, http://www.washingtonpost.com/wp-dyn/content/article/2011/01/01/AR2011010102040.html (accessed November 4. 2016); Janet Quint, Rekha Balu, Micah DeLaurentis, Shelley Rappaport, Thomas J. Smith, and Pei Zhu, "The Success for All Model of School Reform," http://www.mdrc.org/publication/success-all-model-school-reform (accessed November 4, 2016).

69. W. Steven Barnett, Megan Carolan, Jen Fitzgerald, and James Squires, "The State of Preschool 2012" (New Brunswick, N.J.: National Institute for Early Education Research, 2012).

70. Hiro Yoshikawa et al., "Investing in Our Future: The Evidence Base on Preschool" (Washington, D.C.: Society for Research on Child Development, October 2013).

71. William Gormley, Deborah Phillips, and Ted Gayer, "Preschool Programs Can Boost School Readiness," *Science* 320 (June 27, 2008): 1723–1724.

72. Cristina Weiland and Hiro Yoshikawa, "Impacts of a Prekindergarten Program on Children's Mathematics, Language, Literacy, Executive Functioning, and Emotional Skills," *Child Development* 84, no. 6 (2013): 2112–2130.

73. William Gormley, "From Science to Policy in Early Childhood Education," *Science* 323 (August 9, 2011): 978–981; Linda White, *Constructing Policy Change: Early Childhood Education and Care in Liberal Welfare States* (Toronto: University of Toronto Press, forthcoming).

74. Paul C. Light, "The New True Size of Government," Organizational Performance Initiative, Research Brief 2, New York University, Robert F. Wagner Graduate School of Public Service, August 2006, http://wagner.nyu.edu/performance/files/True_Size.pdf; Office of Personnel Management, "Full-Time Permanent Age Distributions," https://www.opm.gov/policy-data-oversight/data-analysis-documentation/federal-employment-reports/reports-publications/full-time-permanent-age-distributions/ (accessed November 4, 2016).

75. Light, "The New True Size of Government"; Louis Peck, "America's $320 Billion Shadow Government," *Fiscal Times*, September 28, 2011, http://www.thefiscaltimes.com/Articles/2011/09/28/Americas-320-Billion-Shadow-Government (accessed November 4, 2016).

Appendix | Web Resources

Federal Government Websites

These are federal government websites, many recently redesigned for improved public access and usability.

ADMINISTRATIVE CONFERENCE OF THE UNITED STATES (www.acus.gov): This website provides access to the work of an independent agency charged with improving the administrative process in areas such as public involvement in notice and comment rulemaking.

CENTERS FOR DISEASE CONTROL AND PREVENTION (www.cdc.gov): This website provides information about birth defects and Zika, as well as links to vaccinations, safe food and water, and other travelers' health issues.

CENTERS FOR MEDICARE AND MEDICAID SERVICES (www.cms.gov): This website contains information about Medicare, Medicaid, and the Children's Health Insurance Program.

CONSUMER FINANCIAL PROTECTION BUREAU (www.consumerfinance.gov): This website provides access to the activities of an agency created in 2010 by the Dodd-Frank Wall Street Reform and Consumer Protection Act.

DEPARTMENT OF HOMELAND SECURITY (www.dhs.gov): This website provides information about counterterrorism, cybersecurity, and the National Terrorism Advisory System, as well as how citizens, first responders, business, and all levels of government can enhance their emergency preparedness.

DEPARTMENT OF TRANSPORTATION (www.transportation.gov): This website addresses issues such as distracted driving and personal use of unmanned drones and provides an array of information about transportation-related regulatory activities.

ENVIRONMENTAL PROTECTION AGENCY (www.epa.gov): This website provides quick links to key topics such as acid rain, bed bugs, climate change, and drinking water.

FEDERAL COMMUNICATIONS COMMISSION (www.fcc.gov): This website, which the FCC designed by studying how people interacted with the previous version of the website, features the agency's consumer complaint center, blog, and Twitter feed and highlights the presidentially appointed commissioners who are charged with regulating interstate and international communications by radio, television, wire, satellite, and cable.

FEDERAL EMERGENCY MANAGEMENT AGENCY (www.fema.gov): This website features information about recent disasters and allows users to search for information about planning for and dealing with the aftermath of disasters.

FEDERAL RESERVE SYSTEM (www.federalreserve.gov): This website provides access to the public activities of Federal Reserve officials, as well as information about monetary policy, banking regulation, and economic data and research.

HEALTHCARE.GOV (www.healthcare.gov): This website provides information for individuals, families, and small businesses seeking health insurance coverage under the Affordable Care Act.

OFFICE OF INFORMATION AND REGULATORY AFFAIRS (www.whitehouse.gov/omb/inforeg_default): This website, part of the White House's website, contains documents related to the president's management of agency regulatory activities, including rules that have been cleared for promulgation and records of communications that have occurred between White House officials and parties from outside government.

REGULATIONS.GOV (www.regulations.gov): This website is a central clearinghouse for information about the regulatory activities of federal agencies, as well as the comments that agencies receive in response to proposed rules.

State and Local Government Websites

These are award-winning websites, as selected by the Center for Digital Government.

BALTIMORE COUNTY GOVERNMENT (www.baltimorecountymd.gov/): This website allows users to submit applications and reports, pay bills and fines, and alerts residents about government news, plans, and resources.

CALIFORNIA DEPARTMENT OF INSURANCE (www.insurance.ca.gov): This website provides information about filing consumer complaints, as well as the Climate Risk Carbon Initiative, in which the state insurance commissioner has asked insurance companies doing business in the state to publicly disclose investments in fossil fuels.

CITY AND COUNTY OF DENVER (www.denvergov.org/content/denvergov/en.html): This website emphasizes top links, such as adopting pets, checking building permit status, renewing vehicle registration, and searching foreclosure records.

STATE OF MISSISSIPPI (www.ms.gov/Pages/default.aspx): This website features access to the government's most popular services, as well as a help center.

eResearch Websites

These are government and nongovernmental websites containing information that is useful for understanding and doing research on government across jurisdictions and policy domains.

AMERICAN ENTERPRISE INSTITUTE (www.aei.org): This website offers analysis of government and policy with an emphasis on the relationship between government policy and the market economy.

BROOKINGS INSTITUTION (www.brookings.edu): This website offers the perspective of Brookings Institution experts on issues such as financial, environmental, and health care regulation.

DATA.GOV (www.data.gov): This website is the home of the U.S. government's open data in such areas as agriculture, climate, and manufacturing.

FEDERAL ADVISORY COMMITTEES DATABASE (www.facadatabase.gov): This website contains information about the meetings, reports, and other activities of the roughly 1,000 advisory committees that operate in the executive branch.

FEDERAL REGISTER (www.federalregister.gov): This website provides access to every document published in the Federal Register since 1994.

GOVERNMENT ACCOUNTABILITY OFFICE (www.gao.gov): This website includes a list of Government Accountability Office reports on a plethora of topics as well as assessments of all major rules issued by federal agencies.

IBM CENTER FOR THE BUSINESS OF GOVERNMENT (www.businessofgovernment .org): This website publishes reports on topics such as e-government, financial management, and innovations in government and leadership.

LIBRARY OF CONGRESS (www.loc.gov): This website has information about legislative affairs, much of which pertains to the executive branch, including presidential nominations, appropriations bills, and delegations of authority from Congress to agencies.

RAND CORPORATION (www.rand.org): This website presents the research of the RAND Corporation, a nonprofit organization that focuses on national security as well as business, education, health, law, and science.

REGBLOG (www.regblog.org): This website, operated by the Penn Program on Regulation, covers regulatory news and provides analysis and opinions on current issues in regulation.

REGULATION ROOM (regulationroom.org): This website, operated by the Cornell eRulemaking Initiative, provides accessible information about proposed rules and facilitates commenting and interactive discussions. The website aims to improve public participation in the rulemaking process.

REGULATORY STUDIES CENTER (regulatorystudies.columbian.gwu.edu): This website provides commentary and research on current issues in regulation.

USA.GOV (www.usa.gov): This website is the official portal of the U.S. government, offering information about programs and services from across federal, state, and local governments.

U.S. EXECUTIVE BRANCH WEB SITES (www.loc.gov/rr/news/fedgov.html): This website presents an official list of executive branch websites, including cabinet departments, independent agencies, and regulatory commissions.

Index

Catalytic control, 290–291
Catastrophic events
  see Disaster management
Categorical grants, 210, 212
Caya, Chris, 229*n*235
CBS News, 277*n*176
Census Bureau, 79 (figure), 201
Centers for Disease Control and Prevention
  (CDC), 21, 189, 264, 277*n*184, 278*n*195,
  278*nn*196–197, 278*nn*198–199, 278*n*202
Centers for Medicare and Medicaid Services
  (CMS), 222*n*68, 222*n*74
  accountability, 9
  childhood immunization policies, 18,
    19 (table)
  nursing home regulations, 173, 174
  performance ratings, 282 (figure)
  primary tasks, 283
Central American immigrants, 41, 42
Central Falls School District (Rhode Island), 96
Central Intelligence Agency (CIA), 12–13,
  201, 251, 257
Centrality
  basic concepts, 177 (figure), 177–178, 218
  disaster reponse and management,
    239, 269
  federal authority concerns, 186
  intelligence community, 257
  intelligence networks, 257
  interagency networks, 200
  intergovernmental networks, 181,
    182–183 (table)
  local governments, 190
  privatized welfare services, 194
Centralized networks, 177, 177 (figure), 180,
  186, 239, 269
CGI Federal, 44
Chaffetz, Jason, 147
Chain of command, 236
Challenger disaster, 10, 245
Chamber of Commerce, 154, 291
Chapman, Gabrielle, 69*n*56
Charleston, South Carolina, 214
Charlotte Observer, 126*n*162
Charter schools, 3, 11
Chattanooga, Tennessee, 39
Cheney, Dick, 91, 93, 256
Chertoff, Michael, 235, 237–238
Chesapeake Bay, 40, 185–186, 288
Chesapeake Bay Commission (CBC), 288
*Chevron U.S.A., Inc. v. Natural Resources
  Defense Council, Inc.* (1984), 114–115,
  128*n*220
Chicago, Illinois, 106, 197
Child Care and Development Block Grant,
  84, 210
Child Care and Development Fund, 84

Child care legislation and implementation,
  84–85, 85 (table), 86 (table), 158
Child immunization rates, 18, 19 (table)
Child nutrition, 215–216
Child protective services, 38–39
Children's Defense Fund, 158
Children's Health Insurance Program (CHIP),
  22, 41–42, 187–188
Choate, Pat, 224*nn*110–111
Chrysler Corporation, 43
Chuck, Elizabeth, 67*n*5
Chukchi Sea, 246
Churning, 188
Cincinnati, Ohio, 197–198
Circuit courts, 113–115
Circulars, 201
Citicorp, 66
CitiStat, 39
Citizenship and Immigration Services (CIS),
  206, 281, 282 (figure), 284–285, 287,
  302*n*10
Civil liberties, 253, 255–256
Civil Service Reform Act (1978), 97
Civil service system
  federal workforce, 300–301
  firings, 96
  political appointees, 14
  reform efforts, 96–98
Clarke, Richard, 251
Clark, Peter, 70*n*80
Clayton, Mark, 274*n*76, 274*n*78
Clean Air Act (1977), 91, 93, 114, 145,
  182 (table), 213, 247
Clean Water Act (1977), 182 (table)
Clement, Scott, 121*n*62
Client participation and influence, 148–151,
  153–161
Client politics
  bureaucratic decision-making process, 248
  Deepwater Horizon oil spill disaster,
    248–249
  disaster reponse and management, 269–270
  Hurricane Katrina, 238–239
  iron triangles, 134, 138, 288–289
  negotiated rulemaking, 144
  notice and comment process, 141, 301
  nuclear power policy, 132
  public policy costs and benefits, 131,
    132 (figure)
  see also Interest group mobilization
Clients, 130–131
Climate change, 37, 48, 96, 230
Climbers, 51, 51 (table)
Clinton administration
  bureaucratic growth and size, 78
  bureaucratic leadership, 292
  Cabinet appointees, 199

child care policymaking, 85, 158
congressional oversight, 109
environmental policymaking, 93, 145, 157
ergonomics regulations, 111
executive orders, 88, 100
health care policymaking, 187
midnight regulations, 101–102
regulatory review, 100, 101
unilateral actions, 87–88
waiver requests, 160, 191
Clinton, Bill
child care policymaking, 85, 158
executive orders, 87–88, 141
political appointees, 54, 199, 233–234
State of the Union address, 300
Clinton, Hillary Rodham, 12–13, 47, 94–95, 123n98, 158, 199
Clinton, Joshua D., 171n157
Clinton Middle School (Oklahoma), 197
Clotfelter, Charles T., 229n241
CNN, 277nn174–175
CNN.com, 124n126
CNNMoney.com, 170n138
Coast Guard, 206, 239–241, 246, 248, 282 (figure), 296, 297 (table)
Coelho, Tony, 47, 69n58
Coercive control, 290–291
Coerciveness, 179–180
Coercive policy tools, 185–186, 189, 212–214
Coglianese, Cary, 168n83, 168n87, 169n109, 228n225
Cohen, Jeffrey, 226n153
Cohen, Mark A., 224n124
Cohen, Sally, 171nn158–159
Collaborative participation
    see Advisory committees; Internet discussions and collaboration
Collins, Eliza, 95
Collins, Susan, 257
Colorado, 55, 193, 300
Color-coded threat level system, 258
Columbia disaster, 22, 286
Columbia, South Carolina, 214
Combination of hierarchical and network arrangements, 301
Comey, James, 12, 95
Comfort, Louise, 273nn51–52, 273n55
Command-and-control regulation, 186, 197
Comment periods
    see Notice and comment process
Commerce Department (DOC), 202, 260
Commercial Space Transportation Advisory Committee, 142
Commission on Civil Rights, 158
Commission on the Intelligence Capabilities of the United States Regarding Weapons of Mass Destruction, 276nn143–149

Commitment, 52–53
Committee Management Secretariat of the U.S. General Services Administration, 171n163
Committee on the Status and Future of Federal e-Rulemaking, 227n181
Common Cause, 156
Common Core State Standards (CCSS), 1, 2, 3, 11
Communications
    failures, 245, 252–253, 269
    information sharing, 214–218, 257, 258–259, 287–288
    Postal Service (USPS), 290
    vertical communications, 238, 269
Community Development Block Grant, 211
Comparative Agendas Project, 136 (figure)
Comparative effectiveness analysis, 45, 47
Competing goals, 284–285
Competitive Enterprise Institute (CEI), 165n35
Complexity, 81–82, 82 (figure), 177, 178, 209, 237
Comprehensive Plan for Reorganizing the Executive Branch, 78
Comprehensive rationality, 33, 50
CompStat, 39
Concentrated effects, 131–133, 132 (figure), 140, 248, 249
Conflict, 284
Congress
    block grants, 212
    budget proposals, 89–90
    bureaucratic control and oversight, 80–81, 103–112, 116, 254–255, 284
    child care legislation, 84–85, 85 (table), 86 (table)
    coercive control, 290–291
    czar positions, 207
    delegated authority, 79–85, 82 (figure), 105–107, 108, 114, 181, 184
    education policymaking, 300
    functional role, 103, 117
    health care policymaking, 187–188
    homeland security grants, 260
    intergovernmental networks, 181, 184
    issue networks, 137
    organizational report cards, 216–217
    policymaking power, 134 (figure), 135
    political appointee confirmations, 92
    post-9/11 terrorism legislation, 253, 257
    presidential power, 88–89
    regulation nullifications, 112, 291
    state and local government lobbying, 159
Congressional Budget Office (CBO), 48, 279nn209–210
Congressional oversight, 9, 11–12

grants-in-aid programs, 181, 189,
210–212, 218
information sharing, 214–218, 257,
258–259, 287–288
interagency networks, 198–207,
203 (figure), 206–207 (table), 214–215
intergovernmental networks, 181,
184–191, 217
public-private partnerships, 191–198
regulations, 212–214, 218, 246–247
Political accountability, 9, 10, 10 (figure), 14
Political appointees
agency heads, 291–292, 298
bureaucratic reputations, 21–22
Bush administration, 14, 21, 94, 102, 116,
234, 237
cabinet departments, 199–200
civil service conversions, 14
Clinton administration, 54, 199, 233–234
firings, 95
Foreign Service officers, 56
Obama administration, 14, 52, 54, 91, 92,
94, 199, 294
performance measurement systems, 40
presidential power, 90–95
Reagan administration, 91, 92, 199, 200
Trump administration, 54, 78–79, 91, 199–200
see also Czars
Political compromise, 105
Political humor, 233 (table), 249,
250 (table), 258
Political interventions, 145–147
Political protest, 147
Political support, 282, 288–291
Political uncertainty, 104–105
Pollard, Michael, 272n27
Pollution problems, 37, 37 (table), 62, 74,
184–185, 212, 216, 288, 289
Pontchartrain Institute for Environmental
Studies, 248
Popely, Rick, 229n231
Port Authority (New York City), 252
Port running, 35
Positive publicity, 293, 294
Posner, Paul, 220n18, 221n39, 221n51, 288,
303n25
Post-9/11 bureaucracies, 253–256, 254 (figure),
258–259, 285
Postal Rate Commission, 291
Postal Service (USPS), 15–16, 22, 281,
282 (figure), 285, 289–290, 291
Potential terrorist threats, 258–259, 261
Potoski, Matthew, 225nn136–138, 225n140
Potter, John, 16
Potter, Rachel Augustine, 111, 125n148,
127n202
Power of the purse, 107

Prakash, Aseem, 225nn136–138, 225n140
Presidential campaigns and elections, 12–13
Presidential Commission on the Space Shuttle
Challenger Accident, 245, 274nn87–90
Presidential memoranda, 87
Presidential power
budget proposals, 89–90
bureaucratic coordination, 86–87
civil service reforms, 96–98
firings, 95–96
midnight regulations, 101–102
policymaking practices, 86–102, 117
political appointments, 14, 21, 54, 90–95, 116
regulatory review, 98–101, 100 (figure),
101 (figure)
unilateral actions, 87–89
President's Daily Brief, 256–257
President's Interagency Task Force to Monitor
and Combat Trafficking in Persons, 202
Pressman, Jeffrey, 302n3
Pressure tests, 243–244, 249
Price, Tom, 48, 83
Primary tasks, 283–287
Principal-agent theory
administrative procedures, 105–107, 112–114
agency clients, 115–116, 130–131,
132 (figure), 161, 162, 269–270
basic concepts, 24, 25 (table), 26, 76–78
bureaucratic structural politics, 104–105
child care legislation implementation,
84–85, 85 (table), 86 (table)
congressional control and oversight,
103–112
contracted services, 174
delegated authority, 79–115, 82 (figure),
161, 237, 266–267
influenza pandemic strategy and
implementation plan, 266–268
judicial review, 112–115
policymaking process, 79–84, 237, 266–267
presidential power, 86–102, 117
principals, 76–78, 115–117, 267, 269
see also Network theory; Policy tools
Principals, 76–78, 115–117, 267, 269
Principled agents, 117
Prior work experience, 292
Prisons, 108, 194–195
Private sector organizations
civil service reforms, 97
economic productivity, 155
influenza pandemic strategy and
implementation plan, 264, 266
information sharing, 218
monetary compensation, 54
network effectiveness, 209
oil and gas exploration, 244–245
public-private partnerships, 161, 191–198

Shapira, Ian, 68*n*14, 221*n*29
Shapiro, Ian, 67*n*10
Shapiro, Stuart, 70*nn*77–78, 125*n*144
Sharp, Elaine B., 165*n*32
Shaw Group, 239
Shear, Michael D., 95, 226*n*160, 229*n*246
Sheehan, Reginald, 128*n*222
Sheppard, Kate, 125*n*134
Sherlock, Ruth, 221*n*34
Sherman Antitrust Act (1890), 133
Sherman, Erik, 170*n*138
Sherrerd, Michael, 170*n*133
Shipan, Charles R., 119*n*11, 120*nn*33–35, 223*n*87, 223*n*90
Shogren, Elizabeth, 273*n*69
Shoichet, Catherine E., 71*nn*91–92
Shore, Jesse, 220*n*25
Shortcuts, 35, 60
Shulman, Stuart W., 166*n*53, 166*nn*55–56
Siddiqui, Sabrina, 121*n*61
Sierra Club Legal Defense Fund, 157
Significant rules, 139
Silver-Greenberg, Jessica, 219*nn*1–2
Simon, Herbert A., 33, 35, 38, 41, 49, 58, 60–61, 66, 67*n*6, 67*n*11, 68*n*18, 68*n*35, 70*n*73, 72*n*130, 72*n*134
Simpson, Cam, 278*nn*200–201
Simulations, 43–44, 236, 261–262, 266, 268, 269
Singer, Paul, 95
Sipress, Alan, 170*n*130, 170*n*131, 170*n*132
Size, 177, 178
Size of the bureaucracy, 78–79, 79 (figure)
Skapinker, Michael, 304*n*48
Skrzycki, Cindy, 125*n*153, 126*n*154, 302*n*1
Slavin, Robert, 299 (figure), 305*n*67
Sledge, Matt, 121*n*61
Sloppy hexagons, 137, 162
Small Business Administration (SBA), 158
Smallpox, 190
Smithberger, Mandy, 274*n*95
Smith, Steven R., 225*n*132, 225*n*134
Smith, Thomas J., 305*n*68
Smokey Bear, 22, 23 (figure)
Smoking bans, 190
Smuggling operations, 35
Smykla, John, 224*n*122
Snider, Annie, 222*n*56
Snowden, Edward, 89
Snyder, Tanya, 123*n*97
Social media, 148–151, 153–154
Social regulation, 214
Social scientific frameworks, 301
    see also Bounded rationality; Interest
        group mobilization; Network theory;
        Principal-agent theory
Social Security Administration (SSA)
    benefits and costs, 131

congressional appropriations, 108
constituency support, 289–290
disaster management, 241
performance measurement, 16, 285
performance ratings, 281, 282 (figure), 297 (table)
primary tasks, 283
regulatory review, 212
websites, 150
Social Services Block Grant, 211
Societal clients, 289–290
Solidary incentives, 50–51
South Carolina, 160–161, 214
South Dakota Department of Game, Fish and Parks, 4
South Dakota v. Dole (1987), 222*nn*76–77
South Fayette Township High School (Pennsylvania), 197
Space shuttle disasters, 10, 22, 245, 274*n*87, 286
Spain, 255–256
Sparks, Jordin, 294
Sparrow, Malcolm, 67*n*13, 68*n*26, 73*n*139, 220*n*26
Speer, Robert, 147
Spence, David B., 126*n*171, 127*n*178, 127*n*180
Spicer, Sean, 48
Spicklemire, Kami, 28*n*13
Spitzer, Eliot, 73*n*147
Spotted owl saga, 157
Spriggs, James F., II, 128*n*210
Springer, Matthew, 72*n*114
Squires, James, 305*n*69
Stack the deck, 106
Stakeholders, 106, 153, 162–163
Standardized testing, 1, 2–3, 55, 298–299, 299 (figure)
Standard operating procedures (SOPs)
    disaster reponse and management, 64–65, 230, 237, 241, 243–244, 249
    financial crisis, 65–66
    functional role, 31–32, 38–40, 64–66, 241
    notice and comment process, 153
    potential terrorist threats, 260
    see also Decision-making process
Standing Rock Sioux Indian tribe, 147
State Children's Health Insurance Program, 222*n*72
State Department (DOS)
    Bureau of Consular Affairs (BCA), 282 (figure), 286
    influenza pandemic strategy and implementation plan, 267
    Office of the Chief Economist, 47, 69*n*54
State educational systems, 1–3
State governments

bureaucratic clients, 158–161
business lobbying, 156
contracted services, 173–174, 192–198, 218
delegated authority, 181, 182–183 (table),
    184–186
diffusion of policy innovations, 41–43,
    42 (figure)
early childhood education programs,
    299–300
empathy and commitment, 52–53
environmental policymaking, 181,
    182–183 (table), 184–186
evidence-based policymaking, 47
grants-in-aid programs, 210–212, 218
health care services, 187–188, 283
influenza pandemic strategy and
    implementation plan, 263–264, 267
information sharing, 258–259
intergovernmental networks, 181,
    182–183 (table), 184–191
legislative professionalism, 83
as organized lobbyists, 158–161
oversight laws, 11–12
partnership agreements, 184–186,
    192–198
performance measurement, 17–18,
    19 (table)
public perceptions, 22
standard operating procedures (SOPs),
    31–32
third-party government, 180
waiver requests, 160
websites, 307
State of Idaho Legislature, 120n36
State of Louisiana, Office of the Governor,
    275n114
State resistance, 189
Statesmen, 51, 51 (table)
StateStat, 39–40
Staton, Tracy, 278n194
Status quo challenges, 34, 41
Statutory deadlines, 75
Stecher, Briam, 27n5
Steinem, Gloria, 130
Stein, Rob, 279n211
Stephenson, Emily, 119n10
Stepp, Laura, 223n79
Sterling Heights, Michigan, automobile
    assembly plant, 43
Stern, Nicholas, 69n60
Stevens, J. Christopher, 94
Stevens, Ted, 149
Stewart, Jon, 233 (table)
Sticks, 10–11
St. Louis, Missouri, 240
Stockpiled drugs, 264
Stolzfoos, Rachel, 120n44

Stone, Clarence N., 225n147
Stone, Deborah, 70n72, 70n74–75
Stop-and-frisk policies, 77
Stovepipe mentality, 62
Stovepipe structure, 234
Strategic uncertainty, 176
Strauss, Valerie, 27n7, 27n9
Street-level bureaucrats, 38, 65
Stretch targets, 20
Strickland, Jim, 236
Strive Together, 197–198, 225n144
Strong ties, 176
Student loan debt, 284
Stump, Scott, 73n148
Subcabinet officials, 91
Substantive controls, 81, 82 (figure)
Substantive uncertainty, 176, 184
Success For All Foundation, 305nn63–64
Success for All program, 298–299, 299 (figure),
    305n65
Suffrage movement, 130
Suicide attacks, 257
Sullivan, Louis, 85
Sullivan, Sean, 121n62
Sunk costs, 41
Sunshine laws, 11–12, 110, 157
Sunstein, Cass R., 99, 124n129, 124n131,
    125n132
Support from diffuse constituencies,
    289–290
Supreme Court, 88, 113–115, 186,
    188–189
Surveillance operations, 88–89,
    256–258
Susskind, Lawrence, 168n81
Suwannee River Partnership, 186
Suzuki-Orff School of Music, 197
Swine flu outbreak, 264–265
Syria, 179
Szabo, Joseph, 94

Tallahassee, Florida, 259
Tamiflu, 264
Task environments, 32–33
Task Force on Export Control Reform, 202
Task forces, 91, 145, 161, 202–203, 213
Tasks, 282, 283–287
Tax gap, 284
Taylor, Kate, 27n8
Teachers
    compensation systems, 54–55
    firings, 96, 293
    performance assessment systems, 55, 96,
        190, 211, 293
    see also Educational systems; Race to the
        Top initiative
Team of rivals, 91, 199